With Spirit and Understanding

With Spirit and Understanding

1369 Meaningful Prayers – Compiled and Classified

Israel Selvanayagam

Christian World Imprints

First Published in 2020 by

Christian World Imprints
Christian Publishing & Books from India
C-3, Wazirpur Industrial Area
Delhi-110052
cwidelhi2017@gmail.com
www.ChristianWorldImprints.com
Phone: +91 11 41526079

ISBN: 978-93-5148-502-5

Printed in India.

To

Donald & Kerstin Eadie

Contents

Preface

Prayer is the lifeline of Christian life. It is the expression of our intimacy with God. It reveals a devotee's spiritual maturity, self-understanding, understanding of God, the Church and the World. It is not limited to asking for our needs – provision, protection, promotion, prosperity, progeny and peace of mind. Every believer in any religion can pray for these. They do not receive all they ask, as is true in our case too. But, interestingly those who do not believe in God and do not ask for their needs do receive those needs and some are 'richly blessed.' At the same time, we all receive many things even when we do not ask for them. For example, how many of us pray for oxygen? Therefore, the meaning of prayer in our faith experience may have a special significance, which we need to explore. Biblical verses like 'Ask, it shall be given' should not be taken out of their context. This famous phrase was said in the context of seeking God's reign and justice. Jesus told his desperate disciples that whatever they asked he would give them. Again, the context is seeking the will of the heavenly Father and engaging in mission in a hostile world. There is a place for sharing our problems and needs with God. As we are finite and weak, we seek the supremely wise God's guidance in our trouble and confusion. But, we must acknowledge that it is a basic human condition and that people of other religions also share this condition, although we learn from Jesus Christ a unique way of handling this condition for the glory of God.

For praying Christians, to pray is basically to spend special time with God. During this time, there are moments of speaking, moments of listening, and moments of silence. After this special time, we feel not only refreshed but also become confident to do something for God. God has created us to be his co-creators. God has made with us a loving covenant which requires us to participate in God's mission of humanizing the world. Justice, uprightness, love, peace, equality and unity are the fundamental virtues of true humanity. Therefore, it is natural that our prayers mainly centre around such virtues. We read them in the prayers of the prophets, Jesus, the apostles and the saints over the centuries. They have experienced not simply 'a sweet hour of prayer' but bitter hours also as they argued, questioned, lamented and remained conspicuously silent. Some of them have found formal prayers unhelpful and have enjoyed living with the constant mindfulness of the presence of God. Groaning in excruciating pain, agonizing over broken relationships, and lighting candles with tears have been their lot. Nevertheless, for strange and mysterious reasons, they have maintained an unshakable faith in God's unfailing love and faithfulness and hope for a life of eternal fulfilment and peace. Their prayers reveal a distilled wisdom, freedom of the spirit, awareness of their surroundings and articulated language. Also, their prayers reveal their allegiance and faithfulness to God and their refusal to accept the subjugation of oppressive regimes. They naturally demonstrate the spiritual organic unity beyond artificial and limiting denominations. In this connection, the written prayers of one may provide the language and articulation for another who may be groaning in pain and groping in darkness without adequate words to express their condition.

Jesus criticized long, repetitive and bluffing prayers. He taught his disciples a short prayer with profound meaning, i.e., The Lord's Prayer (Mt 6:9-13). For him the essence of prayer is to seek and do the will of God. In a context of confusing expressions and emotional manifestations in worship, Paul urged the Corinthian church to 'pray with spirit and understanding' (1 Cor. 14:15). However, not many seem to follow this cardinal principle of prayer. We have cited some statements on prayer in order to help the readers to recover the Christian character and meaning of prayer.

Above all, we humbly acknowledge that our words are limited and imperfect; so also are our imagination and articulation. At the same time, we have good news from Paul: 'In the same way, the Spirit helps us in our weakness. We do not know what we ought to pray for, but the Spirit himself intercedes for us through wordless groans. And he who searches our hearts knows the mind of the Spirit, because the Spirit intercedes for God's people in accordance with the will of God. And we know that in all things God works for the good of those who love him' (Rom. 8:26-28). In other words, the Spirit is in solidarity with the Father and those who groan, translating their groaning or deep sighs into words. In actual fact, the phrase 'prayers of solidarity' is more suitable to the unique biblical vision of God and God's people than 'prayers of intercession.' Intercession perpetuates a dated and distorted understanding of one person (mediator, leader, preacher and 'prayer hero') though in particular circumstances leaders such as Moses and Jesus prayed for people or disciples. Solidarity implies that while all God's children have direct access to address God as *abba, amma* and friend, they are called to have solidarity with the suffering God and suffering humanity (Phil. 3:10). More than manipulative prayer seeking instant response, prayer of solidarity connects us with our suffering God and his people. God hears our prayer and knows our intent, and though in most cases they may be expressions of wishes and frustrations they are a starting point to work out the remedy through concurrent further prayers and actions in collaboration with

God with patience and perseverance. This understanding of prayer is distinctively biblical and Christian. Some illustrious Christians of mature spirituality have written meaningful prayers which are short, thoughtful and inspiring. Many such prayers have been taken as 'collects' (short prayers with certain petitions) and included in western liturgies (e.g. *Book of Common Prayer*, 1549). Since then, several collections of meaningful prayers have been published and as testimonies reveal they have tremendous effect on Christians who have persistently strived to find correct words to pray meaningfully. To hear what other children of God speak is part of our learning experience. The thoughtful language of prayers not only gives meaning to our Christian life, but also indirectly conveys to outsiders our affirmation and conviction about the nature of God, the world and humans – and the relationship between the three – which precisely are the quintessential themes of what we call theology. Therefore, it is not surprising that the best-known theologians and saints, ancient and modern, have left to us best-known collects and prayers. The prayers show their spiritual maturity, theological clarity and creative articulation. Devotional imagination and poetic expression add to the richness of prayers. They provide not only inspiration to create new prayers but in most cases they provide the approximate language for our struggles and questions.

In India, some of the western collections of prayers (e.g. William Barclay's) are well known. Indian liturgies have incorporated western phrases and collects. However, Indian collections of meaningful prayers known widely are very few. Being aware of many well-known collections, prayers in English and other European languages, and of the need in the Indian Church, I have compiled what I consider some of the most meaningful prayers in this book. I have classified the themes and titled each prayer, though many have no titles in the original, but in many cases they are not neat because of different concerns mentioned in one prayer, in which case the main topic is taken. Perhaps more than one prayer for the same topic or situation gives variety and options for appropriate use.

In order to save space and for consistency we have converted many poetic formats into prose except a few. One or two poems and hymns of prayer have been included with some modification of the format. The archaic English words *thou, thee, thy, thine* are generally put in the modern forms *you, your, you, yours*. I have tried to maintain inclusive language with gender equality by adding, for example, 'hu-' to 'man'. Also, in the few group or congregational prayers the people's response is put in bold italics. Also, ending with 'Amen' is often inconsistent with the original, and therefore it is removed so that the users are free to add it if they wish.

I and those who are going to use these prayers should be grateful to the writers of these prayers, ancient and modern. Some prayers have been provided by particular individuals on request. Most of the prayers come from all sorts of collections. Instead of referring to each one of them, I have given the names wherever they are available with basic details in the 'author index.' Perhaps classification into occasions and topics is the specialty of this book which will I hope be a useful resource in Christian life, individual and group.

The original inspiration was Samuel Amirtham (1932-2017), known widely as theological educator (first Principal of the Tamilnadu Theological Seminary, Madurai and Director of the Program on Theological Education of the World Council of Churches), and renowned churchman (bishop in the South Kerala Diocese of the Church of South India). He was my teacher, Principal, mentor, colleague and friend. He and his wife Lily Amirtham compiled several prayers, mainly from their close circle of colleagues, friends and families and published, entitled *Prārthanāñjali,* 'Offering of Prayers' (2004). In 2007, I brought out in Tamil my own one hundred prayers for different occasions under the title 'In Spirit and Understanding.' Magazines of churches and Christian organizations sometimes publish individual prayers. However, in the whole of India, there has been no substantial collection of prayers. In the West, apart from the *Book of Common Prayer* and smaller versions in the Anglican Church, the Methodist Church in Britain publishes annually the *Prayer Handbook* (along with sharing the developments and concerns of particular areas of the Methodist Church worldwide and UK). I have also contributed to this series. Many prayers have been taken from Methodist sources and other major collections (see the bibliography). However, there may be many more meaningful prayers than those I have collected and selected.

Prayers are often approached inter-religiously. In the scientific study of religion, particularly in the phenomenological pursuit of identifying the 'essence' of religion(s), the German scholar Friedrich Heiler claimed prayer as the essence. His classical study was published with the title *Prayer: A Study in the History and Psychology of Religion* (1937). It attracted critical reviews. Since then there have been only a few collections of interreligious sources, despite the affirmation that 'Together they show us that, at their most essential, prayers are the same all over the word, in every religion and every century' (J. Mabey, *One World Book of Prayer*, vii). However, apart from a few, the prayers of this collection are Christian in their unique character with profound love and prophetic intent as informed by the Bible and those great minds which have been guided by it.

Although, I have attempted to provide a classification, there is no claim that they are neat and consistent as there are unavoidable overlaps. There is repetition of ideas too, and I myself am not fully satisfied with assigning all the prayers to various topics. However, I have realized two factors. First, God's children have written and spoken without bothering about conciseness and profundity. Second, we find a global resonance in the prayers offered by Christians from across the world church. It is my hope that the rough classification I have done will help individuals and groups to easily find relevant and meaningful prayers when they need appropriate words for particular occasions. Some prayers are reflective and meditative, and a few prayers are in the form of litanies. Where there is any repetition of the obvious and glaring overlapping I have tried to avoid them so also those seemingly preachy to God and others.

I have acknowledged the source of every prayer if it is available, and have done so in a spirit of gratitude. I have given a suitable title for all prayers as most did not have one in the original. Also, for consistency and space-saving I have often modified the format by aligning the text to the left, thus changing indented or poetic formats. There is a list of authors at the end with their dates, hints of position and place (if known), in alphabetic order. In most cases I did some research.

I am grateful to those who helped by lending some resources. My wife Gnana Leelal deserves appreciation for assisting me by identifying certain prayers, checking the references, dictating from printed materials and my handwritten prayers collected from various libraries and proofreading. She is one of those dedicated Indian ministers' wives who have put up with their workaholic husbands and then experience some kind of fulfilment in their Christian life.

I am immensely grateful to William Allberry who patiently checked, corrected and commented on the text with meticulous care and patience.

Christian World Imprints have once again demonstrated their professionalism and perfection. It is a pleasant experience to work with them and I thank all those who have contributed to this production.

It is my joy to present this book to Donald & Kerstin Eadie, one a senior Methodist minister in Britain and the other a lay theologian from Sweden. I, along with my family, went to Bristol in 1996 to be a World Church Partner of the Methodist Church for teaching. While still struggling to settle down in a strange land, unexpectedly, without acquaintance, we received a call and invitation from them over the phone. They were (and are) living in Birmingham. Since then our friendship has deepened as well as widened. We have had several moments of sharing on challenges for life and resources to sustain faith. The role of prayer is part of the sharing. Probably we found ourselves not so much praying as growing towards being prayerful.

May we all experience that meaningful prayers spring up from prayerful life!

Israel Selvanayagam,
Evesham, UK.

* *Lotus in Indian religious traditions is a symbol of purity, gentleness and graciousness; hence the expression 'lotus-feet of God'.*

On Prayer

1. Prayer as Global Link

We stand today, a link in a chain of prayer joining us to every person who has ever prayed since time began. A pillar of prayer down the ages, arising from desert sands, from the words of patriarchs and matriarchs of many nations. We join our prayers to those of our brothers and sisters in every part of the world, prayer offered in every language at every moment of the day. Thank you, God of all time, God of all places, that you hear each prayer. Lord, hear our prayer.

Diane Clutterbuck

2. Do and Do Not Pray

Please do not pray for me,

If prayer is primarily for protection, prosperity, progeny, promotion and peace of mind; if it is to irritate, manipulate and arm-twist God to come around to our way and fulfil our wish; if it is to display your piety, knowledge of scriptural verses and power of prolonged petition.

Please do pray for me,

If prayer is an act of solidarity in seeking God's will for me and for all those around me; if it is a sharing of joy, pain and doubt with God, the greatest Friend and Companion; if it is to stand in awe, shout in wonder, whisper in love, smile with tears, and end in silence.

Israel Selvanayagam

3. Founded on Love

I ask you to pray for me for I know you love me.
I pray for you whether you expect or not, for I love you.
The Ever-Loving God, Father, Mother, Friend and Fellow Sufferer, longs to hear our voice and our shared aspirations. Jesus Christ, the Supreme Embodiment of God's Love, intercedes in solidarity. The Holy Spirit translates our deep sighs and

inexpressible thoughts into meaningful prayers. May all those who pray know that prayer is founded on love.

Samuel Amirtham

4. The Life of Prayer

Right relation between prayer and conduct is not that conduct is supremely important and prayer may help it, but that prayer is supremely important and conduct tests it.

William Temple (1881-1944)

5. Not Inside the Church Alone

Many times we come to God in Prayer. Over and over again we ask her to show us how to live, how to be just, how to love, how to be faithful. We are people who long to see God's face. Sometimes, God seems to be very far away. We begin to doubt. We become discouraged. Often, our own actions or the actions of the communities to which we belong, deny our prayers. It is easy to say 'Lord, Lord ...' It is much harder to take responsibility, for what needs to be done. Sometimes in our prayers we wish to keep God in church and not in every part of our lives. Sometimes, we prefer pious practices rather than commitment to the works of justice. God helps us not to turn our face from human need. God opens our eyes to what we can do personally, to what we can do as a community, and to what changes need to be made so that justice is available to everyone.

Women's World Day of Prayer, 1990 (adapted)

I. Acclamation and Adoration

1. Blessed be the Name

Blessed be the name of God from age to age,
for wisdom and power are his.
He changes times and seasons,
deposes kings and sets up kings;
he gives wisdom to the wise
and knowledge to those who have understanding.
He reveals deep and hidden things;
he knows what is in the darkness,
and light dwells with him.

(Deutero-Daniel 2:20-22)

2. Exalted for Ever (A)

Blessed are you, O Lord, God of our ancestors,
and to be praised and highly exalted for ever;
And blessed is your glorious, holy name,
and to be highly praised and highly exalted for ever.
Blessed are you in the temple of your holy glory,
and to be extolled and highly glorified for ever.
Blessed are you who look into the depths from your throne on the cherubim,
and to be praised and highly exalted for ever.
Blessed are you on the throne of your kingdom,
and to be extolled and highly exalted for ever.
Blessed are you in the firmament of heaven,
and to be sung and glorified for ever.

Three Jewish Men (Deutero-Daniel 3:29-34)

3. Exalted for Ever (B)

Bless the Lord, all you works of the Lord;
sing praise to him and highly exalt him for ever.
Bless the Lord, you heavens;
sing praise to him and highly exalt him for ever.
Bless the Lord, you angels of the Lord;
sing praise to him and highly exalt him for ever.
Bless the Lord, all you waters above the heavens;
sing praise to him and highly exalt him for ever.
Bless the Lord, all you powers of the Lord;
sing praise to him and highly exalt him for ever.
Bless the Lord, sun and moon;
sing praise to him and highly exalt him for ever.
Bless the Lord, stars of heaven;
sing praise to him and highly exalt him for ever.

Three Jewish Men (Deutero-Daniel 3:35-41)

4. Exalted for Ever (C)

Bless the Lord, all rain and dew;
sing praise to him and highly exalt him for ever.
Bless the Lord, all you winds;
sing praise to him and highly exalt him for ever.
Bless the Lord, fire and heat;
sing praise to him and highly exalt him for ever.
Bless the Lord, winter cold and summer heat;
sing praise to him and highly exalt him for ever.
Bless the Lord, dews and falling snow;
sing praise to him and highly exalt him for ever.
Bless the Lord, ice and cold;
sing praise to him and highly exalt him for ever.
Bless the Lord, frosts and snows;
sing praise to him and highly exalt him for ever.
Bless the Lord, nights and days;
sing praise to him and highly exalt him for ever.
Bless the Lord, light and darkness;
sing praise to him and highly exalt him for ever.
Bless the Lord, lightnings and clouds;
sing praise to him and highly exalt him for ever.

Three Jewish Men (Deutero-Daniel 3:42-51)

5. Exalted for Ever (D)

Let the earth bless the Lord;
let it sing praise to him and highly exalt him for ever.
Bless the Lord, mountains and hills;
sing praise to him and highly exalt him for ever.
Bless the Lord, all that grows in the ground;
sing praise to him and highly exalt him for ever.
Bless the Lord, you seas and rivers;
sing praise to him and highly exalt him for ever.
Bless the Lord, springs;
sing praise to him and highly exalt him for ever.
Bless the Lord, you whales and all that swim in the waters;
sing praise to him and highly exalt him for ever.
Bless the Lord, all birds of the air;
sing praise to him and highly exalt him for ever.
Bless the Lord, all wild animals and cattle;
sing praise to him and highly exalt him for ever.

Three Jewish Men (Deutero-Daniel 3:52-59)

6. Te Deum

We praise you, O God, we acknowledge you to be the Lord. All the earth worships you, the Father everlasting; to you all angels cry aloud, the heavens and all the powers therein.

To you Cherubim and Seraphim, continually do cry: Holy, holy, holy, Lord God of Sabaoth, heaven and earth are full of the majesty of your glory.

The glorious company of the apostles, praise you. The goodly fellowship of the prophets, praise you.

The white-robed army of martyrs, praise you. The holy Church throughout the world does acknowledge you.

The Father of an infinite majesty, your adorable true and only Son, also the Holy Spirit, the Comforter.

You are the King of glory, O Christ; you are the everlasting Son of the Father. When you became human to deliver humankind, you humbled yourself to be born of a virgin.

When you had overcome the sharpness of death, you opened the kingdom of heaven to all believers. You sit at the right hand of God, in the glory of the Father.

We believe that you will come to be our judge. We therefore pray, help your servants whom you have redeemed, with your precious blood. May they be numbered with your saints in glory everlasting.

O Lord, save your people, and bless your heritage, govern them, and lift them up for ever. Day by day we magnify you, and we worship your name, ever world without end.

O Lord, let your mercy alight upon us, as our trust is in you. O Lord, in you is our hope, let us never be put to shame.

Glory be to the Father, and to the Son, and to the Holy Spirit; As it was in the beginning, is now, and ever shall be, world without end.

An Ancient Christian Hymn

7. Wonder of Wonders

For the shining lights and planets which move on their orderly way in space; for the airs and the waters; for the free supply of oxygen we effortlessly breath; for the honey inside the flowers, and the bees and birds that collect and save it carefully; for the multiple and ever-new colours of the butterflies; for the mystery of wind becoming tunes; for the singing birds which had no training; for the flying glow worms giving light without electricity; for the beauty and fragrance of trees, plants and flowers; for cattle, reptiles and pets; for the colourful carpets of crops in the fields; for the natural affection and love inherent in everyone finding different expression through the stages of life, for all these things we acclaim and adore you with awesome wonder.

Israel Selvanayagam

8. Splendid Creation and Salvation

Creator of galaxies and the intricacies of life, we praise you that through your eternal Word you brought the universe into being and made us in your own image. You have woven us into the web of all living things and given us this earth to care for and delight in. When we wandered far from your way, you never lost your loving trust in us. You sent Jesus to be our Saviour. Making his home among us, he reveals your goodness and love. Born of Mary, he shares our life. Eating with sinners, he welcomes us. Leading his followers, he guides us. Dying on the cross, he rescues us. Risen and ascended, his love extends to all the world. We praise and adore you in awe and wonder.

Ascension Rite

9. The Wonder of Creation

Almighty God, whose glory the heavens are telling, the breath of life of all things living: to you be praise from all your creatures, and from humans made in your own image, redeemed and restored by Jesus Christ your only Son, our Lord.

Most glorious Lord God, you created the world and uphold its fabric in order and beauty: give us grace so to meditate on your creative skill and wisdom, your power and great mercies, that we may thank you, and adore you and praise you for ever; through Jesus Christ our Lord.

Daily Prayer 74

10. Worship and Praise

Worship and praise belong to you, Holy God. You have made us – different peoples, cultures and traditions, but one human family. ***All people come within the sweep of your love!***

As a mother tenderly gathers her children, ***you embrace.***

Again and again you call to people to follow you in faith; ***you rescue them from captivity.***

You lead them in the wilderness; ***you give bread to the hungry.***

You speak through the prophets; ***you rebuke greed.***

You comfort those in exile; ***you never give up on your people.***

Showing us the depth of your love, you sent Christ Jesus. He reveals your mercy and compassion and shows us the pattern for our living.

As his witnesses, empowered by the Spirit, we share in building his kingdom. Maranatha! Come, Lord Jesus.

Ascension Rite

11. We Praise and Adore

Concluding each part: God of amazing grace, ***We praise and adore you.***

Gracious and compassionate God, your majesty and glory know no bounds. With our inner eyes we gaze your stunning beauty with all its wonderful colours.

Sovereign God, you are the greatest of the great and subtlest of the subtle. You are the oldest of the old and newest of the new. Your beauty shines on both dirt and dust, and gold and silver.

Loving God, when you created the world you brought light out of darkness, order out of chaos, and fullness out of void. You continue to recreate your world.

When we look above the space, sun, moon and stars, and down upon the waters of the oceans we are overwhelmed by your works of awe and wonder and we stand speechless.

Yet out of your grace you came into the world in Jesus the Christ our Lord. You taught us about the surprising gift of your new reign and opened our eyes.

Your majesty is praised by babes and children. From their mouth you have established a bulwark against your adversaries. You empower the powerless to challenge the powerful.

Israel Selvanayagam

12. Mystery and Mercy

O Lord my God, most merciful, most secret, most present, most constant, yet changing all things, never new, never old, ever in action, yet ever quiet, creating, upholding, and perfecting all: who has anything but of your gift? Or what can any human say when s/he speaks of you? Yet have mercy upon us, O Lord, that we may speak unto you and praise your Name.

St. Augustine

13. Lord of the Universe *(Jegadeesa)*

O Lord of the Universe, the night with its fabulous firmament of heaven, hung firmly as a canopy in the sky, with its moon, and the stars, the day with its dawn, the rising sun and the coloured clouds, the singing birds, the humming bees, the roaming insects, the meandering beasts, the blowing winds, and the blooming blossoms with their fragrance in the air. All proclaim loudly the splendour of your majesty. What a wonder is the sky, what splendour is the sea! How amazing the variety of living things, and what a wonderful phenomenon is life itself! When I ponder over it all and realize you are the Creator of all we know, you are the Almighty Lord; my head bows down in adoration at your feet.

S. Ramachandran Nair

14. Bright and Power

God of beauty and power, wonder and light, we worship you for being who you are: more beautiful than the sunlight you made; stronger than the power that formed the universe; brighter than the light which banishes night; more wonderful than butterfly wings, snow flakes' fall or rising dew. We worship you in adoration and praise.

Donald Hilton

15. Awesome Wonder

Lord of vastness, of colliding galaxies, of an ever-expanding universe, we stand in awe at the magnificence of creation. In all this vastness, our little planet. On this vast planet, our little lives. How small we are, and yet you gave us minds vast enough to reach out, to see the beauty of your plan and the power of your arm.

Annette Kupke

16. Glorious Africa

O Lord, O God, Creator of our land, our earth, the trees, the animals and people, all is for your honour. The drums beat it out, all people sing about it, and they dance with noisy joy that you are the Lord. You have created this glorious, sun-drenched Africa and our friends and families and tribes. You also have pulled the other continents out of the sea. What a wonderful world you have made out of wet mud, and what beautiful people! We thank you for all the beauty of this earth. Everything is like a shiny wreath around your name. The grace of your creation is like a cool day between rainy seasons. We drink in your creation with our eyes. We listen to the birds' jubilee with our ears. How strong and good and sure your smells, and everything that grows there. The sky above us is like a warm, soft Kente cloth, because you are behind it, else it would be cold and rough and uncomfortable. We drink in your creation and cannot get enough of it …

Ghana's Young Christians

17. A Flood of Love

Eternal God of wonder, might and power, how can we offer humble adoration? If we bow our heads, our hearts might still be raised in arrogance. If we kneel, our minds might still stand tall with pride. If we are silent, inner thoughts might overreach themselves. If we speak the lowly word, intention might deny our spoken word. Love us, Lord, and let your love flood through us, heart and mind, and all. Then we will love, and in loving learn to be with you – and thus adore.

Donald Hilton

18. Ever-Creating God

Creator God, in the beauty of moor and coast, river valley and misted tor, natural beauty and human-made wonder, cliff and cathedral, we see reflections of your glory. We praise you for our abilities to work the world you have made to create beauty and for our capacity to appreciate the beauty of your handiwork. Set our minds on the care of your creation and the re-creation of our fallen humanity in Christ.

Peter Pillinger

19. Inadequate Praise

God whose mystery no tongue can describe and whose thoughts no speech can utter; receive the praise of your whole creation and illumine our souls with the glory of your presence, for you live and reign, now and for ever.

Gregory of Nazianzus

20. Greater than the Greatest

Let us fear you, O Lord, beyond whom there is none more holy; love you beyond whom there is none more worthy of praise; and long for you beyond whom there is none more desirable; and grant that thus fearing, loving, and longing we may see you, face to face; through Christ our Lord.

Desiderius Erasmus

21. Unbound Love

Lord of all worlds, your love knows no boundaries, not of ocean, mountain or wilderness, but reaches out constantly, hopefully, willingly: help us we pray, to see your love in unexpected places and to respond with our whole selves.

Fiona Green, LP, Ashbourne Circuit

22. Dwelling in Unapproachable Light

Lord our God, you dwell in unapproachable light, pure Essence and Perfection of being! Self-existent, Necessary, Infinite and Eternal! You comprehend within yourself all nature, all wisdom, all justice, all goodness, all truth and all holiness. Out of the abundance of our reason we adore you and out of the love of our hearts we magnify and praise you, Father, Son and Holy Spirit; one God for ever and ever.

Susanna Wesley (1669-1742)

23. Worship in Spirit and in Truth

Father, help us to worship you in spirit and in truth, that our consciences may be quickened by your holiness, our minds nourished by your truth, our imagination purified by your beauty, our hearts opened by your love, and our wills surrendered to your purpose; may all this be gathered up in adoration as we ascribe glory, praise and honour to you alone, through Jesus Christ our Lord.

Howard Booth

24. Awakened to the Wonder

Grant, O Lord, that through our worship today we may be awakened to the wonder of your love for us; that familiar words may shine with new meaning and that the habit of worship may be cleansed of all stale formality and mere ceremonial observance. Open our eyes to see your loveliness and make our hearts to burn within us as you do speak your word to us in this hour, so that in wondering awe we may know ourselves forgiven, energized with new life and throbbing with new power. Through Jesus Christ our Lord.

Leslie D. Weatherhead

25. Daily Moments

O God our faithful guardian, when we are woken early in the morning by the orchestra of birds with your conducting, our hearts overflow with gratitude. When in the day we see the complex designs and stunning colours of nature and the tiny birds sucking honey from the flowers without damaging them we stand speechless. When we see the mother birds feeding to their chicks the food they gathered and stored in their mouths in such an intimacy, we learn something of love. When we stand before a waterfall with forceful spray and then seeing beside a singing bird unintimidated, we are caught in awe. When we see the moving clouds and the rays of the sun piercing through the woods, we are in wonder. When we watch the fishermen negotiating giant waves to find their way and beekeepers carefully dealing with the ferocious bees, we praise you. When our night is long and, waiting for the dawn, we see the eye-catching morning star which gives us a glimmer of hope, we remain silent with the bursting of gratitude within. Help us to live a Eucharistic life always.

Israel Selvanayagam

26. Holy Majesty

We present ourselves before you in adoration of your holy majesty, conscious of our own indignity, but also of the action of your grace shown in the many gifts which you never cease to give us, gifts both of body and of spirit. We thank you especially that, on this Sunday and this festival, we remember that your well-beloved Son, Our Lord Jesus Christ, did not leave us orphans when he returned to your presence. He wanted, until he returns in glory, to remain close to us through the Holy Spirit, whose reviving strength teaches and comforts us. Grant us to recognise this great benefit, and to praise you for it. Help us, when your Word is preached and understood in this place and wherever your people gather, to call on your name. Sanctify and bless this celebration of the Holy Eucharist in which we are about to share. Let your light illumine us. Let your peace be among us.

Karl Barth

II. Praise and Thanksgiving

1. Countless Gifts

Lord, how much juice you can squeeze from a single grape! How much water you can draw from a single well! How great a fire you can kindle from a tiny spark! How great a tree you can grow from a tiny seed! My soul is so dry that by itself it cannot pray; yet you can squeeze from it the juice of a thousand prayers. My soul is so parched that by itself it cannot love; yet you can draw from it boundless love for you and for my neighbour. My soul is so cold that by itself it has no joy; yet you can light the fire of heavenly joy within me. My soul is so feeble that by itself it has no faith; yet by your power my faith grows to a great height. Thank you for prayer, for love, for joy, for faith; let me always be prayerful, loving, joyful, faithful.

Guigo the Carthusian

2. Cherishing Nature and Surprising us

Living God, our loving parent: you cherish your creation, and we praise you.

With earth, air, water, fire: in our elements as your children, we praise you.

With our lips, with our lives, in all our diversity, each one made in your image, we praise you.

Because your Spirit is at work today: encouraging, enabling, surprising us, we praise you.

Poor as we are, you give us hope: salt of the earth, you give us meaning and purpose and we praise you.

Iona Worship Book

3. Diversity of the Universe

O, God, we thank you for this universe, our great home, for its vastness and its riches, and for the diversity of the life which teems upon it and of which we are part.

We praise you for the arching sky and the blessed winds, for the driving clouds and the constellations on high.

We praise you for the salt sea and the running water, for the everlasting hills, for the trees, and for the grass under our feet.

We thank you for our senses, by which we can see the splendour of the morning, hear the jubilant songs of love, and smell the breath of the springtime.

Grant us, we pray you, a heart wide open to all this joy and beauty, and save our souls from being so steeped in care, or so darkened by passion, that we pass heedless and unseeing when even the thorn bush by the wayside is aflame with the glory of God.

Walter Rauschenbusch

4. Gifts of Nature and Eucharist

Thank you, O God, for all the natural resources of the earth – fruit-bearing trees, beautifying plants, oxygen-providing leaves, fragrance-emitting flowers, milk-supplying cattle and food-producing fields. Thank you for feeding us with the bread and wine signifying the body and blood of Christ. Just as we try to follow his footsteps, give us reverence when treating nature that the heavenly feast may be assured for us.

Israel Selvanayagam

5. From 'A Little *Te Deum* of the Commonplace'

For all the first sweet flushings of the spring; The greening earth, the tender heavenly blue; The rich brown furrows gaping for the seed; For all thy grace in bursting bud and leaf ... For hedgerows sweet with hawthorn and wild rose; For meadows spread with gold and gemmed with stars; For every tint of every tiniest flower, For every daisy smiling to the sun; For every bird that builds in joyous hope, For every lamb that frisks beside its dam, For every leaf that rustles in the wind, For spiralling poplar, and for spreading oak, For queenly birch, and lofty swaying elm; For the great cedar's benedictory grace, For earth's ten thousand fragrant incenses. Sweet altar-gifts from leaf and fruit and flower ... For that sweet impulse of the coming Spring; For ripening Summer, and the harvesting; For all the rich Autumnal glories spread – The flaming pageant of the ripening woods, The fiery gorse, the heather-purpled hills, The rustling leaves that fly before the wind, and lie below the hedgerows whispering; For meadows silver-white with hoary dew; For sheer delight of tasting once again that first crisp breath of winter in the air; The pictured pane, the new white world without; The sparkling hedgerow's witchery of lace, The soft white flakes that fold the sleeping earth; The cold without, the cheerier warmth within ... For all the glowing heart of Christmas-tide, We thank you, Lord!

John Oxenham

6. Earth and All In It

O God, we thank you for this earth, our home; for the wide sky and the blessed sun, for the salt sea and the running water, for the everlasting hills and the never-resting winds, for trees and the common grass underfoot. We thank you for our senses by which we hear the songs of birds, and see the splendour of the summer fields, and taste of the autumn fruits, and rejoice in the feel of the snow, and smell the breath of the spring. Grant us a heart wide open to all this beauty; and save our souls from being so blind that we pass unseeing when even the common thorn bush is aflame with your glory, O God our creator, who lives and reigns for ever and ever.

Walter Rauschenbusch

7. Flowers that Bloom

For flowers that bloom about our feet; For tender grass, so fresh and sweet; For song of bird and hum of bee; For all things fair we hear or see, Father in heaven, we thank You!

For blue of stream, for blue of sky; For pleasant shade of branches high; For fragrant air and cooling breeze; For beauty of the blowing trees – Father in Heaven, we thank You!

For mother-love and father-care; For brothers strong and sisters fair; For love at home and school each day; for guidance lest we go astray – Father in heaven, we thank You!

For Your dear, everlasting arms, That bear us o'er all ills and harms; For blessed words of long ago, That help us now Your will to know - Father in Heaven, we thank You!

Ralph Waldo Emerson

8. Rain

Dear God, thank you for the rain. For the rain that runs and trickles down the window and makes patters on the glass. For the rain that makes the crops and flowers grow and gives the water to drink … Thank you for the rain which makes big puddles in which we can jump. Dear God, thank you for the rain, and please take care of people who don't have enough rain and water to drink and must go many miles to get it.

Virginia Salmon

9. Decorating Power

What power decorates the earth with plants of every colour of the rainbow, and adorns the night sky with a sumptuous lacework of stars? What mind produced so many creatures of grace and beauty, strangeness and complexity as roam the world and fill the seas? Unfathomable designer God, you set in motion the wheel of suns and stars, of infinite universe; you organized the evolution of life on this planet; you gave us senses to brush against your creation, and minds to discover, learn, invent and wonder. Yours is the power, yours the mind and yours the love which surrounds us and supports us through all our experiences, our travels, the changes in our lives. As each day dawns, may we remind ourselves of the joy and wonder of knowing you, and as each day ends may we turn to you again with thankfulness and praise.

Rosy Morgan

10. Nourishing Gifts and Graces

Blessed are you, Lord our God, King of the Universe, for you nourish us and the whole world with goodness, grace, kindness and mercy. Blessed are you, Lord, for you nourish the universe. With wonder and with perplexity, with shame and with gratitude we come before God. 'I will lift up my eyes to the hills but where can I find help? My help comes from the Lord who made heaven and earth.' God of the high mountain ranges and the deep valleys crumbling through earthquakes, God of the weakest, the poorest and the grieving who wait for winter within destroyed villages, God of exhausted medical teams, aid workers, lorry drivers, helicopter pilots, engineers and technicians, of the politicians and of the military, Have mercy upon us, renew our strength, deepen our compassion, grant enough courage, enough wisdom.

The Lord hears our prayer.

Thanks be to God.

God of Magnificat, who lifts up the lowly, who feeds the hungry with good things, who sends the rich empty away; God in the unrest and uprising in many parts of the world, God in the desecrated graveyards, in the blood-stained streets in the city, God of the frightened: God watch over us, our community workers, local councillors and police, the people of the mosques, temples, synagogues, gurudwaras and churches.

Have mercy upon us, renew our strength, deepen our compassion, grant enough courage, enough wisdom.

The Lord hears our prayer.

Thanks be to God.

God of the beatitudes, of those who hunger and thirst to see right prevail, God of the little people of deprived areas in our country and around the world, of the civil rights movement, and of all those who work for justice with peace,

Have mercy upon us, strengthen us, deepen our compassion, awaken our courage, grant us wisdom.

The Lord hears our prayer.

Thanks be to God.

God of those who watch and wait, of the fragile, of the aching heart, who redeems the world through the pain bearers,

Have mercy upon us, renew our strengthen, deepen our compassion, grant enough courage, enough wisdom.

The Lord hears our prayer.

Thanks be to God.

God of the broken bread, bless the broken peoples of our world, bless them and us, and make us signs of resurrection.

The Lord hears our prayer.

Thanks be to God.

God of the great homecoming of the heavenly banquet prepared for all people. Thank you for those in every generation who make grace a reality, who dare to live your love for all, your shocking generosity.

God our Father, thank you for your welcoming us home for receiving us with mercy and gentleness.

'Bless the Lord O my soul, all that is within me bless his Holy name. Bless the lord, my soul, and forget not his benefits.'

We share in the prayer that Jesus taught us, each of us praying in the language of our own …

Donald Eadie

11. Thanksgiving for Ever

ALMIGHTY GOD, and Father in Heaven, who are kind to the unthankful and to the evil; Praise be to you and thanksgivings for ever: your full hand supplies our need.

Praise be to you for the Word of life in ancient scripture and in Holy Gospel; for Jesus Christ the Saviour of the world; and for the Holy Spirit by whom we are born from above.

We bless you for the ministries of your Church in prayer and song, in sacrament and benediction, and in the silent fellowship of believing hearts.

We bless you for all who, taking pleasure in your worship, are at home in your house of prayer, find peace within its walls, and carry your peace with them wheresoever they go.

And may your peace which the world can neither give nor take away, abide in our hearts and be with us, while we praise and bless your Holy Name; through Jesus Christ our Lord.

Donald Eadie

12. Supreme Love

We give you thanks, O God, for your love for us, warm and brooding, which has brought us to birth and opened our eyes to the wonder and beauty of creation; for your love for us, wild and freeing which has awakened us to the energy of creation: to the sap that flows, the blood that pulses, the heart that sinks; for your love for us, compassionate and patient, which has carried us through our pain, wept beside us in our sin, and waited with us in our confusion; for your love for us, strong and challenging, which has called us to risk for you, asked for the best in us, and shown us how to serve.

Iona Community

13. Harmony with Creation

Creator God, as we proclaim our joy in all that you have made, and in the inheritance in which we share, make us to be at one with and within your creation. Open our eyes to our misuse of your gifts, open our minds to new ways of living in harmony with our world, open our hearts to all who share the concern for justice and peace for the whole creation. Open our hands to serve your creation as faithful stewards,

Let All The World …

14. Overwhelmed by Wonders

O God, my Father, I am overwhelmed by the world around me – new knowledge, new wonders; humans reaching out to the moon, to distant planets; possible holidaying in space; microchips producing un-thought-of results; robots with artificial intelligence; sitting in one's room one can reach all kinds of knowledge, or people all over the world, on the Internet. I know this can be both good and bad. Lord, give us the wisdom to know the good from the bad; to choose what is good for us, and for the world, to use it always for good, never to misuse or abuse it. So help us, O Father.

Samuel Amirtham

15. Justifying Righteous

We bless you, O God, who have kept us in life, shielded us, led us by your goodness in the land of the living.

We praise you that you call into your fellowship not the self-righteous, nor those wise and prudent in their own conceits, but rather the broken-hearted, the ruined and undone; for such were we. And we bless you for your amazing love in giving us of the Holy Spirit, by whose gracious influence our evil is changed to good, and our enmity to love and peace.

Fulfil in us, O Lord, the work of your mercy; and more and more conform us to the image of your Son, our Lord Jesus Christ.

James Ferguson

16. Unfathomable Wisdom

O Eternal Lord Christ, we praise you that since the beginning of the universe, you have worked unrecognised as the wisdom of men and women. We praise you that your name became known in a human life, in the humility of Bethlehem, the love of Calvary and the glory of resurrection. Help us to see you working in everything that is true, holy, and loving, and grant that we, too, may delight to work humbly and unrecognised, desiring only that your purposes shall go forward, until all come to see you as the hidden heart of all things. In your name we pray.

George Appleton

17. Unfailing Care

O God, giver of all good, you continually pour your benefits upon us, age after age the living wait upon you and find that of your faithfulness there is no end and that your care is unfailing. We praise you that the mystery of our life is a mystery of infinite goodness. We praise you for the order and constancy of nature; for the beauty and bounty of the earth; for the day and night, summer and winter, seed time and harvest; for the varied gifts of loveliness and usefulness which every season brings. We give you thanks for all the comforts and joy of life, for our homes, for our friends, and for all the love and sympathy and good will of all people.

A Book of Worship for Free Churches

18. All Good Things

Giver of all good things, we thank you for health and vigour, for the air that gives the breath of life, the sun that warms us, and the good food that makes us strong; for happy houses and for the friends we love; for all that makes it good to live. Make us thankful, and eager to repay, by cheerfulness, kindliness, and by a readiness to help others. Freely we have received; let us freely give. In the name of Him who gave his life for us, Jesus Christ our Lord.

Bishop Ken

19. Overflowing Gratitude

Lord of deep wisdom, you keep us waiting. You the God of all time, want us to wait for the right time in which to discover who we are, where we must go, who will be with us, and what we must do. We give you thanks for the waiting time.

You keep us looking. You, the God of all space, want us to look in the right and wrong places for signs of hope, for people who are hopeless, for visions of a better world which will appear among the disappointments of the world we know. We give you thanks for the looking time.

You keep us loving. You, the God of whose name is love, want us to be like you – to love the loveless and the unlovable, to love without jealousy or design or threat, and, most difficult of all, to love ourselves. We give you thanks for the loving time.

And in all this, you keep us through hard questions with no easy answers, through failing where we hope to succeed and making an impact when we felt we were useless, through the patience and the dreams of the love of others, and through Jesus Christ and his Spirit, you keep us. We give thanks for the keeping time, and for now, and for ever.

Let All The World ...

20. Varied Gifts

O God, help me to be grateful for the things which come so regularly that we can forget that they are gifts. Help me to be grateful for the things which so often we do not value until we lose them. Above all, make me grateful to you for my health, for strength of body and for health of mind, for accuracy of hand and eye, and mind and brain, to do my work. Give me sympathy for those who are ill; and help me never to be impatient and annoyed and irritated with those who are not strong as I am. Help me to give my strength to the weak, and grant that my own good health may never make me forget those who are less fortunate than I am.

William Barclay

21. Resources of Culture

Lord, your glory fills the world and is seen in the life and work of all people. You are present in the experience and cultural heritage of all races. You inspire our use of colour, sound and movement and the rich resources of the earth. You made us in your image and gave us your creative ability.

Thank you, Creator and Provider of all.

Thank you for gifts of communication, speech and language; for the art of storytelling, enabling us to pass on traditions from one generation to another; for the gift of writing and the enrichment of mind that comes from the literature, poetry and wise sayings of people of many countries and periods of history.

Thank you, Creator and Provider of all.

Thank you for gift of dramatic art, the development of radio and television and the wealth of talent from many cultures they bring into our homes.

Thank you, Creator and Provider of all.

Thank you for varieties of sound and rhythm and the power of music and dance to make us forget ourselves and become one with the community.

Thank you, Creator and Provider of all.

Thank you for works of art and architecture, woodcarvings and sculpture, beautiful jewelry and ornaments, and fashioning and design of cloths and textiles.

Thank you, Creator and Provider of all.

Thank you for the gift of knowledge and the development of science; that we can look through microscopes at the smallest units of your creation and discover wonders invisible to the naked eye; for the use of radiation in the diagnosis and treatment of disease; for new methods of agriculture to combat soil erosion, cultivate deserts and provide food for everyone.

Thank you, Creator and Provider of all.

Maureen Edwards

22. Garland of Thanksgiving

In the quiet we give thanks to God:
For strength released within weakness,
For hope borne in testing places,
For joy and laughter in places of sorrow and pain,
For the power to be gentle,
For strength to forgive,
For the patience to understand,
For the courage to live the truth we know,
For the love that transforms us,
For the vision of a new world rising from the ruins of the old,
For the renewing power of God within all circumstances,
We give thanks and praise.

Donald Eadie

23. Redeeming Presence

We give thanks for the cross of Christ at the heart of creation, for the presence of Christ in our weakness and strength, for the power of Christ to transform our suffering, in darkness and in light, in trouble and in joy. Help us to trust your love, to serve within your unfolding purposes, and in every circumstance praise your Holy name.

The Daily Office Revised (adapted)

24. Music

Lord, I thank you that you have spoken to us in the music of words and melody, in so many marvellous instruments in unison and in harmony; thank you for song writers and musicians, for bands, groups, and orchestras. Sometimes, Lord, I hear sounds that speak of heaven: I am 'lost in wonder, love and praise.' How good it is to sing your praises, to know you bless creativity, that you speak in the music of life, and that so many kinds of music can tell of you. May we honour you in the music we sing. May we praise you always with words and thought that are honest and true. May we forever sing Hallelujah! May our shout be Hallelujah!

Tony Jasper

25. Revelation through Children

Loving Creator, we recognize you in a baby's eyes, and smile before we have thought; we hear you in a child's cries, and feel your pull in our heart; we know your delight in children's jokes and laughter, and relax in their spirit of joy.

Thank you for the children in our churches. We love them in your name. Thank you for children's workers, who learn, pray and serve with your worldwide Church. Thank you for the child in us, who knows you as Mother and Father and enjoys your smiles, your tears, your laughter and your love for us all.

Steve Pearce

26. Timely Help

O God of love, grace and truth, we give you thanks for family and friends, for hope in times of despair, for light in times of darkness, for showing us the way to life, for strength to endure to the end, and for your love and the blessings we cannot count.

Lesley G. Anderson

27. Spirit of Creation

Spirit of creation, spilling into rivers and oceans, cleanse the life-giving waters. Spirit of creation, rushing through mighty forests, spread the seeds of new life. Spirit of creation, burning in the hearts of your people, give life, reborn and renewed. Spirit of God, water, wind and fire, fill us with your love.

Diane Clutterbuck

28. Trees and Foliage

The tree, dependent on the soil in which it grows, a home for animals, birds and insects, fungi and other parasites, the beautiful orchid ... absorbing the impurities of the air we breathe and giving out oxygen, it heals and gives life to the world. Fragile, it can be broken and smashed by wind and hurricane, but in the process of falling to the ground and dying, it gives life again to the soil that nourished it. Trees hold the land together and save it from becoming a desert, shedding leaves to be broken down by the forces of nature to renew the earth.

Creating God, trees speak to us of the mystery of your presence, and your words to us; 'I created you. I love you and care for you. You belong to me like branches of the tree. My name is Emmanuel. I will be with you until the end of time and beyond with all the energy and love that are needed to heal and nourish the nations and their peoples; and to bring all things into a unity in Christ.'

Creator God, help us to care for the trees which you planted that we may have abundant life.

Maureen Edwards

29. Water

Creator God, you made the wells of this earth and continue to replenish them. You send rain on the righteous and on the unrighteous and invite us to drink the water of life. We pray for all lands which cry out for rain, that they may be blessed. We pray also for those places where floods destroy. May we thirst until we find a vital harmony with the earth, replenished and whole. To you we turn.

World Council of Churches

30. Mysterious Love

Lord, I am grateful to you that you in your mysterious love have taken away from me all earthly wealth, and that you now clothe and feed me through the kindness of others.

Lord, I am grateful to you that since you have taken away from me the sight of my eyes, you care for me now through the eyes of others.

Lord, I am grateful to you that since you have taken away from me the strength of my hands and heart, you are for me now strength through the hands and hearts of others.

Lord, I pray for them that you will reward them in your love; that they may continue to faithfully serve and care until they come to a happy end and live in eternity with you.

Mechthild of Magdeburg

31. Marriage and Family

For the day of our marriage, and the years we have shared together,
we praise and thank you, Lord.
For faithfulness and friendship, for love and security,
we praise and thank you, Lord.
For the hours of happiness and joy, for the hours of sadness and tears,
we praise and thank you, Lord.
For difficulties shared and problems overcome,
we praise and thank you, Lord.
For your gift of children, and all that you have blessed us with,
we praise and thank you, Lord.
For your protecting power, and your presence in our home,
We praise and thank you, Lord.
For the love you have shown us, and your peace and grace given us,
we praise and thank you, Lord.
Almighty and Heavenly Father, for all that lies ahead of us
we trust and praise you.
For the future together without fear,
we trust and praise you.

Pamela Wilding

32. Canticle of the Sun

O most high, Almighty, good Lord God, to you belong paradise, glory, honour, and all blessings!

Praised be my Lord God for all his creatures, especially for our brother the sun, who brings us the day and who brings us the light; fair is he and shines with a very great splendour; O Lord, he signifies you to us!

Praised be my Lord for our sister the moon, and for the stars, which he has set clear and lovely in heaven.

Praised be my Lord for our brother the wind, and for the air and clouds, calms and all weather by which you uphold life in all creatures.

Praised be my Lord for our sister water, who is very serviceable to us and humble and precious and clean.

Praised be my Lord for our brother fire, through whom you give us light in the darkness, and he is bright and pleasant and very mighty and strong.

Praised be my Lord for our mother the earth, who sustains us and keeps us and brings forth various fruits and flowers of many colours, and grass.

Praised be my Lord for all those who pardon one another for his love's sake, and who endure weakness and tribulation; blessed are they who shall peaceably endure, for you, O Most High, will give them a crown.

Praised be my Lord for our sister, the death of the body, from which no man escapes. Woe to him who dies in mortal sin!

Blessed are they who are found walking by your most holy will, for the second death shall have no power to do them harm.

Praise and bless the Lord, and give thanks to him and serve him with great humility.

Francis of Assisi

33. Holy and Almighty

You are holy, Lord, the only God and your deeds are wonderful. You are strong, you are great. You are the most High, you are almighty, You, holy Father, are King of heaven and earth. You are Three and One, Lord God, all good. You are good, all good, supreme good. Lord God, living and true. You are love, you are wisdom. You are humility, you are endurance. You are rest, you are peace. You are joy and gladness, you are justice and moderation. You are all our riches, and you suffice for us. You are beauty, you are gentleness, You are our protector, you are our guardian and defender. You are courage, you are our haven and our hope. You are our faith, our great consolation. You are our eternal life, great and wonderful Lord. God almighty, merciful Saviour.

Francis of Assisi

34. For Multifarious Gifts

O God, our Father, we thank you that you have made all things and made them well.

We thank you for the world in which we live. For the light of the day and the dark of the night; For the glory of the sunlight, for the silver splendour of the moon, and for the star-scattered sky; For the hills and the sea, for the busy city streets, for the open road and the wind on our faces:

We thank you, O God.

We thank you for ourselves. For hands to work, and eyes to see, and ears to hear; For minds to think, and memories to remember, and hearts to love:

We thank you, O God.

We thank you for all that makes life worthwhile. For a task to do, and for health of body, for accuracy of hand and eye; For skill of mind and brain to do it; For homes and for friends and for loved ones:

We thank you, O God.

We thank you that this life is not the end. That we are preparing ourselves for another and a greater life; That there is a place where all questions will be answered, and all hopes realized; That we will meet again those whom we have loved and lost awhile:

We thank you, O God.

We thank you most of all for Jesus, our Friend and our Example, our Saviour and our Lord. Help us to try to deserve a little better all the gifts which you have given to us.

William Barclay

35. Home

Lord of the stable and of the hillsides, we thank you for the homes that you have given us; for a door to shut against the night; for a roof and walls to keep out the cold and rain; for a fire at which we can warm ourselves; for a table at which we can gather to eat and talk. We pray for those who have no homes and who must live without privacy or security. We pray for those whose only home is a crowded tenement room or a rough shelter of planks or corrugated iron. Lord, in our comfort, remind us of the uncomfortable, in our plenty, give us concern for all those in need.

Beryl Bye

36. Joy

Lord of righteousness, make all your treasures our pursuit. You brought into the turmoil of this world all good and great joy. Help us to focus our lives on all that you have given us. Guide us to live lives that show the joy of your creation.

Moravian

37. Life in Fullness

We thank you, O God, for all the interesting things in life.

For music and for rhythm; For pictures and for plays; For wireless and for television; For the things which make us laugh; For the things which command our interest; For the things which widen our knowledge;

We thank you, O God.

For our work and for our study; And for the real satisfaction of a difficult task mastered, completed and done;

We thank you, O God.

O God, forgive us for the things in us which have spoiled life. If we have been lazy at work; If we have been difficult to get on with at school, at our work, or in this fellowship; If we have been inconsiderate and ungrateful at home; If we have been forgetful of you:

O God, we thank you for all the possibilities of life. Help us to work so hard; To study so diligently; To discipline ourselves so firmly, that we may turn the possibilities into realities and so make all our plans and dreams come true. So grant that we may ever be, a credit to ourselves; a help to others; a joy to you.

Bless our friends and our comrades and our loved ones. Bless all those in trouble of any kind; and bless each one of us.

William Barclay

38. The Word

Thank you, God, for your Word: made known through prophets; made firm through scripture; made flesh in Christ; made present by your Spirit. Thank you also, God, that you speak to us and through us. Thank you, God, for all who have laboured long and hard to hear and to know and to show your word for all the world. Thank you, God, that you are never without witnesses, that countless quiet and faithful people, listening, wait on you; ready to hear, willing to speak. In the clamour of competing voices, thank you that your Word still can be heard. Make us expectant to hear, ready to respond and willing to change. In Christ's name.

Donald Hilton

39. Study

O God, we thank you for everything which widens our knowledge and which equips us more fully for the task of life and living.

For school and college and university; For all wise teachers and instructors; For those who teach not only by their words but also by their example;

We thank you, O God.

For all good books; For all that makes available for us the wisdom which has gone before; For all the knowledge in the printed page with which we can store our mind;

We thank you, O God.

For all the precious things the past has left us; For great poetry to linger in the memory; For great pictures and sculpture to delight the eye; For great music to sound in the ear and to thrill the heart; For all the heritage of beauty and loveliness into which we have entered;

We thank you, O God.

For wireless and for television; For all that brings the distant places to our own fireside; For every opportunity to gain knowledge and wisdom; For everything whereby we learn our profession, our trade, our craft. And above all else for Jesus to show us how to use it all for your sake and for the sake of mankind;

We give you thanks, O God.

William Barclay

40. Source of all Life

O God, Giver of all good, and Foundation of mercies, in whom are the springs of our life; All glory, thanks and praise be unto thee for thy ever-flowing goodness; for thy faithfulness which is from one generation to another; for thy mercies which are new every morning, fresh every moment and more than we can number; for seed-time and harvest, summer and winter, day and night throughout the year; for food and raiment and shelter, for health and reason, for childhood and age and youth and manhood; for thy fatherly hand upon us in sickness, in health, in joy and sorrow, in life and in death; for fiends and kindred and kind benefactors; for home and country; for thy church and for thy Gospel.

Yea, Lord, for that there is nothing for which we may not bless and thank thee; therefore do we call upon thy Name, and pay our vows now in the presence of all thy people; humbly beseeching thee to accept this our thanksgiving, even as we offer it in the Name and through the infinite merits of thy Son, Jesus Christ our Lord.

James Ferguson

41. Fun Times

Thank you, God, for sunny days, for my favourite colours, and dogs with wagging tails.

Thank you, God, for trees to climb, and cubbies to hide in, for parks with slides and swings.

Thank you, God, for my gum boots and my rain coat, for puddles to splash in, and leaves to kick.

Thank you, God, for beach balls and surf boards, for warm sand and the cool sea to swim in.

Thank you, God, for friends to play with, and for everyone who loves me very much. ***Thank you, God, for me.***

Terry C. Falla (+)

42. Past, Present, Future

O God of past, present and future, in the challenge and excitement of the new, help us to be grateful for the past. May we have the grace to be open to what is different in a fast-changing world, to allow our faith to be stretched, as we explore new ways of worship while retaining the richness of what we already know. As we give thanks for the wonder of easy communication with those who are far away, enable us always to be aware of people nearby who need our help. May your whole church experience the invigoration of the Holy Spirit who links us to the earliest followers of Christ, so that we and all who profess the faith may go forward in hope into what is yet to be, in the name of Jesus who shows us the Father, and who is always with us in the power of Holy Spirit.

Thomas Kingston

43. Hope and Joy

And now unto him who is able to keep us from falling and lift us from the dark valley of despair to the bright mountain of hope, from the midnight of desperation to the daybreak of joy; to him be power and authority, for ever and ever.

Martin Luther King

44. Wisdom and Experience

Thank you, Lord for the gift of years, for wisdom and experience, for the ability to look back on our lives and to discern how you have been working out your loving purpose in us. Thank you for those who have shared our journey and have been woven into the tapestry of our lives, enriching our experience. Help us to adjust now to different circumstances and learn that although we may have white hair and wrinkles, and our physical and mental abilities may limit us, we can grace the world with our smiles and our love. Lord, more than ever we want to stand in your presence, to be near you.

Susan Dutton

45. From Clay to Jewel

Loving God, your grace makes diamonds from our leaden words of praise. You take the clay of our humanity, and make of it a jewel in your hands. You take our faith that drifts like sand that finds itself in pooled shallows, and make it a mirror for your love. Transforming God, we praise you and thank you for your willingness to enter into our lives and live alongside us.

Fiona Green

46. Gifts of Winter

Thank you, Father God, for making winter-time when so many things you have made can sleep and rest – flowers, trees and hedges, squirrels and dormice. We thank you for the loveliness of bare tree branches and of sparkling frost and icicles; for the cheery song of the robin; for winter fun and games. Thank you, Father God, for winter time.

J. M. Macdougall Ferguson

47. Wisdom Infinite

For the wisdom that fashioned the universe and can be read in the earth's dark depths and in heaven's infinity of lights, thanks be to you, O God. For the wisdom of teachers before me and their words and imaginative seeing, for the wisdom of those I have known and their silence and humility of speech, and for wisdom's wellspring in my own soul and in the soul of every human being from which ancient truths and new realizations spring forth, thanks be to you. Let wisdom unfold in my own heart and mind and in the men and women of every nation. Let us see the foundations for a new harmony within us and between us, the foundations for a recovered unity with the earth and all its creatures, for the ground of life is in you, O God, the ground of all life is in you.

J. Philip Newell

48. Gift of Time

Eternal God, thank you for your gift of time and the measure death gives to our days. They pass so quickly as to dent our pride. May we neither rely on our achievements nor be downcast at our failures. Keep us but faithful to your love, and dependent on your grace alone. We ask this in the Spirit of the One who died a human failure, and died so young.

Jim Cotter

49. Thanksgiving at Planting

Father God, maker of all that is beautiful in the world; we praise you for light and colour, for sound and scent, for softness and strength, and for all the other wonderful things which only you could make. Especially we thank you today for the bulbs we are going to plant. Help us take care of them in the right way, so that we do not spoil your lovely handwork.

J. M. Macdougall Ferguson

50. Beauty

Thank you God for all good men and women, who have put new beauty into the world: those who have made us see it in pictures and hear it in music; those who have carved haunting sculpture made uplifting building, woven beauty into fabrics and shown it in glass and metal and substances now-formed. Give us minds appreciating all such beauty and hearts filled with gratitude for it.

Sid G. Hedges

51. Truth Inscribed

That truth has been inscribed into my heart and into the heart of every human being, there to be read and reverenced, thanks be to you, O God. That there are ways of seeing and sensitivities of knowing hidden deep in the palace of the soul, waiting to be discovered, ready to be set free, thanks be to you. Open my senses to wisdom's inner promptings that I may give voice to what I hear in my soul and be changed for the healing of the world, that I may listen for truth in every living soul and be changed for the well-being of the world.

J. Philip Newell

52. For Faithful Servants

Bounteous God, we praise and thank you for all those who have helped us to see your world in new light, to have new life freed from clutches of slavery and oppression and to have new hope with which we can journey on with confidence. We acknowledge the inadequacy of our language and modes of praise when we think of all those who have contributed to our life, individual and collective. Give us a grateful heart in the altar of which there will be unbroken chain of praise and thanksgiving.

Israel Selvanayagam

III. Confession, Forgiveness, Deliverance

1. Introspection

Gracious God,
Help us to realise our true condition before your presence.
Let us not cover up our weaknesses and shortcomings with shining carpets.
Give us more light that we may see the depth of our darkness.
Give us more strength that we may feel our weakness.
Give us more knowledge that we may know more our ignorance.
Give us greater purity of heart that we may realise our inner dirt.
Melt our frozen hearts that our relationship with you and all your children may become warmer.
In all we do, let us seek your glory alone, now and always.

Israel Selvanayagam

2. Self-Examination

O Lord, you have searched me and known me.

You know when I sit down and when I rise up; you discern my thoughts from far away. You search out my path and my lying down, and are acquainted with all my ways.

Even before a word is on my tongue, O Lord, you know it completely. You hem me in, behind and before, and lay your hand upon me.

Such knowledge is too wonderful for me; it is so high that I cannot attain it.

Where can I go from your spirit? Or where can I flee from your presence? If I ascend to heaven, you are there; if I make my bed in Sheol, you are there. If I take the wings of the morning and settle at the farthest limits of the sea, even there your hand shall lead me, and your right hand shall hold me fast.

Search me, O God, and know my heart; test me and know my thoughts. See if there is any wicked way in me, and lead me in the way everlasting.

Psalms 139:1-10;23-24

3. True Condition

Gracious God,
When we are tormented by thoughts of our past guilt,
Bring to our minds that you have already blotted out and forgotten it.
When we feel that we are tainted by dirt and filth all around,
Make us know that we are washed by the torrent of your pardoning love.
When we are tempted to swell in self-righteousness and pride,
Remind us of how failing we are in fulfilling your commandments of love.
Just as the wiper of a windscreen wipes away the splashing water,
Let us feel that your grace overcomes our faults at every moment.
Make us sensitive to avoid that which will grieve your Holy Spirit.
And help us to seek always to do your will and accept others as you accept them.
In the name of the one who never turned away even the wicked and vile,
Even Jesus Christ your Son and our Saviour.

Israel Selvanayagam

4. To Overcome Temptation

I'm at the end of my tether, Lord. I am shattered, I am broken. Since this morning I have been struggling to escape temptation, which now subtle, now persuasive, now tender, now sensuous, dances before me like a glamour girl at a fair. I don't know what to do. I don't know where to go. It spies on me, follows me, engulfs me. When I leave a room I find it seated and waiting for me in the next … It has seeped into the crevices of my memory and sings into the ear of my imagination. It plays on my nerves as on the strings of a guitar. I don't know where I stand, Lord. I don't know whether or not I want this sin that beckons to me. I no longer know whether I pursue it or am pursued. I am dizzy, and the void draws me as it draws the rash mountaineer who can neither advance nor retreat. Lord, help me!

Michel Quoist

5. Shortcomings

All knowing God, we confess that in our lives we do not always choose the way of peace. We spread gossip which fans the flame of hatred. We are ready to make any sacrifice when the world demands, but few when God invites. We worship the false god of security. We hold out one hand in friendship, but keep a weapon in the other behind the back. We have divided your body of people into those we trust and those we do not. Huge problems challenge us in the world, but our greed, fear and selfishness prevent us from uniting to solve them. Lord, we need your help and forgiveness, your reconciling power, now and always.

Let All The World ...

6. Cruelty and Insensibility

O Lord, forgive the cruelties of humans of every age, their insensibility to others' pain, the deliberation that gives pain to satisfy and express the evil that rebels from love's surrender to others' needs to exalt itself.

O Lord, forgive the carelessness that passes by the blunted conscience that will not see or fear to see the wrongs humans do to each other.

Most merciful, most loving Judge, Redeemer of humankind, you restore the fallen, you seek out the scattered sheep.

Gilbert Shaw

7. Omission and Commission

Forgive them all, O Lord: our sins of omission and our sins of commission; the sins of our youth and the sins of our riper years; the sins of our souls and the sins of our bodies; our secret and our more open sins; our sins of ignorance and surprise, and our more deliberate and presumptuous sin; the sins we have done to please ourselves and the sins we have done to please others; the sins we know and remember, and the sins we have forgotten; the sins we have striven to hide from others and the sins by which we have made others offend; forgive them, O Lord, forgive them all for his sake, who died for our sins and rose for our justification, and now stands at your right hand to make intercession for us, Jesus Christ our Lord.

John Wesley

8. Wrong Choices

O God, our Father, forgive us that we so often give our best to the wrong things.

Sometimes, we put far more enthusiasm and thought and effort into our pleasures and our games and our amusement than we do into our work.

Sometimes we keep our best behaviour for strangers and our worst behaviour for our own homes; and often we treat our nearest and dearest with a discourtesy and a disregard we would never show to strangers.

Sometimes we get irritated and annoyed and angry about things which in our calmer moments we know do not matter.

Sometimes we lose our temper in an argument about trifles.

Sometimes we allow very little things to cause a quarrel with a friend.

Help us to see what is important and what is unimportant, so that we may never forget the things that matter, and so that we may never allow the things which do not matter to matter too much.

William Barclay

9. Failings in Using the Gifts

Gracious God, where love is replaced by domination or trivialized for commercial gain, forgive us for neglecting the gifts of your Spirit. Where joy is snuffed out by pessimism or stifled by apathy, forgive us for undermining the gifts of your Spirit. Where peace is destroyed by violence and broken by ambitious nationalism, forgive us for failing to use the gifts of your Spirit. Where patience is paralysed by greedy demands for instant success, forgive us for manipulating the gifts of your Spirit. Where kindness is treated as weakness or rejected through lack of grace, forgive us for underestimating the gifts of your Spirit. Where goodness is crucified by the power-hungry and passes unrecognized by a noisy, busy world, forgive us for losing sight of the gifts of your Spirit. Where faithfulness is abandoned and no one trusts another anymore, forgive us for wiping out the gifts of your Spirit. Where gentleness is ridiculed and people build their lives around aggression, forgive us for misrepresenting the gifts of your Spirit. Where we lose self-control, giving into the violence of our emotions, forgive for not trusting the gifts of your Spirit. Holy Spirit, forgive us our rejection of your riches; open the hearts of the nations and peoples to receive love, joy, peace, patience, kindness, goodness, faithfulness, gentleness and self-control; but start with us.

David Jenkins

10. Failures to be True

My failure to be true even to my own accepted standards; my self-deception in face of temptation; my choosing of the worse when I know the better. O Lord, forgive my failure to apply to myself the standards of conduct I demand of others; my blindness to the suffering of others; and my slowness to be taught by my own. My complacence towards wrongs that do not touch; my own case and my over sensitiveness to those that do; my slowness to see the good in my fellows; and evil in myself. My hardness of heart towards neighbours` faults; and my readiness to make allowance for my own; my unwillingness to believe that you called me to a small work and my brother to a greater one. O Lord, forgive.

William Barclay

11. Faults and Failures

O God our Father, Jesus has taught that we need forgiveness. Help us then to remember our faults and failures, to think of them quietly in our hearts, and to ask to be forgiven. For greediness and wanting the best for ourselves, for laziness and not trying hard, for bad temper and gloominess, for bearing grudges and nursing grievances, for cheating or meanness in work or play, for rudeness and lack of care for others, for the times when we have hurt anybody, for repeating unkind gossip, for thinking too much about ourselves and too little about others. Forgive us, Lord – may we be strong to correct these faults, and may we not fail like this again.

Roderic and Gregor H. Dunkerley

12. Failing to be Helpful

Forgive me when I haven't been much of a saint; when I have caused brokenness, tears or pain. Forgive me when I haven't been a friend to the weak; when my heart has been cold and I haven't shared my bread. Forgive me when I haven't given shelter or refuge; whenever I have prevented your freedom or peace. Give me compassion and warmth in my heart, change my love from a spark to a flame.

Josette Crane

13. Clearing the Mind in Night

O God, our Father, we have come to you tonight to say that we are sorry for all the wrong things that we have done. For the work that we did carelessly; For the work that we have left half-finished; For the work that we have not even begun:

Forgive us, O God.

For the people we have hurt; For the people we have disappointed; For the people we have failed when they needed us most:

Forgive us, O God.

For the friends to whom we have been disloyal; For the loved ones to whom we have been untrue; For the promises we have broken; For the vows we have forgotten:

Forgive us, O God.

For the way in which we have disobeyed you; For the way in which we have grieved you; For our failure to love you as you have loved us:

Forgive us, O God.

William Barclay

14. Selfishness and Ugliness

O God, forgive us for the faults which make us difficult to live with.

If we behave as if we were the only people for whom life is difficult; If we behave as if we were far harder worked than anyone else; If we behave as if we were the only people who ever got a raw deal; If we are far too self-centred and far too full of self-pity:

Forgive us, O God.

If we are too impatient to finish the work we have begun; If we are too impatient to listen to someone who wants to talk to us, or to give someone a helping hand; If we think that other people are fools, and make no attempt to conceal our contempt for them:

Forgive us, O God.

If we too often rub people the wrong way; If we spoil a good case by trying to ram it down someone's throat; If we do things that get on people's nerves, and go on doing them, even when we are asked not to;

Forgive us, O God.

Help us to take the selfishness and the ugliness out of life and to do better in the days to come.

William Barclay

15. Eyes of Compassion

Living God, look on us with eyes of compassion; call us with the word of forgiveness, again and again, to seventy times seven, that we may at last hear and see, and turn our stricken and wounded faces, and know ourselves accepted and embraced, loved beyond measure and without reserve.

Jim Cotter

16. Sin and Pride

Take us to yourself, compassionate God, we who hurt so much in the depths of our being, caught up in the pain of life, and so often inflicting yet more on to others; embrace us with the hands that show the marks of the nails, your love swallowing up all our sin and pride. So we pray that broken bones may joy, in the dance of Yeshua who embodies your redeeming power.

Jim Cotter

17. Anger and Rage

O God, forgive our murderous deeds and blind, unthinking rage. Give us your Spirit of compassionate anger, that we may live and work in harmony with you for the healing of the body of this planet, gasping for air, sores weeping on its skin. Make us a people of one earth, our bodies no longer violated, but cherished and loved.

Jim Cotter

18. Deviations

For my deceitful heart and crooked thoughts: for barbed words spoken deliberately: for thoughtless words spoken hastily: for envious preying eyes: for ears that rejoice in iniquity and rejoice not in the truth: for greedy hands: for wandering and loitering feet: for haughty looks: have mercy upon me, O God.

John Baillie (1886-1960)

19. Self-doubting and Self-loathing

Heavenly Father, the world has worked on us and taken us from you. We have forgotten you, closed our ears to your call, and closed our hearts to those whom you would have us love. We have known this long before we were sorry for it. So now we come, self-doubting and often self-loathing, willing to be changed by you and for you. Grant us that we may start anew through your live-giving forgiveness.

Fiona Green

20. Transform Us

God: take fire and burn our guilt and lying hypocrisies. Take water and wash away our brothers' blood which we have caused to be shed. Take hot sun light and dry the tears of those we have hurt, and heal the wounded souls, minds and bodies. Take love and root it in our hearts, so that brotherhood may grow, transforming the dry desert of our prejudices and hatred. Take our imperfect prayers and purify them, so that we mean what we pray and are prepared to give ourselves to you along with our words, through Jesus Christ, who did not disdain to take our humanness upon him and live among us, sharing our life, our joys, and our pains.

Malcom Boyd

21. Break the Chains

Merciful God, break the chains that keep us in bondage; break the chains that cause us to hurt others; break the chains on our hearts that stop us from caring. For the sake of your Son, Jesus Christ, our Lord.

Ascension Rite

22. When we forget the Cost

When we forget what it means to be your people, ***Lord have mercy.***

When we find it easier to close our eyes to the cries of those in need, ***Christ have mercy.***

When we take for granted the Gospel message and lose our passion to share the good news, ***Lord have mercy.***

Ascension Rite, United College of the Ascension

23. Frivolous Self

O God, save me from my self, save me from my self; this frivolous self which plays with your creation, this vain self which is clever about your creation, this masterful self which manipulates your creation, this greedy self which exploits your creation, this lazy self which soothes itself with your creation; this self which throws the thick shadow of its own purposes and desires in every direction in which I try to look, so that I cannot see what it is that you, my Lord and God, are showing to me. Teach me to stand out of my own light, and let your daylight shine.

Austin Farrer

24. Many to be Nailed

O God our Father, help us to nail to the cross of your dear Son the whole body of our death, the wrong desires of the heart, the sinful devising of the mind, the corrupt apprehensions of the eyes, the cruel words of the tongue, the ill-employment of hands and feet; that the old man being crucified and done away, the new may live and grow into the glorious likeness of the same your Son Jesus Christ, who lives and reigns with you and the Holy Ghost, one God, world without end.

Eric Milner-White

25. Faithlessness

O God, you are always true to us in love and we are left wanting to say sorry for our faithlessness to you and to one another for our forgetting of the poor and the broken, for our failure to cherish creation. Give us life, O God, to change and enable us to change, that we may live.

O God, gladly we live and move and have our being in you. Yet always in the midst of this creation-glory, we see sin's shadow and feel death's darkness: around us in the earth, sea and sky, the abuse of matter; beside us the broken, the hungry and the poor, the betrayal of one another; and often, deep within us, a striving against your Spirit. O Trinity of love, forgive us that we may forgive one another, heal us that we may be people of healing and renew us that we also may be makers of peace.

Iona Community

26. Wavering Mind

God help my thoughts! They stray from me, setting off on the wildest journeys; when I am at prayer, they run off like naughty children, making trouble. When I read the Bible, they fly to a distant place, filled with seductions. My thoughts can cross an ocean with a single leap; they can fly from earth to heaven, and back again, in a single second. They come to me for a fleeting moment, and then away they flee. No chains, no locks can hold them back; no threats of punishment can restrain them, no hiss of a lash can frighten them. They slip from my grasp like tails of eels; they swoop hither and thither like swallows in flight. Dear, chaste Christ, who can see into every heart, and read every mind, take hold of my thoughts. Bring my thoughts back to me, and clasp me to yourself.

Celtic (source unknown)

27. Slow to Love

I was slow to love you, Lord, your age-old beauty is still as new to me: I was so slow to love you! You were within me, yet I stayed outside seeking you there; in my ugliness I grabbed at the beautiful things of your creation. Already you were with me, but I was still far from you. The things of this world kept me away: I did not know then that if they had not existed through you they would not have existed at all. Then you called me and your cry overcame my deafness; you shone out and your light overcame my blindness; you surrounded me with your fragrance and I breathed it in, so that now I yearn for more of you; I tasted you and now I am hungry and thirsty for you; you touched me, and now I burn with longing for your peace.

St. Augustine

28. Self-Contradiction

Lord, forgive us when we listen, but do not hear; when we look, but do not see; and when we feel, but do not act; and by your mercy and grace draw us into the righteous deeds of your kingdom of justice and peace; through Christ our Lord.

Maria Hare

29. Sloth and Idle Talk

Take from us, O Lord, all sloth, love of power and idle talk. Of your mercy grant us clarity of mind, strength of purpose and humility of heart. Beholding our own faults let us not be the judge of others, for you alone are truly blessed, now and to the ages of ages.

Ephrem the Syrian

30. Thoughtlessness and Negligence

Almighty God, we confess before you and before one another that we have broken your laws and forgotten our promises; we have been thoughtless in our actions and we have wasted your gifts; we have neglected opportunities for good and we have gone our own way; we pray to you for forgiveness.

Norman Wallwork

31. Being Slow to Trust

God of compassion, in whom grace is certain, mercy ever flowing and peace deep stillness, we confess our sin; we are slow to trust, have no longing to forgive and we fail to notice the holy in your world. Speak of your love, that we may live in your freedom. Touch us with healing, and we will be whole.

Philip Turner

32. For Mercies

Father, we come to you as sinners. You know our deepest faults and wayward deeds. Yet you invite us to your table, welcome us as disciples, and forgive us our trespasses. For these mercies, we thank you every day.

Moravian

33. Lack of Openness

Eternal and most gracious God; we confess that we have esteemed ourselves better than others, we have refused to help those who need us most, we have closed our gates on the poor and oppressed, we have ignored the cries of hurt and pain, we have forgotten to feed the hungry, we have neglected the homeless, we have not cared for the naked, we have lived for ourselves, obsessed with race, colour and nationality.

O God, in your mercy forgive our sin, free us from pride, give us humility in all our relationships, and grace to choose your will.

O God, in your love consecrate us anew for your mission, that we may go in faithfulness, and the assurance of your love, through Jesus Christ our Lord.

Lesley G. Anderson

34. Prejudice and Discrimination

God, merciful and gracious, you breathed life into all beings; you blessed us with minerals and waters as well as fruits and flowers and beautiful living creatures great and small. We confess our fault and those of the world. Your Son Jesus gave us peace but we chose to divide ourselves and hold on to values of this broken world: we waste the land and pollute the seas. Fear and prejudice set us against other beings; we discriminate on the basis of race; we violate your image in those we dislike; we oppress others and refuse them freedom; we are prisoners of our racism, oppressions and xenophobia.

Creator God of heaven and earth, the icon of justice, peace and creation, help us to love each other as you loved us. Teach us to share the earth and to live in harmony with all who inhabit it.

Naboth Nuchopa

35. Careless Handling

Lord, what a wonderful world! Forgive us that we spoil it. Life is a precious possession: forgive us that we waste it. Love is the greatest gift: forgive us that we devalue it. Lord God, Creator, recall us to your purpose; Lord Jesus, Redeemer, renew in us your life; Spirit of the Living God, renew us with your gifts.

Michael Wearing

36. Deliver from Ghosties

From the ghosties of our un-understood feelings and misunderstood hostilities, from the ghosties of our outworn ideas to which we cling and the illusions of our wisdom and competence, from the long-leggedy beasties of our ignorance and prejudices and self-satisfaction, and from all the things that we don't even know enough about to be afraid of that exist in the mysterious night beyond our limited sight, may the good Lord deliver us – you, me, and the whole of our struggling infant humanity.

Scott Peck

37. In Penitence

Before God and you who are near us, we release anything we hold against you. We regret all we have done to harm you. We stand beside the wrong in our lives and ask God's forgiveness.

The Lord Jesus Christ says to us, each one, 'Go and sin no more, come and follow me.'

Now bind our hands with honesty as we offer them to each other and our prayer to you.

Iona Community

38. In Need of Grace

As a fish that is dragged from the water gasps, so gasps my soul. As one who has buried his treasure, and now cannot find the place, so is my mind distraught. As a child that has lost his mother, so am I troubled. My heart is seared with sore anguish. O merciful God, you know my need, come, save me, and show me your love.

Tukaram

39. True Worth

O Lord Jesus, Son of the living God, forgive us the many times we have judged others without knowing or loving them. Give us an awareness of our sins and shortcomings and make us see ourselves as you know us. Guide us in all our contacts with those around us and fill us with mercy and love; through Jesus Christ, our Lord.

Church Army

40. Thoughtlessness

Almighty God, we confess before you and before one another that we have broken your laws and forgotten our promises; we have been thoughtless in our actions and we have wasted your gifts; we have neglected opportunities for good and we have gone our own way; we pray to you for forgiveness.

Norman Wallwork

41. Greatest Error

The error of not realising the error is the greatest error of all errors. God Save us!

V. P. K. Sundaram

42. Repentance and Forgiveness

Gracious God, we find some satisfaction in pronouncing absolution following a routine confession of sin in our worship services. Those who hear it seem to feel comforted and accepted. Is it right, O God? If it is true that your gospel is the inseparable pair of both repentance and forgiveness, help us to no more despise your grace but call everyone who is nominally religious for a new orientation in life. May we do it in love!

Israel Selvanayagam

43. Wounding Words and Hurting Actions

Gracious God, with sorrow we admit how well we know that our lives have not been wholly as you will. We confess the sin we know and regret the shame we feel. We confess that some thoughts have been unworthy: centred on self, others denied. We confess that some words have been wounding: barbed and harsh, twisting deep. We confess that some actions have been unfitting: kingdom-destroying, love-denying. We confess that sometimes we have been silent and still in the face of need: hesitant to give, slow to care.

Stephen Brown

44. Scars of Greedy Abuse

Loving God, we are sorry that we have marred the beauty of your world with the source of pollution, the scars of greedy abuse. We are sorry that we have been poor stewards of its bounty, heedlessly plundering its natural resources and selfishly holding its wealth. We are sorry that we have not treated your creation with respect, that we have taken and taken with no thought for tomorrow. We are sorry that we do not act as your true children towards the world that you have made and towards one another. Loving God, you have the power and the will not only to create, but to re-create. Re-create your loving image within us, that we might strive with you for the healing of all creation. In the name of your Son, Jesus Christ, our Saviour, who died that all might be made new.

Christine Odell

45. Pollution and Waste

We have disfigured the face of the beautiful earth you, O God, have given. We have dirtied the walking paths with heaps of litters and wastes. Our industrial smoke and personal smoking have polluted the atmosphere. The scourge of plastic has toxicated our waters and other resources. In the name of development, we have cherished greed over against need; we have overused and abused the resources often induced by the manipulative media. We are truly sorry, O God; forgive our lack of sensitivity, and give us seriousness and a sense of the sacred in treating and using the earth's resources. May Jesus who walked on the dusty paths of Galilee and shared simple food with the poor be still our master and model. In his holy name we pray.

Israel Selvanayagam

46. Unworthy Pursuits

Precious God, when we consider the things we exalt in this life, the things we honour, the things that receive our homage and devotion, too often they are less than worthy and are not what would please you. We make this confession, seeking your forgiveness.

Moravian

47. Afflicted and Suffocated

Loving God, we are afflicted with the human condition: what we shouldn't do, we do anyway, what we know is right, we neglect. The weight of our sin is suffocating. Yet you still love us. We acknowledge that your love is unmerited; that we are unworthy; and that your grace is a gift. We accept this gift with gladness and praise!

Moravian

48. Burdensome and Painful Remembrance

O merciful God, full of compassion, long-suffering, and of great pity, who sparest when we deserve punishment, and in thy wrath think upon mercy, make me earnestly to repent, and heartily to be sorry for all my misdoings, make the remembrance so burdensome and painful, that I may flee to thee with a troubled spirit and a contrite heart; and, O merciful Lord, visit, comfort, and relieve me; cast me not out from your presence, and take not your Holy Spirit from me, but excite in me true repentance; give me in this world knowledge of your truth, and confidence in your mercy, and in the world to come life everlasting, for the sake of our Lord and Saviour, your Son Jesus Christ.

Samuel Johnson

49. Scarlet to Turn White

Forgiving Saviour, what solace we find in knowing that our scarlet sins are washed white as snow; in knowing that you not only forgive but that you also forget. The weight of our sin is great; yet, you have taken it from us with your own life so that we might live. We praise you and thank you for this greatest of all gifts!

Moravian

50. Remove Blockages

Peel the scales from our eyes, remove the blockages from our ears and hearts, O Lord, so that we may receive you. Let not this day pass without us drawing nigh unto you, our Saviour, Redeemer, and Sustainer.

Moravian

51. Covetousness and Greed

The hatred which divides nation from nation, race from race, class from class, Father, forgive. The covetous desires of men and nations to possess what is not their own, Father, forgive. The greed which exploits the labours of men, and lays waste the earth, Father, forgive. Our envy of the welfare and happiness of others, Father, forgive. Our indifference to the plight of the homeless and the refugee, Father, forgive. The lust which uses for ignoble ends the bodies of men and women, Father, forgive. The pride which leads to trust to ourselves and not in God. Father, forgive.

Author Unknown

52. Squandering the Gift of Life

We have squandered the gift of life. The good life of some is built on the pain of many; the pleasure of a few on the agony of millions. To you we lift our outspread hands. We thirst for you in a thirsty land. We worship in our quest to possess even more things; we worship death in our hankering after our own security, our own survival, our own peace, as if life were divisible, as if love were divisible, as if Christ had not died for all of us. To you we lift up our outspread hands.

Used at 6th Assembly of the WCC, Vancouver, 1983

53. In Shame and Humility

We remember, O Lord, our land and our nation before you. In shame and humility we confess that we are a hopelessly divided people, ruthlessly selfish, arrogant and conceited … We are prone to despise rather than to love … We are suffocating goodness, beauty and truth and are rushing down the precipice of ruin and destruction. Lord have mercy on us, miserable offenders, renew and re-clothe us with goodness, beauty and truth … In Christ's name we pray.

From Kolkota (India)

54. Tried and Failed

Lord, I confess that I have tried and failed! I thought I could follow Jesus and do it in my own strength; that I could serve my neighbour without relying on you; that I could live the Christian life and rarely turn to you in prayer; that I could plan my own life; make my decisions and live each day never listening to your voice, never opening your word. Lord, I confess that I have tried and failed! Now send your living fire that the Holy Spirit may refine, reform and renew – even me! Lord, I have made my confession; come now, that the living fire may make me new.

David Clowes

55. Forgive Being Unaware

Surprising God, your presence in the life of the world often goes unnoticed; forgive us when we do not have eyes to see. You sometimes speak to us in uncomfortable ways, forgive us when we do not have ears to hear. You call us to walk the way of the cross, forgive us when we do not have hearts to follow where Jesus leads.

John Hellyer

56. Being a Thorn

Forgive me, Jesus, for being a thorn. I confess that when I find signs of hope, I respond with the prick of cynicism; when I watch your spirit alive in people, I fail to give encouragement; when I see sprouts of growth, I pour scorn; when you offer the seeds of new life, my hands reach out to choke the new shoots. Forgive me, Lord, for being jealous when I see you working in others. Help me to rejoice in what you are doing, and to be open enough to allow you to work in me.

Ken Kingston

57. Straighten the Crooked

Father, we cannot undo the past or make it never have happened, so we humbly ask that you would write straight on our crooked lines. Will you make something beautiful for you out of the mistakes we have made? Teach us to live at peace with you, to make peace with others and to make peace with ourselves. Give us fresh vision. Let us experience your love so deeply that we are free to face the future with a steady eye, strong in your purpose, forgiven and strong in hope.

Richard

58. Enslaved in Selfishness

Liberating God, you come to us as we are: enslaved in selfishness; imprisoned in prejudices and pride; trapped in long-established habits of resistance to change and growth. You come to us, to set us free in Christ. You meet us in your grace and you melt us by your love. You call out what and who we might be. Release us, this day, freely to live holy and just lives. And empower us with your freedom, so that all our words and actions may point to your redeeming love and glorify your name.

Roger Walton

59. Selfish and Stingy

Lord, we know we can be selfish at times, and our desire for material goods and over-indulgence fills our minds. We become reluctant to give up what we feel is ours and only sparingly give of our time, effort and money. Help us to be generous with our gifts; turn our greed into generosity, our wants into needs, and help us not to be selfish, but selfless. Teach us to be content with what we have and trust in the promise that you will give us what we need. We pray that in our world of temptation, all may have the courage to make the right choices and the faith to be led by your Spirit. We ask this in the name of our friend and Saviour, Jesus Christ.

Megan Thomas

IV. Nearer my God

1. Mysterious God

Living mysterious God, greater than the human heart, greater than all the peoples of the world, greater than the faiths that try to cage you, shatter the idols which we make to keep us safe, to claim you for ourselves, to portray you in superior ways. Humble us, living God, and draw us by the magnet of your love into the glory of your presence and the harmony of a new Jerusalem.

Jim Cotter

2. Desire to Love

Let me desire you, O Lord, with my whole heart. Thus desiring you, may I seek you; seeking you, may I find you; finding you, may I love you; loving you, may I be parted from those sins which separate me from you; and this I beg for Jesus' sake.

St. Anselm

3. All Encompassing Love

Lord, in the silence, we hear your love; in the stillness, we feel your love, and when stumbling on the pathway, we are enveloped in your love. In this busy and complex world, we are humbled to know that your love will never change, never fail and never end. Help us, Lord, to be true witnesses to your love.

Susan Robinson

4. Open My Life

Loving God, open our hearts, so that we may feel the breath and play of your Spirit. Unclench our hands so that we may reach out to one another, and touch and be healed. Open our lips that we may drink in the delight and wonder of life. Unclog our ears to hear your agony in our inhumanity. Open our eyes, so that we may see Christ in friend and stranger. Breathe your Spirit into us, and touch our lives with the life of Christ.

Anon

5. Bond of Unity

O God, who are the unsearchable abyss of peace, the ineffable sea of love, the fountain of blessings and the bestower of affection, who send peace to those that receive it; open to us this day the sea of your love and water us with plenteous streams from the riches of your grace and from the most sweet springs of your kindness. Make us children of quietness and heirs of peace, enkindle in us the fire of your love; sow in us your fear; strengthen our weakness by your power; bind us closely to you and to each other in our firm and indissoluble bond of unity.

Syrian Clementine Liturgy

6. Goodness and Love

God of all goodness and grace, you are worthy of a greater love than we can either give or understand. Fill our hearts with such love towards you that nothing may seem too hard for us to do or to suffer in obedience to your will. In loving you may we grow daily more like you and finally receive the crown of life which you have promised to those who are faithful to the end: through Jesus Christ our Lord.

Brooke Foss Westcott

7. Fortress and Refuge

I love you, O God: my strength, my crag, my fortress, and my deliverer, the rock to which I cling for refuge, my shield, my saviour, and my stronghold. I called to you with loud lamentations, and you released the trap which held me fast.

Jim Cotter

8. Undivided Love

Grant, O God, that we may be united to you and to our neighbour with an undivided love; serve you and your children with an undivided heart and revere you and your creation with an undivided will; through Christ our Lord.

John Scotus Erigena

9. Hen-Like God

Hen-like God,

You surprise us with your awakening act of immeasurable compassion and love.

You hatched us, injected life into us and your Spirit brooded over us.

You formed us so mysteriously and gave us as neighbours the rest of your creation that surrounds us.

You nurtured us with warmth of your love and the touch of your embrace.

When we stray towards dangerous predators, you signal to us that we may rush back and look out upon the world through the feathers of your wings.

When you encourage us to go out, your eyes watch over us.

You feed us by sharing what you have gathered and reserved for us in your store.

When we encounter others of your broods of different colours and looks,

let us not push them aside nor look indifferent,

but make them feel welcome, creating a space for each of them.

Fill us with the joy of fellowship and neighbour us with your constant loving care and welcome within the shelter of your wings.

Joining the host of your children, past, present and future, we say Amen, Amen, Amen.

Leela and Israel Selvanayagam

10. Sea of Mercy

Lord, open to us the sea of your mercy and water us with full streams. From the riches of your grace and the springs of your kindness. Make us children of quietness and heirs of peace; kindle in us the fire of your love; sow in us your fear; strengthen our weakness by your power and bind us close to you and to each other.

Syrian Church (Iona Community: A WEE Worship Book)

11. Greater than Any Imagination

Gracious God, you are almighty and greater than anything we can imagine, and yet you are a friend and closer to us than every breath we can take. You are forever generous and there are no boundaries to your love. In a world that is ever changing, you remain constant. Help us to remain firm in you. As your people, may we seek to build each other up. May walking together strengthen our pilgrimage, trusting in Christ's name, and by the power of the Spirit.

Paul Davies

12. Service to Christ

Jesus, I wish you would let me wash your feet, since it was through walking about in me that you soiled them. I wish you would give me the task of wiping the stains from your feet, because it was my behaviour that put them there. But, where can

I get the running water I need to wash your feet? If I have no water, at least I have tears: let me wash your feet with them, and wash myself at the same time.

Ambrose of Milan

13. Open to Love

Mysterious God, choosing the small, the unnoticed, the obscure, to renew the ways of your covenant when your followers wander and fail you, strive yet with our intractable clay, open us to the love you revealed to us in Yeshua, emptied of power, untouched by delusion, dying unrecognised, yet for those with eyes to see the decisive clue to the mystery of your being.

Jim Cotter

14. Despairing Depths

Through the dark despairing depths, through the drought of the desert, through the abyss opened up by our failings and folly, we dare to risk our cry to the living God. For you will not let us escape from our greatest good. In our struggle with you, fierce, fiery lover, let some new glory wrought, and new and unexpected life come to birth.

Jim Cotter

15. Peace Beyond Complacency

Come Lord, do not smile and say you are already with us. Millions do not know you, and to us who do, what is the difference? What is the point of your presence if our lives do not alter? Change our lives, shatter our complacency. Make your word our life's purpose. Take away the quietness of a clear conscience. Press us uncomfortably. For only thus that other peace is made, your peace.

Dom Helder Camara

16. Priceless Treasure

Lord, we bring to you a priceless treasure, greater than the mountains, wider than the world, and deeper than the ocean. We offer you the greatest of all gifts, higher than the heavens, more glorious than the sun and weightier than the whole earth; even the offering of our own heart, to be yours now and for ever.

Mechthild of Megdeburg

17. We Turn to You

We turn to you, trusting your promise that your kingdom will come, your new world of peace and healing.

We turn to you as Lord of truth and right; you alone can lead us from our twisted values and misguided notions.

We turn to you as Lord of peace; you alone can turn us from our hatreds,

from our mistrust of others that leads to violence.

We turn to you as Lord of compassion; you alone can save us from the greed destroying our world, you alone can transform our hearts with active love for those in need.

We turn to you as Lord of the Cross, risen from death; you alone can make us more faithful in following your way, your way of self-giving.

We come to you, Lord of our hearts, in trust and repentance, sad for the destructive ways of our world; sure of your redeeming grace, seeking more urgently your forgiveness, your guidance for each step of our journey.

May we hear this day that word of assurance – 'Your sins are forgiven you, go in peace' – the word of our Lord Jesus Christ.

Eric Lott

18. Allegiance to the Incomparable

O God all powerful, true and incomparable, present in all things yet limited by none, untouched by place, unaged by time, unhurried by years, undeceived by words, not subject to birth, nor in need of protection: you are above corruption, you are beyond all change, living in light that none can approach, invisible, yet you yourself make known and you are found by all who seek you with their whole heart; you are the God of Israel and all who hope in Christ. You are our God!

Let All The World ...

19. Relief and Renewal

Almighty and everlasting God, the comfort of the sad, the strength of them that suffer: let the prayers of your children who cry out of any tribulation come unto you; and unto every soul that is distressed grant your mercy, grant relief, grant refreshment; through Jesus Christ our Lord.

The Divine Liturgy of Mark

20. Commending All

We commend unto you, O Lord, our souls and our bodies, our minds and our thoughts, our prayers and our hopes, our health and our work, our life and our death; our parents and brothers and sisters, our benefactors and friends, our neighbours, our country people, and all Christian folk this day and always.

Bishop Lancelot Andrewes

21. Hidden Sanctuary

Consecrate, O Lord, in my heart, a hidden sanctuary, where you alone enter; where secret sacrifices are offered up, which no one knows, but you only, to the glory of your Name. Blessed Spirit of God, pour upon us such gifts of faith, purity and love, that we may have your temple within us, and you in that temple, and life everlasting in you; through Jesus Christ our Lord.

O you who dwell in every humble heart, and consecrate it for your sanctuary: hallow, we pray you, our hearts within us that they may be houses of prayer, dwelling-places of your Spirit, wherein you reveal your holy mysteries; through Jesus Christ our Lord.

Jeremy Taylor (adapted)

22. Tune the Limbs

Strengthen, O Lord, the hands which have been stretched out to receive your holy things, that they may daily bring forth fruit to your divine glory. Grant that the ears which have heard your songs may be closed to the clamour and dispute; that the eyes which have seen your great love may also uphold your blessed hope; that the tongues which have uttered your praise may speak the truth; that the feet which have walked in your courts may walk in the region of light; that the souls and bodies which have fed upon your living body may be restored to newness of life. And with us may your great love for ever abide, that we may abundantly render back praise, praise to your Sovereignty. Amen, Amen.

A Liturgy of Malabar

23. Purify

Almighty God, to whom all hearts are open, all desires known, and from whom no secrets are hid: cleanse the thoughts of our hearts by the inspiration of your Holy Spirit, that we may perfectly love you, and worthily magnify your holy name; through Christ our Lord.

Book of Common Prayer

24. Covenant

I am no longer my own but yours. Your will, not mine, be done in all things,

wherever you may place me, in all that I do and in all that I may endure; when there is work for me and when there is none; when I am troubled and when I am at peace. Your will be done when I am valued and when I am disregarded; when I find fulfilment and when it is lacking; when I have all things, and when I have nothing. I willingly offer all I have and am to serve you, as and where you choose.

Glorious and blessed God, Father, Son and Holy Spirit, you are mine and I am yours. May it be so for ever. Let this covenant now made on earth be fulfilled in heaven.

John Wesley

25. Being Close to Christ

O Christ, you are within each of us. It is not just the interior of these walls: it is our own inner being you have renewed. We are your temple not made with hands. We are your body.

If every wall should crumble, and every church decay, we are your habitation.

Nearer are you than breathing, closer than hands and feet.

Ours are the eyes within which you, in the mystery, look out with compassion on the world.

Yet we bless you for this place, for your directing of us, your redeeming of us, and your indwelling.

Take us outside, O Christ, outside holiness, out to where soldiers curse and nations clash at the crossroads of the world.

So, shall this building continue to be justified. We ask it for your own name's sake.

Iona Community

26. Want and Need

O God, set your blessing on us as we begin this day together. Confirm us in the truth by which we rightly live; confront us with the truth from which we wrongly turn. We ask not for what we want, but for what you know we need, as we offer this day and ourselves for you and to you, through Jesus Christ our Saviour.

Iona Community

27. Trinity of Love

O God of the high heavens, O Christ of the deep earth, O Spirit of the flowing waters, O Trinity of love, you have offered your love to us, and here we pledge our love to you. Strengthen us in our desire and breathe into our bodies the passion of your love. We pray this in the name of Jesus, to whom we commit ourselves.

Iona Community

28. A Day with God

God in the midst, come close to us, and help us come close to you, as for a fraction of time, we step back from the activities of the day. May we treasure such moments with you. Moments when we can bring to you the things we are doing, and find new meaning for them, and new strength for doing them. And moments for recalling how we are meeting you already, in the stuff of daily living and engagement, when faith is tested and compassion is translated into action. So if, as the day goes on, we forget you, do not forget us O God.

Iona Community

29. Bless the Whole Life

Bless to us, O God, the earth beneath our feet.
Bless to us, O God, the path whereon we go.
Bless to us, O God, the people whom we meet.
Bless to us, O God, our souls that come from on high.
Bless to us, O God, our bodies that are of earth.
Bless to us, O God, each thing our eyes see.
Bless to us, O God, each sound our ears hear.
Bless to us, O God, each odour that goes to our nostrils.
Bless to us, O God, each taste that goes to our lips,
each note that goes to our song,
each ray that guides our way.

Iona Community

30. Deep Peace

Deep peace of the running wave to you, deep peace of the flowing air to you,
Deep peace of the quiet earth to you, deep peace of the shining stars to you,
Deep peace of the Son of Peace to you.
Peace between nations, peace between neighbours,
Peace between lovers, in love of the God of life.
Peace between person and person, peace between wife and husband,
Peace between parent and child, the peace of Christ above all peace.
Bless O Christ our faces, let our faces bless everything.
Bless O Christ our eyes, let our eyes bless all they see.

Iona Community

31. Face of Eternity

Lord, your ways are not our ways; your thoughts are not our thoughts; what to us seems like eternity is only a moment to you. In the face of eternity, help us to be humble.

Worshipping Ecumenically, WCC

32. Lead to Life, Truth, Hope

Eternal Guide, lead us from death to life, from falsehood to truth, from despair to hope, from fear to trust. Lead us from hate to love, from war to peace. Let the peace that comes from hope fill our hearts.

Worshipping Ecumenically, WCC

33. Fulfilment

Eternal God, our beginning and our end, be our starting point and our haven and accompany us in this day's journey. Use our hands to do the work of your creation and use our lives to bring others the new life you give this world in Jesus Christ, Redeemer of all.

Worshipping Ecumenically, WCC

34. Life Overcoming Death

I am no longer afraid of death: I know well its dark and cold corridors leading to life. I am afraid rather of that life which does not come out of death, which cramps our hands and retorts our march. I am afraid of my fear and even more of the fear of others, who do not know where they are going, who continue clinging to what they consider to be life, which we know to be death! I live each day to kill death; I die each day to beget life, and in this dying unto death, I die a thousand times and am reborn another thousand through that love from my people, which nourishes hope!

Julia Esquivel

35. All in All

I bless you, O Lord, that you have worked wondrous mercies upon me, a sinner, and have been most loving to me in all things: nurse and governor, guardian and helper, refuge and Saviour, protector of both soul and body. I bless you, O Lord, for you have granted me the power to repent from my sins and have shown to me myriad occasions to return from my malice. For you have mercy and save us, O God, and to you we send up glory, thanksgiving and worship, and your all-holy, good and life-creating Spirit, now and ever and unto ages of ages.

St. Basil the Great, 4th Century

36. Fashion us for Shining and Service

Come, O Creator, O Immensity of love, O Eternity of mercy. Come, and be with us and in us and beside us and over us. Be as hands upon us and fashion us for shining. Be as warmth within us, and fire us for caring. Be as strength beside us and shape our lives for healing. Abide in our prayers, the spoken and the unspoken; and make your Word come true in our flesh; through Jesus Christ our Redeemer.

Arnold Kenseth

37. Reshape and Activate

Almighty God, whose breath quickened us, whose tongue named us, whose language we are: grant us grace to be true words – not gentle when it is in anger that we live, not smooth when it is desperation that we know, not patient when time has narrowed down to now, not wise, not neat, not all our fences mended, but words, broken yet honest words, and lost, stumbling their way towards silence. Take us back. Recall us. Then speak us once again. Set us in order. Mend our shattered syntax. Set all our commas straight. Imbue in us a power that keeps company with pain, then march us across the pages of this beautiful, fragile, tormented, and perishable earth to sing the songs of Zion. In the name of the Word made flesh, made dead, and made alive again.

Barbara Sargent

38. Rest and Disturbance

Eternal One, Silence from whom my words come; Questioner from whom my questions arise; Lover of whom all my loves are hints; Disturber in whom alone I find my rest; Mystery in whose depths I find healing and myself: enfold me now in your presence; restore to me your peace; renew me through your power; and ground me in your grace.

Ted Loder

39. Renewal

My spirit is one with you, Great Spirit. You strengthen me day and night to share my very best with my brothers and sisters. You whom my people see in all of creation and in all people, show your love for us. Help me to know, like the soaring eagle, the heights of knowledge. From the Four Directions, fill me with the four virtues of fortitude, generosity, respect, and wisdom; so that I will help my people walk in the path of understanding and peace

Lakota Prayer

40. Pledge of Love

O God of the high heavens, O Christ of the deep earth, O Spirit of the flowing waters, O Trinity of love, you have offered your love to us, and here we pledge our love to you. You have been faithful to your people through the ages, and here we pledge our faithfulness to one another. You have sustained in love the earth, sea and sky around us, and here we pledge our sustaining love for creation. You have identified with the powerless and the weak of the world, and here we pledge our identification with them. O God, strengthen us in our desire, and breathe into our bodies the passion of your love. We pray this in the name of Jesus, to whom we commit ourselves.

Iona Community

41. Reliance on Grace

Gracious God, Holy Trinity, God above us, God below us, God around us, blessed are you and worthy of all praise. Teach us at this time to rely on your grace, to trust in your mercy and to respond to your love, that we may welcome the opportunities this day brings and know the encompassing presence of your Holy Spirit through Jesus Christ our Lord.

John Taylor

42. Religious Life

Help me, Lord, to remember that religion is not to be confined to church or closet, nor exercised only in prayer and meditation, but that everywhere I am in your presence; so may my every word and action have a moral context.

Susanna Wesley

43. Love of Wonder

Lord God, your love has called us here as we, by love, for love were made; your living likeness still we bear, though marred, dishonoured, disobeyed; we come, with all our heart and mind, your call to hear, your love to find.

We come with self-inflicted pains of broken trust and chosen wrong, half-free, half-bound by inner chains, by social forces swept along, by powers and systems close confined, yet seeking hope for humankind.

Lord God, in Christ you call our name, and then receive us as your own, not through some merit, right or claim, but by your gracious love alone; we strain to glimpse your mercy-seat, and find you kneeling at our feet.

Brian A. Wren

44. Hearts Cold and Weak

Lord God, we come to you with hearts that are cold, that they may be warmed by your selfless love. We come to you with hearts that are sinful, that they may be cleansed by the Saviour's precious blood. We come to you with hearts that are weak that they may be strengthened by your Holy Spirit. We come with hearts that are empty that they be filled with your divine presence, Father, Son and Holy Spirit.

St. Augustine

45. Refreshing Spirit

As the dew refreshes and cleanses fragile blades of grass, as gentle rain feeds and lifts sun-dried leaves and flowers, and as the snow covers the earth and holds it in frozen stillness, so Lord, may we recognize your Spirit at different times, answering our many needs, challenging us to understand ourselves, helping us to accept the waiting and stillness, the moving and growing, the resting and healing, the planning and doing, as constant stages of a journey with One whose love holds us in each step. God, in your goodness and endless generosity we think you that you are with us on the journey and in the coming home.

Margaret Matta

46. Gladness in Your Presence

When we come to you, we find you have already come to us; you fill the silence and we hear your voice above the noise. We meet you in the peace and quiet of the soul and know your challenge in the pleading beggar. Help us not to turn our eyes from you, and make us glad in your presence.

Kenneth Hext

47. Silence of Humility

Saviour, teach me the silence of humility, the silence of wisdom, the silence of love, the silence of perfection, the silence that speaks without words, the silence of faith. Lord, teach me to silence my own heart that I may listen to the gentle movement of the Holy Spirit within me and sense the depths which are of God.

Source Unknown

48. Rest for the Restless

Great, O Lord, is your power and infinite your wisdom; therefore we bless you without ceasing and delight in your praise. You have made us for yourself and our hearts are restless until they find their rest in you.

St. Augustine

49. Infinite Love

Deepen within us, holy and blessed Jesus, a true sense of your infinite love; that adoring you and believing in you, we may trust in your infinite merits, imitate your holy example, obey your wise commandments and finally enjoy your promises; for you live and reign with the Father and the Holy Spirit, one God now and for ever.

John Wesley

50. You Alone

O Lord God who are all in all to me, Life of my life and Spirit of my spirit, have mercy on me and so fill me with your Holy Spirit and with love that there may be no room for anything else in my heart. I ask not for any blessing, but for yourself, who are the giver of all blessings and of all life. I ask not for the world and its pomp and glory, nor for heaven, but I need you yourself, for where you are, there is heaven. In yourself alone is satisfaction and abundance for my heart; you yourself, O Creator, have created this heart for yourself, and not for any other created thing. Therefore, this heart cannot find rest in anything but you: only in you, O Father, who has made this longing for peace. So now take out of this heart whatever is opposed to you and abide and rule in it yourself.

Sadhu Sundar Singh

51. Self-Offering

Dear Lord, my heart is full of gratitude for your various gifts and blessings. The gratitude of heart and lips alone is insufficient until I devote myself to your service with my life and prove it by my deeds. To you be thanks and praise for bringing me, a worthless creature, out of non-being into being, and making me glad in your love and fellowship. I do not know you fully, and do not know even my own needs; but you, O Father, know well your creatures and their needs. I am not able to love myself as much as you love me. In reality, to love oneself means that I should love with heart and soul the boundless love which created me and which is yourself. It is for this very reason that you have created in me only one heart, that it should be joined only to One, to you who did create it.

Lord, to sit at your feet is many times better and grander than sitting before any royal throne on earth; indeed, it means to be enthroned for ever in the eternal kingdom. Now I offer myself as a burnt-offering on the altar of those holy feet. Accept it as and where you wish; use me according to your pleasure. For you are mine and I am yours. You did make me in your image out of this handful of dust and grant the right of becoming your child. May all honour and glory and praise be yours for ever and ever.

Sadhu Sundar Singh

52. Sustaining Presence

Lord, you are my leader, I have all I need, you calm me down when I am moody, you give me energy and love. You lead me down the right path, even if I'm scared or upset. I will not be afraid, because you are with me and will protect me. You have given me more than I deserve. I know you will always be there and your house will be my home for evermore.

Clare Hardwicke

53. Enlivening Presence

Loving God, may we see your presence in the tears and laughter of our lives; in our wilderness experience may we find hope; in the faces of others may we discern your beauty; and in our abandonment may we be found by you. In Jesus Christ we pray.

Stuart Burgess

54. Sufficient Word

Lord, in the wilderness we all hunger after something. It may be for justice or freedom or simply to be heard. It may be for a smile or compassion or to be loved. You are here in the wilderness, and your voice, often like a murmur says – My word is sufficient for you, this word feeds you. Today, again in the wilderness, having left my home country, my family, my friends, I hear your voice, and your voice feeds me. Having my fill, I will go on my way, becoming for the people around no longer a wasteland but a haven of restoration. This is my prayer Lord.

Josiane Bidaux

55. Renewing Spirit

Spirit of God, present with us now, renew in us the character of the community of Jesus.
Grant us the courage and the grace to live the shared pilgrimage within our differences.
Strengthen us to live as those who enter the long work of forgiveness – not seven but seventy times seven.
Set us free to live simply and generously.
Deepen the trust that draws us into the mystery of death and resurrection,
Help us to live as those who wait on God, the God who also waits.
Form us into a people thankful for God's daily providing.
May the Spirit first clearly seen to be at work in Jesus of Nazareth also be seen to be clearly at work even among us.
Help us to live the prayer that we offer in the name of Jesus Christ.

Donald Eadie

56. Presence and Enlightenment

Strengthen in our weakness with your compassion, O Lord, and comfort us with your loving kindness. Amidst the changing fortunes of this world may we find rest in your peace. May we find cleansing in your presence, and the enlightenment of your Holy Spirit all our days; through Christ our Lord.

Nestorian Liturgy

57. Ever Present

O God, in mystery and silence you are present in our lives, bringing new life out of destruction, hope out of despair and growth out of difficulty. We thank you that you do not leave us alone but are working with us to bring new things to birth. Help us to perceive your hand in the unfolding of our lives, to know the dignity of acceptance within your family and to work to make all human life full of purpose and joy.

Kathleen Richardson

58. Discord and Restart

Lord of life, when the rhythm of my life is disturbed by fear or sorrow, when harmony is jarred by discord, when I am out of tune with you and the world – help me to sing a new song of faith and hope, peace and love, joy and praise.

Gwen Charlton

59. Claiming the Divine Peace

May the calm of our Lord's presence still the storm of our stress; may the coolness of his touch assuage our anxieties; may the clarity of his vision clear our confusion; and may he give us courage to claim his peace.

Rosemary Watters

60. One More Step

Dear Lord, when your way is hard to find, guide my next step; when your truth is hard to know, inform my next decision; when life is hard to bear, help me through this day.

Thomas McKnight

61. Always in All

Compassionate God, console us as we mourn loss in our attempts to establish your commonwealth. Encourage us to continue the struggle and accept us again as we fall at your feet. In our success and failure, strength and weakness, life and death, let us always seek your glory.

Israel Selvanayagam

62. Holy Life

Sometimes, O God, I am so bursting with life that all I can say is, "Holy, holy, holy." Life is glorious because you are glorious. Or is it that *you* are glorious because life is? I won't quibble, nor analyse or divide you and life in this way. You are you. Life is life. You are life. And life is you. You are more than life, dearer than life. Yet since it is only life that brings you to us, only in life are we aware of you, you and life are one – both glorious. So, life is to be glorified – affirmed. As you are. To be lived, then, affirmatively. Openly. Graciously. How else can we live if we live you – or want to live you? Not just to live *toward* you but to *live* you. Not just to say, 'Holy, holy, holy' but to be holy. Wholly. Holy Lord. Holy life. Yes.

John B. Coburn

63. Worthy Offerings

You know us, God. You know all about us. We tell you what we want, not to inform you but to be honest with ourselves in your light.

What we want now is to make our offerings to you. Help us to know what to do with those things we want that are not worthy of you or us.

Accept our lives, our loves, our integrity. What we offer to you make whole, so that we may go on from strength to strength and continue to find your meaning in our lives, now and always.

John B. Coburn

64. Above, Beyond, Around

O God, you are above us, beyond us, around us, beneath us, within us. We sense within ourselves some goodness, and we long for more. We see some beauty around and would bring more to what we see. We know some truth and search for more to be true ourselves. You are, we believe, the source of all that is good and beautiful and true. So, we thank you for what you have already given us.

As we seek more goodness, to create more beauty and to know more truth, let us remember that you have already found us; and that as we live in you, and you in us, the sense of your presence will grow. In that presence goodness, beauty and truth will come as we are able to bear them – And thus to express them.

John B. Coburn

65. Realization in Pilgrimage

Was the pilgrimage I made to come to my own self, to learn that in times like these and for one like me God will never be plain and out there, but dark rather and inexplicable as though he were in here?

R. S. Thomas

66. Draw Me

Draw me God, to your heart, your compassion, your silence.

Donald Eadie

67. The Spirit's Work

Eternal God, your Spirit creates and renews the face of the earth; deepens and marks our humanity; helps us in our weakness; strengthens us to follow in the way of Jesus; ignites within and among us the fires both of passion and compassion.

Donald Eadie

68. Aching Body

Lord my body is hurting, my inner world is hurting and you have chosen to make of both your dwelling place and home. Help us to embrace the wound in such a way that it becomes part of our greater wholeness, with God's help.

Donald Eadie

69. Marks of Resurrection

May we discern the marks of resurrection in the wounds that we carry.

Bishop John Austin

70. Discovery on Pilgrimage

Lord of every pilgrim heart, bless our journeys on these roads we never planned to take but through your surprising wisdom discovered we are on.

Peter Millar

71. Journeying God

Through fire and water, ***you have brought us.***
Through storm and bitter hurt, ***you have brought us.***
Through searing pain and bitter wound, ***you have brought us.***
Through years of searching and of longing, ***you have brought us.***
Day after day, night after night, ***to this time and place.***
Scarred yet beautiful, ***you have brought us.***
Limping but able to dance, ***you have brought us.***
Wounded yet able to love more deeply, ***you have brought us.***
Hurt yet somehow still able to embrace where the anguish has been greatest, ***you have brought us.***
Day after day, night after night, ***to this time and place.***
With friends and companions, ***you have brought us.***
With searching, discovery and delight, ***you have brought us.***
With pilgrims of age and the laughter of childhood, ***you have brought us.***
With pilgrims of many faiths and of none, ***you have brought us.***
Surrounded by, and one with all the saints in light, ***you have brought us.***
Day after day, night after night, ***to this time and place.***

Bill Denning

72. Unto Yourself

Take Lord, unto yourself
My sense of self and let it vanish utterly.
Take Lord, my life
Live you your life through me.
I live no longer, Lord
But in me now you live.
Aye, between you and me, my God
There is no longer room for 'I' and 'mine.'

Tukaram

73. Sanctify Our Love

O God, you who are love, search our hearts. Reveal to us in the way that is best known to you, and in your own good time, whether we bear for each other that pearl of your bestowing, human love. Sanctify our feelings towards each other. Help us to come before you in prayerful silence during this time of waiting. O Father, help us to see your will for us. This we ask in the name of our common Saviour Jesus Christ.

Chandran Devanesan

74. A Longing for the Divine

I am thirsting for your love, my beloved! I shall make this body a lamp, and my tender heart shall be its wick. I shall fill it with the scented oil of my young love and burn it night and day at your shrine, O beloved! For Your love I shall sacrifice all the wealth of my youth.

Your name shall be the crown of my head. I am longing for you, O my Lord: for the season of the sowing has come; but You are not beside me. Clouds gather on my brows and my eyes shed heavy showers. My parents gave me to You, I have become Yours for ever; who but You can be my Lord? This separation troubles my breast; make me Your own; make me perfect like you, O Lord of perfection!

Mirabai

75. Your Light and Thunder

When the heart is hard and parched up, come upon me with a shower of mercy.
When grace is lost from life, come with a burst of song.
When tumultuous work raises its din on all sides shutting me out from beyond, come to me, my Lord of silence, with thy peace and rest.
When my beggarly heart sits crouched,
shut up in a corner, break open the door, my King,
and come with the ceremony of a king.

When desire blinds the mind with delusion and dust,
O Thou Holy one, Thou wakeful,
come with Thy light and Thy thunder.

Rabindranath Tagore

76. My Everything

Be you a light unto my eyes, music to my ears, sweetness to my taste, and full contentment to my heart. Be you my sunshine in the day, my food at table, my repose in the night, my clothing in nakedness, and my succour in all necessities. Lord Jesus, I give you my body, my soul, my substance, my fame, my friends, my liberty and my life. Dispose of me and all that is mine as it may seem best to you and to the glory of your blessed name.

John Cosin

77. To Be Better

O most merciful Redeemer, Friend and Brother, may we know you more clearly, love you more dearly, and follow you more nearly day by day.

Richard of Chichester

78. Life with Light

God make my life a little light within the world to glow; a little flame that burns bright wherever I may go. God make my life a little flower that gives joy to all; content to bloom in native bower although the place be small. God make my life a little song that comforts the sad; that helps others to be strong and makes the singer glad. God make my life a little staff whereon the week may rest; that so what health and strength I have may serve my neighbours best.

Matilda Betham-Edwards

79. Inward Vision

O God, who have given me eyes to see the light that fills my room, give me the inward vision to behold you in this place. O God, who have made me to feel the morning wind upon my limbs, help me to feel your presence as I bow in worship of you.

Chandran Devanesan

80. Partnership

Good Lord, with this faith in you may we be able to work together, to pray together, to struggle together, to go to jail together, to stand up for freedom together, to realise the dream together, knowing that we will be free one day.

Martin Luther King

81. Worship for Yourself

O my Lord, if I worship you from the fear of hell, burn me in hell; If I worship you from the hope of Paradise, bar me from its gates; but if I worship you for yourself alone, grant me the beauty of your face.

Rabia of Basra

82. Yourself the Greatest Gift

My Lord God, my all in all, life of my life, and spirit of my spirit, look in mercy upon me and so fill me with your Holy Spirit that my heart shall have no room for love of aught but you.

I seek from you no other gift but yourself, who are the Giver of life and all its blessings. From you I ask not for the world or its treasures, nor yet for heaven even make request, but you alone do I desire and long for, and where you art, there is heaven. The hunger and the thirst of this heart of mine can be satisfied only with you who has given birth.

O Creator mine! You have created my heart for yourself alone, and not for another, therefore this my heart can find no rest or ease save in you, in you who has both created it and set in it this very longing for rest. Take away then from my heart all that is opposed to you and enter and abide and rule for ever.

Sadhu Sundar Singh

83. Divine Comrade

Holding my hand, you lead me, my comrade, everywhere; as I go on and lean on you, my burden you lovingly bear. If as I go, in my distress, I, frantic words should say, you set right my foolishness, and take my shame away. Thus, you to me new hope send, a new world you bring in, now know I, every person a friend, and all I meet, my kin. So, like a happy child I play, in your dear world, O God. And everywhere – I, Tuka, say, your bliss is spread abroad.

Tukaram

84. Bring out the Hidden

God, there are corners in my soul that I don`t know yet. How can I ever understand myself? How can I ever fathom my answer to the challenge of life? Where are you? Are you possibly present in those unknown corners? Lighten up what is hidden. Reveal my soul, untie your secret in me, I would like to meet the others with only light in my eyes, with an unbiased heart, I would like to be an oasis in the desert of life. A home where they can rest, a tree in whose shade they can finally meet you.

André Quintelier

85. In Search of Grace

O God, who dwell in the hearts of your saints, I have not the mind to seek the great object of life. Father, what can I do to get your grace? Rule me with your grace. I do not know the medicine, the jewel, the mantra, the knowledge, the rule and conduct of life. I do not know the way of repentance, the power of your grace and the path of righteousness. I do not know the place where I can live the controlled life, nor how to enter into the society of the wise, nor how to approach the holy place where the Lord resides. I do not know the direction in which to go. How can I enter? Whom can I speak to? What can I do? I know not anything. I have not abandoned a coil of caste, creed and sect. I have not abandoned plunging into the mire of theological wrangling. I do not know the beginning nor the end, nor how to abide in the wave-less sea of your bliss. I have not walked in the way of holiness, nor do I know the inward will of Him who abides in the assembly of the Holy One. How can I enter the world of my foes? To whom can I speak? What can I do? I know not.

Ramalinga Swami

86. Vision of Hope

God, the stranger, help us to welcome you to our land, our street, our home, our Church. God, the anonymous, help us to know you in lives that touch ours at a thousand points. God, the helpless one, may we see you, when you are cradled in a mother`s arms. God, the seed, the new born, the beginning, help us to find our hope in you. We thank you, pioneering God, for the visionaries of faith who see more clearly and work more boldly because they have seen you in love, in suffering and in new life.

Bernard Thorogood

87. The Way of Love

It is not far to go for you are near. It is not far to go, for you are here. And not by travelling, Lord, persons come to you, but by the way of love, and we love you.

Amy Carmichael

88. Christ is All to Me

Christ be with me, Christ within me, Christ before me, Christ beside me. Christ to win me, Christ to comfort and restore me, Christ beneath me, Christ above me, Christ in quiet, Christ in danger, Christ in hearts of all that love me, Christ in mouth of friend and stranger.

St. Patrick

89. Sharpen the Inner Tools

O gracious and holy Father, give us wisdom to perceive You; Intelligence to understand You; Diligence to seek You; Patience to wait for You; Eyes to behold You; A heart to meditate upon You; and a life to proclaim You: through the power of the Spirit of Jesus Christ our Lord.

St. Benedict

90. Art of Life

O Divine Spirit, who in all the events of life are knocking at the door of my heart, help me to respond to You. I would not be driven blindly as the stars over their courses. I would not be made to work out Your will unwillingly, to fulfil Your law unintelligently, to obey Your mandates unsympathetically. I would take the events of my life as good and perfect gifts from You; I would receive even the sorrows of life as disguised gifts from You. I would have my heart open at all times to receive – at morning, noon and night; in spring and summer and winter. Whether You come to me in sunshine or in rain, I would take You into my heart joyfully. You are Yourself more than the sunshine; You are Yourself compensation for the rain; it is You, and not Your gifts, I crave; knock and I shall open unto You.

George Mathesan

91. Delight in Work

O Lord, renew our spirits and draw our hearts unto Yourself, that our work may not be to us a burden, but a delight; and give us such a might love to You as may sweeten all our obedience. O, let us not serve You with the spirit of bondage as slaves, but with the cheerfulness and gladness of children, delighting ourselves in You and rejoicing in Your work.

Benjamin Jenks

92. God's Voice

We ask you, Gracious Saviour, to calm our thoughts and our spirits so that we may hear from you when you need to speak to us. The still small voice reminds us that you are never far away and we only need to quiet ourselves before your throne. Have mercy upon us we pray.

Moravian

93. Renew Your Promises

Thank you, God that we have access to you and your Son Jesus Christ by the one Spirit. We behave at times as though we have no communication with you and need to fix all things on our own. Forgive us, gracious Father, and show us today that your promises never fail us when we stand on your word.

Moravian

94. Stronger Faith

Eternal King, we call you both Father and Friend; yet, you are beyond our imaginations in power and grandeur. We recognize you as the source of every blessing in our lives; nonetheless, we sometimes find ourselves saying, 'I believe, but help me in my unbelief!' In our uncertainty, lead us to stronger faith. Remove our doubt and comfort us with your almighty hand.

Moravian

95. Infinite Power and Beauty

Lord, we believe that you are excited to share your wonders with us, so that we, together, may marvel at your infinite power and the beauty of your hands. Help us to believe the unbelievable and to not be ashamed to be perceived as fools.

Moravian

96. Constant Caring

Caring and constant God, you know how our hearts ache –

You have been there too.

Like a mother nursing a sick child on her knee, like a father who has not given up on his runaway son, like a friend who is there for someone who would otherwise die alone, like a partner coping with a crisis, or patiently working through a time of change – you know how our hearts ache –

You have been there too.

When we feel most alone, when it seems as though everyone has deserted us; when it would be much easier to give up and deny the vision; when we take a step in faith that is in fact a leap in the dark; when we face death, and when we struggle to begin again; you know how our hearts ache –

You have been there too.

We take courage from your love which has no limits, your compassion which never fails – they are new every morning: caring and constant God.

Jan Sutch Pickard

97. Treat Me Like a Child

Parent God, thank you for adopting me as your child. You have nursed me patiently and nurtured me kindly. You want me to grow into maturity weaning away from milk and taking on solid food. I hear you sharing your concerns so that I may help you by participating in your plans. However, irrespective of my age, experience and achievements, treat me still like a child, playing with me with your profound sense of humour and guiding me to the right place in right time until I am in your infinite realm of joy.

Israel Selvanayagam

98. Joyful Presence

Grant us, O Lord, the royalty of inward happiness, and the serenity which from living close to you. Daily renew in us the sense of joy and let the eternal spirit of the Father dwell in our souls and bodies, filling every corner of our hearts with light and grace, so that, bearing about with us the infection of a good courage, we may be diffusers of life, and may meet all ills and accidents with gallant and high-hearted happiness, giving you thanks always for all things.

Robert Louis Stevenson

99. To Love Creatively

Lord God, we are called to love you with all our heart and soul and strength and mind. Give us pure hearts so that in the encounter with others we always see you. Fill our souls with delight in our love that we might share with everyone we meet. Help us to be strong in the face of discouragement or difficulty so that even then we may feel your presence with us. Open our minds to new ideas and possibilities so that your will be done, not ours.

Jane Bingham

100. Fullness of Goodness

Creator, Redeemer and Saviour God, in you is the fullness of goodness, mercy and gentleness. You alone are just and holy, innocent and pure. Only in you is all pardon, all grace and all glory, without beginning and without end.

St. Francis of Assisi

101. Near and Far

Father, you are closer to us than the air we breathe, and yet, Almighty God, you are beyond the range of radio wave, telescope sight or radar search. Father, your touch is as gentle as a snow flake, and yet, Almighty God, yours is the power which spoke the universe into being. Father, we know you as a loving parent, intimate and close, and yet, Almighty God, we can never comprehend you – our imagination is not lively enough, our minds too small. Near us and beyond us, Father and Almighty God, help us to worship you.

Simon Oxley

102. Teach the Truth

Lord, let silence speak and teach its own truth: let the sleeping child speak of vulnerability; let the silent dawn speak of hope; let the urgency of spring speak of growth; let the single rose in its vase speak of earth's beauty, and silent prayer be eloquent praise.

Donald Hilton

103. Be My All

Weave a web of your presence around me today. Be with my hands as they work. Be with my eyes as they see. Be with my ears as they hear. Be with my tongue as it speaks. Be with my feelings and thoughts. Be with the people I meet. Be with the things I make. Be with the decisions I take. Be in and through, over and under all, that doing and hearing and seeing, speaking and making and being, I may glimpse your glory, hear your voice, and joyfully work with you to create a new heaven and new earth.

Kate McIlhagga

104. Pleasing You

O Lord, we open our hearts to you. May they be found not wanting, but ideal for your kingdom here on earth and your home in heaven. While we walk in your creation, may all that we do be pleasant to your sight.

Moravian

105. Grace in Fullest Measure

Fill us, O Lord. Fill us with your grace to fullest measure that we may have it in abundance, that it may grow through our spirits, and that it may be an offering unto you and a gift to all whom we serve in your love.

Moravian

106. Mystery of Love

In us, O Lord, you have entrusted a sacred obligation. To us you have shown the great mysteries of your love; in humility you find greatness, in weakness you find strength, to self-giving you find abundance, and in death you find life. May we always be guided by the mystery of your love.

Moravian

107. Kind Shepherd

Great Shepherd, we are your flock, honoured to hear our names called by you. You, Lord, give us green pastures to lie down in and still waters to walk beside.

In you we find all that we need for true purpose for our lives. Call on us; we are yours.

Moravian

108. With Humble Spirits

Lord of all blessings, we often become content with our lives, thinking we will never be shaken; but when hardship arises, we fear losing you. You are never far from us, and we need only to reach out to you with humble spirits, acknowledging your grace and love even in the most difficult times.

Moravian

109. Blessing of Joy

From the first morning of our lives to the last evening that falls upon us, we live in your joy, Creator God. It is a blessing to be one with you and with all those who serve you. As we continue our journeys here in your creation, may we hold each moment dearly.

Moravian

110. Enfold Us

Heavenly Father, we come to you as strangers, yet are welcomed as your children. Fold your loving arms around us, protect us from evil and show us the right path to follow. With hope we pray.

Moravian

111. Test our Faith

Heavenly Father, this world tests our resolve and our faith in you. Too many times we feel the fear and heartache of a life without you. Yet your smiling face and gentle hand remind us of your love and give us the power to live lives of goodness and hope.

Moravian

112. Warmth and Hope

God of hope, pour out your Spirit upon us; let us feel the warmth of your abounding love and your merciful grace. Let us feel surrounded by your calmness and gentleness as we daily gain our victory over sin.

Moravian

113. Love and Grace

Gracious King, every day we seek your love and grace. We are pilgrims – sometimes lost, sometimes on the right path. Sometimes tired of travelling – yet we always hope to see your face throughout our journey and at its end.

Moravian

114. Closer in Communion

We stand amazed at your goodness and greatness, gracious Saviour, as we seek to walk closer in communion with you. Sin is so prevalent in our human societies. Give us a clear vision of who we are and remind us that we are your representation here on earth. Let us act justly and walk humbly before our God.

Moravian

115. The House of the Soul

O Lord, the house of my soul is narrow; enlarge it, that you may enter in. It is ruinous, O repair it! It displeases your sight; I confess it, I know. But, who shall cleanse it, to whom shall I cry but to you? Cleanse me from my secret faults, O Lord, and spare your servant from strange sins.

St. Augustine

116. All Sufficient

God, of your goodness, give me yourself; for you are sufficient for me. I cannot properly ask anything less, to be worthy of you. If I were to ask less, I should always be in want. In you alone do I have all.

Julian of Norwich

117. All in You

Sever me from myself that I may be grateful to you; may I perish to myself that I may be safe in you; may I die to myself that I may live in you; may I wither to myself that I may blossom in you; may I be emptied of myself that I may abound in you; may I be nothing to myself that I may be all to you.

Desiderius Erasmus

118. Power of Love

God of compassion and understanding, we always tend to think that your power is like the forms of power we know – muscular, torrent, storm, electric, nuclear and the like. When we do not see the manifestation of your power in such fashion and speed, we question your power and goodness. You have taught us through the cross of your son Jesus that your power is powerlessness yet powerful in love as a child's power that moves her parents. Give us patience to wait for realising your power in mysterious ways and help us to rely on your perfect justice and wisdom.

Israel Selvanayagam

119. Thought of You

Father in heaven, when the thought of you wakes in our hearts, let it not wake like a frightened bird that flies about in dismay, but like a child waking from its sleep with a heavenly smile.

Søren Kierkegaard

120. You are My Remedy

In me there is darkness, but with you there is light; I am lonely, but You leave me not. I am feeble in heart, but with You there is help. I am restless, but with You there is peace. In me there is bitterness, but with You there is patience; Your ways are past understanding, but You know the way for me.

Dietrich Bonhoeffer

121. Abide with Me

Lord Jesus Christ, You were poor and in misery, a captive and forsaken as I am. You know all man's distress; You abide with me when all others have deserted me; You do not forget me, but seek me. You wish that I should know You and turn to You. Lord, I hear Your call and follow You; do You help me.

Dietrich Bonhoeffer

122. The Difficulties of Praying

Why, O Lord, is it so hard for me to keep my heart directed toward you? Why do the many little things I want to do, and the many people I know, keep crowding into my mind, even during the hours that I am totally free to be with you and you alone? Why does my mind wander off in so many directions, and why does my heart desire the things that lead me astray? Are you not enough for me? Do I keep doubting your love and care, your mercy and grace? Do I keep wondering, in the centre of my being, whether you will give me all I need if I just keep my eyes on you?

Please accept my distractions, my fatigue, my irritations, and my faithless wanderings. You know me more deeply and fully than I know myself. You love me with a greater love than I can love myself. You even offer me more than I can desire. Look at me, see me in all my misery and inner confusion, and let me sense your presence in the midst of my turmoil. All I can do is show myself to you. Yet, I am afraid to do so. I am afraid that you will reject me. But, I know – with the knowledge of faith – that you desire to give me your love. The only thing you ask of me is not to hide from you, not to run away in despair, not to act as if you were a relentless despot.

Take my tired body, my confused mind, and my restless soul into your arms and give me rest, simple quiet rest. Do I ask too much too soon? I should not worry about that. You will let me know. Come, Lord Jesus, Come.

Henri Nouwen

123. Kingdom Within

See this kingdom of God is now found within us. The grace of the Holy Spirit shines forth and warms us, and overflowing with many and varied scents into the air around us, regales our senses with heavenly light as it fills our hearts with joy inexpressible.

Author Unknown

124. Let Me Sleep, Mother

My loving heavenly mother, I am returning to your bosom on which I laid my head many times, on which you stroked, cuddled and suckled me. I am finishing my race that you pushed me into, and preparing to come to the place of my origin. Calm my short breaths, anxiety and tensions. Kindle my imagination that I am going to those millions of your servants and children, from the ancestors of old and the recent ones who are sleeping in your presence. If any memory of my shortcomings, failures and even blunders disturbs me let me feel your embrace with an absolute absolution. Let me not carry on any sack loads of grudges or resentments against those who have harmed or backbitten, been indifferent or unresponsive. Let me fully rely on your judgment which is always just, true and understanding. Give your grace that my last breath will be combined with a spell of smile and a drop of tears. I am eager and longing to sleep on your bosom, my welcoming mother, with my eyes closed yet with every breath praising you, joining the orchestra of the whole creation and all loved ones.

Israel Selvanayagam.

125. Rejoice in the Lord

Our spirit shall rejoice in you, O Lord, Heavenly Father, and unto you will we give thanks; because of all your benefits known and unknown, your mercies new every morning, your faithful love and providence.

We will rejoice in all the riches of your world, in the truth you have unfolded, the beauty and goodness you have given us to love.

We will rejoice in every experience, however hard, bitter or costly, by which we are schooled to walk with humble faith in you, and in charity with our fellow men and women.

And in this will we rejoice with joy unspeakable, that you gave Jesus Christ to be our Saviour, and have vouchsafed the comfort of your Holy Spirit, the pledge and foretaste of victorious life; through him who for our victory suffered the semblance of defeat, and for our life went down to death.

Make us willing, O Lord, we beseech you, so to lose our life, even as he did, that with him we may keep it unto life eternal; through the same Jesus Christ our Lord.

James Ferguson

126. Our Call and Commission

God our Father, we need reminding, because our memories are short.

We forget that there is a hand that holds us, a heart that thinks of our good; we forget that you throw bridges across the chasms we fear and consider impassable.

Lord, we need you to sweep the dust from our minds and the cobwebs from our hearts.

When in the face of adversity we have said, 'We can't go on', you have replied, 'I will be with you.'

When in times of depression and doubt we have said, 'We have failed, we are defeated', we heard you saying 'Do not be afraid, for I am your God. It is I – not your doubt or anxiety – you must allow to be master of your life.'

Terry C. Falla

127. Alpha and Omega

Before galaxies burned in empty night, planets hurled through deepest space, waves broke upon primeval shores, volcanoes roared with molten rock;

Before lightning split an angry sky, glaciers cut through tortured steeps, flowers danced in zephyr winds, streams chattered by forest glades.

You were already God.

And when in unimagined aeons the earth ignites in flames of dying sun; or missiles flash to cities doomed, ash drifts, boughs break, unheard, unseen.

You will still be God.

Christ risen, what futile, cold assurance, if he were not our God! But Alpha, cosmic, crucified, he comes in grace confounding: Omega, Father, Saviour, Friend;

Our Judge, our Breath, our Joy.

Terry C. Falla

128. Inner Power, Love and Fullness

We pray, O God, that out of your glorious riches you may strengthen us with power through your Spirit in our inner being, so that Christ may dwell in our hearts through faith. And we pray that we, being rooted and established in love, may have power, together with all the saints, to grasp how wide and long and high and deep in the love of Christ, and to know this love that surpasses knowledge – that we may be filled to the measure of all your fullness.

Based on Paul's prayer (Ephesians 3:16-19)

129. Mind to Know and Soul to Love

Eternal God, the light of the minds that know you, the light of the souls that love you, the strength of the wills that serve you; help us so to know you that we may truly love you, so to love you that we may fully serve you, whom to serve is perfect freedom.

Pope Gelasius

130. Late have I Loved You

Late have I loved You, O Beauty so ancient and so new; late have I loved You: for behold You were within me, and I outside; and I sought You outside and in my unloveliness fell upon those lovely things that You have made. You were with me, and I was not with You. I was kept from You by those things, yet had they not been in You, they would not have been at all. You did call and cry to me to break open my deafness: and You did send forth your beams and shine upon and chase away my blindness: You did breathe fragrance upon me, and I drew in my breath and do now pant for You: I tasted You, and hunger and thirst for You: You did touch me, and I have burned for Your peace.

St. Augustine

131. Your Sweetness

You will seek me and find me when you seek me with all your heart – Jeremiah 29

Lord, we are rivers running to your sea, Our waves and ripples and derived from you: A nothing we should have, a nothing be, Except for you.

Sweet are the waters of your shoreless sea, Make sweet our waters that make haste to you; Pour in your sweetness, that ourselves may be Sweetness to you.

Christina Rossetti

132. Faith and Steadfastness

Give me O Lord, a steadfast heart, which no unworthy affection may drag downwards; give me an unconquered heart, which no tribulation can wear out;

give me an upright heart, which no unworthy purpose may tempt aside. Bestow on me also, O Lord, my God, understanding to know you, diligence to seek you, wisdom to find you, and a faithfulness that may finally embrace you, through Jesus Christ our Lord.

St. Thomas Aquinas

133. Fix our Steps

Fix You our steps, O Lord, that we stagger not at the uneven motions of the world, but steadily go on to your glorious home; neither censuring our journey by the weather we meet with, nor turning out of the way for anything that befalls us. The winds are often rough, and our own weight presses us downwards. Reach forth, O Lord, your hand, your saving hand, and speedily deliver us. Teach us, O Lord, to use this transitory life as pilgrims returning their beloved home; that we take what our journey requires, and not think of settling in a foreign country.

John Wesley

134. In the Depths of Heart

Lord, enfold me in the depths of your heart; and there hold me, refine, purge, and set me on fire, raise me aloft, until my own self knows utter annihilation.

Pierre Teilhard de Chardin

135. Life Can Begin Again

Most gracious God, Father of our Lord Jesus Christ, we thank you that all our days are lived in the presence of your eternal love.

We thank you that to experience the reality of your love in Jesus Christ is to step from a living death to life itself.

We know, and know so well, what it means to exist in a world where life is not real life at all, but a deadness of spirit – a deadness in which the possibility of the flowering of goodness and truth seem to be just a wishful dream.

But, because of your steadfast love, there is always the possibility for life and light to enter into our own life to transform and heal us.

Alan Wade (Terry C. Falla)

136. Teach to Serve

Dearest Lord, teach me to be generous; Teach me to serve you as you deserve; To give and not to count the cost, To fight and not to heed the wounds, To toil and not to seek for rest, To labour and not to seek reward, Save that of knowing that I do your will.

St. Ignatius Loyola

137. Royalty of Inward Happiness

Grant me, O Lord, the royalty of inward happiness and the serenity which comes from living close to you. Daily renew the sense of joy, and let the eternal spirit of the Father dwell in my soul and body, filling every corner of my heart with light and grace, so that bearing about with me the infection of a good courage, I may be a diffuser of life and may meet all ills and crosses with gallant and high-hearted happiness, giving you thanks always for all things.

Robert Louis Stevenson

138. Draw us Entirely to Yourself

Yes, Lord Jesus Christ, whether we be far off or near, far away from you in the human swarm, in business, in earthly cares, in temporal joys, in merely human highness, or far from all these, forsaken, unappreciated in lowliness, and with this the nearer to you, do you draw us entirely to yourself.

Soren Kierkegaard

139. Steadfast Heart

Give us, O Lord, a steadfast heart, which no unworthy affection may drag downwards; give us an unconquered heart which no tribulation can wear out; give us an upright heart, which no unworthy purpose may tempt aside. Bestow upon us also, O Lord our God, understanding to know you, diligence to seek you, wisdom to find you and a faithfulness that may finally embrace you; through Jesus Christ our Lord.

St. Thomas Aquinas

140. You Understand

Lord, you understand me, you know my every thought, my brain is not a mystery to you. Enter into my mind, Lord, guide and direct my thoughts. Be before me when I speak, be beside me when I act, be within me when I listen, that I might possess the wisdom born of love, for you are love, the love which understands everything.

Frank Topping

141. Great Gifts

Almighty God, give us wisdom to perceive you, intellect to understand you, diligence to seek you, patience to wait for you, eyes to behold you, a heart to meditate upon you and life to proclaim you, through the power of the Spirit of our Lord Jesus Christ.

Attributed to St. Benedict

142. Take My Liberty

Take, Lord, all my liberty. Receive my memory, my understanding and my whole will. Whatever I have and possess, you have given me; to you I restore it wholly and to your will I surrender it for my direction. Give me the love of you only, with your grace and I am rich enough; nor ask I anything beside.

St. Ignatius Loyola

143. Batter Me to Free

Batter my heart, three-person'd God, for you as yet but knock! Breathe, shine and seek to mend; that I may rise and stand, o'erthrow me, and bend your force to break, blow, burn and make me new. I, like an usurp'd town, to another due labour to admit you, but O, to no end! Reason, your viceroy in me, me should defend, but is captiv'd and proves weak or untrue. Yet dearly I love you, and would be loved fain, but am betrothed unto your enemy; divorce me, untie, or break that knot again, take me to you, imprison me, for I except you enthrall me, never shall be free, nor ever chaste, except you ravish me.

John Donne

144. I Abandon Myself

My Father, I abandon myself to you. Do with me as you will. Whatever you may do with me I thank you. I am prepared for anything. I accept everything, provided your will is fulfilled in me and in all creatures. I ask for nothing more, my God. I place my soul in your hands. I give it to you, my God, with all the love of my heart, because I love you. And for me it is a necessity of love, this gift of myself, this placing of myself in your hands without reserve in boundless confidence, because you are my Father.

Charles de Foucauld

145. God of All Goodness and Grace

O God, the God of all goodness and grace, who are worthy of a greater love than we can either give or understand: Fill our hearts, we beseech you, with such love towards you that nothing may seem too hard for us to do or suffer in obedience to your will; and grant that thus loving you, we may become daily more like unto you, and finally obtain the crown of life which you have promised to those that love you; through Jesus Christ our Lord.

Brooke Foss Westcott

146. Draw Hearts and Guide Minds

Almighty and eternal God, so draw our hearts to you, so guide our minds, so fill our imaginations, so control our wills, that we may be wholly yours, utterly dedicated unto you; and then use us, we pray you, as you will, but always to your glory and the welfare of your people, through our Lord and Saviour Jesus Christ.

William Temple

147. Undoubting Faith

Look in compassion, O heavenly Father, upon this troubled and divided world. Though we cannot trace your footsteps or understand your working, give us grace to trust you with an undoubting faith; and when your own time is come, reveal, O Lord, that new heaven and new earth wherein dwells righteousness, where the Prince of Peace rules, your Son our Saviour Jesus Christ.

Charles Vaughan

148. My Pledge

Despite superficial positivity, truthful God, there are authentic voices about human rejection of your loving reign and its values, about a declining Church. In this context this is my pledge: Even if there is only one person who loves and obeys your commandment, let me be that person; if there is only one person who can speak the truth in love, let me be that person; if the membership of your church is reduced to only one person let me be that person; if there is only one person who has the confidence of sharing the good news of God's love and his waiting to welcome, let me be that person. But when I am surprised by your showing of many such ones, dear Lord, humble me to the dust. Whether I live or die let your name be glorified!

Israel Selvanayagam

149. Unfold Mysteries

Gracious Lord, flood our nature with your presence, unfold to us the mysteries of your love and reveal to us the depth of your compassion. Create within us a longing for your healing purity and grant us the gift of your cleansing truth; through Christ our Lord.

Walter James

150. Join with Me

Rising to joy, you laugh with me. Rising to toil, you work with me. Rising to sorrow, you weep with me. Rising to fear, you wait with me. Each returning day, accompanying God, I give you thanks.

Ruth Gee

151. Living in Your Presence

Perfect within us, O Lord, the work of grace which you have begun. May we think, speak and do only what is pleasing in your sight. Keep us from falling back into the sins of which we have repented. May we live our lives in your presence and finish them in your fear; through Jesus Christ our Lord.

William Bright

152. Covenant of Love

Of your mercy and goodness, O God, grant to your servants a covenant of love from which they cannot be separated, a fire of love to consume all their sins and a gift of love to heal their wounds; through Christ our Lord.

Miles Coverdale

153. Generous and Healing Presence

Extravagant God, in the arid sparsity of my faith expectations may your generous presence surprise my questioning mind with moments of quenching inspiration. In the voices of the unloved and unseen may your prophetic presence challenge my myopic ways with an invitation to deeper insight. In the warmth and words of others may your healing presence gently tend my soul with unfathomable compassion. So, may each present moment of my life shine with your extravagant presence, and may your living word of grace in Jesus become ever more fully and freely expressed in the loving kindness of my heart.

David Perry

154. Trusting Your Unfailing Love

Not trusting in our own power, merit and resources, God of unfailing love, let us trust in your supreme wisdom and mysterious guidance. In a perplexing world we seek clarity in confusion, confidence in desperation and hope in despair. Even when none of these seems to work or it works beyond our understanding, may we surrender to your will and take refuge under your wings. May we humbly trust that your goodness will triumph in the end.

Israel Selvanayagam

155. Never Separated

Blessed Lord God, be to me at all times my unending joy, my eternal bliss and my enduring comfort. Be to me light in the darkness, strength in temptation and refreshment in the desert. Grant that, penitent for my sins, I may never be separated from you and, longing for your face, I may behold you in heaven; for your own name's sake.

Margery Kempe

156. Fill Gaps

God of the gaps: you are the bringer of genuine hope to our lives and the life of the world. Help us today and tomorrow to live out and share that hope with confidence. God beyond the gaps: you are with us and alongside us in the good and bad experiences of life. Help us today and tomorrow to encourage celebration and to stand alongside those in need. God around the gaps: you embrace us with your free gifts of forgiveness, love and compassion. Help us today and tomorrow to own these gifts for ourselves and to offer them to those around us. God of all time and space: may I sense your peace and blessing and be a channel for these priceless gifts to those around me.

Ward Jones

157. Illumining Flame of Love

Let the flame of your love never be quenched in our hearts O Lord. Waking or sleeping, living or dying, let us delight in your presence. Let the flame of your love brighten our souls and illumine our path, and let the majesty of your glory be our joy, our life and our strength now and for ever.

Johann Arndt

158. Liberating Truth

Father of all, pour into our hearts the love that casts out fear, the truth that sets us free and the grace that is sufficient for all our needs, and grant we may rejoice that though you are unseen, you are not unknown and that, though you are hidden from our eyes, we may behold your beauty at the last; through Christ our Lord.

Louisa May Alcott

159. Timely Needs

Dear Lord, we pray for the things we need to come quickly: to the hungry, food; to the weeping, joy; to the thirsty, water; to those living with war, peace; to those in poverty, a truly human life. Give us patience to work for your kingdom. Give us hope, that we may not weary in proclaiming it. Give us vision to see your kingdom around us in the ordinary. Give us light to see the horizon where your kingdom is fully known, in Jesus Christ.

Richard Teal

160. Closest Companion

Be to us, O Lord, the closest of our companions, our everlasting love and our enduring happiness. Through your Spirit, create in us holy fire and purity of life, that loving you above all things and our neighbours ardently, we may come to the glories of your everlasting kingdom; through Christ our Lord.

Thomas à Kempis

161. Love Divine

O love divine, to you we cry in the day and in the night, for you alone can speak to our condition. For you alone can search the mind and purify the heart. You alone are infinite and you alone can flow over our darkness with the ocean of eternal light. O love divine, to you we cry in the day and in the night.

George Fox

162. The Depth of Trinity

You, O eternal Trinity, are a deep sea, into which the more I enter the more I find, and the more I find the more I seek. The soul cannot be satiated in your abyss, for she continually hungers after you, the eternal Trinity, desiring to see you with the light of your light. As the hart desires the springs of living water, so my soul desires to leave the prison of this dark body and see you in truth.

O abyss, O eternal Godhead, O sea profound, what more could you give me than yourself? You are the fire that ever burns without being consumed; you consume in your heat all the soul's self-love; you are the fire which takes away cold; with your light you illuminate me so that I may know all your truth. Clothe me, clothe me with yourself, eternal truth, so that I may run this mortal life with true obedience, and with the light of your most holy faith.

Catherine of Siena

V. God the Father

A note on addressing separately the Father, Son and Holy Spirit: *From the creation to completion of salvation the Bible presents glimpses of the unique vision of Trinity. The Father, Son and Holy Spirit love, glorify, collaborate and are humble to one another, thus providing an inspiring model for common human life. Even if there is a hierarchy it is different, graciously coming down to earth and moving upwards and sideways, thus challenging hard-core and unmoving hierarchies. It is mysterious but revealing. In Christian prayers and songs they are mentioned both individually and together. When one is addressed the others are behind the scene and their profound love refuses to remain in one position as they form a dynamic life in unity.*

1. Merciful Father

Our merciful Father, who in teaching us to pray by the Son Christ has commanded us to call you Father, and to believe that we are your beloved children, who stirs up none of you to pray, but to the intent that you would hear them, giving unto us also all things more effectually and plenteously than we can either ask or think. We do beseech you, for your Son's sake, to give us grace to believe, and know assuredly, that your Son and our Saviour Christ, is given of you unto us to be our Saviour, our righteousness, our wisdom, our holiness, our redemption, and our satisfaction. O Lord suffer us not to trust in any other salvation, but in your Son our Saviour Jesus Christ: So be it.

Elizabeth Oxenbridge Tyrwhitt

2. Your Kingdom

O God, you have set before us a great hope that your kingdom will come on earth, and have taught us to pray for its coming: make us ever ready to thank you for the signs of its dawning, and to pray and work for the perfect day when your will shall be done on earth as it is in heaven. Through Jesus Christ our Lord.

Iona Community

3. Guard and Guide

May the wisdom of God instruct us; may the hand of God protect us; may the way of God direct us; may the shield of God defend us and may the hosts of God guard us.

St. Patrick

4. Tower of Defence

Be to us, O Lord a strong tower of defence; a comforter in every tribulation; and a deliverer in times of distress. In all our troubles be to us a present help, and guide us through all dangers and temptations, till we come at length to the glory and habitation of heaven; this we ask through Jesus Christ our Lord.

Thomas à Kempis

5. Work with Love and Joy

God of truth and grace, by taking the risk of coming among us, you showed us that you trust us to care for this wonderful planet and for each other. Open our eyes and ears to your anger and grief; help us to trust you and to take the risk of travelling vulnerably into the unknown, to do your work joyfully in the love of our risen Saviour, Jesus Christ.

Mary Ann Ebert

6. Calmness of Faith

Guide us, O Lord, in all the changes of this uncertain world, that we may live in your peace. Let us not complain in our troubles, nor grow proud in our prosperity. With calmness of faith, let us rejoice in the goodness of your perfect will; through Christ our Lord.

Jeremy Taylor

7. Delight in Beauty

Give to me, O God, a heart of joy that rests in your peace and a soul of tranquillity that delights in your beauty; a spirit of glory that sings your praise, a life of serenity at home in your presence and a mind of quietness renewed by your Spirit; through Jesus Christ our Lord.

Evelyn Underhill

8. Receive All We Offer

Receive, O Lord, every heart that desires to love you. Fill every mouth that longs to praise you and strengthen every hand that seeks to serve you; through Christ our Lord.

François Fénelon

9. Recharge Power

Father, Creator of this warm and rain-washed Celtic land, we feel your power in the majesty of towering cliff and restless sea; in wooded creek and sandy cove, adorned with flowers and teeming with wildlife. Recharge us with the power of your Spirit, which surges with sacrificial love for others, that conflict and pain may be burnt up in hope and harmony as we follow the path of our Living Lord.

Daphne Train

10. Stay with Us

Stay with us, O Lord, when we are swamped by weariness and seeming impossibilities. Turn our faces gently towards you, keep our hearts loving and our will determined to fight on to the end.

Mother Janet Stuart

11. Guide us in Love

Parent God, like a mother hen you gather us under your protecting wing; like a nurse you bind our wounds and tenderly restore our health; like a Father you guide our footsteps along safe paths; show us through your Son the way that we should speak and act in love to others.

Donald Hilton

12. Your Son for Us

Grant us grace, O God, to take your Son for our Redeemer; his life for our example; his word for our rule; his Spirit for our guide, his wounds for our healing and his cross for our salvation, that he may take possession of our hearts, now and for ever.

Jeremy Taylor

13. Your Holy Spirit

Eternal Father, we thank you for giving us your Holy Spirit; for the comfort it brings; for its guidance as we seek your truth; for its enlightenment as we read your word; for the changes in heart that it provokes. As we persevere in the course that you have set for us, we ask that you continue to pour out your Spirit that we might grow in our discipleship.

Moravian

14. Our Space and Time

God, you stand up for us like a father for his child or a human for his/her friend. And you do more than this, so deeply you care for us and no one can prevent you from being our God. We rely on you, we wait for you and we trust in your name. You are too great a truth to be expressed in our words. You are our space and time now and for ever.

Huub Oosterhuis

VI. God the Son

1. Teach us How to Pray

Jesus of Nazareth, supreme teacher of God, often we do not know how to pray when crisis strikes and needs overwhelm. Help us to be mindful of the fact that you know our real needs better than we do and you are more concerned about our well-being than we ourselves are. Fill us with your wisdom that we may be able to discern your will. When tossed by waves and wavering, quieten our mind and calm our spirit. Give us the courage to speak to you, our friend and brother, even if we are not sure of the right words. While relying on your guiding presence, let us be silent waiting for new glimpses into meaningful words. Just as in the words you taught your disciples – hallowing God's name, coming of his kingdom, doing of his will, safeguarding from trial, deliverance from evil and attributing to the heavenly Father reign, power and glory.

Israel Selvanayagam

2. Increase our Faith

Increase our faith, O Lord, to move mountains, uproot obstructing trees and find sprouting seeds. Just like those who made hole in the roof to let a paralytic to you, help us to dare the impossible; like the woman of un-curable bleeding who squeezed through the crowd and touched your garment, let us have the courage to break the oppressive cultural norms; and like the Samaritan cured of leprosy who only came back to you in thankfulness, may we be not carried away by the currents of peer influences. No longer confused by clinging to familiarity, tradition and dogma, help us to learn from you that faith which has the ability to move on and power to make things anew.

Israel Selvanayagam

3. Show us the Way

Jesus, show us your way, lead us into your path, hold us within the new companionship, transform us into signs of your generosity. May the life that flows from the heart of God form and mark us.

Donald Eadie

4. Carpenter

O Christ, the Master Carpenter, who at the last, through wood and nails, purchased our whole salvation, wield well your tools in the workshop of your world, so that we who come rough-hewn to your bench may here be fashioned to a truer beauty of your hand. We ask it for your own name's sake.

Iona Community

5. On a Journey

Lord Jesus, Leader in our journeys, king of life and death, and resurrection, creator of light and darkness, revealer of mystery and eternity, don't let us rest or go back either.

You have called us to life. Keep us tagging along. When the crises come, help us to be true to ourselves, true to you, and so more ourselves transformed by you into you so that we may bring life.

And so go on our journey rejoicing in you and with those whom you have given us – our companions along the way.

John B. Coburn

6. You and Our Loves Together

Lord Jesus, you know us better than we know ourselves. Help us therefore to keep our eyes on you, so that we may come to ourselves, to be ourselves, and so become more of you.

You take our fears now, our anxieties, our worries, and turn them into your own, so that we may be turned away from obsession with ourselves into possession by you.

We give you also all thoughts that are unworthy of us, all sins that separate us from one another and from you so that we may see more clearly, live more purely, and love more deeply – with our deepest, purest selves.

Take our longings, our yearnings, and our agonies. Transform them as they become yours into joy and glory with peace and love as we become yours. We do not want so much the fruits of our spirit as we want you.

John B. Coburn

7. Prisoners of Conscience

Lord Jesus, you experienced torture and death as a prisoner of conscience. You were beaten and flogged and sentenced to an agonizing death though you had done no wrong. Be now with prisoners of conscience throughout the world. Be with them in their fear and loneliness in the agony of physical and mental torture, and in the face of execution and death. Stretch out your hands in power to break their chains. Be merciful to the oppressor and the torturer, and place a new heart within them. Forgive all injustice in our lives, and transform us to be instruments of your peace, for by your wounds we are healed.

Amnesty International

8. Not Forsaken

Lord Jesus Christ, whether in the quietness of my own resting place or in the busy storms of the day, amidst all the cares and joys of life, may I never feel forsaken or alone. Of your grace draw me entirely to yourself, now and for ever.

Soren Kierkegaard

9. Touch Me and Turn Me

May your touch on my life, Lord Jesus, be as a vine to a branch – a constant communication. Nudge me forward when there is opportunity for witness. Hold me back when I needlessly rush about. Turn me in the right direction when I go wrong. Silence my voice when I hog the conversation. Embrace me in the arms of your mercy. And when my life touches another, may it always be in love. May my touch on your life, Lord Jesus, be as a branch to a vine – a constant communication.

Peter Good

10. Help in Darkness and Weakness

O Blessed Jesus, immortal and victorious, by the sorrow you suffered when all the powers of your heart failed you, have mercy on us and help us in our days of darkness and in our hours of weakness, that we do not lose hold of you either in this life, or in the life of the world to come. This we ask for your own name's sake.

St. Bridget of Sweden

11. Tree of Life

Jesus, you are the Christ who is the Tree of Life. Your leaves are for the healing of all people. Grant us this day to shelter in your shade, that we may clearly see the things which lead to health and healing, well-being and peace. Grant us to eat of your fruit, that we may be strong to work for the health of our communities. Grant us the use of your branches, that we may shelter the homeless, defend the weak and discover creative work for unemployed hands. Grant us the sweet perfume of your flower, that in all our efforts we may never lose the wonder and delight of your presence.

David Moore

12. Life-giving Spirit

O Lord Jesus Christ, on the cross you shed your most precious blood to bring peace with God; and by your resurrection you revitalized us with new hope that 'love is stronger than hate, good is stronger than evil and truth is stronger than falsehood'. Come to your world today by your life-giving Spirit. Come, heal the sick and restore the broken. Come, release the fearful, renew the weak with grace and save us all for your glory.

Ken Todd

13. On the Way to Golgotha

Lord we cannot properly reflect on the meaning of the cross while life is easy and comfortable. Let us follow you on your way to Golgotha again and again, bearing the pain and sin of humanity, yet directing all our deep questions to you, you alone. Loving God, you create and recreate; you allow all things to die and you bring to life. Let us not aspire to glory without suffering, confidence without self-denial, or eternal life without dying.

Israel Selvanayagam

14. Sufficient Grace

Lord Jesus Christ, come to us in the power of the Spirit that we may take initiatives in mending broken relationships. Give us perseverance in breaking down barriers of suspicion and mistrust; insight to recognise our prejudices; courage to admit our failures; honesty to acknowledge our festering hurts and willingness to repent of our personal and community sins. Help us to prove that your grace is sufficient for every need.

Ian D. Henderson

15. Together with You

When what has been regarded sacred and sacrosanct become irrelevant and alienating, give us, O Son of God, our Saviour, courage to cleanse, as you cleansed the temple in Jerusalem, and lay it bare. When traditions have become idols and been safeguarded with claims of truths, may we prayerfully question them on our knees and be empowered to move them for your name's sake! In the midst of threatening words and jeering voices let our 'Hosanna' continue to echo proclaiming your majesty and meekness in perfect balance.

Israel Selvanayagam

16. Transform Us

Risen Christ, as ice melts and rivers flow when spring comes, breath your life-giving Spirit into our frozen hearts. Set our minds on fire and feet running, to seek and serve your truth. Free us from all that captivates us. Give us a deeper understanding of your truth. Increase our wisdom. Remind us that you have written our names on the palms of your crucified hands and help us to know that you call us by name.

Donald Hilton

17. Gift of Grace

Jesus, we set our sights and hopes on your gift of grace; a gift unearned. It is with great joy that we await the revealing of this great mystery of love – one day face-to-face with its Giver.

Moravian

18. Freedom of Your Spirit

Lord Jesus Christ, alive and at large in the world, help me to follow and find you there today, in the place where I work, meet people, spend money and make plans. Take me as a disciple of your kingdom to see through your eyes and hear the questions you are asking, to welcome all people with your trust and truth and to change the things that contradict God's love by the power of the Cross and the freedom of your Spirit.

John Taylor

19. Joyful Cooperation with Your Woodwork

Christ the carpenter, who sanctifies our daily labour, I will praise you with my hands at the workbench and my arms on the production line. I will honour you in my trade and business. In my office the thoughts of my head shall be yours, and you will be in my heart when I am caring for others. Let my integrity bear witness to you. I will proclaim you by my joy, for my spirit adores you in my work and in my church. Lord Jesus, you are my redeemer.

Selwyn Veater

20. Jesus All to me

Jesus: I offer to you all my weakness, my inability to cope. In all my weakness – not being able to say 'no' - you will be there to say 'no' for me. In all my waste of time, you will be there to direct me. In all my lack of concentration you will be there to guide me. In all my panic, you will be there to calm me. In all my wilfulness you will be there to rebuke me, and show me your scarred hands. In all my lack of loving, you will be the one who loves. Take all of me, Lord Jesus, mould me to the pattern you have planned for me, for I can neither live nor die without you.

Thelma Wilson

21. Neighbour and Stranger

Christ our neighbour, you come to us in the stranger, the one we have been conditioned to despise, the one from whom we recoil. You are moved by our pain, you tend our wounds, you bring us to a place of healing. Teach us to love you as we love ourselves and, loving you, to welcome the stranger, to recognize the dignity of the despicable, and draw close to those are difficult to love, so that together we may bring healing to a beaten and neglected world.

Jonathan Kerry

22. Christ the Essence

Christ be the power in my purpose and the passion in my pace, be my fight and my fervour, and the calm in my haste. Be my breath when I am breathless, and the wind at my back, the strength in my knees and the courage I lack. Be my guide at each corner, and my bridge over the stream, my stamina in my weakness, and my boldness to dream. Be the towel which sooths and mops the cost from my face, my stimulant and tonic, when I could give up the race. Be my victory, my joy, my objective and prize, let me share in the podium with you by my side.

Gill Daniel

23. Solidarity with You

Jesus, abject and despised, let us not be ashamed to follow you. Jesus, hated and persecuted, let us not be afraid to walk in your footsteps. Jesus, blasphemed and condemned, let us be counted your friends. Jesus, mocked and scourged, let us bear all things patiently. Jesus, crowned and derided, let us not be overwhelmed by our injuries and grief.

John Wesley

24. Jesus, the Glimmer

Jesus, light of the world: in the darkness of anxiety be the glimmer of peace; in the darkness of sorrow be the glimmer of joy; in the darkness of suffering be the glimmer of comfort; in the darkness of rejection be the glimmer of welcome; in the darkness of despair be the glimmer of hope. So, may the light that cannot be overcome shine through the darkness, shine through our lives, shine in the world.

Ruth Gee

25. Come, Lord Jesus

Come to us, O Christ, as the wind that blows the autumn leaves, as the song that soothes the troubled child, as the melody that lifts the anxious spirit, and fill us with affection for you that is unbounded, desire for you that is unrestrained and a yearning for you that throws caution to the winds, and this for your own love's sake.

Richard Rolle

26. Way, Truth, Life

O Jesus, the Christ, Lord and Saviour, continue to teach us the implications of your claim that you are the way, the truth and the life. Let us not stand on the way but move on, helping those who faint, challenging those who block it by perpetuating oppression and injustice, not backtracking from the way to the cross. Let us not remain with the truth we know but explore into the depths of the truth yet to be known. Just as you gave your life for the salvation of others, let us too spend our life and all its resources for the new life of the 'lifeless.' Let us never think that we will move on only when we have full clarity and certainty.

Israel Selvanayagam

27. To Centre and Heart

Draw us, O Christ, by grace irresistible to the centre of all faith and to the heart of all sacrifice; to the deepest of all wells and to a work that is not our own; even your holy Cross, to which we cling and by which we are; for your own name's sake.

Dora Greenwell

28. Be My Stronghold

O Jesus, be my rock that stands when the tide has come and washed the soil away; be the foundations of my life that hold me up; be my wind-filled sail that will send me on the best course; be the morning breeze that gets me ready for the day; be the lion in my heart that gives me bravery; be the plough that provides for my people; but, most of all, be in my heart, my soul and my spirit; for when I am with you Jesus, I feel at peace.

Sophie Temple

29. Grant us the Basics

Loving Jesus, let us step out with you in faith; grant us understanding to know what we need to do, grant us courage to go where we are needed, grant us strength to face our difficulty, grant us determination to overcome our disappointments, grant us wisdom to serve you well. Lord Jesus, let us step out with you in faith, so that your light shines far beyond our way, bringing your truth to many.

Andrea Davies

30. Eternal Contemporary

Lord Jesus Christ, you were there when the Spirit hovered over the waters at creation and you will be there when a new heaven and new earth come into being. You were there when we took our first breath and you will be there when we breathe our last. You have begun a good work in us, and you will continue that work to its completion as we make ourselves available to you and to the work of your Spirit in us. Thank you that there is nothing that has been, or is, or will be, in our lives or in the life of the world, which is not known to you or of concern to you. Thank you that, because all things, past, present and future are in your hands, that there is nothing in our past, present or future with which we cannot trust you.

Gill Newton

31. The Way in the Labyrinth of Life

Lord Jesus, your way spreads like a labyrinth before my sight. Today, your Spirit may lead me to the outer edge where I shall feel far from your presence; or I may be drawn towards the centre where I shall sense you tantalizingly near. Thank you that I am never led to a dead end. Help me to trust that your path will unfailingly lead me home where I shall find both my end and my beginning in the Creator's love.

Rachel Parkinson

32. Fellow Traveller

Lord Jesus Christ, in the loneliness of our journey may we never feel abandoned, and in the days of our affliction may we know your comfort. In the hour of our despairing may our faith be strengthened, our hope fortified and our love purified; for your own name's sake.

Marie Bernarde Soubirous

33. Warmth of Genuine Welcome

Lord Jesus, you are the source of all that is good, all that is joyful, and all that is loving, and we thank you for each and every way in which you show yourself to us; for your presence in the small things, as well as the great and magnificent: the comforting touch of a friend's hand, the warmth of genuine welcome, a human smile or the wag of a dog's tail. In so many ways, Lord, you reveal your love for us. Help us to see and truly understand that you want us as your friends and that, as we open our hearts and minds to you, you will always be there to welcome us into yours. For this we are truly grateful.

Ren

34. Sweet One

Grant me, O most sweet and loving Jesus, to rest in you above every creature, above all health and beauty, above all glory and honour, above all power and dignity, above all knowledge and subtility, above all riches and arts, above all joy and exultation, above all fame and praise, above all sweetness and consolation, above all hope and promise, above all desert and desire, above all gifts and presence which you are able to bestow or infuse, above all joy and gladness which the mind is capable of receiving and feeling; finally, above angels and archangels and above all the heavenly host, above all things visible and invisible and above all that you are not, O my God!

Thomas à Kempis

35. Share the Gifts of Your Presence

O Lord, give us yourself above all things. It is in your coming alone that we are enriched. It is in your coming that your true gifts come. Come, Lord, that we may share the gifts of your presence. Come, Lord, with healing of the past, come and calm our memories, come with joy for the present, come and give life to our existence, come with hope for the future, come and give a sense of eternity. Come with strength for our wills, come with power for our thoughts, come with love for our heart, come and give affection to our being. Come, Lord, give yourself above all things and help us to give ourselves to you.

David Adam

36. Christ of Immeasurable Love

Lord Jesus Christ, draw our hearts to yours with a love that is irresistible; unite our hearts to yours with a love that is immeasurable, and bind our hearts to yours with a love that is inseparable; now and for ever.

Miles Coverdale

37. In Your Face, Jesus

Jesus, in your face we catch a glimpse of the anger of the loving God. We feel the heat of the holy fire. We hear the sounds both of judgment and mercy rumbling from the depths among the people. Help us to see that fire that spreads everywhere, that pervades all things. Draw us into that travail that transforms evil into good.

Donald Eadie (from a friend's letter)

38. Risen Lord

Risen Lord, as you met your troubled followers on the road, walked with them, and shared their doubts, their despair, their disappointments, help all your people to find you there, present with them, longing to share in all their troubles, to lead them further on their journey:

Lord, in your mercy; ***Hear our prayer.***

Risen Lord, you met your despairing disciples with words of Peace; we pray for all who live in places of great violence, that your world may yet find the peace that is your will for us, that our warring ways seeking power over others may yet be changed:

Lord, in your mercy; ***Hear our prayer.***

Risen Lord, you sent out your followers to be witnesses to your new way, we pray that we too may find new ways to serve you in our changing world, that others, far and near, may come to recognise the signs of your presence:

Lord, in your mercy; ***Hear our prayer.***

Risen Lord, always ready to stretch out your hand in healing, touch, we pray, those wounded and weakened by the ills of our world, and bring a new wholeness to the lives of the needy; for we pray with faith in you as our fellow-traveller on the road of life, even Jesus Christ our Lord.

Eric Lott

39. Emmaus Journey

Gracious Christ, our Risen Lord, Thank you for your presence with us. You are worthy of all honour yet you have chosen to walk with us as our greatest companion and fellow sufferer. You marvel us by embracing those who are pushed aside on the way. You often set our hearts on fire opening the scriptures to us in new light. When we invite you to be our guest, you turn to be our host breaking bread with us. When we take part in the communion you open our eyes to see you vanishing from our sight. We belong to you and you belong to us and to the whole world. Show the beauty of your grace again and again that all who live in fear of uncertain future and death may find hope in you. Help us to be mindful of your instant appearances and rejoice over the fellowship of your friends who are ours too. Just as you are one with the Father and the Holy Spirit, make us one and give us a glimpse of your divine fellowship. Let us walk together and work together having fixed our eyes on your imminent glory. In your holy name we pray.

Israel Selvanayagam

40. Always Journeying with us

You are with us, Risen Lord, with us and with all your people for ever;

You are with us, the Beginning and the End of all life, with us as the one who was, and who is, and who for ever will be;

You are with us, our unfailing Friend on the road of life, even when we do not know you, ever drawing near in unexpected ways;

You are with us, our sin-bearer, our sorrow-sharer, ever seeking to rekindle faith, to revive our weakened vision and quicken our flagging footsteps;

Help us, Risen Lord, to respond to you in this time of worship together, that we may truly break the bread of life with you, and find forgiveness for all the times we have failed you; for we pray with faith in you as the One who can set us free from our past, even Jesus Christ our Lord.

Eric Lott

41. Help to Live the Truth

Jesus, help us to live the truth that we know with both courage and humour. Jesus, show us, as we can bear, the marks of God's passion and lead us within these mysteries. Jesus, give us courage not to hide our faces when the tears flow. Give us courage not to wash away the stains. Release in us that breaking of the waters both of grief and joy that flow from the heart of God. Give us courage to live openly with the stains of these tears.

Donald Eadie

VII. God the Spirit

1. Adoration

Everlasting Spirit, one with the Father and the Son, the love of the divine family, as we celebrate Pentecost, when you descended upon a festival gathering on such a day as this, we think of your wonderful work. You participated in the creation by brooding over the deep waters of darkness. You mingled in the breathing of the spirit in the nostrils of the humans and in the life energy of every creature. We worship and adore you.

Almighty Spirit, Spirit of power and wisdom, you empowered the powerless Hebrew slaves when they were longing for liberation in Egypt. You filled them with joy when they crossed the Red Sea and celebrated your victory. You filled the crafts and other workers with the gift of art when they were making the Tabernacle. You energized the leaders and prophets to guide the community in the ways of justice and peace. We worship and adore you.

Loving Spirit, you conceived the divine Son in the womb of Mary, you anointed Jesus for the ministry of liberation, you were poured into the fellowship of his disciples, and you directed them into new places teaching them the new truth. You blessed the church with spiritual gifts and continue to lead it, reminding them of all that Jesus did and said. You unite the church as one body with diverse gifts. Above all you have flooded the hearts of the believers with love, the greatest gift. We worship and adore you.

Israel Selvanayagam

2. Confession

Holy spirit, holy of all holies, we come to you with broken hearts and wounded spirits. Before your presence we are unclean with many shortcomings and failures. We fear the most terrible sin against you, twisting your purpose and resisting your guidance. We have grieved you by choosing easy ways of comfort and pleasure in preference to a simple life-style with honesty and thankfulness. We have divided ourselves by our vested interests instead of contributing to the body of Christ by sharing our gifts for common good. Forgive us and make us new. Help us to feel the healing you are bringing into our bodies, minds and fellowships. Fill us with your love. We ask this in the name of Christ who reigns with you and the Father, now and always.

Israel Selvanayagam

3. Blowing Wind

Wind of God, blow far from us all dark despair, all deep distress, all groundless fears, all sinful desires, all Satan's snares, all false values, all selfish wishes, all wasteful worries.

Blow into us your holy presence, your living love, your healing touch, your splendid courage, your mighty strength, your perfect peace, your caring concern, your divine grace, your boundless joy.

Wind of God, blow strong, blow fresh, blow now.

Pamela Wilding

4. Fall Afresh and Renew

God the Spirit, you hovered over the surface of the deep water covered with darkness in the beginning. You created light out of darkness, order from chaos and fullness from void. We still need light, order and fullness.

Fall afresh on us and renew us.

Gracious Spirit, you have guided fathers and mothers and prophets of many generations. You filled them with your power and used them effectively. We need your guidance and strength.

Fall afresh on us and renew us.

Filling Spirit, you have filled rulers, particularly your chosen ones, with the gifts of wisdom and understanding, counsel and power, knowledge and fear of the Lord. We need the balance of these gifts in their perfect combination.

Fall afresh on us and renew us.

Spirit of joy, you filled Elizabeth and Mary and hosts of your servants whom you have used as instruments for carrying out your will. You looked with favour on these lowly servants. We need your joy and assurance.

Fall afresh on us and renew us.

O Holy Spirit, you descended like a dove and alighted on Jesus at his baptism. You guided him in the wilderness and sustained him in his trial and temptation.

You assured him of your ever-continuing presence.
Fall afresh on us and renew us.
Divine Comforter and Advocate, you descended on the disciples of Christ on the day of Pentecost. You sounded like a strong driving wind. You gave them flames like tongues of fire and filled them with power. You sent them to be the witnesses of Christ throughout the world. We need your flame of fire and power of discernment.
Fall afresh on us and renew us.
Spirit of love, pour out your love into our hearts. Let us have the harvest of your love in joy, peace, patience, kindness, goodness, fidelity, gentleness and self-control.
Fall afresh on us and renew us.
When we hesitate to cross boundaries, to be open to learn from others and to risk our safety, O Guiding Spirit, blow upon us and move us in the right direction so that we will not miss unique opportunities.
We pray in the name of Christ whom you glorify in the fellowship of the Father.

Israel Selvanayagam

5. Create and Revive

Spirit of God, creating and reviving,
Renew our hearts and minds and revive our commitment to your cause.
Blow away from us and from our churches
The dead leaves of outdated ideas and irrelevant words.
Blow away from us the accumulated dust
Of biases and prejudices.
Blow away from us all coverings that conceal our real true nature.

Spirit of the oldest of the old and newest of the new,
Blow upon us with wisdom, courage and counsel;
Blow upon us with new vision and openness;
Blow upon us with strength to move on in our journey with confidence.
Spirit of all truth,
Guide us into the path of absolute truthfulness;
Guide us to new avenues of imagination and action;
Guide us on the way of the cross as willed by the Father and taken by Christ.
Spirit of love,
As you go between the Father and the Son,

Between everything in your creation and everything in us,
Go between us, among us and around us,
And give us a share in your eternal love and unity
With the Father and the Son, now and always.

Israel Selvanayagam

6. Past, Present, Future

O God of past, present and future, in the challenge and excitement of the new, help us to be grateful for the past. May we have the grace to be open to what is different in a fast-changing world, to allow our faith to be stretched, as we explore new ways of worship while retaining the richness of what we already know. As we give thanks for the wonder of easy communication with those who are far away, enable us always to be aware of people nearby who need our help. May your whole church experience the invigoration of the Holy Spirit who links us to the earliest followers of Christ, so that we and all who profess the faith may go forward in hope into what is yet to be, in the name of Jesus who shows us the Father, and who is always with us in the power of Holy Spirit.

Thomas Kingston

7. Breathe on our Fragile Frame

Loving God, breathe your Spirit of healing into us, for we are like clay jars, easily broken, shattered by the fragility of life and relationships in which you place us, and may your healing grace flow through us into others. Deepen our awareness of our own need that we may recognise when others are broken and be able to share their emptiness and darkness. In the name of Christ who brings healing.

Maureen Edwards

8. Disturbing Questions

Holy God, beneath the deepest peace and most turbulent strife you hold all things together, and in Jesus you show us your love that nothing can break. Help us in our calm certainties and in our disturbing questions to rest in your strength, to be fed by your Spirit, and to trust in Christ's way, that in all seasons of life we may walk with you, through Jesus Christ our Lord.

Robin Hutt

9. Spirit of the North

We greet you, Spirit of the North. You are the cold, biting wind that blows across our land, that strips the earth of all that is dead and decayed, that robs us of the false securities, so easily blown away. Teach us to plant our feet securely on the earth and to see things as they really are, that your coming may find us standing firm in integrity. It is you whose winds bring the snow of winter, with their fury and their solitude. It is you who blanket the earth for sleep. Teach us, Spirit of the North, in the solitude of winter, to wait in darkness with the sleeping earth, believing that we, like the earth, already hold within ourselves the seeds of new life.

A Canadian Indian

10. Wings of the Spirit

Gracious God, you seek us at every moment of our lives. When the sun is shining it is not too difficult to believe in you and to live thankfully. But, the hardest times are when our minds are filled with anxiety and dread, or when we are tired out with caring for others. Give us then the wings of your Spirit, not to escape from all that we must do, but to face it with calm mind, aware of your unfailing presence.

Nigel Collinson

11. Wisdom, Vision, Justice

Come, Spirit of Wisdom, be that inner sense to be present in us for decisions hence. Come, Spirit of Vision, and give us sight to perceive your future and do what you might. Come, Spirit of Justice, set us on fire to stand up in all lands for what you desire.

Uniting Church of Australia

12. Liberate and Comfort

O Holy Spirit, our liberator and comforter, we are thankful that you have renewed us and given us courage and new confidence. Help us recapture our sense of mission and share in your ministry of reconciliation. Help us rediscover how to enrich the world with your justice, peace and love. Strengthen us that we may stand firm against all forms of domination, exploitation, discrimination.

Strengthen us that we may meet the challenges and opportunities of the present age to proclaim with urgency: 'Good News to the poor, liberty to the captives, recovery of sight to the blind, freedom for the oppressed and to announce the year when the Lord will save his people' (Luke 4:18,19).

Strengthen us that we may move ahead, out of the paths of divisiveness, hopelessness, powerlessness.

Strengthen us that we may go into the world with your power to fulfil our calling as servants of our Lord and Saviour Jesus Christ.

Lesley G. Anderson

13. Holy Spirit of God

Holy Spirit of God, blow over the spoiled earth and renew creation.

Holy Spirit of God, blow among the torn peoples of the earth and form one family.

Holy Spirit of God, blow through your Church and form that Christ who will be recognised only by its markings.

Donald Eadie

14. Penetrate into Spirits

O Spirit of God, who speak to spirits, who created us in your own likeness; penetrate into the depths of our spirits, into the storehouse of memories, remembered and forgotten, into the depths of being, the very springs of personality; and cleanse and forgive, making us whole and holy, that we may be yours and live in the new being of Christ our Lord.

George Appleton

15. Inner Life

Holy Spirit, Spirit of the living God, you breathe in us on all that is inadequate and fragile. You make living water spring even from our hurts themselves. And through you the valley of tears becomes a place of wellsprings. So, in an inner life with neither beginning nor end, your continual presence makes new freshness break through.

Brother Roger of Taizé

16. Radiance of Light

Come Holy Spirit, send from highest heaven radiance of your light. Come, Father of the poor; come, giver of all gifts; come, light of every heart. Of comforters the best dear guest of every soul refreshment ever sweet. Without thy Holy Presence all is dark: nothing free from sin. Give Thy faithful ones who in Thee confide sevenfold hallowing. Give Goodness its reward; give journey safe through death; give joy that has no end.

Stephen Langton

17. Inner Presence and Stimulus

Come, Spirit of Wisdom, be that inner sense to be present in us for decisions hence. Come, Spirit of Vision, and give us sight to perceive your future and do what you might. Come, Spirit of Justice, set us on fire to stand up in all lands for what you desire.

Uniting Church of Australia

18. Spirit of Creation

Spirit of creation, spilling into rivers and oceans, cleanse the life-giving waters. Spirit of creation, rushing through mighty forests, spread the seeds of new life. Spirit of creation, burning in the hearts of your people, give life, reborn and renewed. Spirit of God, water, wind and fire, fill us with your love.

Diane Clutterbuck

19. Help Us

Spirit hovering over our chaos, help us to acknowledge our sin; lead us to deeper repentance in unity with Christ. Help us to admit our emptiness, that we may turn to be filled with the love that rushes to meet us. May we be more conscious of God's goodness than that of our own guilt. May we allow ourselves to be embraced and kissed by the father who delights in us, and if we look out of the eye of the other, the elder brother, in jealousy and pain, help us to admit our emptiness, that we may turn to be filled with the love that says: 'My son, my daughter, you are with me always, and all I have is yours.' When we see the happiness of a father and children through the smoke of the cooking fire, from behind the daily juggling act of unfinished tasks, may our tears be ones of joy as we admit our emptiness, our longing for fulfilment, and receive the understanding love which empowers and enables us to serve by being ourselves.

Kate McIlhagga

20. Ever Moving Wind

As the wind is your symbol, so forward our goings. As the dove so launch us heavenwards. As water so purify our spirits. As a cloud so abate our temptations. As dew so revive our languor. As fire so purge out our dross.

Christina Rossetti

21. Transform Us

Refining fire, you take us as we are: the raw material of nature, thrust into the furnace of the world where you reform us. Reforming wind, you buffet us in the maelstrom of life: the tempest-tossed debris of emerging being propelled into the whirlpool where you transform us. Transforming love, you cherish us as we grow; the budding potential of creation given a place in the kingdom of grace where we blossom. Refining, reforming, transforming God, take us as we are, make us as you would have us be.

Anne Smith

22. Sacred Flame

Holy Spirit, Fire of Pentecost, let us partake of your sacred flame. Take possession of our hearts and cast your fire into our souls. Kindle within us the flame of love and consume our sins. Welcome us into the burning light of your presence that we may dwell there for ever.

Richard Challoner

23. Refine Us

O Holy Spirit, we look for ways to refine our thinking, our living and our being, so that we may be able to see ourselves and the world around us more clearly and with love and compassion. We look for your reforming power to enable us to see our own weakness and to feel that we are being restored to that image of God which truly reflects your love and the interconnectedness of all loving. We look for your transforming power to change hatred into love, oppression to freedom, diversity into unity, unity into cooperation, misunderstanding into mutual understanding, rejection into recognition, injustice to justice and turmoil into peaceful transformation.

Ngurliana

24. Breath of Life

Breath of life, untamed and uninvited, disturb and caress the sleeping coals of our faith: spark us into life, draw us into your dancing flame; and from the crucible of your white-hot presence pour for the gift of an urgent energy charged with renewing the face of the earth. Divine flame, spark us, astonish us, re-birth in us your burning promise of life in all its fullness: open our eyes to the holy ground beneath our feet, and help us walk in wisdom and in peace.

Liz Smith

25. Divine Spark

Divine spark, just as the candle goes out before its flame translates into a spiral, as a cobweb spouts before its flame translates to grey-white, there waits atop a charred wick almost dead, sitting in pliable wax, a spark of most vivid red staying stubbornly and acting as a hope-filled signal. I see when darkness to light turns, divine luminosity waiting for me and burning … transformationally. Eternal source of peace and strength, permeate our lives with a sense of your presence. Restore to us a sense of your nearness, renew within us enthusiasm for the truths of your gospel, base our lives in your grace, so that we will receive from our worship every good thing you offer to us.

Wesley Blakey

26. Transform and Reform

Refining Spirit, purify our hearts, clarify our vision, and clean our souls, that we may come into your presence, and worship you. Reforming Spirit, remould our wills, amend our lives, and rework us into your likeness, that we may continue your presence, and know ourselves loved. Transforming Spirit, convert our ways, rekindle our faith, and remake our mission, that we may live in your presence, and be your people in the world.

Adrian Burdon

27. Empower Us to Exercise True Spirituality

Spirit of the living God, save us from the narrow views of your presence and action in our solitary and pious pursuits. Empower us to exercise true spirituality where people struggle to relate, to save relationships, to struggle for survival, to free from the clutches of unmeaning and outmoded religious practices. Equip us to exercise true spirituality in political hustings, governmental controversies and corridors of administration. Spirit of truth, help us to discriminate between weakness and wickedness, failures and blunders, and truth and half-truth or falsehood which may appear to be the truth. Firm up our feet, clarify our minds, warm our hearts and move us into creative and transformative action, for your glory.

Israel Selvanayagam

28. Sevenfold Gifts

Pour upon us, O Holy Spirit, your sevenfold gifts: of understanding, that we may be enlightened; of counsel, that we may follow in your footsteps; of courage, that we may face the enemy; of knowledge, that we may discern the good; of piety, that we may be compassionate; of fear, that we may draw back from evil; and of wisdom, that we may taste the sweetness of your love.

Bonaventure of Bagnoregio

29. Vital Forces

O Holy Spirit, God, all loveliness is yours; great things and small are both in you, the star-world is your shrine. You are the stream of love, the unity divine; good people and true are in you, and in your radiance shine. The heroes and the saints your messengers became; and all the lamps that guide the world were kindled at your flame. Give fellowship, we pray, in love and joy and peace, that we in counsel, knowledge, might and wisdom, may increase.

Percy Dearmer

30. Breath of All Life

O Holy Spirit, breath of all creatures, purifier of all souls and healer of all wounds; be fire to our heart, light to our path and friend for our journey.

Hildegard of Bingen

31. Immeasurable Good

O God the Holy Ghost, most loving Comforter of the fainthearted, I beseech you ever to turn that which is evil in me into good and that which is good into that which is better; turn my mourning into joy, my wandering feet into the right path, my ignorance into knowledge of your truth, my lukewarmness into zeal, my fear into love, all my material good into a spiritual gift, all my earthly desires into heavenly, all that is transient into that which lasts for ever, everything human into that which is divine, everything created and finite into that sovereign and immeasurable good, which you yourself are, O my God and Saviour.

Thomas à Kempis

32. Fill with Wonder

Come, free, abundant Spirit of God; fill this place with the wonder of your presence; fill our hearts with your love; fill the whole Church with the power of Christ. Come in all the mystery signified by wind and fire, beyond human definition, not held in the grasp of anyone, or any thought, or any programme. Come, Sovereign Spirit, and move our hearts to awe and wonder.

Michael Fooler

33. Spirit of Life

Spirit of life, quicken us; Spirit of power, renew us; Spirit of truth inspire us; Spirit of holiness, purify us; Spirit of love, make us whole.

Ermal Kirby

34. Boundless Life

O come, Holy Spirit, inflame my heart, set it on fire with love. Burn away my self-centredness so that I can love unselfishly. Breath your life-giving breath into my soul so that I can live freely and joyously, unrestricted by self-consciousness, and may be ready to go wherever you may send me. Come like a gentle breeze and give me your still peace so that I may be quiet and know the wonder of your presence, and help diffuse it in the world. Never let me shut you out; never let me try to limit you to my capacity; act freely in me and through me, never leave me, O Lord and giver of life!

Michael Hollings and Etta Gullick

VIII. Triune God

1. We Adore

We adore you, Mighty Father, Giver of life, Lover of all;

we lift our hearts to the light of your eternal love.

For you have blessed us with a world of great beauty, a world of plenty, a world of mystery; you have blessed us with life of great promise and diversity, a world with brightness and shadows, with joy and with pain, with hope and with fear.

Life-blessing Father, we lift our hearts to you in worship.

We adore you, Mighty Saviour, our Healer, our Friend,

For you have forgiven us; even though we fail in your good purpose for us, even though we cause you pain, you have welcomed us into your great family.

Cross-bearing Saviour, we lift our hearts to you in worship.

We adore you, Spirit of the Living God,

For you continue to lead us through times of great change and painful challenge,

you are present within us on the long journey of our seeking, as we travel on in faith and hope.

Life-sharing, indwelling Spirit, we lift our hearts to you in worship.

Eric Lott

2. Love and Unity

Loving God, we thank you for revealing to us your love and unity as Father, Son and Holy Spirit.

Help us to reflect that love in our lives as members of the Body of your Son, Jesus;

kindle our imagination to realize that you three love, glorify and sustain one another.

Lead us not into the temptation of sticking to only one of you, thus creating an idol.

Nurture in us as children of God a spirit of freedom, but keep us from using it for selfish gain, and make us open to the unity that exists within and between you.

Give us, we pray, grace to accept one another everywhere, as sisters and brothers in Christ.

May we be tireless in the pursuit of the unity we see in you, the one God, who is Father, Son and Holy Spirit, and in whose Holy Name we pray.

Israel Selvanayagam

3. For Renewal and Unity

Blessed Trinity, Father-Son-Holy Spirit, show us the dynamic movement within you and in between you. While there is growing apathy to know the truth and pursue it, adamance to move forward in unity, your dynamic unity is our only hope. Break the stony hearts, move the status quo that is zealously guarded for personal comfort and selfish interest. Replace the protocols with friendly behaviour and speeches within a framework of partnership yet with courtesy, honesty and integrity.

Israel Selvanayagam

4. Litany

Holy God, Holy Mighty, Holy Immortal,

have mercy on us.

Glory to the Father and the Son and the Holy Spirit,

now and for ever and to the ages of ages.

All-holy Trinity, have mercy on us.

Lord, forgive our sins.

Master, pardon our transgressions. Holy One, visit us and heal our infirmities for your name's sake.

Lord, have mercy. Lord, have mercy. Lord, have mercy.

Daily Prayer

5. True Humanity

Triune God, we come before you with our deep longing for true community; between young and old, between men and women, rich and poor, between all races. We long to overcome the divisions between Christians. Help us to overcome the many barriers we erect. Help us to dispel our suspicions that we may see the good intentions in those we meet. Help us to put aside our uncertainty that we may appreciate the dignity of others. Help us to cast out our fears that we may allay the fears of others. Help us to conquer our pride that we may love our neighbours as ourselves. Grant us the gift of true community in reconciliation with others.

European Ecumenical Assembly, Graz

6. Triune Love

Gracious divine family – Father, Son and Holy Spirit, let the love existing between you encompass our families.

Just as each of you subject yourself to the other in love and glorify the other in joy, let us reflect this attitude in our relationship in family.

Help us to grow towards the perfect love of your family in which our diverse identities find their true meaning in the immersion of your loving unity.

Compassionate God, the Father of the whole human family, thank you for the gift and resources you provide in the form of your children.

Your beloved Son Jesus Christ has asked us to look at the children, to learn innocence, trust and confidence for a life of your loving reign.

Let us learn innocence from the moments of the rolling of their eyeballs, trust from the sight of clinging to their parents, and confidence from watching their growing day by day.

O Holy Spirit, inspire and empower as to recognise your presence in the whole world and in all history.

Forgive our falling and failing, and hold on our hands at each of our steps. Through the one who had only the power of love, even Christ, our Lord.

Israel Selvanayagam

7. Blessed Trinity

Blessed Trinity, God of Jubilee, we turn to you for the life of the Churches. Where there is generosity found in us, expand it with your grace; where our longing for newness has run dry, refresh it with your truth; where there is creativity of heart, deepen it with your wisdom; where there is hope of reconciliation, add your power to make us one. Raise up in us honesty of mind, passion for justice and courage to choose your prophetic way.

Turn your face to us in grace, O God, and breathe into us the life of your Spirit.

World Council of Churches

8. Abyss of Beauty and Wisdom

O eternal Trinity, ocean of love, source of light and abyss of beauty, bathe us in the glory of your creation, save us by the wounds of your grace and transform us by the gift of your Spirit. O abyss of wisdom we glorify you! O Godhead we worship you! O deep sea of eternal love we bless you, now and for ever.

Catherine of Siena

9. Holy Ambition

Creator God, inspire us with holy ambition that we may seek the prize that you set before us. Saviour Christ, be our pace-setter and our coach that we might run with perseverance and hope. Life-giving Spirit, refresh us and renew us that we might finish our course with joy.

Ermal Kirby

10. Wrap in Majesty

O Eternal and glorious Trinity, deeper than the deepest sea, and the abyss of love for whom we thirst and long; let us forever desire your light, forever seek your face and forever wrap ourselves in the robe of your majesty and Godhead; world without end.

Catherine of Siena

IX. The Word of God

1. In Jesus' Way

Living God, the source of all wisdom, thank you for the scripture and all those who have contributed to its making. Guide us to grasp its profound insights. When we are confused by different approaches to your Word, help us to follow the way of your Son Jesus our Lord. As he did, may we reject a literalist interpretation put forward by the devil in the wilderness, revise the customary laws, select texts of progressive thinking and reflect contextually. Above all, may what he regarded as the greatest commandment, to love you and our neighbours, be our scale to measure claims of experiences and popular preaching. May the light of your word direct our feet when we stumble on the way.

Israel Selvanayagam

2. Before Reading

Lord, before we open the Bible, we invoke the Holy Spirit to open our hearts and minds so that the words we read and hear will become the word of God for us. Let these words whisper all day long in our lives. Convert our imprisonment into open-mindedness, covert our shyness into courage and covert our selfishness into fraternity and diversity. So together, listening your still, calm voice, we will work to build your kingdom.

Dorothée Bouillon

3. Open Your Word

You wait for us until we are open to you. We wait for your word to make us receptive. Attune us to your voice, to your silence, speak and bring your Son to us – Jesus, the word of your peace.

Your word is near, O Lord our God, your grace is near. Come to us, then, with mildness and power. Do not let us be deaf to you but make us receptive and open to Jesus Christ your Son, who will come to look for us and save us today and every day for ever and ever.

Huub Oosterhuis

4. Mixture of Sources

Gracious God, author of a thousand words, Father of the Word made flesh; we praise you for the Bible, your open word. We thank you for the rich mixture of myth and mystery, legend and law, poetry and prophecy, history and story, wisdom and apocalyptical literature, Gospel and letter. We rejoice that your word speaks today through the interpretation of commentators, the study of historians, the work of archaeologists, the fellowship of study groups and the spoken word of preachers. We are grateful for the work of translators and the sacrifice of martyrs that have brought this precious gift to us, and that by the power of the Holy Spirit your word today reveals your love in Jesus, the Word made flesh.

Ray Cornick

5. Light on My Path

Your word is a lamp for my feet, a light on my path. I have taken an oath and confirmed it, that I will follow your righteous laws.

Psalm 119:105-106

6. Grace to Study Scripture

Blessed Lord by whose providence all holy scriptures were written and preserved for our instruction, give us grace to study them this and every day with patience and love. Strengthen our souls with the fullness of their divine teaching. Keep from us all pride and irreverence. Guide us in the deep things of your heavenly wisdom, and of your great mercy lead us by your Word unto everlasting life; through Jesus Christ our Lord and Saviour.

Brooke Foss Westcott

7. Living Word

Gracious God, we thank you for your living word that refreshes us, stirs us, and guides us throughout each new day. Be with us this and every day that we might be alive to the words of Christ, and love others as you love us.

David Lawton

8. Precious Jewel

Fix the precious jewel of your holy word within our hearts, O God, that we may be comforted by its message, reformed by its laws and perfected by its teaching; through Christ our Lord.

The Geneva Bible (1560)

9. Seed of Life

Lord, you likened God's word to seed that is sown. May it take root deeply in our hearts, producing a great harvest. May we, your co-workers, be diligent in preparing the ground, unstinting in spreading the seed and joyful in reaping the harvest. We pray that those who are hardened to the gospel may be softened by grace, love and mercy. We pray that your word may not be crowded out by the cares of the world, the lure of wealth and the desire for other things. We pray that all who receive your word would come to maturity, and to fruitful labour for the Lord of the harvest. We pray in the name of Jesus Christ, the Word become flesh.

Paul Dunstan

10. Bitter and Sweet

Healing God, when your word does a spiritual surgery analysing my life, give me the strength to bear the pain. Let me not reject your word when at first it tastes bitter. Give me patience for the moments when I find it sweet. Give me wisdom and commitment so that your word runs its course, healing, warning and filling my pores with joy. However difficult to gain insights and discern your will, let me not stop reading it and preaching from it.

Israel Selvanayagam

11. Like Rain and Snow

As the rain and snow come down from heaven, and do not return to it without watering the earth and making it bud and flourish, so that it yields seed for the sower and bread for the eater, so is your word, O God, that goes out from your mouth: it will not return to you empty, but will accomplish what you desire and achieve the purpose for which you sent it. May we go out in joy and led forth in peace and bear good fruits.

Based on Isaiah 55:10-13

12. Double-Edged Sword

Loving God, your Word is alive and active. Sharper than any double-edged sword, it penetrates even to divide soul and spirit, joints and marrow; it judges the thoughts and attitudes of the heart. Nothing in all creation is hidden from your sight. Everything is uncovered and laid bare before your eyes, and to you we must account. Let us then approach your throne of grace and confidence, so that we may receive mercy and find grace to help us in our time of need.

Based on Hebrews 4:12-13, 16

13. Ever-Speaking God

Ever-speaking God, we thank you for the many ways in which you have opened your word to us and for the many people whose stories have brought that word to life. Help us always to be open to that word, that by your Spirit we may be challenged and changed by it. Through Christ, your living Word.

Leo Osborn

14. Ever-Living Word

We bless you, Lord, for all who teach us to love the Scriptures and for all who help us to understand them. Grant that in the written word we may encounter the living Word, your Son, our Saviour Jesus Christ.

Norman Wallwork

15. People of the Scriptures

Gracious God, we thank you for the Scriptures and for those inspired to write them; for those skilled to translate them; for those who read them daily; for those who are challenged by them; for those whose lives are changed by them and that you have called us to live by them.

David Jones

16. Handle with Fear

Just God, when we handle your double-edged-sword-like Word, give us fear of you and humility. May we seek proper training in order to draw the profound insights of your written Word. Give your wisdom to those who are engaged in sophisticated and highly specialized research so that they will translate the findings for ordinary peoples' daily lives. May we preach from your Word with reverence, truth and love, with no personal motives of gains or fear of any opposition.

Israel Selvanayagam

X. Life and its Fullness

1. Use our Life

God of celebration and daily bread, you see us gather in our Sunday best, and scatter to farm, office, school and backyard; you hear us singing hymns and calypsos, sharing gossip and good news; you remember the past with the old, and wonder about the future with the young. You touch the world with our hands – often hard at work, sometimes forced to be idle. Use our hands, our skills, our energy, our generosity, and build your Church through our lives.

Jan Sutch Pickard

2. Clear Light

Grant to us, Lord, purity of heart and strength of purpose; that no passion may hinder us from knowing your will and no weakness from doing it; that in your light we may see light clearly, and in your service find perfect freedom; through Christ our Lord.

St. Augustine

3. To be Transformed

We bring to you, O Lord, our poverty of soul to be transformed by your beauty; our waywardness of passion to be tamed by your love; our stubbornness of will to be conformed to your commandments and our coldness of heart to be enkindled by your grace; now and for ever.

Catherine of Genoa

4. Holy Wisdom

Holy wisdom, free us to participate more deeply in the divine dance of creating, redeeming and healing our world. Liberating God, release in us a passionate energy for seeking justice; for investing in peace; for tending the needs of fragile human communities; for befriending and healing the planet. Companion at the well, help us to draw and to share fresh clean water, for the health of our bodies, the clarity of our thinking, and the wholeness of our soul-making.

Liz Smith

5. Free us for Life

Liberating Lord, under the burden of your cross you walked free of constraint; and by your resurrection you lead us into the glorious freedom of the children of God. As you free us from fear, let us live out your love; as you free us from anxiety, let us live in your joy; as you free us from hatred, let us live in your peace; as you free us from shortness of temper, let us live with your patience; as you free us from callousness, let us live by your kindness; as you free us from greed, let us live with your goodness; as you free us from violent impulse, let us live with your gentleness; as you free us from inconstancy, let us live through your faithfulness; as you free us from disobedience, let us live in your self-control.

Andrew Lunn

6. Your Power

Your power is seen in roaring waves that surge on the coast; your creative hands in the lush green of hills and forests; your tender touch in the sleeping child wrapped on a mother's back; your joy in the laughter of the young and in the greetings of those who pass in the street. Amid the greatness of your creation, here we stand small and pathetic, but with a hope in the power of the risen Lord. Like the mustard seed may the small things that we do, the small prayers that we say, the insignificant deeds of each day be a part of the growth of your kingdom as you change the inconspicuous into the mighty for your glory.

Sheila Holland

7. Mental Rust

Lord, still me. Let my mind be inquiring, searching. Let my heart be open. Save me from mental rust. Deliver me from spiritual decay. Keep me alive and alert. Teach me, that I may teach them.

Donald Coggan

8. Gift of Humour

Give us a sense of humour, Lord and also things to laugh about; give us the grace to take a joke against ourselves, and to see the funny side of the things we do; save us from annoyance, bad temper, resentfulness against our friends. Help us to laugh even in the face of trouble, fill our minds with the love of Jesus; for his name's sake.

Michael Hollings and Etta Gullick

9. Source of Joyful Heart

Almighty and merciful God, who are the strength of the weak, the refreshment of the weary, the comfort of the sad, the help of the tempted, the life of the dying, the God of patience and all consolations; you know full well the inner weakness of our nature, how we tremble and quiver before pain, and cannot bear the cross without your divine help and support. Help me, then, O eternal and pitying God, help me to possess my soul in patience, to maintain unshaken hope in you, to keep that child-like trust which feels a Father's heart hidden beneath the cross; so shall I be strengthened with power according to your glorious might, in all patience and long-suffering; I shall be enabled to endure pain and temptation, and, in the very depth of my suffering, to praise you with a joyful heart.

Johann Habermann

10. Reverence for Life

Eternal Father, source of life and light, whose love extends to all people, all creatures, all things: grant us that reverence for life which becomes those who believe in you; lest we despise it, degrade it, or come callously to destroy it. Rather let us save it, serve it and sanctify it, after the example of your Son, Jesus Christ our Lord.

Robert Runcie

11. Fullness of Humility

We give you thanks, Gentle One, who touched our soul. You have loved us from the moment of our first waking and have held us in joy and in grief. Stay with us, we pray. Grace us with your presence and with it, the fullness of our own humanity. Help us claim our strength and need, our awesomeness and fragile beauty, that encouraged by the truth we might work to restore compassion to the human family and renew the face of the earth.

Janet Schaffran and Pat Kozak

12. Shine Light on My Child

O Lord, my God, shine the warm light of your love on my child. Hold her safe from all illness and harm. Come into her little soul and comfort her with your happiness. Let her feel your peace. She is too tiny to speak to me, and her cooing and gurgles are hard to translate into human words. But to you, her sounds are prayers. Her cries are cries for your blessing and grace. Let her learn your ways while she is still a child. In adulthood let her live the whole span of a human life, fulfilling your purposes. And in her old age, let her die joyfully, secure in the knowledge of your eternal love. I am not asking that she should be wealthy or famous, but I do ask that she will live prayerfully, serve others in true humility, loving you. Smile on her, my God.

Johann Starck

13. God of Jubilee

Blessed Trinity, God of Jubilee, we turn to you for the life of the Churches. Where there is generosity found in us, expand it with your grace; where our longing for newness has run dry, refresh it with your truth; where there is creativity of heart, deepen it with your wisdom; where there is hope of reconciliation, add your power to make us one. Raise up in us honesty of mind, passion for justice and courage to choose your prophetic way.

Turn your face to us in grace, O God, and breathe into us the life of your Spirit.

World Council of Churches

14. Caring God

Caring and constant God, you know how our hearts ache –

You have been there too.

Like a mother nursing a sick child on her knee, like a father who has not given up on his runaway son, like a friend who is there for someone who would otherwise die alone, like a partner coping with a crisis, or patiently working through a time of change; you know how our hearts ache –

You have been there too.

When we feel most alone, when it seems as though everyone has deserted us; when it would be much easier to give up and deny the vision; when we take a step in faith that is in fact a leap in the dark; when we face death, and when we struggle to begin again; you know how our hearts ache –

You have been there too.

We take courage from your love which has no limits, your compassion which never fails – they are new every morning: caring and constant God.

Jan Sutch Pickard

15. Life-giving Love

'*While love is making all things new,*' Lord, in love, you were in the fertile seed of our beginning and in the communion of our conception; in love, you were in our eager growth in the womb, and you were present at the rawness of our birth; in love, you were in the dependency of our childhood, and when we broke free to be ourselves; in love, you are there in our daily joys and sorrows, our triumphs and our failures, and in the warmth and cold of daily experience; in love you will be there when the wounds of life sap our strength and bring the darkness of death. Lord of love, of life, of healing, of all-knowing, quieten the anxiety of our isolation with the experience of our presence through which all things are made new and united in your purpose.

Peter Fox

16. Creator and Creating

Energising, life-giving, playful God, whose Spirit teases out of creation things old and new, be creative in and through us; be creative beyond us, so that what you hope and will for the world may come into being, justly, abundantly and joyously. Help us to face honestly and boldly all the flaws and frailties that flow from the freedom you have given us. Open us up with the whole of creation, to the future that is yours alone to give. Involve us not to create your kingdom but to welcome its arrival in our actions and words. We pray in the name of Christ, who proclaims and embodies the kingdom we seek.

Clive Marsh

17. Blessing of Various Cultures

Wondrous and holy God, Creator of the universe, you make all people in your own image, you live and work in our midst. You bless us with an immense variety of cultures and ways of responding to you. You show us new patterns of living and loving in Jesus. You give us strength by your Holy Spirit.

We bless and thank you.

Forgive all among us who put boundaries around your presence, love and work; who use diversity to divide people – to demonise some and accord privileged status to others; who seek to dominate or destroy those who are different.

Have mercy on us all.

Show us all how to live and work with others; to receive diversity as a gift and not as a threat; to move beyond tolerance of those who are different to mutual respect and trust. Show us the art of listening with respect to one another. Grant us the help of your Spirit that, in humility, we may share with others our faith and story.

In the name of Christ. Amen.

Inderjit Bhogal

18. Highest Friendship

O God, our heavenly Father, you have commanded us to love one another as your children, and have ordained the highest friendship in the bond of your Spirit, we beseech you to maintain and preserve us always in the same bond, to your glory, and our mutual comfort, with all those to whom we are bound by any special tie, either of nature or of choice; that we may be perfected together in that love which is from above, and which never fails when all other things shall fail. Send down the dew of your heavenly grace upon us, that we may have joy in each other that passes not away; and having lived together in love here, according to your commandment, may live for ever together with you, being made one in you, in your glorious Kingdom hereafter, through Jesus our Lord.

George Hickes

19. Guide in the Straight Path

In the name of the God, the merciful Lord of mercy. Praise be to God, the Lord of all beings, the merciful Lord of mercy, master of the day of judgment. You alone we serve. To You alone we come for aid. Guide us in the straight path, the path of those whom You have blessed, not of those against whom there is displeasure nor of those who go astray.

The first chapter of the Holy Qur'an

20. Right Spirit

Almighty God, from whom every good prayer comes, and who pours out on all who desire it the spirit of grace and supplication: deliver us, when we draw nigh to You from coldness of heart and wanderings of mind, that with steadfast thoughts and kindled affections we may worship You in spirit and in truth: through Jesus Christ our Lord.

William Bright

21. Wholesome Blessing

O God, our Father, our life reaches out in ever-widening circles; bless us in each one of them.

Bless us in our homes and help us to remember all that we owe to them. Bless us in our schools and help us to learn well and to play fair. Bless us in our universities and colleges and help us to use to the full every opportunity which is given to us to equip our minds with knowledge and to widen our horizons. Bless us in the places where we work and help us to be workers who will never need to be ashamed of anything we do or make. Bless us in the places where we rest and help us to put as much as more into the life of the community as we take out. Bless us in our churches; make us in our church to worship with reverence and with gladness to serve the church with whatever gifts we have. Bless us in our country, and help us to study, to learn and to train that we may be good citizens of it. Bless us in the world, and in our day bind the nations together in peace.

Author Unknown

22. Love One Another

O God of love, who has given us a new commandment through Your only-begotten Son, that we should love one another, even as You did love us the unworthy and the wandering and gave Your beloved Son for our life and salvation: we pray You give us, your servants, in all time of our life on earth, a mind forgetful of past ill-will, a pure conscience, sincere thoughts and a heart to love our brethren; for the sake of Jesus Christ, Your Son, our Lord and Saviour.

St. Cyril

23. Usefulness

Use me then, my Saviour, for whatever purpose and in whatever way You may require. Here is my poor heart, an empty vessel; fill it with Your grace. Here is my sinful and troubled soul; quicken it and refresh it with Your love. Take my heart for Your abode; my mouth to spread abroad the glory of Your name; my love and all my powers for the advancement of Your believing people; and never suffer the steadfastness and confidence of my faith to waver – that so at all times I may be enabled from the heart to say, Jesus needs me, and I him.

D. L. Moody

24. Be in Every Part

O God, touch every part of us with your Spirit and your power.

Be in our hearts, that every unclean and impure thought may be banished from them. Be in our minds, that they may be eager to learn, adventurous to think, and retentive to remember. Be in our eyes that they may never linger on any forbidden thing, or find delight in looking at that which is soiled. Be in our ears that, above the many voices of the clamorous world, we may hear your still small voice speaking to us. Be upon our hands, that we may do an honest day's work for ourselves and that we may ever help others. Be upon our feet that we may never stray from the way in which we ought to go.

So, be on every part of us that we may be able to take all life and bring it as an offering to you.

Author Unknown

25. Help from Above

We beseech You, Lord and Master, to be our help and succour. Save those who are in tribulation; have mercy on the lonely; lift up the fallen; show Yourself unto the needy; heal the ungodly; convert the wanderers of Your people; feed the hungry; raise up the weak; comfort the faint-hearted. Let all the peoples know that You are

God alone, and Jesus Christ is Your Son, and we are Your people and the sheep of Your pasture: for the sake of Christ Jesus.

Clement of Rome

26. True Community

Lord, the lover of communes and communal harmony, by our pursuit of individual interest we have lost our way of building up community. Individual concerns often drag us away from concentrating on common good. Our communities including the churches are paralysed by this tendency. Forgive us and give us a new vision to rebuild us as a community of love, understanding and sharing. As we appreciate and applaud displays of talents, skills and achievements, may we acknowledge those millions in the world community who do not have equal opportunities to realise their potential and develop their skills. Help us to work together as a true community which will reflect your glory.

Unknown

27. Right Mindset

Lord Jesus Christ, come to us in the power of the Spirit that we may take initiatives in mending broken relationships. Give us perseverance in breaking down barriers of suspicion and mistrust; insight to recognise our prejudices; courage to admit our failures; honesty to acknowledge our festering hurts and willingness to repent of our personal and community sins. Help us to prove that your grace is sufficient for every need.

Ian D. Henderson

28. To Be Open

Loving God, open our eyes to the beauty of your holiness; open our ears to the message of your word; open our minds to the challenge of your truth; open our hearts to the power of your love; open our lives to the coming of your Spirit, that we may truly worship you, now and for ever.

Peter Sheasby

29. To Bring Up Children

Father, forgive us the foolish mistakes we make. We raise children out of your gift of love and then turn them into pale reflections of ourselves. We know the purpose of life is to move to maturity but take offence when our children grow beyond us. We long for our children to find the wings of freedom but hold on to them when we ought to let go. We want to give our children the values that have served us well but forget that the world has changed since we accepted them ourselves. Teach us, Lord, when to speak and when to be silent; when to move forward and when to stand back; when to declare our own beliefs and when to leave the moment to you Spirit. And more, when to influence and when to let our children to influence us; when to teach and when to know that we have become learners again; and all this for their growth, and ours.

Donald Hilton

30. Develop Me

I am only a spark, make me a fire. I am only a string, make me a lyre. I am only a drop, make me a fountain. I am only an anthill, make me a mountain. I am only a feather, make me a wing. I am only a rag, make me a king!

From Mexico

31. All for God

Let my heart always think of you. Let my head always bow down to you. Let my lips always sing your praise. Let my hands always worship you. Let my body always serve you with love. O Lord of grace, immense like a mountain peak full of goodness! Do you forgive my sins! When my spirit leaves my body, let me behold your divine face, radiant like the lotus even on the cross on which your enemies nailed you, and let my heart rejoice in your sacred name. Grant you this boon to me, O Lord!

Krishna Pillai

32. To Know the Triune God

Glorious God, refine us on the threshing floor of your grace; reform us on the potter's wheel of your love. Transform us through the fire of your Spirit and bring us to know the grace of the Son, the love of the Father and the power of the Spirit in all things.

Graham Thompson

33. Teach and Train Me

God, when you give me good soil, show me how to plant seeds in it. When I need encouragement, train my heart and lips to sing your songs of courage. When I am buffeted by trials, teach me to laugh. When I am being criticized, teach me to give thanks and try again. When I have failed, give me the determination to succeed. God, I know you intend me to live your gospel even though it is not easy. Help me not to falter.

Wesley Blakey

34. Seeds of New Life

Great God, when we have glorious petals, tinged with the Spirit's fire, may we stand in your strength and blaze forth into your creation. When our heads droop, heavy with pain, as petals fall, help us to remember that the seeds of new life are within us ready to repair, reconcile, renew. Give us the courage and vision to trust in their harvest.

Josette Crane

35. Housewarming

O God, make the door of this house wide enough to receive all who need human love and fellowship, and a heavenly Father's care; and narrow enough to shut out all envy, pride and hate. Make its threshold smooth enough to be no stumbling block to children or straying feet, but rugged enough to turn back the tempter's power; make it gateway to your eternal kingdom.

Thomas Ken

36. Everlasting Hope

Helper of all who are helpless, we call on you in times of stress and in times of devastation. Pick up the broken pieces of our hearts, our homes, our history and restore them to the way they were, or give us the means of starting over when everything seems lost. O God, our help in ages past, we place all our hope in you.

Miriam Therese Winter

37. Fullness of Daily Life

Give me this day, a lung full of spirit, an eye full of beauty, a step full of joy, a mouth full of praise, and hands full of nothing but desire to do your will.

Stephen Cherry

XI. Stages of Life

1. Dedication of Baby

God of all life and new life, we come to your presence lifting this new-born baby in your presence, a new fruit of your creation and of the love of the parents. Thank you for all those who have helped to bring this baby out of his/her mother's womb with care and gentle handling. May this baby continue to be a joy of his/her parents and the wider family. In his/her rolling movements and probing looks let us see the glory of your grace. In his/her growing may we also grow into the full maturity of your kingdom. Protect this baby from all ills and evil effects. In the name of the one who moved in an open manger, even Jesus Christ our Lord we pray.

Israel Selvanayagam

2. Holding Child in Arms

Lord, the life we hold in our arms is the life you have given to us in trust. This child is not our own property to use for the fulfilment of our own ambitions; this child is yours, whom one day you will call to confess your name and become your disciple. May we be wise in these short years when our influence will be more important than anyone else's. In our love may our child begin to learn the perfect love that casts out fear. In the life that we share as a family, in our talking together, and the discipline we impose, may our child learn that we are worthy of trust.

Further Everyday Prayers

3. Newborn Child

Through all the years of marriage we have happily shared with others. But God, you have given us one priceless gift that belongs exclusively to us, not to be shared with another, the beautiful gift of physical intimacy. Thank you for its mystery, its wonder, its delight. May we never mishandle it. May we respect and cherish it always. May our self-giving continue to be an expression of oneness, a celebration of wholeness. Keep it alive, fulfilling and always full of surprises. O God, what a marvelous expression of your own fathomless love!

Ruth Harms Calkin

4. Gift of Children

Almighty God and heavenly Father, we thank you for the children you have given us. Give us grace to train them in your faith, fear and love, that as they advance in years they may grow in grace, and may hereafter be found in the number of your elect children; through Jesus Christ our Lord.

Bishop Cosin

5. Upbringing Child

Teach me to let go, Lord; to let my child take his/her own steps into the big world, to watch and care but let him/her grow, as you, Lord, let us all grow, all of us your children. You let us make our own choices, our own mistakes, although you love us. She is ours, Lord, yours and mine; upheld by both our loves. We both want the best for him/her. Let him/her be sure of that, now and wherever s/he goes.

More Everyday Prayers

6. Communication with Children

Give us the grace, Lord, to tell our children the truth and nothing but the truth. To issue no idle threats or promises, to keep our word. To apologize when we have been wrong. To be disciplined over time. To be courteous in all our dealings. To answer children's questions as honestly and as simply as we can. To let them help in all the way we can devise. To expect from them no longer standard of honesty, unselfishness or politeness than we are prepared to live up to ourselves.

Joan Kendall (adapted)

7. Laughter and Happiness

Father, whose Son called children to him, we pray for boys and girls everywhere, that their childhood may be filled with laughter and happiness. As they learn so many facts and enter into so many new experiences, may they learn of your love, and how to serve Jesus as Master and Lord.

Bernard Thorogood

8. Dreaming and Drawing

Dear Lord, please bless these children and give them understanding. Break down the barriers that are keeping them from grasping these skills, this knowledge. Stir and awaken their now dreaming mind. Bless their books and notebooks. Let your power and love work through them to excite and delight them so that the message is clear and strong. Bless their tools – their papers and pencils and crayons, so that they become lovely and sure, a source of joy to their hands. Bless their teachers and give them patience, understanding and the ability to guide them out of dark confusion into the light of comprehension and command, for in you is all wisdom, and that wisdom is a part of each of these children.

Marjorie Holmes (adapted)

9. Learn from Children

Just as you commanded us, O Christ, help us to observe the life of the children and learn about the ethos of the commonwealth of God. Just as they move things with the power of their love, remain humble and yet move with vigour, let us practise every day. Just as they symbolize the powerless, in your grace join us in their holy company. When we are affected by wavering, naivety and immaturity, give us the wisdom to distinguish between being childish and childlike. In our conscious living in and for your commonwealth, transforming Christ, teach us in your wisdom that true maturity is to be born again and again. Save us from the pride of long experience and achievements and conservative stubbornness and inspire us to be creatively sportive so we may continue to grow. May we come to your presence and see the glimpses of your face always as your children.

Israel Selvanayagam

10. Birthday

Gracious and compassionate God,

My heart overflows with gratitude for the way you have guided me thus far.

In the moments of my walking through the dark valley of death you have held my hand fast.

In the moments of confusion, you have given me wisdom and diligence.

In the midst of uncertainties you have helped not to miss any opportunity to learn and work.

Thank you for my parents who sustained my life in great difficulties.

I am thrilled to think of their daily living as sacrifice to feed me and my siblings.

Thank you for my friends, teachers, pastors and mentors who supported and encouraged me.

Thank you for my spouse and children for the love and joy shared.

Give them all a sense of fulfilment of having been associated with my life, now and always.

Loving Father, Mother, Greatest companion, whatever may happen to my life in the days to come,

Let me be firm in directing it for your glory that many people may be touched by your love.

Even when my words fail to talk to you and talk about you, accept my deep sighs and silence.
Through the one who walked on the dusty roads and unclean beaches, in the power of the Holy Spirit.

Israel Selvanayagam

11. Baptism

Gracious Lord, in response to your grace and invitation 'Let the children come to me', we bring this child/ren to be baptized in your holy name. Thank you for this gift which we gratefully accept while being aware of our responsibilities to help them grow in your love and knowledge. Help us to perceive in each drop of the water poured on their heads the ocean of your unfailing love. Give us the urge to explore the deeper dimensions of this love so that these children and others may see the reflections of this love in our life. May we grow along with these children and realise again and again that true maturity is being child-like. Lead us to the immersion into your pool of love so that the remembrance of all our baptisms renews our minds.

Israel Selvanayagam

12. Education Sunday

Eternal Educator, instruct us in all truth and enlighten us to live accordingly. Impress upon our minds that fearing you is the beginning of all wisdom. Safeguard our wisdom and knowledge that it may not drift into craftiness. Move us away from following hidden strategies to a mature behaviour of simplicity and straightforwardness. Bless all our educational and training institutions so that those who pass through them may become blessings for society, particularly for the vulnerable. Give us the joy of searching, researching and serving. We ask these in the name of our friendly teacher, Jesus Christ.

Israel Selvanayagam

13. Puberty

Living God, thank you for the stages of a lifecycle through which you lead us into greater maturity. Thank you for the precious body you have given to me. Give me the courage to face changes in my body, mind and spirit. Help me not to be washed away by the waves of wavering and excess. Teach me the way of introspection and self-awareness so that by your grace I may have control over my instincts and emotions. As I have a long journey to glorify your name through my body, help me to take this decisive moment to celebrate and move forward with determination.

Israel Selvanayagam

14. Young People

O God our Father, we pray for our young people growing up in an unstable and confusing world. Show them that your ways give more meaning to life than the ways of the world and that following you is better than chasing after selfish goals. Help them to take failure not as a measure of their worth but as a chance for a new start. Give them strength to hold their faith in you and to keep alive their joy in your creation; through Jesus Christ our Lord.

Episcopal Church of USA

15. Creative Culture for Young People

Lord, we place into your hands the young people of our world. Keep your eyes for ever on them, and your heart eternally surrounding them. Allow your love to fill them and shine out through them into a dark world. Help them to hear your call clearly and believe in your words, no matter the obstacles that are presented by others. Give them the strength to accept failure and success, in the light of your love. Give them love and respect for your creation. Keep their natural energies and passions alive, to be poured out for you. Create in them a heart of love and peace, for all peoples of the world. Create a culture and future of love and praise in them, so that the people of this world might always feel your presence.

Sarah Malik

16. Confirmation

Generous God, touch us again with the fire of your Spirit and renew us by your grace, that we may profess the one true faith and live in love and unity with all who follow Christ.

Confirmation Service from the Methodist Worship Book

17. Wedding Day

God of grace, source of all love, we pray for this couple that they may live together in love and faithfulness to the end of their lives. Enrich their friendship, that each may be for the other a companion in joy and a comforter in sorrow. Help them to be patient, gentle and forgiving, that their marriage may reflect Christ's love for all people. Enable them to make their home a place of welcome and friendship, that their life together may be a source of strength to others.

Lord of life, Hear us in your love

Based on the prayer of the Marriage Service of the Methodist Worship Book.

18. Couple's Delight

Creator Spirit, we thank you for your gift of sexual love, by which husband and wife may express their delight in each other, find refreshment, and share with you the joy of creating new life. By your grace may – and – remain lovers, rejoicing in your goodness.

Anglican Church of New Zealand, Prayer Book

19. Working Life

Lord, we pray for those who are struggling with the pressures and busyness of adult life. Give wisdom to those whose professions call for accurate skill and critical decision-making. Give courage and endurance to those whose daily work is hard or monotonous. Strengthen and reassure all those who are bringing up families: struggling with broken nights and childhood illnesses; dealing with teenage rebellion and self-will. Give patience and love to those endeavoring to make their marriage good and enduring. For all we ask your peace and encouragement. Through Jesus Christ our Lord.

Author Unknown

20. Miracle of Friendship

God, you are the source of love and you join us together in the miracle of friendship, marriage and family life. Let faithfulness, freshness and unselfishness fill the deep relationship we cherish and be a sign to the nations that this is the way you love the world in Jesus Christ our Lord.

Further Everyday Prayers

21. Power of Wedding

Almighty God, in whom we live and move and have our being, look graciously upon the world which you have made and for which your Son gave his life, and especially on all whom you make to be one flesh in holy marriage. May their lives together be a sacrament of your love to this broken world, so that unity may overcome estrangement, forgiveness heal guilt, and joy overcome despair.

Alternative Service Book of the Anglican Church of Canada

22. Wedding Anniversary

God of love, greater than all loves we have seen, known and experienced,
with grateful hearts we come to your loving presence on this our wedding anniversary day.
You graciously united us in holy matrimony and have guided us all these years.

You have helped us to understand one another and grow into greater dimensions of love.

You have given us the gift of children and grace to be in solidarity with childless couples.

Thank you for the fellowship we have enjoyed with many people related to our life and work.

Forgive us if we have caused our children to stumble and harden their hearts, and help us to amend.

Help us to renew our marital vows with sincerity and resolve.

Just as plants discard dried leaves and gain new ones for new flowering,

let our life blossom today and proceed to flower and bear fruits for your and others' delight.

Help us and all the couples around us to fulfil the purpose of your creation of married life.

Let us hear the sound of your walking in our garden of Eden, and live in your presence.

In the name of the one who has accepted the weak church as his bride, even Christ our Lord.

Gnana Leelal and Israel Selvanayagam

23. Marriage at Risk or Broken

We remember before you, Lord, those whose marriages are at risk or broken down. You alone know the story behind each unhappy and broken marriage. We remember especially just now – and –. Make them willing to recognize where they may be at fault; give them a sincere desire to put things right; and teach them in their desperate need to turn to you, whose love is unfailing and whose power can make all things new, in Jesus our Lord.

Llewellyn Cumings

24. Harmony and Happiness

Eternal God, author of harmony and happiness, we thank you for the gift of marriage in which men and women may seek and find the consummation of bodily union, the satisfaction of life-long companionship, and the fulfilment of creative and responsible parenthood. Give patience to those who look forward to marriage; give courage to those who face trials within their marriage; give comfort to those whose marriage has broken; and to those whose marriages are successful and fruitful give gratitude and understanding, that they may be examples to all of your great love. Through Jesus our Lord.

Michael Saward

25. Parenthood and Children

Heavenly Father, from whom all parenthood comes, teach us so to understand our children that they may grow in your wisdom and love according to your holy will. Fill us with sensitive respect for the great gift of human life which you have committed to our care; help us to listen with patience to their worries and problems, and give us the tolerance to allow them to develop as individuals. For your name's sake.

Michael Buckley

26. Unafraid of Ageing

Don't let me be so afraid of ageing, God. Let me rejoice and reach out to be replenished; I know that each day I can be reborn into strength and beauty through you.

Marjorie Holmes

27. Grandmother

Lord, teach me to love my grandchildren as a grandmother should: not interfering, only understanding; not pushing myself, just being there when wanted. Teach me to be the sort of grandmother my children and my children's children would want me to be.

Rosa George

28. Facing Old Age

God of infallible remembering, thank you for the assurance that our names are written on your palms and that those who touch us touch the apple of your eyes. Remember us in your kingdom even if our condition is that of a thief on the one side of your Son our Lord Jesus' cross. Stir us to rejoice over the moments of our new initiatives, of having new friends and achievements. Let our memory of achievements overcome the frustration of what we could not do in our frailty. We pray for those who have shared our life and work and continue to use them for your glory. Let your goodness absolve our failings. Help us to be thankful for those who still sustain our life in different ways. Prepare us to sleep peacefully when the moment comes. May we feel the peace as the flowing of crystal clear stream in a full moon light.

Michel Quoist

29. Growing to Ageless Life

Dear God, Holy Spirit, the things of the spirit are the only realities that age cannot weary. And the spirit that reaches out to Spirit is, in time, set free from the flesh and quiver of ambition, the fleeting joys of status and possessions, and the physical indignities of age. Lord, as I grow older, may I be blessed with faith enough to make the journey from ageing body to ageless life.

Frank Topping

30. With Failing Memory

Loving God, we pray for those whose memory is failing; for those who are forgetting the simplest of things; cherished names, treasured experiences, loved ones' faces. Be with them in their fear, reassure them in their frustration, calm them in their anger, comfort them in their depression. Loving God, we pray for those who care for those whose memory is failing, for those who must repeat things time and time again, reassurance given, explanations offered, love assured. Strengthen them in their decision-making, unburden them of their guilt, hold them in their grief. And as memories fade, may your love be known by both carer and cared for, now and always.

Richard Vautrey

31. Touch My Mind

When the signs of age begin to mark my body (and still more when they touch my mind); when the ill that is to diminish me or carry me off strikes from without or is born within me; when the painful moment comes in which I suddenly wakened to face that I am ill or growing old; and above all at the last moment when I feel I am losing hold of myself and am absolutely passive in the hands of the great unknown forces that have formed me. In all those dark moments, O God, grant that I may understand that it is you (provided only my faith is strong enough) who are painfully parting the fibres of my being in order to penetrate to the very marrow of my substance and bear me away within yourself.

Pierre Teilhard De Chardin

32. Old Age and Young Heart

I thank you, Lord, that my heart has not grown old, that it still skips a beat at the beauty of a sunset, a stormy sea, or a spider weaving webs. I thank you, Lord, that my heart has not grown old, that it still is full of urges, longing, energy and hope which has not yet found its fulfilment. I thank you, Lord, my heart has not grown old, that love's exchange still has greatest power, for all love comes from that ageless eternal source: your heart. Lord, may my heart remain for ever young, and may it beat in time with yours.

Jo Jacobs

33. Prepare for Dying

Ever living God and the Eternal I AM, thank you for all the moments of my life, from conception to grave, when your presence has been constant. Thank you for good thoughts, good deeds and right decisions throughout my life in spite of aberrations and deviations. When I was walking on slippery paths you held my hands tightly, and when the going was heavy you bore me on your shoulders. My heart is full of the unceasing waves of gratitude. Thank you for the many opportunities to share love within the family and without. Just as the cow licks up the dirt of her calf you have removed my guilt. Even in difficult and ambiguous times you have understood and accepted me. Keep me away from tormenting memories so that I will rest peacefully in your bosom. Just as your Son Jesus died on the cross, let me commit my spirit into your hands of compassion. With a vision of life beyond the horizon where my risen Lord Jesus is waiting to welcome me and others, may I come with eager anticipation, with a smile on my face and tears of joy.

Israel Selvanayagam

34. At a Funeral

Ever living God, we celebrate your presence and acclaim your glory. You fill the vacuum of death with your enlivening Spirit.

Ever loving God, your love is higher than all heights, deeper than all depths and broader than all breadths.

Ever guiding God, you have guided us through rugged paths, steep hills and deep valleys, through shadows of death and lights of hope.

May your departed son/daughter/servant continue to experience your guidance beyond our horizon and imagination. As s/he finds rest in you, may those of us who live a restless life in a restless world find the same in your warm embrace.

In the name of your beloved Son who calls all people to rest from their hard labour, even Jesus Christ our Lord.

Israel Selvanayagam

XII. Daily Cycle

1. To Greet the Day

Grant me, O Lord, to greet the coming day in peace. Help me in all things to rely upon your holy will. In every hour of the day, reveal your will to me. Bless my dealings with all who surround me. In unforeseen events, let me not forget that all are sent by you. Teach me to act firmly and wisely, without embittering or embarrassing others. In all my deeds and words, guide my thoughts and feelings. Direct my will; teach me to pray; pray thou thyself in me.

Philaret of Moscow

2. Each Returning Day

Those who have climbed the steep hillside, stumbling in the dark to wait and watch for first light of dawn are surprised occasionally by a dramatic sunrise, but more often by the gentle watery light of a landscape receiving back its colour and contours. May we be attentive each returning day to glimpse afresh, around us and within us, the light of grace caressing the colours and contours of our shared living. Surprise and renew your people in the breaking of the dawn from on high, that we may see clearly the path beneath our feet and may find courage and companionship for our continuing journey.

Liz Smith

3. To Wake Up Afresh

Generous God, as we wake each day and remember afresh the greatest news we ever heard, may our eyes reflect your light, our mouths speak your truth and our voices sing your praise. May our ears hear your call, our minds seek your wisdom and our hearts be filled with your love. May our feet bear us to the places of need and our hands reach out in compassion. May our thoughts be kind, our words comforting and our deeds helpful, and may our souls find the true worth, as we respond to your generous gift of grace.

Yvonne Williams

4. Rejoice in Grace and Do Your Will

Let your peace rule in our hearts, O Lord, that each day we may delight in your strength, rejoice in your grace and find joy in the doing of your will. Keep us free from sin and grant us your blessing that we may serve you faithfully all our days; through Christ our Lord.

Matthew Henry

5. Rising and Preparing

Let me rise to the rising sun, gracious God, just as plants and flowers do. Focus your face on me and shine on my face, my mind and spirit, my whole self.

Prepare me for this new day so that it does not pass without fulfilling work. Let your love flood within me that I share it with those I see and work with today.

Give me a kind heart and brisk hand to remove hurdles of stones and thorns on the public ways I walk. Hold my hands tightly when I have to tread on slippery paths.

Give me clarity of thought and purity of mind when I deal with issues with colleagues, customers and clients. Help us to help one another and grow together in maturity.

Let me do my duty faithfully having my mind fixed on you and discarding any craving for profit and selfish benefit. What I deserve let me gracefully receive and surrender myself and all I have to your lotus-feet today and every day.

Israel Selvanayagam

6. Amazing Grace

Awesome God of grace, may we never cease to be amazed by the miracle of every returning day. Just as you looked upon each day in creation and saw it was good, may we learn to pause in each returning day to see, treasure and ponder in our hearts all that is good.

Jenny Ellis

7. Dawn and New Day

Thank you, Father, that even the longest night ends in dawn and a new day. Thank you that your mercies are new every new morning. Clear from my mind now all black thoughts of the night and give confidence in your loving care as I face today. Give me your strength in my tiredness and sure hope that your love will guard and keep me. Through Jesus Christ our Lord.

'Prayer after a sleepless night' (Author unknown)

8. Assurance of My Origins

In the silence of the morning I am alive to the new day's light, alert to the early stirrings of the wind and the first sounds of the creatures. In the silence of my heart I hear the yearnings that are in me and the fears, the hopes that rise from within and the doubts that trouble my soul. In the beginnings of this day, O God, before the night's stillness is lost to the day's busyness, open to me the treasure of my inner being that in the midst of this day's busyness I may draw on wisdom. Assure me again of my origins in you, assure me again that my true depths are of you.

J. Philip Newell

9. Rising with Power

I rise today with the power of God to guide me, the might of God to uphold me, the wisdom of God to teach me, the eye of God to watch over me, the ear of God to hear me, the word of God to give me speech, the hand of God to protect me, the path of God to lie before me, the shield of God to shelter me, the host of God to defend me against the snares of the devil and the temptations of the world, against every man who meditates injury against me, whether far or near.

St. Patrick

10. Fresh Energy

Thanks be to you, O God, for the stirrings of new life in me this day, for rising from the dreams of the night to a fresh flowing of energy, for the vitality that awakened my body and the desires that stir my soul. Let me know the power for life that is in me, the life-force that is in my senses and the might that is in my heart. Let me know you as the source of such force and be wise to its true streams and false currents. Let me serve you this day with my love and strength. In my heart and mind and body this day let me serve love.

J. Philip Newell

11. In Solidarity

Lord, we rejoice with those for whom each returning day dawns brightly with new opportunities and old duties, all embraced with love and eagerness. We rejoice with those who see each returning day as full of fresh and exciting things to see, to learn or to do. We pray for those for whom each returning day dawns grey and miserable: those who are caught up on the treadmill of work or debt or the search for a job, struggling to cope with demands made upon them, with no sense of fulfilment. We pray for those for whom each returning day seems to be without hope, just the same as the day before, those who are weighed down by depression, bereavement, pain, disability or disappointment. And we pray for ourselves, that we may receive each day as a gift from you, walk through it with you as our guide and companion and use to the full every opportunity for service and enjoyment which it offers.

Jackie Chinnakone

12. Freshness and Gentleness

Gracious God our heavenly Father, Mother and Companion,

we thank you for the freshness of this morning and all the new opportunities before us today to glorify your name.

Give us purity of heart, clarity of mind, courtesy of speech, gentleness of our movements and generosity of our hands. Help us today to see your image on every person we meet, your love in every fellowship we share and your truth in every conversation.

May we seek to be more faithful than successful, more prayerful than praying, more listening than speaking. Give us the imagination what Jesus would have done while dealing with difficult issues.

Israel Selvanayagam

13. Morning Wish

Eternal God, we say good morning to you. Hallowed be your name. Early in the morning, before we begin our work, we praise your glory. Renew our bodies as fresh as the morning flowers. Open our inner eyes, as the sun casts new light upon the darkness which prevailed over the night. Deliver us from all captivity. Give us wings of freedom, like the birds in the sky, to bring a new journey. Restore justice and freedom as a mighty stream running continuously as day follows day. We thank you for the gift of this morning and a new day to work with you.

Masao Takenaka

14. Spiritual Resource

Lord give us wisdom before we speak, understanding while we listen, sensitivity towards those we meet, and the perspective of your kingdom in which to see the things of earth. Bring us to the day's ending, blessed through having shared the day's beginning. In Christ's name we ask this.

Iona Community

15. Precious Peacefulness

Slow me down, O Lord! Ease the pounding of my heart by the quieting of my mind. Steady my hurried pace with a vision of eternal reach of time. Give me amidst the confusion of my day the calmness of the everlasting hills. Allow me to know the magical restoring power of sleep. Teach me the art of taking one-minute vacations ...of slowing down to look at a flower, to pat a dog, to read a few lines from a good book. Let me look up into the branches of the towering oak and know that it grew great and strong because it grew slowly and well. Slow me down Lord, and inspire me to send my roots deep into the soil of life's enduring values that I may grow toward the stars of my greater destiny.

Toc H

16. Doors of Mercy

Open your doors of mercy, Lord: hear our prayer and have mercy upon our souls. Lord of the morning and rulers of the seasons: hear our prayer and have mercy upon our souls. Shine on us, Lord, and make us light like the day: let your light shine in our minds and drive away the shadows of error and night. The creation is full of light, give your light also to our hearts: that we may praise you all the day long. The morning and the evening praise you, Lord: they bring you the praise of your church. Light which gives light to all creatures: give light to our minds that we may thank you, Lord.

Syrian Orthodox Church

17. New Gift

I accept this day as your gift, and enter it now with eagerness; I open my senses to perceive you; I lend my energies to things of goodness and joy.

Rita Snowden

18. Daily Surprise

My Lord, my God, I will seek you this day in silence and in words, in the street and in the church, in the immediate and in the strange, in work and in prayer. Help me not to be too surprised that when I find you, you are more beautiful than I had expected. And help me to discover that even when I have not searched for you, you have been searching out me.

Stephen Plant

19. Imaginative Living

Who can tell what a day may bring forth? Cause me therefore, gracious God, to live every day as if it were to be my last, for I know not but that it may be such. Cause me to live now as I shall wish I had done when I come to die. O grant that I may not die with any guilt on my conscience, or any know sin unrepented of, but that I may be found in Christ, who is my only Saviour and Redeemer.

Thomas à Kempis

20. Teach Me to Ask

Teach me, O Father, how to ask you each moment, silently, for your help. If I fail, teach me at once to ask you to forgive me. If I am disquieted, enable me, by your grace, quickly to turn to you. May nothing this day come between me and you. May I will, do, and say, just what you, my loving and tender Father, will me to will, do, and say. Work your holy will in me and through me this day. Protect me, guide me, bless me, within and without, that I may do something this day for love of you; something which shall please; and that I may, this evening, be nearer to you, though I see it not, nor know it. Lead me, O Lord, in a straight way unto yourself, and keep me in your grace unto the end.

Edward Bouverie Pusey

21. To Find a Pearl

God of grace, may I find a pearl today; in the deep see of faith, in the secure shell of intimacy, in the irritation that gives birth to new possibilities, in the death that leads to new life. And finding that pearl may I discern its beauty, grasp it and share it, that others may see the pearl of great price, the pearl of your grace.

Ruth Gee

22. *Kairos* Moments

We wake each day to the sounds of the morning. Help us to begin with the silence of your presence. So often we, who live within the constraints of the clock, fail to see the *Kairos* moments to which you call us. The opportunities, through thoughts, words and deeds to share your love. When we begin with stillness, in your presence, then each human moment becomes an opportunity to live for you! And for this great privilege, we thank you.

Peter Fox

23. Refreshing Love

Almighty God, we thank you that your love for us is new every morning, despite the things we did yesterday or what we plan for tomorrow; despite the pain we feel for the past and our anxieties about the future; despite the memories we treasure and the hopes we have. Help us to glimpse your love today, that we may make the most of now.

Graham Thompson

24. All This Day

O God, our Father, help us all through this day so to live that we may bring to others, credit to ourselves and to the name we bear, and joy to those that love us, and to you. Help us to be cheerful when things go wrong; persevering when things are difficult; serene when things are irritating. Enable us to be helpful to those in difficulties, kind to those who are in need, sympathetic to those whose hearts are sore and sad. Grant that nothing may make us lose our tempers, nothing may take away our joy, nothing may raffle our peace; nothing may make us bitter towards any person. So, grant that through all this day all with whom we work, and all those whom we meet, may see in us the reflection of the Master, Whose we are, and Whom we seek to serve. This we ask for your love's sake.

William Barclay

25. Until the Shades Lengthen

Support us, O Lord, all the day long, until the shades lengthen, and the evening comes, the busy world is hushed, the fever of life is over, and our work is done. Then, Lord, in your mercy grant us a safe lodging, a holy rest and peace at last; through Jesus Christ our Lord.

John Henry Newman

26. Bless Me

O God, who have ordained that whatever is to be desired, should be sought by labour, and who, by your blessing, bring honest labour to good effect, look with mercy upon my studies and endeavours.

Grant me, O Lord, to desire only what is lawful and right, and afford me calmness of mind, and steadiness of purpose, that I may so do your will in this short life, as to obtain happiness in the world to come; for the sake of Jesus Christ, our Lord.

Samuel Johnson

27. Do the Maximum

Lord, may we do all the good we can, by all the means we can, in all the ways we can, in all the places we can, at all the times we can, to all the people we can, as long as ever we can. May we earn as much as we can, save as much as we can and give as much as we can.

Let us always remember that goodness means love, and love means justice and dignity, freedom and equality for all.

John Wesley (adapted by Samuel Amirtham)

28. Body Life

O Lord, we have a busy world around us. Eye, ear and thought will be needed for all our work to be done in the world. Now are we again enter into it, we would commit eye, ear and thought to You. Do You bless them and keep their work Yours, that as through Your natural laws our hearts beat and our blood flows without any thought of ours for them, so our spiritual life may hold on its course at those times when our minds cannot consciously turn to commit each particular thought to Your service: through Jesus Christ our Lord.

Thomas Arnold

29. Morning Light

O God, our Father, who ever make the light to shine out of the darkness, we thank You for waking us to see the light of this new day. Grant unto us to waste none of its hours; to soil none of its moments; to neglect none of its opportunities; to fail in none of its duties. And bring us to the evening time undefeated by any temptation, at peace with ourselves, at peace with our fellow-men, and at peace with You. This we ask for your love's sake.

William Barclay

30. Morning of Today

O God, help me to live one day at the time, not to be thinking of what might have been and not to be worrying about what may be. Help me to accept the fact that I cannot undo the past, and I cannot foresee the future. But even as I think of this, and even as I face today, help me always to remember that I will never be tried beyond what I can bear; that a father's hand will never cause his child a needless tear; that I cannot ever drift beyond your love and care. So, help me to live today in courage, in cheerfulness and in peace. This I ask for Jesus' sake.

William Barclay

31. To Face the Truth

O God, our Father, bless us and keep us all through today. At our work, make us diligent, every showing ourselves to be workers who have no need to be ashamed. In our pleasure, help us to find delight only in such things as bring no regrets to follow. In our homes, make us kind and considerate, every trying to make the work of others easier, and not harder. In our dealings with our fellow humans, make us courteous and kindly. In our dealings with ourselves, make us honest to face the truth.

And in every moment of this day make us ever to remember that You, God, see us, and that in You we live and move and have our being. So, grant that we may do nothing which would bring shame to ourselves, grief to those who love us, and sorrow to You; through Jesus Christ our Lord.

William Barclay

32. To Live in Fellowship

O God, our Father, who have bidden us to live in fellowship with one another, keep us from everything which would make us difficult to live with today.

Help us never thoughtlessly or deliberately to speak in such a way that we would hurt another's feelings, or wound another's heart.

Keep us from all impatience, from all irritability, and from a temper which is too quick. Keep us from eyes which are focused to find fault and from a tongue which is tuned to criticise. Keep us from being touchy, and quick to take offence, and slow to forget it. Help us not to be stubborn and obstinate, and keep us from the selfishness which can see nothing but its own point of view, and which wants nothing but its own way.

Grant unto us all through this day something of the grace and beauty which shone upon our blessed Lord.

Hear this our prayer, for Your love's sake.

William Barclay

33. To Think of Others

O God, our Father, who have bidden us to be lights in this dark world, help us throughout all this day to be a help and an example to all whom we meet.

Help us to bring comfort to those in sorrow, and strength to those who are tempted. Help us to bring courage to those who are afraid, and guidance to those who do not know what to do. Help us to bring cheer to those who are discouraged, and encouragement to those who are depressed.

And grant that, as we move among men and women this day, they may catch a glimpse in us of the Master, whose we are and whom we seek to serve. This we ask for Your love's sake.

William Barclay

34. Awareness of Your Presence

O God, our Father, before we go out on the duties and the tasks of this day, we ask You to direct, to control, and to guide us all through its hours.

Grant that today we may never for one moment forget Your presence. Grant that we may take no step, and that we may come to no decision, without Your guidance, and that, before we act, we may ever seek to find Your will for us.

Be on our lips, that we may speak no evil work. Be in our eyes, that they may never linger on any forbidden thing. Be on our hands, that we may do our own work with diligence and serve the needs of others with eagerness. Be in our minds, that no soiled or bitter thought may gain an entry to them. Be in our hearts, that they may be warm with love for You, and for our fellow humans.

Help us to begin, to continue, and to end this day in You: through Jesus Christ our Lord.

William Barclay

35. Steady Mind

O God, our Father, help us all through this day so to live that we may bring help to others, credit to ourselves and to the name we bear, and joy to those who love us, and to You.

Help us to be, cheerful when things go wrong; persevering when things are difficult; serene when things are irritating.

Enable us to be, helpful to those in difficulties; kind to those in need; sympathetic to those whose hearts are sore and sad.

William Barclay

36. A Mind to Serve

O God, our Father, deliver us this day from all that would keep us from serving You and from serving our fellows as we ought.

Deliver us from all coldness of heart; and grant that neither our hand nor our heart may ever remain shut to the appeal of someone's need. Deliver us from all weakness of will; from the indecision which cannot make up its mind; from their resolution which cannot abide by a decision once it is made; from the inability to say No to the tempting voices which come to us from inside and from outside. Deliver us from all failure in endeavour; from being too easily discouraged; from giving up and giving in too soon; from allowing any task to defeat us, because it is difficult.

Grant unto us this day the love which is generous in help; the determination which is steadfast in decision; the perseverance which is enduring unto the end; through Jesus Christ our Lord.

William Barclay

37. To Seek Truth

O God, our Father, grant us Your blessing as we go to meet this day.

Grant unto us this day lips which speak the truth, but whichever speak the truth in love. Grant unto us minds which seek the truth; and grant that we may face the truth even when it hurts and condemns us, and that we may never shut our eyes to that which we do not wish to see. Grant unto us hands which work with diligence, and which yet have time to help another with his task. Grant unto us resolution to stand for principle; but save us from stubbornness, and from magnifying trifles into principles. Grant unto us grace to conquer our temptations and to live in purity; but save us from the self-righteousness which would look down on anyone who has fallen by the way.

All through this day grant unto us the strength and the gentleness of our blessed Lord. This we ask for Your love's sake.

William Barclay

38. A Pilgrim's Prayer

With each returning day you are with me, O Lord. May the embrace of your arms protect me; the wisdom of your love guide me; and the power of your creative glory refresh and renew me, as I follow The Way in faith, this day and every day.

Sue Sowden

39. Daily Priorities

Lord Jesus Christ, who so often paused to talk with those you met on the way, save me from being so preoccupied with the tasks before me today that I have no time for the person on the edge of the crowd who is in need of my help, for the unexpected visitor who makes demands upon me, for the sudden emergency that interrupts my plans. Give me a right sense of priorities and readiness to change them when need arises, yielding first place always to what love of you requires of me. For your name's sake.

Pauline Webb

40. This Day's Purpose

Enable us Lord within the life of this day to live with openness, wisdom and generosity.

Donald Eadie

41. God of Adventure

Creator God of adventure and surprise, we thank you for the new hope brought by each returning day. Whatever the burdens we must bear this day, help us to trust in your greater sustaining power which holds us in being, delights in us and has a challengingly alternative perspective on our view of success and failure. Each day afresh may we listen deeply to the drawing of your Spirit, with lives increasingly shaped by the life of your Son.

Jenny Ellis

42. Way to Serenity

Lord, this day, may my business become the way to serenity, may my pride be turned into humility, may my prejudices turn to perceptive understanding, may my narrowness open into wide vision, and may the darkness in me become light through your transforming love.

Margaret James

43. The Gifts I Ask

Lord, give me this day a mind that is eager to seek, memory that is strong to remember, will that is dedicated to obey, a heart surrendered to love, and a life committed to service. At all times Lord, grant me to be most mindful to your grace, and so save me.

Thayumanavar (tr. T. I. Thumbyah)

44. Family Prayer

Lord, behold our family here assembled. We thank you for this place in which we dwell, for the love that unites us, for the peace accorded us this day, for the hope with which we expect the morrow; for the health, the work, the food and the bright skies that make our lives delightful; for our friends in all parts of the earth... Give us courage and gaiety and the quiet mind. Spare us to our friends, soften us to our enemies. Bless us, if it may be, in all our innocent endeavours; if it may not, give us the strength to endure that which is to come that we may be brave in peril, constant in tribulation, temperate in wrath, and in all changes of fortune and, down to the gates of death, loyal and loving to one another. As the clay to the potter, as the windmill to the wind, as children of their sire, we beseech of you this help and mercy for Christ's sake.

Robert Louis Stevenson

45. At Noon

God of all times and every moment. We stand between unsatisfactory morning and promising afternoon. The intense flames of a thousand suns cannot match your shining. May we sit for a while and meditate and move on. May the afternoon be less burdensome and the evening refreshing. Let the coolness of the moon shine upon our life force and mind.

Israel Selvanayagam

46. In the Evening

Go with each of us to rest; if any awake, temper to them the dark hours of watching; and when the day returns, return to us, our sun and comforter, and call us up with morning faces and with morning hearts, eager to labour, eager to be happy, if happiness should be our portion, and if the day be marked for sorrow, strong to endure it.

Robert Louis Stevenson

47. To be Thankful

O God, our Father, we thank You for this day which is passing from us now. For any glimpse of beauty we have seen; for any echo of Your truth that we have heard;

for any kindness that we have received; for any good that we have been enabled to do; and for any temptation which You did give us grace to overcome: We thank You. O God.

We ask Your forgiveness for anything which has spoiled and marred this day. For any word which now we wish that we had never spoken; for any deed which now we wish that we had never done.

William Barclay

48. To be Restful

Eternal and ever blessed God, we give You thanks, as this day comes to an end, for those who mean so much to us, and without whom life could never be the same.

We thank You for those to whom we can go at any time, and never feel a nuisance. We thank You for those to whom we can go when we are tired, knowing that they have, for weary feet, the gift of rest. We thank You for those with whom we can talk, and keep nothing back, knowing that they will not laugh at our dreams or mock at our failures. We thank You for those in whose presence it is easier to be good.

William Barclay

49. Seeking Forgiveness

O God, our Father, forgive us for the failures of today.

Forgive us for any failure in self-control, through which we said or did things for which we are sorry now. Forgive us for any failure in self-discipline, through which we were slack, when we should have been doing with our might that which our hand found to do.

William Barclay

50. To be Free of Anxiety

O God, our Father, take from our minds this night the worries and anxieties which would keep us from sleeping. Help us to make up our minds bravely to deal with the things which can be dealt with, and not to worry about the things about which we can do nothing.

Take from our hearts this night the feeling which would keep us from resting; take from us all discontent, all envy and jealousy, all vain and useless longings for the things which are not for us. Take from our bodies the tension which would keep us from relaxing; and help us to lean back in the clasp of the everlasting arms.

Into Your hands we commit our loved ones, knowing that, even if they are absent from us, they are forever present with You. Into Your hands we commit ourselves that in Your keeping, in light and in dark, in life and in death, we may be safe.

Hear these our prayers, through Jesus Christ our Lord.

William Barclay

51. Seeking Rectification

O God, our Father, be with us as this day ends.

If we are feeling depressed, if we have honestly done our best and yet feel that we are a failure, help us know that You do understand. If we are well aware that we have done something wrong today, save us from the foolishness of trying to hide it from You; and help us to tell You about it, knowing that, if we are truly sorry, You will forgive. If things have hurt us today, if people have been unkind and friends have been unfaithful, help us to remember that Jesus too knows what it is like, because He went through it. If today has been a happy day, and life has been sweet, help us not to forget now to give You thanks.

Before we sleep, we give You thanks for all Your goodness; we ask Your pardon for all our sins and our mistakes; and we ask Your blessings on ourselves and on those we love; through Jesus Christ our Lord.

William Barclay

52. To be Free of Tormenting Thoughts

O God, our Father, there are things in today which make us ashamed when we remember them.

Forgive us if we have lost our temper with the people who get on our nerves. Forgive us if we have been cross and irritable with those who are nearest and dearest to us. Forgive us if at any time we were discourteous and impolite to those with whom we came in contact in our work. Forgive us if we have thoughtlessly or deliberately hurt anyone's feelings today.

O God, our Father, there are things in today which make us glad when we remember them.

We thank You for any lovely thing that we have seen, for any wise thing that we have heard and for any good thing that were have been enabled to do. We thank You for the time we have spent with our friends and comrades, and with those we love.

O God, our Father, accept our sorrow for our sins and our gratitude for Your gifts before we sleep this night; through Jesus Christ our Lord.

William Barclay

53. To be Calm

At last, O God, the sun's heat has given way to the cool evening. Take, we pray, the heat out of our desires and our tempers, and in this evening hour calm us, that we may experience the peace and serenity which come from you.

At last, O God, the sun's brightness has given way to the rich colours of the evening. Prevent us, we pray, from being dazzled by the apparent brilliance of human achievement. And, in this evening hour, help us to rediscover the varied beauty of your creation, and appreciate afresh, in the stillness, the value of your abiding presence. For the sake of Jesus Christ,

For African Congregations (United Church of Christ)

54. God's Watching

Watch, dear Lord, with those who wake, or watch, or weep tonight, and give your angels charge over those who sleep. Tend your sick ones, O Lord of Christ, rest your weary ones. Bless your dying ones. Pity your afflicted ones. Shield your joyous ones. And all for your love's sake.

St. Augustine

55. Thanksgiving

Eternal and ever-blessed God, We give you thanks, as the day comes to an end, for those who mean so much to us, and without whom life could never be the same. We thank you for those to whom we can go at any time and never feel a nuisance. We thank you for those to whom we can go when we are tired, knowing that they have, for the weary feet, the gift of rest. We thank you for those with whom we can talk, and keep nothing back, knowing that they will not laugh at our dreams or mock our failures. We thank you for those in whose company joys are doubly dear, and sorrow's bitterness is soothed. We thank you for those who by their warning counsel and their rebuke have kept us from mistakes we might have made, and sins we might have committed. And above all, we thank you for Jesus, the pattern of our lives, the Lord of our hearts, and the Saviour of our souls. Accept our thanksgiving and grant us tonight a good rest; through Jesus Christ, our Lord.

William Barclay

56. At the Closing of the Day

O Lord my God, thank you for bringing this day to a close; thank you for giving me rest in body and soul. Your hand has been over me and has guarded and preserved me. Forgive my lack of faith and any wrong that I have done today, and help me to forgive all who have wronged me. Let me sleep in peace under your protection, and keep me from all the temptations of darkness. Into your hands I commend my loved ones and all who dwell in this house; I commend to you my body and soul. O God, your holy name be praised.

Dietrich Bonhoeffer

57. The Night Comes

Come Lord and cover me with the night. Spread your grace over us as you assured us as you would do. Your promises are more than all the stars in the sky. Your mercy is deeper than the night. Lord, it will be cold. The night comes with the breath of death. Night comes, the end comes, but Jesus Christ comes also. Lord, we wait for Him day and night.

Young Africans in Ghana

58. Christ's Peace

May our hearts be rested in the mystery of Christ's peace: may we lay down all the unfinished business of the day – allowing our spirit to be enfolded in that embrace which holds together all the wonder, surprise, and contradiction of our human journey – and much more.

Peter Miller

59. Before Reading Scripture

O Lord, heavenly Father, in whom is the fullness of light and wisdom, enlighten our minds by your Holy Spirit, and give us grace to receive your Word with reverence and humility, without which no one can understand your truth. For Christ's sake.

John Calvin

60. Grace for Meal

O God, you are the final source of all our comforts and to you we give thanks for this food. But, we also remember in gratitude the many men and women whose labour was necessary to produce it and who gathered it from the land and the sea for our sustenance. Grant that they too may enjoy the fruit of their labour without want, and may be bound up with us in a communion of thankful hearts.

Walter Rauschenbusch

61. Blessing the Meal

Generous God, our loving Mother, while sitting around for sharing this meal we acknowledge your presence with thanksgiving. We thank you for those who produce rice, tapioca, grains and pulses, spices, vegetables, fruits, meat, fish and eggs; those who help us to keep the fire and assist in the cooking. Just as we share this meal and receive nourishment, we remember those who are hungry or do not have enough to eat. Help us to commit ourselves to work for their welfare and fulfilment. We pray in the name of the one who has promised a banquet for all in his reign, even Jesus Christ, our Lord and Saviour.

Gnana Leelal Selvanayagam

62. Remembering the Hungry

O Lord, our meal is steaming before us and it smells very good. The water is clear and fresh. We are happy and satisfied. But now we must think of our sisters and brothers all over the world who have nothing to eat and only a little to drink. Please, please let them have enough to eat and enough to drink. That is most important. But, give them also what they need every day in order to get through in this life, just as you gave enough to eat and drink to the people of Israel in the desert, please give it also to our hungry and thirsty brothers, now and anytime.

An African Christian

63. For Food Producers

For all the food we have at our table, for all the farmers who produce it, for all the shop keepers or vendors who sell it, for parents or servants who cook it, I thank you, O God. Help us to care for people who do not have enough food; bless all the efforts of those whose struggle to eliminate poverty from our land.

Lily Amirtham

64. Before Going to Bed

Compassionate God, as the birds and cattle have retired from their busy life, let me too retire for renewal and refreshment. Relax me from all stresses and strains.

Accept the flowers of my gratitude and tears of joy for the fruitful day I have had. Forgive my shortcomings and purify me of all dust and dirt that I may have acquired today.

Just as a tortoise withdraws its limbs into its covering shell let me subdue all my parts and thoughts into myself. Control and calm my mind from leaping and hoping like a monkey.

Give me deep sleep without nightmares while my every exhalation and inhalation and heartbeat remain in the rhythm of continuous offering of my loving devotion to you.

Thank you for the love and concern shared between friends and colleagues, help received and values cherished, and let them be stored within me for fulfilling my life in future. All glory, power and honour be yours now and always.

Israel Selvanayagam

65. Free from Dreadful Dreams

The God of Angels and humans, the founder of all creatures visible and invisible, in whose hand is life and death, light and darkness, and all the motions of soul and body, without whom there is no good gift, nor perfect quietness of conscience, but only vanity and vexation of mind, and utter confusion of soul and body, and final torments in the pit of darkness: now my Lord God, darkness approaches, this day has lost its beauty, I as unworthy of your benefits , most humbly pray you this night to bless me with your holy Angels assist me, your Holy Spirit lighten me … And banish Satan from me that neither my own conscience now vex me, nor my old offences trouble me … Save me good Lord this night sleeping, from dreadful dreams and painful slumber deliver me, that I may awake in Christ, and rest in peace: So be it.

Elizabeth Oxenbridge Tyrwhitt

66. Peaceful Night

Before we go to rest, we would commit ourselves to God's care through Christ, beseeching him to forgive for all our sins of this day past, and to keep alive his grace in our hearts, and to cleanse us from all sin, pride, harshness, and selfishness, and to give us the spirit of meekness, humility, firmness and love. O Lord, keep yourself present to us ever, and perfect your strength in our weakness. Take us and ours under your blessed care, this night and ever more; through Jesus Christ our Lord.

Thomas Arnold

67. Night Commendation

Loving God, this night I lay at your feet, the faces I have seen, the voices I have heard, the words I have spoken, the hands I have shaken, the service I have given, the joys I have shared, the sorrows revealed, the memories remembered, the journey travelled.

Author Unknown

68. In the Night of Weariness

In the night of weariness let me give myself up to sleep without struggle, resting my trust upon you. Let me not force my flagging spirit into a poor preparation for your worship. It is you who draw the veil of night upon the tired eyes of the day to renew its sight in a fresher gladness of awakening.

Sadhu Sundar Singh

69. Restful Night

Go with each of us to rest; if any awake, temper to them the dark hours of watching; and when the day returns, return to us, our sun and comforter, and call us up with morning faces and with morning hearts, eager to labour eager to be happy, if happiness should be our portion and if the day be marked for sorrow, strong to endure it.

Robert Louis Stevenson

70. God the Rest Giver

O God, in whose unsleeping love there is no variableness; and in whom, when all else changes, we can most surely confide; Grant us this night to know your everlasting arms beneath us; that, safe in your power, we may sleep and take our rest.

Or if, in wakefulness, pain or sorrow, we must count the hours of night, fill our minds with such thoughts of you, that both soul and body may rest in your goodness, and be revived unto your service. This we pray for Jesus Christ's sake.

Crompton Jones

71. Regularly Grant

Grant unto us, in our hearts, O God, as we come to you, gratitude for all your gifts; Sorrow for all our sins; Trust in your power and will to help. So, grant that we may find here tonight: Forgiveness for the past; Strength for the present; Confidence that the future can bring nothing that in your strength we cannot meet: through Jesus Christ our Lord.

William Barclay

72. The Silence of Sleep

O God, give me sound and refreshing sleep, give me safety from all perils; give me sleep, freedom from restless dreams; give me control of my thoughts, if I should lie awake; give me wisdom to remember that the night was made for sleeping and not for the harbouring of anxious or fretful or shameful thoughts. Give me grace, if as I lie in bed I think at all, to think upon you.

St. Augustine

73. Speak to Us

O God, help us tonight to say to you, just as Samuel did; Speak, Lord, your servant is listening. Speak to us the word we need, and help us to hear it.

Speak to us the word of encouragement when we are discouraged and depressed; The word of warning when we are likely to go astray; The word of guidance when we do not know what to do and where to go; The word of strength to enable us to resist our temptations; The word of power to make us able for work and ready for any burden. Whatever word we need, speak it to us now.

Take from us everything which would keep us from hearing your voice. Take from us the inattentive mind and the wandering thoughts; The cold heart and the weak will; The self-will which disregards the truth; The prejudice which cannot hear or see the truth, but which sees only what it wants to see; The desire not to be disturbed, which is afraid of the truth.

Help us in this place to hear your word, and to go out and obey it.

William Barclay

74. Bodies of Night Life

Hear, Lord, before you, tonight, are the bodies of sleeping humans: the pure body of the tiny child, the soiled body of the prostitute, the vigorous body of the athlete, the exhausted body of the factory worker, the soft body of the playboy, the surfeited body of the rich man, the starved body of the poor man (or woman), the neglected body of the slum child, the feverish body of the sick, the painful body of the injured, the paralyzed body of the cripple, all bodies, Lord, of all ages. Here is the body of the fragile new-born baby, plucked like ripe fruit from its mother. Here is the body of the light-hearted child who falls and gets up, unmindful of its bruises. Here is the body of the worried adolescent who doesn't know that it is a fine thing to grow up. Here is the body of a grown man, powerful and proud of his strength. Here is the body of the old man, gradually failing. I offer them all to you, Lord, and I ask you to bless them, while they lie in silence, wrapped in your night. Left by their sleeping souls, they are there before your eyes, your own. Tomorrow, shaken from their sleep, they will have to resume work. May they be servants and not masters, welcoming homes and not prisons, temples of the living God and not tombs. May these bodies be developed, purified, transfigured by those who dwell in them, and may be find them, at the end of their days, faithful companions, illumined by the beauty of their souls. In your sight, Lord, and in your Mother's, since you both belong to our earth, all the bodies of humans will be guests in glory of your eternal heaven.

Michel Quoist

75. Presence and Clarity

I seek your presence, O God, not because I have managed to see clearly or been true in all things this day, not because I have succeeded in loving or in reverencing those around me, but because I want to see with clarity, because I long to be true and desire to love as I have been loved. Renew my inner sight, make fresh my longings to be true, and grant me the grace of loving this night that I may end the day as I had hoped to live it, that I may end this day restored to my deepest yearnings, that I may end this day as I intend to live tomorrow, as I intend to live tomorrow.

J. Philip Newell

76. Loving-Kindness

Show your loving-kindness tonight, O Lord, to all who stand in need of your help. Be with the weak to make them strong, and with the strong to make them gentle. Cheer the lonely with your company and the worried with your peace. Prosper your church in the fulfilment of her mighty task, and grant your blessing to all who have toiled today in Christ's name.

John Baillie

77. Transforming Sleep

Lord of the night, be with me through the hours of darkness, let all my questions, problems, decisions, be enveloped in sleep that through the mystery of the sleeping mind the difficulties of the day will be seen to be easier in the morning light. Into your hands, O Lord, I commit my spirit.

Frank Topping

XIII. Courage, Guidance and Strength

1. Faith to Venture

Lord, we come before you in trembling and fear: there are so many changes taking place in the world today, changes that will affect our private lives and our church lives. We are happy with the tried and tested ways, the way we have professed our faith over many years: we know where we stand. Let us remind ourselves that you are an unchanging God – and yet, you are a God of surprises. You are always making all things new. Forgive us when we fail to notice that you are calling us to become involved in some new venture for you … Your Son Jesus challenged people by what he said and did, and by his death and resurrection. When we are in the place where you expect us to be, may we be open to being used by you, as instruments of your honour and glory.

John Lawley

2. Be My Guide

Your way, not mine, O Lord, however dark it be; lead me by your own hand, choose out the path for me. Smooth let it be or rough, it will be still the best; winding or straight, it leads right onward to your rest. I dare not choose my lot; I would not if I might: choose thou for me, my God, so shall I walk aright. The kingdom that I seek is yours, so let the way that leads to it be yours, else I must surely stray. Take you my cup, and it with joy or sorrow fill, as best to you may seem; choose you my good and ill. Choose for me my friends, my sickness or my health; choose my cares for me, my poverty or wealth. Not mine, not mine the choice in things or great or small; be you my guide, my strength, my wisdom, and my all.

Horatius Bonar

3. Guidance of Wisdom

Grant us, Lord, to know in weakness the strength of your incarnation: in pain the triumph of your passion; in poverty the riches of your Godhead; in reproach the satisfaction of your sympathy: in loneliness the comfort of your continual presence; in difficulty the efficacy of your intercession; in perplexity the guidance of your wisdom, and by your glorious death and resurrection bring us at last to the joy of seeing you face to face.

Source Unknown

4. Promised Land

God, our promised land; Christ, our way; our journey has become long and hard because we wander about like nomads not knowing where to go. We are strangers in our own land without bread, a roof, a future. But, you came to find us with your life-giving breath. You, who are also displaced, have become an exile with us. You offer us anew the promised land. Your spirit urges us toward that joyous homecoming.

From 'Displaced campesinos', Lima, Peru

5. Fixed on the Goal

O God of the loving, keep our eyes fixed on the goal of our journey, that we may be fleet of heart, and in all our doings leap to the embrace of the One who lures us with love, the pioneer of our salvation, Jesus, our elder brother and our faithful friend.

Jim Cotter

6. Divine Mercy

Almighty and everlasting God, who are always more ready to hear than we to pray and are willing to give more than either we desire or deserve. Pour down upon us the abundance of your mercy, forgiving those things where of our conscience is afraid and giving us those good things which we are not worthy to ask, but through the merits and mediation of Jesus Christ, your Son, our Lord.

Book of Common Prayer

7. Interdependence

O God, who have bound us together in this bundle of life, give us grace to understand how our lives depend on the courage, the industry, the honesty, and integrity of our fellow human beings; that we may be mindful of their needs, grateful for their faithfulness, and faithful in our responsibilities to them; through Jesus Christ, our Lord.

Reinhold Niebuhr

8. To Salvation

Lord, in your great generosity heal my sickness, wash away my defilement, enlighten my blindness, enrich my poverty, and clothe my nakedness. May I receive the bread of angels, the King of Kings and Lord of lords, with humble reverence, with purity of faith, repentance and love, and the determined purpose that will help to bring me to salvation.

St. Thomas Aquinas

9. Graceful Acceptance

God grant me the serenity to accept the things I cannot change, the courage to change the things I can, and the wisdom to know the difference.

Reinhold Niebuhr

10. Deliver from Snares

Save us, O Lord, from the snares of a double mind. Deliver us from all cowardly neutralities. Make us go in the paths of your commandments, and to trust for our defence in your mighty arm alone; through Jesus Christ our Lord.

Richard Hurrell Froude

11. Lift from Depression

My strength fails; I feel only weakness, irritation and depression. I am tempted to complain and to despair. What has become of the courage I was so proud of, and that gave me so much self-confidence? In addition to my pain, I have to bear the shame of my fretful feebleness. Lord, destroy my pride; leave it no resource. How happy I shall be if you can teach me by these terrible trials, that I am nothing, that I can do nothing, and that you are all!

Francois Fénelon

12. Struggle Against Injustice

Lord, in these times, when we fear we are losing hope or feel that our efforts are futile, let us see in our hearts and minds the image of your resurrection, and let that be our source of courage and strength. With that and in your company, help us to face challenges and struggles against all that is born of injustice.

Filipino Church (Iona Community)

13. Glowing Centre

Give me courage, pillar of flame, as I begin to follow you on the pilgrim way. Create a calm and glowing centre within me that I may resist the cruelties of those who seem to love me. May I be firm in refusing all collusion. May I be harmed no more. Keep me steady when I arouse unresolved conflicts in others, for you love them as much as you love me. Loose my chains in the dungeons, and free them from their prisons too.

Jim Cotter

14. Grant Us a Vision

God of mercy and hope, in the struggle for freedom grant us strength; in decisions about freedom grant us wisdom; in the practice of freedom grant us guidance; in the dangers of freedom grant us protection; in the life of freedom grant us joy; and in the use of freedom grant us vision; for your name`s sake.

Latin American Council of Churches

15. Faithful Partner God

Faithful God, when you call, may we respond; when we falter, be our guide. When you speak may we hear; when we question, be our wisdom. When you ask, may we answer; when we hesitate, be our resolve. When you show, may we see; when we disregard, be our conscience. When you lead, may we follow; when we stray, be our shepherd. When you send, may we go; when we fear, be our courage. When you challenge, may we listen; when we fail, be our rock. When you gave, may we receive; and may we love, as you first loved us.

Paul Martin

16. God of Journey

Pilgrim God, there is an exodus going on in my life: desert stretches, a vast land of questions. Inside my head your promises tumble and turn. No pillar of cloud by day or fire by night that I can see. My heart hurts at leaving loved ones and so much of the security I have known. I try to give in to the stretching and the pain. It is hard, God, and I want to be settled, secure, safe and sure. And here I am, feeling so full of pilgrim's fear and anxiety. O God of the journey, lift me up, press me against your cheek. Let your great love hold me and create a deep trust in me. Then set me down, God of the journey; take my hand in yours and guide me ever so gently across the new territory of my life.

Joyce Rupp

17. Carrying Heavy Luggage

O my Lord, I am carrying too much luggage, and it's weighing me down, holding me back. I worry about losing it, but I don't need much of the stuff I am dragging about. It blocks out the isles and gangways, getting in the way, making people cross and wrapping itself round my ankles. I need to learn to travel light, but I don't know what to do with all this stuff. Here, you take it. I am leaving it with you. Perhaps you can find a better use for it.

Kathy Galloway

18. Strange Places

God beyond borders, we bless you for strange places and different dreams, for the demands and diversity of a wider, for distance that lets us look back and re-evaluate, for new ground where broken stems can take root, grow and blossom. We bless you for the friendship of strangers, richness of other cultures and the painful gift of freedom.

Kathy Galloway

19. From Idea to Enfleshment

Lord God, in Jesus, you came in the body: flesh of our flesh, bone of our bone, one with us in searing pain and delirious laughter. We thank you that you did not remain an idea, even a religious idea, but walked, wept and washed feet among us. By your love, change our ideas, especially our religious ideas, into living signs of your work and will.

Iona Community

20. Clear the Debris

Gracious Lord, clear away all the debris we carry that is slowing us down, impeding our progress. All the hurts and failures, prejudice and faults, preventing us becoming the people we could be. We lay them before you. Free us from these chains so we can run with you and live again the life that we were created for.

John Birch

21. God of Pilgrims

O God of the desert pilgrims, we who are wearied by monotonous days of sun or cloud, who are battered by the monstrous whirling winds, surprise us yet with a monstrance of wonder, a revelation of love, oasis of refreshment, a taste of the harvest, a moment of grace.

Jim Cotter

22. Strength and Warmth

Look upon your servant, O Lord, weak in faith and asking for your strength; cold in heart, but seeking the warmth of your love; assailed by doubt, but longing to trust you; abounding in sin, yet begging to be filled with your righteousness; now and for ever.

Martin Luther

23. Growing Up

God of new beginnings, we are walking into mystery. We face the future, not knowing what days and months will bring us or how we will respond to them. Give us faith to go out with courage not knowing where we go, knowing only that your hand is leading us and your love supporting us, through Jesus Christ our Lord.

Liam Kelly

24. Your Hand is Enough

As the rain hides the stars, as the autumn mist hides the hills, as the clouds veil the blue of the sky, so the dark happenings of my lot hide the shining of your face from me. Yet, if I may hold your hand in the darkness, it is enough. Since I know that, though I may stumble in my going, you do not fall.

Celtic (Source Unknown)

25. Uneasy Travel

Living God, the path you wish for us to travel is not always easy to see, as when the returning tide sweeps across the causeway. But, today we thank you for those moments when our hearts are lifted, when hope is reawakened, when we receive new insights and a new confidence, when the way ahead becomes clear and our destination more sure.

David Coote

26. Acceptance

Dear Father, help us accept each other as Christ accepted us; teach us as sister, brother each person to embrace. Be present, Lord among us and bring us to belief that we are ourselves accepted and meant to love and live. Teach us, O Lord, your lesson, as in our daily life; we struggle to be human, and search for hope and faith. Teach us to care for people, for all; not just for some, to love them as we find them or as they may become. Let your acceptance change us, so that we may be moved in living situations to do the truth in love, to practise your acceptance until we know by heart, the table of forgiveness and laughter's healing art. Lord, for today's encounter with all who are in need, who hunger for acceptance, for righteousness and bread, we need new eyes for seeing, new hands for holding on. Renew us with your spirit. Lord, free, us, make us one!

Fred Kaan

27. Guiding Spirit

O Lord our God, teach us, we beseech you, to ask you aright for the right things. Steer you the vessel of our life towards yourself, you tranquil haven of all storm-tossed souls. Show us the course wherein we should go. Renew a willing spirit within us. Let your Spirit curb our waywardness and guide and enable us unto that which is our true good, to keep your loss, and in all our works ever more to rejoice in your glorious and gladdening presence. For yours is the glory and praise from all your saints for ever and ever.

Basil the Great

28. Head and Mind

Give us, O Lord, a mind after Your own heart, that we may delight to do Your will, O our God; and let Your law be written on our hearts. Give us courage and resolution to do our duty, and a heart to be spent in Your service, and in doing all the good that possibly we can the few remaining days of our pilgrimage here on earth. Grant this, we humbly beseech You, for the sake of Jesus Christ Your Son our Lord.

John Tillotson

29. Strength to Keep Pure

O God, our Father, we come to you tonight to find strength: to keep our hearts pure; to keep our minds clean; to keep our words true; to keep our deeds kind; through Jesus Christ our Lord.

William Barclay

30. Guide Through Scripture

Blessed Lord, by whose providence all holy Scriptures were written and preserved for our instruction, give us grace to study them this and every day, with patience and love. Strengthen our souls with the fullness of their divine teaching. Keep from us all pride and irreverence. Guide us in the deep things of Your heavenly wisdom, and of Your great mercy lead us by the word unto everlasting life: through Jesus Christ our Lord and Saviour.

Brooke Foss Westcott

31. Courage to Combat

We pray you today for your strong courage to combat your enemies and to suffer in your cause. Spur us in this day to challenge the grim realities of pain, disease, injustice and sin, and by gallant service to conquer these your foes.

J. S. Hoyland

32. In Unfavourable Conditions

God, make each moment of our lives a miracle; God, make us laugh at the utterly impossible; God, give us hope when all things seem hopeless, peace where no peace could be, love for the unlovable. Make us to gamble all on your Almightiness, and to dare everything in your great service.

M. E. Procter

33. Steer Our Vessel

Be our captain O God even when our sailing is rough-going and storm-tossed. As Paul and his companions experienced on their way to Rome may we also realise your presence around us. We thank you for the islanders of Malta who received the stranded passengers of the shipwreck with kindness and looked after them with generous spirit. Whatever may be the challenges we face on our troublesome voyage, help us to be effective witnesses.

Israel Selvanayagam

34. Fellow Traveller

Blessed are all your saints, O God and King, who have travelled over the tempestuous sea of this life and have made the harbour of peace and felicity. Watch over us who are still in our dangerous voyage; and remember such as lie exposed to the rough storms of trouble and temptations.

Frail is our vessel and the ocean is wide; but, as in your mercy you have set our course, so steer the vessel of our life toward the everlasting shore of peace, and bring us at length to the quiet haven of our heart's desire, where You O our God, are blessed, and live and reign for ever and ever.

St. Augustine

35. Guide in the Straight Path

O God, by whom the meek are guided in judgment, and light rises up in darkness for the godly; grant us in our doubts and uncertainties the grace to ask what you would have us to do; that the Spirit of wisdom may save us from all false choices, and that in your light we may see the light, and in your straight path may not stumble: through Jesus Christ our Lord.

William Bright

36. Sharing Faith Through Love

Loving God, we know you and see you in Jesus; so come to us in friendship and walk with us along the way, that when the pathway is rocky and uphill we may know your strength and, in all circumstances, have eyes which are open to others, that we may be to them instruments of your purpose, sharing faith through encouragement and love.

Geoffrey Clark

37. Ideal Life

Eternal and ever-blessed God, equip us, not only to see, but also to attain, the ideal.

Grant unto us, the wisdom to know what is right, and the courage to do it; The clear sight to see the right way, and the perseverance to walk in it; The vision to see the ideal, and the discipline to toil towards it.

Help us never to be satisfied with words without deeds; With plans without performance; With schemes without results; With dreams without toil to make the dream come true.

Teach us that the way to the stars is always steep; That sweat is the price of all things precious; That there never can be any crown without a cross.

So make us willingly to spend life that we may gain life, and to take up our cross and follow in the footsteps of our Lord and Master, Jesus Christ.

William Barclay

38. Unburden

O God, who has drawn over the weary day the restful veil of night, enfold us in your heavenly peace. Life from our hands our tasks, and all through the night bear in your bosom the full weight of our burdens and sorrows, that in untroubled slumber we may press our weariness close to your strength, and win new power for the morrow's duties from you who give to your beloved in sleep: through Jesus Christ our Lord.

An Unknown Saint

39. Strength to Love and Serve

Give us the strength lightly to bear our joys and sorrows. Give us the strength to make our love fruitful in service. Give us the strength never to disown the poor or bend our knees before insolent might. Give us the strength to raise our minds high above daily trifles. And give us the strength to surrender our strength to your will with love.

Rabindranath Tagore

40. Help to Resist

O God, Source of all strength and goodness, help us to resist the things which by ourselves we cannot resist, to overcome the temptations which fascinate us; To break the habits which enslave us; To say No to anything which invites us to set foot on the wrong way.

Help us to do and to be all the things which by ourselves we cannot do and be. We have never been as good as we could be; We have never done anything as well as it could be done; Life has never been what it might have been and could have been.

Give us the strength and wisdom to be what you meant us to be, and to do what you meant us to do, so that we may fulfil the purpose for which you sent us into this your world.

William Barclay

41. In Our Isolation

As infants, so recently from the womb, we cry and with our mother's touch are calmed and made secure,

In our isolation, Lord we cry to you!

As children, shaken by the pain of a fall, seeking solace in a parent's arms,

In our isolation, Lord we cry to you!

As confused adolescents, enduring the pain of transition from child to adult,

In our isolation, Lord we cry to you!

As adults in a hostile world seeking others to share our personal island,

In our isolation, Lord we cry to you!

As age leads to loss of those whose touch we have valued,

In our isolation, Lord we cry to you!

(Pause)

Your healing touch we recognise in the touch of others, but in our lonely times, when no human touch is near and the fears of life beset us, hold us in your love.

In our isolation, Lord we cry to you!

Peter Fox

42. Lead Us

Lead us, O Lord, from the night of doubt and despair into the daylight of dialogue and hope. Lead us out of the tomb of suspicion and fear, into the life of faith and trust. Lead us out of the darkness of terror and hate into the sunlight of security and love; and lead us out of the gloom of isolation and hurt into the healing presence of your glory; through Jesus Christ our Lord.

Norman Wallwork

43. Shield and Defend

May the wisdom of God instruct us; may the hand of God protect us; may the way of God direct us; may the shield of God defend us and may the hosts of God guard us.

St. Patrick

44. Times of Distress

Be to us, O Lord, a strong tower of defence; a comforter in every tribulation; and a deliverer in times of distress. In all our troubles be to us a present help, and guide us through all dangers and temptations, till we come at length to the glory and habitation of heaven; this we ask through Jesus Christ our Lord.

Thomas à Kempis

45. Protect from Fear

Lord, you are my leader, I have all I need, you calm me down when I am moody, you give me energy and love. You lead me down the right path, even if I'm scared or upset. I will not be afraid, because you are with me and will protect me. You have given me more than I deserve. I know you will always be there and your house will be my home for ever more.

Clare Hardwicke

46. Risk and Vulnerability

God of truth and grace, by taking the risk of coming among us, you showed us that you trust us to care for this wonderful planet and for each other. Open our eyes and ears to your anger and grief; help us to trust you and to take the risk of travelling vulnerably into the unknown, to do your work joyfully in the love of our risen Saviour, Jesus Christ.

Mary Ann Ebert

47. Tears and Laughter

Loving God, may we see your presence in the tears and laughter of our lives; in our wilderness experience may we find hope; in the faces of others may we discern your beauty; and in our abandonment may we be found by you. In Jesus Christ we pray.

Stuart Burgess

48. Wilderness

Lord, in the wilderness we all hunger after something. It may be for justice or freedom or simply to be heard. It may be for a smile or compassion or to be loved.

You are here in the wilderness, and your voice, often like a murmur says – MY word is sufficient for you, this word feeds you. Today, again in the wilderness, having left my home country, my family, my friends, I hear your voice and your voice feeds me. Having my fill, I will go on my way, becoming for the people around no longer a wasteland but a haven of restoration. This is my prayer Lord.

Josianne Bidaux

49. Disturbing Questions

Holy God, beneath the deepest peace and most turbulent strife you hold all things together, and in Jesus you show us your love that nothing can break. Help us in our calm certainties and in our disturbing questions to rest in your strength, to be fed by your Spirit, and to trust in Christ's way, that in all seasons of life we may walk with you, through Jesus Christ our Lord.

Robin Hutt

50. Moments of Distress

Lord, when I walk in the darkness be my light; when I am lonely be my companion; when I am weak come to my help; when I am restless grant me your peace and when I am bitter fill me with your patience and love; for Jesus' sake.

Dietrich Bonhoeffer

51. Divine Map

Lord, I can only see a little of the road ahead. I can't see my final destination. I can't even see over the next hill, and I know there will be other ups and downs beyond it – high points from which one can see quite a long view, valleys where the hills shut one in. And some of those clouds may mean storms. But, the great thing is to have got started! Lord, thank you for calling me, and setting my feet on the way. Thank you for the map of the way, which is yourself. Lord, help me to persevere.

Margaret Dewey

52. Earthly Pilgrimage

God our Father, in this house of prayer you bless your family on its earthly pilgrimage; so quicken our consciences by your holiness, nourish our minds by your truth, purify our imaginations by your beauty, and open our hearts to your love, that, in the surrender of our wills to your purpose, the world may be renewed in Jesus Christ our Lord.

William Temple

53. To Golgotha

Lord we cannot properly reflect on the meaning of the cross while life is easy and comfortable. Let us follow you on your way to Golgotha again and again, bearing the pain and sin of humanity, yet directing all our deep questions to you, you alone. Loving God, you create and recreate; you allow all things to die and then you bring to life. Let us not aspire to glory without suffering, confidence without self-denial, or eternal life without dying.

Israel Selvanayagam

54. Presence and Enlightenment

Strengthen our weakness with your compassion, O Lord, and comfort us with your loving kindness. Amidst the changing fortunes of this world may we find rest in your peace. May we find cleansing in your presence and the enlightenment of your Holy Spirit all our days; through Christ our Lord.

Nestorian Liturgy

55. Teach Us

Living God, when we feel the shaking of the foundations and try to retreat into the security of the past,

Teach us that you are the God of the future.

Living God, when we are tempted to despair, when events move so quickly and it seems that there is no way forward,

Teach us that you are the God of hope.

Living God, when things happen beyond our understanding and we find our trust in you is threatened,

Teach us that you are the God of all faith.

Living God, in a fast-moving world, when we find our values questioned and it is not easy to perceive what is right,

Teach us that you are the God of all wisdom.

So may we learn to live each day in company with you and it follow you wherever you will lead us.

Nigel Collinson

56. Give Me Joy

Give to me, O God, a heart of joy that rests in your peace and a soul of tranquillity that delights in your beauty; a spirit of glory that sings your praise, a life of serenity at home in your presence and a mind of quietness renewed by your Spirit; through Jesus Christ our Lord.

Evelyn Underhill

57. Refresh and Recharge

Father, Creator of this warm and rain-washed Celtic land, we feel your power in the majesty of towering cliff and restless sea; in wooded creek and sandy cove, adorned with flowers and teeming with wildlife. Recharge us with the power of your Spirit, which surges with sacrificial love for others, that conflict and pain may be burnt up in hope and harmony as we follow the path of our Living Lord.

Daphne Train

58. Stay with Us

Stay with us, O Lord, when we are swamped by weariness and seeming impossibilities. Turn our faces gently towards you, keep our hearts loving and our will determined to fight on to the end.

Mother Janet Stuart

59. Work with Us

O God, in mystery and silence you are present in our lives, bringing new life out of destruction, hope out of despair and growth out of difficulty. We thank you that you do not leave us alone, but are working with us to bring new things to birth. Help us to perceive your hand in the unfolding of our lives, to know the dignity of acceptance within your family and to work to make all human life full of purpose and joy.

Kathleen Richardson

60. Song of Hope

Lord of life, when the rhythm of my life is disturbed by fear or sorrow, when harmony is jarred by discord, when I am out of tune with you and the world, help me to sing a new song of faith and hope, peace and love, joy and praise.

Gwen Charlton

61. Calm in Storm

May the calm of our Lord's presence still the storm of our stress; may the coolness of his touch assuage our anxieties; may the clarity of his vision clear our confusion; and may he give us courage to claim his peace.

Rosemary Watters

62. Firm and Integrity

We greet you, Spirit of the North. You are the cold, biting wind that blows across our land, that strips the earth of all that is dead and decayed, that robs us of the false securities, so easily blown away. Teach us to plant our feet securely on the earth and to see things as they really are, that the coming of your Spirit may find us standing firm in integrity. It is your Sprit whose winds bring the snow of winter, with their fury and their solitude. It is your Spirit who blankets the earth for sleep. Teach us, Spirit of the North, in the solitude of winter, to wait in darkness with the sleeping earth, believing that we, like the earth, already hold within ourselves the seeds of new life.

A Canadian Indian

63. Wings of the Spirit

Gracious God, you seek us at every moment of our lives. When the sun is shining it is not too difficult to believe in you and to live thankfully. But, the hardest times are when our minds are filled with anxiety and dread, or when we are tired out with caring for others. Give us then the wings of your Spirit, not escape from all that we must do, but to face it with calm mind, aware of your unfailing presence.

Nigel Collinson

64. Lead us Into Mysteries

Lord, deepen our understanding of your nature; increase in us the awareness of your ways. Draw us into those paths that lead to the transforming both of nations and of people. Strengthen us in our weakness, hold us in our trembling and form us into the servants of your mysteries, through Christ our Lord.

Donald Eadie

65. To Fight for Truth

Lord Jesus, make us people who fight for truth without self-righteousness, who can be wrong and know ourselves forgiven, who can love and go on loving, and who can suffer if need be. May our neighbours see something of you in us and may you not be ashamed of us when you come in glory.

Christina Le Moignan

66. Dying and Rising

Living Christ, bring us from death to life: from being the kind of church we try to maintain to becoming a community of love, and excite us with the truth; that to die and rise again is the great mystery and challenge of the gospel for each generation. Strengthen us through prayer and give us courage to take the first step, knowing that you, whose name is Emmanuel, travel with us.

Maureen Edwards

67. Guardian and Friend

Protector God, our strength for meeting life's trials comes from you. You are our shield, our foundation, our Guardian and our Friend. Help us to stay strong in faith, hope and love so that we may serve others in your name.

Moravian

68. Comfort and Care

O God, when we think we can fly like eagles we come crashing back to earth; when we trust in the ways of the world, the battle increases. We race to your side for comfort and care. Help us rise to new heights of faith, hope and love.

Moravian

69. Respect Other Thoughts

Keep us, Lord, from the snare of spiritual arrogance; teach us to listen to what others believe, seeking to understand and respect their thoughts, and to find our common ground in relationship with Christ; in his name we pray.

Moravian

70. Save in Raging Waters

Saving God, when we are caught in raging waters, when vicious winds toss us about, when demeaning actions and statements come from ever those we love, throw us the lifeline of your mercy, love and grace.

Moravian

71. Trustworthiness

Approachable God, worthy of our trust in all things and places, strengthen us when we are tempted to choose the path of least resistance, seeking peace at any price, putting on blinders instead of binoculars. We want to please and honour you now and always.

Moravian

72. Waiting with Patience

God of the living word, you have commanded us to be still, to wait patiently, and to listen more attentively for your voice. Help us to slow down, put on the brakes, shift into neutral, and remain in place awaiting your call through Jesus.

Moravian

73. Renew and Lead

God of the stillness, remind us to stop to refresh and renew our lives. May we wait patiently in the silence and truly listen to your voice and leading, rededicating ourselves in service to you and your children.

Moravian

74. Slow us Down

Lord of patience, our spirits are willing but our lives are so busy! We mean well but forget. Remind us that in doing your will we become sisters and brothers in love. Slow us down to see what you require of us.

Moravian

75. Repentant and Repair

God, today we say more than a simple, "I am sorry." We ask forgiveness for all of the ways that we fall short, resolving to truly repent and repair the brokenness in our lives and in the world. Guide us in Jesus' name.

Moravian

76. Cry for Strength

Lord Jesus Christ, have mercy on our blindness! Forgive our failure to see those who need our help and our ignorance to the sufferings of those around us. We cry out for strength and sight. Lord Jesus Christ, have mercy on us.

Moravian

77. Amazing God

Lord God, you amaze us by not rejecting your sinful children! Thank you for choosing to love us and to work wonders through us. Your love never ends and never fails! In Jesus' name, alleluia!

Moravian

78. Keep Close

Merciful Lord, your patience is amazing! You wait for us when we stray, search for us when we are lost, and open your arms when we come turning back! Keep us close to your heart as we find our way home.

Moravian

79. Light of Justice

Jesus, let the knowledge of your love and sacrifice burn so brightly within us that all who meet us today will know that we are yours. Let the light of justice shine in our lives as we work for peace.

Moravian

80. Awareness of Presence

Mighty God! Sometimes we forget your majesty. How blessed we are that you choose us as your family to share in all creation! Increase our awareness of your presence and of our stewardship over all entrusted to us.

Moravian

81. Renewed Life

Lord, there are times when our pain seems too much to bear. In realizing that you have experienced the same pain and still choose to bear ours, we are comforted. Help us in our grief to find joy, healing and renewed life.

Moravian

82. Unity in Essentials

Father, we grieve you with our pettiness! People know we are Christ's by the love we have for each other. Remind us: in essentials, unity; in non-essentials, liberty; and in everything, love. Reconcile us to one another in you.

Moravian

83. To Honour and Praise

Lord, make your home in our hearts and guide us to live in your ways. Give us strength to honour you through our words and actions, to praise you alone, and to shine your light in the world.

Moravian

84. Justice and Righteousness

Gracious heavenly Father, teach all those in positions of power about your justice and righteousness. Be with those living in poverty and oppression that they may find a life of abundance through you. Empower us to do your mission, to be your sheep, and to take the time to listen for your each and every day.

Moravian

85. Path of Life

Teacher, light the path that you have laid for us to follow so that we might see your plans for us and know your will. Give us the strength and courage to follow where you lead, trusting in you with our whole selves.

Moravian

86. Open Our Hearts

Lord, open our hearts to love all those we meet, our eyes to see all those in need, our hands to hold and help where we can, our minds to learn from others and to allow you to lead, and our ears to listen more than we speak and to hear your words.

Moravian

87. Grant to Know

Grant to me, O Lord, to know what I ought to know, to love what I ought to love, to praise you what delights you most, to value what is precious in your sight, to hate what is offensive to you. Do not suffer me to judge according to the sight of my eyes, nor to pass sentence according to the hearing of the ears of ignorant men, but to discern with true judgement between things visible and spiritual, and above all things to enquire what is the good pleasure of your will.

Thomas à Kempis

88. Lead Through All Odds

Faithful shepherd, lead us; through trial and injustice, lead us; through stress and business, lead us; through illness and loss, lead us. Carry us when we are weak and tired, find us when we are lost. Heal us when we are sick; leave no one behind. Faithful Shepherd, lead your flock.

Moravian

89. Deliver and Lead

Strong Deliverer, shower us with your healing strength; be our Shield as we move as pilgrims in this land. Be our Pillar of fire that leads us on our journey. Be our Guide and Redeemer as we await your approaching return.

Moravian

90. Fill with Abundant Love

Creator God, Lord of all the living, fill our hearts with the abundant warmth of your abounding love. Light up our contrite hearts so that we will remain faithful and ablaze for you until your return!

Moravian

91. Mind of Christ

Mighty God, as your chosen people, let the mind of Christ richly dwell in us. Grant us the power to surrender ourselves to your leading as we look beyond this earthly home toward our heavenly home.

Moravian

92. Power to Finish the Race

As the days and years edge on, help us, Lord to not be weary and to not faint. Let our zeal for you never run dry. Daily renew us by the power of your Spirit. Let us by your power and strength finish the race.

Moravian

93. Great I Am

With each waking day, great I AM, purify and guard our hearts. Clothe us in your armour from the crowns of our heads to the soles of our feet. Until you return, may we be unshaken, unmoved by every false wind. In Jesus' name we pray.

Moravian

94. Help in Perplexities

O God, from whom to be turned is to fall, to whom to be turned is to rise; and with whom to stand is to abide for ever; grant us in all our duties your help, in all our perplexities your guidance, in all our dangers your protection, and in all our sorrows your peace, through Jesus Christ our Lord.

St. Augustine

95. Eternal God

Eternal God, the light of the minds that know you, the life of the souls that love you, the strength of the wills that serve you; help us so to know you that we may truly love you, so to love you that we may fully serve you, whom to serve is perfect freedom.

Gelasian Sacramentary

96. Desire for God

O Lord our God, grant us grace to desire you with our whole heart, that so desiring we may seek and find you, and so finding you; may love you, and loving you, may hate those sins from which you have redeemed us.

Anselm

97. Day by Day

Thanks be to you, Lord Jesus Christ, for all the benefits which you have won for us, for all the pains and insults which you have borne for us. O most merciful Redeemer, Friend and Brother, may we know you more clearly, love you more dearly, and follow you more nearly, day by day.

Richard of Chichester

98. A Steadfast Heart

Give me, O Lord, a steadfast heart, which no unworthy affection may drag downwards; give me an unconquered heart, which no tribulation can wear out; give me an upright heart, which no unworthy purpose may tempt aside. Bestow on me also, O Lord my God, understanding to know you, diligence to seek you, wisdom to find you, and a faithfulness that may finally embrace you, through Jesus Christ our Lord.

Thomas Aquinas

99. To Be True

Lord, since you have taken from me all that I had from you, yet of your grace leave me the gift which ever dog has by nature: that of being true to you in my distress, when I am deprived of all consolation. This I desire more fervently than your heavenly kingdom!

Mechthild of Magdeburg

100. Write Your Name

Write your blessed Name, O Lord, upon my heart, there to remain so indelibly engraved, that no prosperity, no adversity shall ever move me from your love. Be to me a strong tower of defence, a comforter in tribulation, a deliverer in distress, a very present help in trouble, and a guide to heaven through the many temptations and dangers of this life.

Thomas à Kempis

101. Submission to Your Will

O Lord, you know what is best for me. Let this or that be done, as you please. Give what you will, how much you will and when you will.

Thomas à Kempis

102. Aptness to Learn

Hear our prayers, O Lord Jesus, the everlasting wisdom of the Father. You give to us, in the days of our youth, aptness to learn. Add, we pray, the furtherance of your grace, so to learn knowledge and the liberal sciences that by their help, we may attain to a fuller knowledge of you, whom to know is the height of blessedness; and by the example of your boyhood, may duly increase in age, wisdom and favour with God and man.

Desiderius Erasmus

103. To Honour Parents

O Lord God, whose will it is that, next to yourself, we should hold our parents in highest honour; it is not the least of our duties to beseech your goodness towards them. Preserve, I pray, my parents and home, in the love of your religion and in health of body, and mind, Grant that through me no sorrow may befall them; and finally, as they are kind to me, so may you be to them. O supreme Father of all.

Desiderius Erasmus

104. Love and Longing

Glorious God, give me grace to amend my life, and to have an eye to my end without begrudging death, which to those who die in you, good Lord, is the gate of a wealthy life.

And give me, good Lord, a humble, lowly, quiet, peaceable, patient, charitable, kind, tender and pitiful mind, in all my works and all my words and all my thoughts, to have a taste of your holy, blessed Spirit.

Give me, good Lord, a full faith, a firm hope, and a fervent charity, a love of you incomparably above the love of myself.

Give me, good Lord, a longing to be with you, not to avoid the calamities of this world, nor so much to attain the joys of heaven, as simply for love of you.

And give me, good Lord, your love and favour, which my love of you, however great it might be, could not deserve were it not for your great goodness.

These things, good Lord, that I pray for, give me your grace to labour for.

Thomas More

105. The Empty Vessel

Behold, Lord, an empty vessel that needs to be filled. My Lord, fill it. I am weak in the faith; strengthen me. I am cold in love; warm me and make me fervent, that my love may go out to my neighbour. I do not have a strong and firm faith; at times I doubt and am unable to trust you altogether. O Lord, help me. Strengthen my faith and trust in you. In you I have sealed the treasure of all I have. I am poor; you are rich and came to be merciful to the poor. I am a sinner; you are upright. With me, there is an abundance of sin; in you is the fullness of righteousness.

Therefore, I will remain with you, of whom I can receive, but to whom I may not give.

Martin Luther

106. When Persecuted

O God, give us patience when the wicked hurt us. O how impatient and angry we are when we think ourselves unjustly slandered, reviled and hurt! Christ suffers strokes upon his cheek, the innocent for the guilty; yet we may not abide one rough word for his sake. O Lord, grant us virtue and patience, power and strength, that we may take all adversity with good will, and with a gentle mind overcome it. And if necessity and your honour require us to speak, grant that we may do so with meekness and patience, that the truth and your glory may be defended, and our patience and steadfast continuance perceived.

Miles Coverdale

107. In Weariness

O Lord Jesus Christ, who art as the shadow of a great rock in a weary land, who behold your weak creatures weary of labour, weary of pleasure, weary of hope deferred, weary of self, in your abundant compassion, and fellow feeling with us, and unutterable tenderness, bring us, we pray you unto your rest.

Christina Rossetti

108. As Needle and Thread

O God I am Mustafah, the tailor, and I work at the shop of Muhammed Ali. The whole day long I sit and pull the needle and the thread through the cloth. O God, you are the needle and I am the thread. I am attached to you and I follow you. When the thread tries to slip away from the needle it become tangled up and must be cut so that it can be put back in the right place. O God, help me to follow you wherever you may lead me. For I am really only Mustafah, the tailor, and I work at the shop of Muhammed Ali on the great square.

Author Unknown

109. O Tree of Calvary

O Tree of Calvary, send your roots deep down into my heart. Gather together the soil of my heart, the sands of my fickleness, the stones of my stubbornness, the mud of my desires, bind them all together, O Tree of Calvary, interlace them with your strong roots, entwine them with the network of your love.

Chandran Devanesen

110. King's Son

Lord, isn't your creation wasteful? Fruits never equal the seedlings' abundance. Springs scatter water. The sun gives out enormous light. May your bounty teach me greatness of heart. May your magnificence stop me being mean. Seeing you a prodigal and open-handed giver, let me give unstintingly like a king's son, like God's own.

Helder Camara

111. God the Consoler

Help us, O Lord, to pray always, and not to lose heart; and in everything to give thanks, learning how to use abundance and how to suffer want, and in whatsoever state we are, therewith to be content, and referring all our cares and concerns unto thee, who know and love us all; that we may tread with cheerful confidence the path thou hast appointed for us, and may press on toward the goal; knowing that what is impossible for us by nature, is possible for us with God.

Crompton Jones

112. Unfading Light

O Lord, Let not the light that gleams within us in these moments of meditation and prayer fade and die out; but may your Word of comfort, of rebuke, of promise, which we have heard when our souls were hushed in your house speak to us with power when we return to the busy world.

Be you still our light and our strength in the labours, cares and temptations by which we are tried. Enable us in everything to show forth your truth and love; and thus may we live to your glory; who with the Father and the Holy Ghost, art worshipped One God, both now and ever, world without end.

James Ferguson

113. To Feel the Wonder

God, help me to feel wonder – in a leaf, in a ray of sun, in a snowfall. To laugh and cry with somebody else or all by myself. To let gaiety into my life and to show someone else how. To take a friend's hand for no special reason. To value the small things but to want to do great things. To believe what your Son said about becoming like little children. May I be at home in your kingdom.

Author Unknown

114. Imperfection and Feebleness

O God, our Leader and our Master and our Friend, forgive our imperfections and our little motives, take us and make us one with your great purpose, use us and do not reject us, make us all servants of your kingdom, weave our lives into your struggle to conquer and bring peace and union to the world.

We are small and feeble creatures, we are feeble in speech, feebler still in action; nevertheless let but your light shine upon us, and there is not one of us who cannot be lit by your fire and who cannot lose himself in your salvation. Take us into your purposes, O God; let your kingdom come into our hearts and into this world.

Herbert George Wells

115. Inspire and Strengthen

Inspire and strengthen us by your Holy Spirit, O Lord God, to seek your will and uphold your honour in all things; in the purity and joy of our homes, in the trust and fellowship of our common life, in daily service of the good; after the pattern and in the power of your Son, our Lord and Saviour, Jesus Christ.

Jeremy Taylor

116. Handing over Body for Medical Research

God, you offer your self through everything, the membranes of our lives, the intermingling of joy and sorrow, surprising, unfolding, enfolding. 'In the heights and in the depths be praise.'

God, you sustain us through wilderness times, Gethsemane times. You strengthen us through angels, angels in so many forms. 'In the heights and in the depths be praise.'

God, you mark our body with the sign of the cross, children of the Way of Jesus. You party with us. You hold us in your pain-bearing. You draw us into a future we could not have imagined. 'In the heights and in the depths be praise.'

God, help us with our letting go, our handing over, our entrusting, our yielding into the flow, divine life within all life. 'In the heights and in the depths be praise.'

God, you draw us into the bumpy road that leads into your deep love. You draw us into your heart, your silence, your compassion. 'In the heights and in the depths be praise.'

Donald Eadie

117. Direct and Guide our Steps

O Lord our God and God of our fathers! Mercifully direct and guide our steps to our destination and let us arrive there in health, joy and peace! Keep us from snares and dangers and protect us from any enemies that we might meet along the way. Bless and protect our journey! Let us win favour in your eyes and in the sight of those around us. Blessed are you, O Lord, who hear and grant our prayers!

Jewish

118. Deliver Us

O Lord, we beseech you to deliver us from the fear of the unknown future, from fear of failure, from fear of poverty, from fear of sickness and pain, from fear of age, and from fear of death. Help us, O Father, by your grace and love to fear you only. Fill our hearts with cheerful courage and loving trust in you; through our Lord and Master Jesus Christ.

Akanu Ibiam

119. Protect from Despair

O Holy Spirit, give me faith that will protect me from despair, from passions and from vice, give me such love for God as will blot out all hatred and bitterness, give me hope that deliver me from fear and faintheartedness.

Dietrich Bonhoeffer

120. Free My Soul

Set free, O Lord, my soul from all restlessness and anxiety; give me that peace and power which flow from you; keep in all perplexities and distresses, in all fears and faithlessness; that so upheld by your power and stayed on the rock of your faithfulness, I may through storm and stress remain in you, through Christ Jesus our Lord.

New Every Morning

121. Candle of the Spirit

Give me a candle of the Spirit, O God, as I go down into the deeps of my being. Show me the hidden things, the creatures of my dreams, the storehouse of forgotten memories and hurts. Take me down to the spring of my life and tell me my nature and my name. Give me freedom to grow, so that I may become that self, the seed of which you planted in me at my making. Out of the deeps I cry to you, O God.

George Appleton

122. Set at Rest

O Spirit of God, set at rest the crowded, hurrying conscious thoughts within our minds and hearts. Let the peace and quiet of your presence take possession of us. Help us to relax, to rest, to become open and receptive to you. You know our inmost spirits, the hidden unconscious life within us, the forgotten memories of hurts and fears, the frustrated desires, the unresolved tensions and dilemmas. Cleanse and sweeten the springs of our being that freedom, life and love may flow into both our conscious and hidden life. Lord, we lie open before you, waiting for your healing, your peace and your word.

George Appleton

123. Calm the Waves

O Lord, calm the waves of this heart; calm its tempest! Calm yourself, O my soul, so that the divine can act in you! Calm yourself, O my soul, so that God is able to repose in you, so that his peace may cover you! Yes, Father in heaven, often have we found that the world cannot give us peace. O but make us feel that you are able to give peace; let us know the truth of your promise; the whole world may not be able to take away your peace.

Søren Kierkegaard

124. Perfect Way

O Lord, whose way is perfect, help us, we pray, always to trust in your goodness, that walking with you and following you in all simplicity, we may possess quiet and contented minds and may cast all our care on you, who care for us. Grant this, O Lord, for your dear Son's sake, Jesus Christ.

Christina Rossetti

125. Praising and Participating

O God, we want to praise and thank you for giving us so much to enjoy in your world. Open our eyes to see all the beauty around us, to appreciate your greatness in giving us the different seasons, each fulfilling our needs. And if we do not understand why nature is sometimes cruel and harsh and why people suffer from earthquakes and other disasters in your world, help us to trust where we cannot see, knowing that you love us all. Help us to do what we can to relieve the sufferings and hardships caused by those disasters and those caused by human errors. Make us willing and eager to share the many good things you have provided for the benefit of all.

Nancy Martin

126. Courage to Stand Up

Give us courage, O Lord to stand up and be counted, to stand up for those who cannot stand up for themselves, to stand up for ourselves when it is needful for us to do so. Let us fear nothing more than we fear you. Let us love nothing more than we love you, for thus we shall fear nothing also. Let us have no other God before you, whether nation or party or state or church. Let us seek no other peace but the peace which is yours, and make us its instruments, opening our eyes and ears and our hearts, so that we should know always what work of peace we may do for you.

Alan Paton

127. Courage and Obedience

O God, our Father, the fountain of love, power and justice, the God who cares, particularly for the least, the most suffering and the poorest among us. O God, Lord of creation grant us today your guidance and wisdom so that we may see the human predicament for what it is. Give us courage and obedience so that we may follow you completely. Help us, Lord, to bear witness to the cross of your Son, our Lord Jesus Christ, who alone is the reason for hope, and in whose name we pray.

Koson Srisand

128. Understanding Better Each Day

God of all creation, yours is the majesty, the power and the glory. Unbelievable is your gracious compassion and boundless love for all you have made. May I understand you better as each day unfolds and in understanding you, better understand myself. Nurture me in your ways, enlighten me through your Spirit, recreate me after the pattern and example of your Son. Then, today and every day, may I, in some small way, embody your presence in my thoughts, words and deeds.

Ward Jones

129. Still Liberate Us

Lord, liberate us from a risk-free life where we never try anything because it might fail, never invest in anything because it might be lost. Arrest us when we are about to bury our talents in the ground and escort us to the place of faith-speculation where miracles become possible. Give us the courage to die with you so that we may also live with you, now and for ever.

Peter Hancock

130. Education

Ever-living and enabling God, thank you for teaching your ways through preachers, teachers, tutors, books, papers, personal conversations and your inspiration within us. As you taught your people on their long journey in the wilderness and reminded us by your Son Jesus, may we relearn the meaning of your supreme lesson that humans shall not live by bread alone but by every word that comes from your mouth. We pray for all who are engaged in the vocation of education at different levels and in different institutions. May all kinds of our education lead us to enlightenment and exploration into the hidden source of our life and all gifts.

Israel Selvanayagam

131. Race of Life

Lord of the race, help me to fix my eyes on you for it is to you I travel. Keep me from fainting or from being side-tracked by my own inclinations. May I be strong to resist temptation. Let me draw others to you, that together we may journey in Christian fellowship and arrive to hear your greeting: "Well done, for you have not strayed from the path that leads to eternal life. Enter with joy for your race has been won."

Maureen Tullett

132. For the Highest Purpose

Energising God, when I falter, lift me up to reach new heights. Breath of Life, when life's knocks take my breath away, inspire me. Faithful Saviour, may I pass on the baton of faith and in all things may I strive to give my utmost for your highest purpose, by the grace of Christ who, for the finishing of the race, endured the cross, gave his all, and rose again.

Keith Beckingham

133. Delightful Journey

God you are always alongside us. When our plans are knocked off course, help us to depend on your leading. When the goal seems to be unattainable, help us to delight in the journey. When we lack the energy to keep going, teach us to depend on your grace. We ask these things through him who set his face towards Jerusalem, the way to the cross and the empty tomb.

John Hellyer

134. Encourage for a New Start

We thank you God that you know each of us, not by number, but by name. As we journey with you, may that intimate knowledge inspire us, not to be complacent in our discipleship, but to follow more perfectly the way of Christ. When we are downhearted and feel that we have let you down, give us the encouragement to make a fresh start, over and over again, never giving up, but determine to stay the course until we meet you face to face.

Anne Brown

135. Revive, Restore, Renew

Faithful God: when we faint, revive us; when we falter, restore us; when we fail, renew us; when we fall, raise us up. In the strength of the Spirit and with the courage Christ.

Paul Martin

136. Help Me Appropriately

Lord, when I feel weak and uncertain, reassure me that I am held in your love; when I feel confident and strong, challenge me by your cross and tomb; when I lack hope, open my eyes to your life at the heart of all life; that, today and every day, I might walk my life's journey with you, my Saviour, Lord and friend.

Jim Booth

137. Presence in Our Journey

Creator God, I love to run with you. May I persevere on the uphill slopes and endure the difficult paths in the strength of Jesus. Then, with the wind of your Spirit behind me, I can praise you on the downward road and we can enjoy the spectacular views together.

Josette Crane

138. Sustain Our Discipleship

God, keep us faithful and persistent in the disciplines of discipleship that we may be ready for new tasks when you call us to our marks. Settle and keep us steady when we are nervous with anticipation at the challenges you set before us. Then, wherever we go and whatever happens, we may keep our eyes on Jesus who sets the pace and on whose grace we depend from start to finish.

Peter Sulston

139. Border Crossings

God of surprises, in Jesus you were often found on the borderlands: leading people beyond the frontiers of the familiar to discover new truth. Equip us with the wisdom and imagination to negotiate those boundaries that isolate individuals and divide communities, so that even chasms of difference may become channels of your transforming grace.

Stuart Jordan

140. Breath Upon Us

Come from the four winds, O Lord, and in your holiness breathe upon us with your Spirit, that we may be gathered into your kingdom; for yours is the glory and the power throughout all ages, world without end.

The Didache

141. City Life

God, who are with us in the midst of traffic chaos and noisy commerce, remind us to stop and listen to the sounds of longing hearts. In the dark loneliness of crowded living, remind us to look for glimpses of your light. When tempted to see only struggle and bad news, remind us that the city is full of stories of hope and human flourishing. Help us to be the human agents of your divine grace.

Michaela Youngson

142. Loving Sacrifice

Holy God, too great to be trifled with and too wise to be deceived by insincerity; compose our thoughts as we enter your presence, order our minds as we bring our petitions, and grant us grace to offer you the loving sacrifice of hearts both steadfast and obedient; through Jesus Christ our Lord.

Susanna Wesley

143. Hope of Our Journey

Gracious God, you are the hope of our journey and the light on our way. Accompany us as we step forward in faith. Be close to us as we seek to witness and serve. When we flag, give us new energy; when we are afraid, fresh courage; when we feel overwhelmed, a sense of your enduring faithfulness; and let our joy and delight in the gift of your love shine from us to inspire hope in others. For Jesus' sake.

Roger Walton

144. To Grow in Grace and Holiness

Gracious God, you call us on a journey to grow in grace and holiness. As we travel on that journey give us an assurance of your loving presence, that filled with your Spirit, we may work with you, and our fellow pilgrims, in the transformation of our churches and our communities, so that they become signs of your kingdom of justice and joy.

Ian Howarth

145. To Walk Steadily

Gracious God, when the way is easy, may we walk it joyfully. When the way is hard, may we walk it faithfully. And when the way seems unclear, may we trust the one who walks alongside us, Jesus, our companion and friend.

Stephen Wigley

146. To Travel with Confidence

Generous God, as your pilgrim on the journey of faith, help me to face each day confidently. When I feel overwhelmed, help me to fix my attention on your cross. When I find myself in deep darkness, help me to trust in your resurrection power. When my heart feels cold, fill it with your warmth and delight. Generous God, let your Spirit fill my life, to bring encouragement and hope. Enable me to honour you throughout this day and to give proper attention to your love and grace, as I serve you in and through other people.

Richard Teal

147. Into Depths and Fullness

When the beauty and the fragility of life stop us in our tracks, when the cruelty and injustices of life confront us with deep questions, when our walking and living are energised and purposeful, when our feet falter and our hearts are hesitant, when our souls are attuned in hope to singing and dancing, when our spirits are crushed and we feel alone in our despair, let us turn to you, ever-present and constant companion. Whatever this day's journey requires of us, remind us of earthly companions and colleagues, mentors and loved ones, seen and unseen, who journey with us, pilgrims on a shared journey into your depths and fullness, O God, and accept our profound wonder and thanks.

Liz Smith

148. Race in the Royal Road

Let us run the race that is set before us in the royal road of love. Let us keep an even pace rooted in the faith of the saints. Let us be grounded in true catholic love until we are consumed by the fire of your grace for ever.

John Wesley

149. To Face Unpopularity

Lord and King, we pray you for courage to face unpopularity for the sake of truth; for courage to declare boldly our convictions, though they make us despised; for courage to break with evil custom and evil opinions. Give us strong hearts that will not fear what any human may do to us. Give us, O Lord, the spirit of boldness, that being delivered from all fear of our fellows, we may be strong in you, and very courageous; through Jesus Christ our Lord.

J. S. Hoyland

150. To Leave Behind

God of green and pleasant places and of dark uncomfortable situations, you call your people to be in every part of your creation. Give us courage and wisdom to leave behind some of those that are easy to cherish, and to walk in love where we are needed most, with Jesus Christ.

Alan Anderson

151. With Prayer and Faith

God, Lord of History, many barriers still remain before us. Casting aside our arrogance, let us resolve all things by wisdom and courage, prayer and faith. So, that our people may be tested no longer; so that we may no longer be divided ... until at last God's Kingdom comes. In the name of Jesus Christ we pray.

National Council of Churches in Korea

152. Settlement and Peace

O Saviour Christ, Light of the world and Prince of Peace; give to those who pray a longing for your Kingdom of justice and love. Grant to those who lead the nations the true welfare of their people, and to those at war the wisdom of settlement and peace. Take from our hearts all greed, envy and pride and equip your Church throughout the world with the gift of prophetic speech and the ministry of true reconciliation; all this we ask for your own name's sake.

Norman Wallwork

153. Holding On

O Blessed Jesus, immortal and victorious, by the sorrow you suffered when all the powers of your heart failed you, have mercy on us and help us in our days of darkness and in our hours of weakness, that we do not lose hold of you either in this life, or in the life of the world to come. This we ask for your own name's sake.

St. Bridget of Sweden

154. Step by Step

Dear Lord, when your way is hard to find, guide my next step; when your truth is hard to know, inform my next decision; when life is hard to bear, help me through this day.

Thomas McKnight

XIV. Virtues and Values

1. Depth of Insight

We pray, our loving God, that our love may abound more and more in knowledge and depth of insight, so that we may be able to discern what is best and may be pure and blameless until the day of Christ, filled with the fruit of righteousness that comes through Jesus Christ – to your glory and praise.

Based on Paul's Prayer (Philippians 1:9-11)

2. Love Freedom of All

God of love, we know that all is not right in your world. We concentrate on what is broken, and not on how it might be mended. We criticise often and praise little; we see the darkness and not the glimmers of light. We are jealous of our own freedoms, and trample on the freedom of others. We look to ourselves and not to you. Forgive us and turn us around, Lord, that we might see possibilities: hope, promise, grace, healing and love. In the name of Jesus.

Connie Jeffery

3. One Hope in Calling

God of all grace, good beyond all that is good, fair beyond all that is fair and loving beyond all that is loving; grant us to be of one mind in our faith, of one hope in our calling and of one heart in our loving; through Christ our Lord.

Dionysius of Alexandria

4. Truthful Living

Almighty God, you have sent the Spirit of truth to us to guide us into all truth: so rule our lives by your power that we may be truthful in thought, word and deed. Keep us, most merciful Saviour, with your gracious protection, that no fear or hope may ever make us false in act or speech; cast out from us whatever loves or makes a lie, and bring us all into the perfect freedom of your truth; through Jesus Christ our Lord.

Brooke Foss Westcott

5. Learn to Listen

That we may be ready to learn from the wisdom of the past and not least from the Scriptures; that we may be ready in stillness and quietness to wait for and listen to the inner voice; that we may have all the time and the patience we shall need to listen and pay heed to what others would say to us; Lord, grant us hearts with skill to listen.

Edmund Banyard

6. Poor in Spirit

Make us poor in spirit, God, unselfish and ready to receive you. Make us sincere and pure in heart so that we may recognise the signs of your presence. Let us hunger for peace and thirst for justice and righteousness. Make us gentle and forgiving. And be yourself merciful to us. Teach us to pardon each other and give us the strength to bear the suffering of others.

Huub Oosterhuis

7. Well-grounded Hope

O Lord, who are the hope of all the ends of the earth, let me never be destitute of a well-grounded hope, nor yet possessed with a vain presumption: suffer me not to think you will either be reconciled to my sins or reject my repentance; but give me, I beseech you, such a hope as may be answerable to the only ground of hope, your promises, and such as may both encourage and enable me to purify myself from all filthiness, both of flesh and spirit; that so, it may indeed become to me an anchor of the soul both sure and steadfast.

The Whole Duty of Man

8. Childlike and Lowly

O Lord, who in every age reveal yourself to the childlike and lowly in heart, and from every race write names in your book of life: Give us the simplicity and faith of your saints, that loving you above all things, we may be what you would have us be, and do what you would have us do. So, may we be numbered with your saints in glory everlasting; through Jesus Christ our Lord.

George Appleton

9. Unselfish Kindness

Pour into our hearts the spirit of unselfishness, so that, when our cup overflows, we may seek to share our happiness with our brethren. O God of love, who makes your sun to rise on the evil and on the good, and send rain on the just and the unjust, grant that we may become more and more your true children, by receiving into our souls more of your own spirit of ungrudging and un-wearying kindness; which we ask in the name of Jesus Christ.

John Hunter

10. Never Be Self-sufficient

Suffer me never to think that I have knowledge enough to need no teaching, wisdom enough to need no correction, talents enough to need no grace, goodness enough to need no progress, humility enough to need no repentance, devotion enough to need no quickening, strength sufficient without your Spirit; lest, standing still, I fall back for ever more.

Eric Milner-White

11. Spirit of Wisdom

O God, by whom the meek are guided in judgement, and light rises up in darkness for the godly; give us, in all our doubts and uncertainties the grace to ask what you would have us to do; that the spirit of wisdom may save us from all false choices, and that in your light we may see light and in your straight path may not stumble: through Jesus Christ our Lord.

William Bright

12. Service to Reveal Sacrifice

Loving God, may our service reveal your sacrifice, may our discipleship confirm your dependability, may our kindness build your kingdom, may our presence bring your peace, may our words express your wisdom, may our living show your loving, may our giving reflect your generosity, may our caring mirror your compassion, may our journeying be with Jesus, our seeking be through the Spirit and may our prayers be said confidently to you, our patient and providing, and ever-present parent.

Paul Martin

13. Remind us of Truth

All-embracing One, ease the paranoia from our hearts, grown cold in a time of fear. Remind us of the truth that even those who terrify us – eyes harsh and vengeful – are created and loved by you. Show us how to be reconciled and so to live in peace.

Jim Cotter

14. Open to Love

Mysterious God, choosing the small, the unnoticed, the obscure, to renew the ways of your covenant when your followers wander and fail you, strive yet with our intractable clay, open us to the love you revealed to us in Yeshua, emptied of power, untouched by delusion, dying unrecognised, yet for those with eyes to see the decisive clue to the mystery of your being.

Jim Cotter

15. Strengthen the Weak

Look upon your servants, O Lord, weak in faith but praying for your strength; cold in heart, but seeking the fire of love; assailed by doubt, but awaiting assurance; abounding in sin, yet longing for righteousness; now and for ever.

Martin Luther

16. To Serve as You Deserve

Teach us, good Lord, to serve you as you deserve; to give and not to grudge the cost; to fight and not to heed the wounds; to toil and not to seek for rest; to labour and not to seek for any reward, save that of knowing that we do your will; through Christ our Lord.

Ignatius Loyola

17. Whole Body at Service

Strengthen for service, Lord, the hands that have taken holy things; may the ears which have heard your word be deaf to clamour and dispute; may the tongues which have sung your praise be free from deceit; may the eyes which have seen the tokens of your love shine with light of hope; and may the bodies which have been fed with your body be refreshed with the fulness of your life; glory to you for ever.

Malabar Liturgy

18. Retrain and Regulate

Holy and just God, receive the feelings of our outraged and wounded hearts. Console our grief, melt our fear, lift the burden of our shame. Restrain our desire for revenge, and channel the energies of our anger in the service of justice and truth.

Jim Cotter

19. To Rejoice in Work

Lord, renew our spirits and draw our hearts unto yourself, that our work may not be to us a burden, but a delight. Oh, let us not serve you with the spirit of bondage as slaves, but with the cheerfulness and gladness of children, delighting ourselves in you, and rejoicing in your work.

Benjamin Jenks

20. From Self-Centredness to Sacrifice

O Lord of grace, lead us and guide us from a life of self-centredness and satisfaction for what we are and what we do to a life of dependence on you. Inspire our hearts that we rise beyond the daily trifles of our existence and join with you in love and concern for the whole creation, that we may always remind ourselves that we are the disciples of one who did not help himself but was a man for others. Grant that we may, through our life and example, work for a world where God is praised and we all live like salt and leaven in the midst of this mass of humanity and in a bond of charity. O God the Holy Spirit, inspire, hallow and guide us in this vocation of wholeness and healing, through Jesus Christ our Lord.

Church of Bangladesh

21. Seeking the Great

Give me, O Lord, a steadfast heart which no unworthy affection may drag downwards. Give me an unconquered heart which no tribulation can wear out. Give me an upright heart which no unworthy purpose may tempt aside. Bestow upon me also, O Lord my God, understanding to know you, diligence to seek you, wisdom to find you and a faithfulness that may finally embrace you; through Jesus Christ our Lord.

Thomas Aquinas

22. Fruitful Life

We kindly ask our gracious God to fill us with the knowledge of your will through all spiritual wisdom and understanding. And we pray this in order that we may live a life worthy of the Lord Jesus and may please him in every way: bearing fruit in every good work, growing in the knowledge of God, being strengthened with all power according to your glorious might so that we may have great endurance and patience.

Based on Paul's Prayer (Colossians 1:9-11)

23. Light for Others

Lord, we thank you for the transformation of a shrivelled seed into food or flower, the movement of night to day and your eternal love seen in Jesus. May we be transformed for fruitfulness, become light for others and know that your love is broader, higher, wider and deeper than we will ever comprehend.

Graham Thompson

24. Hospitality

As the poor widow welcomed Elijah, let us be open tonight to the richness and miracle in meeting. As Abraham and Sarah welcomed passing strangers, let us entertain the possibility of angels in disguise. Let our eyes be open, that we may recognize in our neighbour the divine presence of Christ.

Iona Community

25. Thankful Heart

O Lord, give me a heart that I may pour it out in thanksgiving, give me life that I may spend it in working for the salvation of the world; Lord, give me understanding that I stray not from the path. Give me light to avoid pitfalls; give me eyes which see nothing but your glory; give me a mind that finds delight in your service.

Jogendra Singh

26. Hunger and Thirst for Peace

Vulnerable God, you challenge the powers that rule this world through the needy, the compassionate, and those who are filled with longing. Make us hunger and thirst to see right to prevail and single-minded in seeking peace; that we may see your face and be satisfied in you, through Jesus Christ.

Janet Morley

27. Candle for Peace

We light this candle for peace, Lord. May its light scatter the darkness; may its flame be a symbol of hope; may its burning be a sign of faith joining with many other lights for peace. We light this candle for peace. May our lives be an expression of peace making; may we seek to be lights in a dark world, pointing to you, Jesus, the Prince of Peace, and following you in the way of peace. Let the candle burn as a sign for peace offered to you.

John Johansen-Berg

28. Make the Door Wide

Lord God, make the door of my house wide enough to receive all who need love and fellowship, and narrow enough to shut out all envy, pride and hate. May its threshold be smooth enough to put no stumbling block in the way of your lost or little ones; and may it be rugged enough to foil the tempter's power. May the entrance to my home be for some the gateway to your eternal Kingdom, through Christ our Lord.

Thomas Ken

29. The Art of Love

All loving and all-embracing God, our hearts overflow with gratitude when we think and feel of your love that was manifest in Jesus Christ and poured into our hearts by the Holy Spirit. Let our response be to be spontaneous, praying fervently, reading your words passionately and willingly welcoming strangers. Give us a charismatic smile, courteous words and sacrificial action when we approach others with your love in our hearts. Help us to overcome the temptation of being engaged in pious acts to win your favour and teach us to live in solidarity with you and with needy and suffering others. Let us and our churches thus reflect your love in a love-hungry world, now and always.

Israel Selvanayagam

30. In the Service of Others

O God, the giver of all good gifts, we thank you for all the many blessings which we have. Give us always contended minds, cheerful hearts, and ready wills, so that we may spend and be spent in the service of others, after the example of him who gave his life a ransom for many, our Lord and Master, Jesus Christ.

David Sellick

31. Truly Educated

Almighty Lord, may we be so truly educated that we not merely do the right things, but enjoy the right things; not merely prove industrious, but love industry; not merely learn, but love knowledge; not merely are pure, but love purity.

John Ruskin

32. Power to be Gentle

Lord, for the power to be gentle, for the strength to forgive, for the patience to understand, for the endurance that holds on to what is right, for the good that overcomes evil, for the vision of a new world arising from the ruins of the old, we give thanks and pray.

Donald Eadie

33. Good Manners

God of all wisdom and all goodness, preserve in us good manners. Let us not be discourteous, not mock at others, not quarrel, not despise the poor, nor use harsh words indiscriminately, nor be vindictive, nor injure others, nor praise ourselves. But may we be polite and sweet in speech, grateful for kindnesses, living in harmony with others, doing not unto others what we would not think acceptable if done to us.

Adapted from Persian Book of Advice

34. To Bathe in the Sea of Grace

Lord, keep me from wanting always to outstrip others in my conceit, crushing those in my way. Wipe from my face the look of dark, dominating anger. Rather, Lord, grant that I may live my days calmly and fully, as the sea slowly covers the whole show. Make me humble like the sea as, silently and gently, it spreads out, unnoticed. May I wait for my brothers and sisters and match my pace to theirs, that I may move upward with them. Grant me the triumphant perseverance of the waters. May each of my retreats turn into an advance. Give my face the light of clear waters. Give my soul the whiteness of foam. Illumine my life that it may sing like sunbeams on the surface of the sea. But above all, Lord, may I not keep this light for myself, and may all those who come near me return home eager to bathe in your eternal grace.

Michel Quoist

35. Resentment

O God, it is better to speak frankly about things than bottle them up. I can't help wondering why this should have happened to me. I can't help feeling bitter and resentful. I know that I shouldn't feel that way, and I don't really want to feel that way. I can't help feeling angry when people who have never known any trouble come and tell me that it is all for the best. Whatever happens, keep me from querulous self-pity. At least teach me that I have got to accept things, whether I like it or not, and bring me in the end to that faith which can accept even what it cannot understand.

William Barclay

36. Courage to Bear Discomforts

Give me, O God, all the courage I need in this place. Give me courage to bear discomfort without grumbling, and pain without complaint. Give me courage to bear uncertainty with hope, and long delays with patience. Give me courage to keep on trusting when I cannot understand, and help me always to remember that, in this as in everything, it is the one who sticks it out gallantly to the end who will be saved.

William Barclay

37. Physician's Attitude

O God, when people come to me, help me always to ease the pain and to strengthen the weakness of their bodies, and to calm the anxieties of their minds. Help me never to think of them as cases, but always as persons. Help me to be patient, when I need to be patient, and to be stern, when I need to be stern. Help me to remember that when I bring health to the sick and the suffering, the healing work of Jesus is being continued through me, and that I am helping you to defeat the world's disease and pain. This I ask for your love's sake.

William Barclay

38. A Nurse's Behaviour

O God, help me to be a good nurse. Make me quick and eager in learning, and wise and efficient in action. Give me patience with people who are irritating and demanding and annoying. Give me firmness with people who are foolish and stubborn, and disobedient and uncooperative. Give me sympathy with people who are nervous and anxious and frightened. Help me to be kind when I need to be kind, and severe when I need to be severe. Help me always to remember that, when I share in the work of healing, I share in the work of Jesus, who healed all those who had need of healing. This I ask for your love's sake.

William Barclay

39. Enlighten, Purify

Grant, O Lord, even to me, your unworthy servant, your salvation. Enlighten my mind with the light of the understanding of your holy gospel, my soul with the love of your cross, my heart with the purity of your word, my body with your passionless passion. Preserve my thought in your humility, and rouse me at the fit time to glorify you. For you are glorified above all, with your eternal Father and the most Holy Spirit for evermore.

St. Ignatius of Antioch (William Barclay)

40. Contentment

O God, our Father, save us from these thoughts and feelings which only succeed in making life wretched and unhappy for ourselves and for others.

Save us from foolish discontent and help us at all times to do the best we can with the resources we have. Save us from the envy which forgets to count its own blessings, because it thinks so much of those of others every gift and every success. Save us from vain regrets about things which cannot be altered; and give us grace to accept this situation in which we are, and there to serve You with our whole heart. Save us from the bitterness which poisons life for ourselves and for others.

So grant that, cleansed from self and cleansed from sin, our lives may bring joy to others and contentment to ourselves; through Jesus Christ our Lord.

William Barclay

41. Where Needed Most

God of green and pleasant places and of dark uncomfortable situations, you call your people to be in every part of your creation. Give us courage and wisdom to leave behind some of those beings that are easy to cherish, and to walk in love where we are needed most, with Jesus Christ.

Alan Anderson

42. Unending Love

Generous God, you never cease to pour out your love on all people in spite of what we do in our selfishness and narrowness. Strengthen us that we may be generous in our love; that we may never fail to welcome others, even if their standards are different from our own; that we may always respond to the needs of others, though it may be costly to ourselves; and that we may have confidence that our loving will help to change the world; through Jesus Christ whose death on a cross marks the victor of love.

Graham Carter

43. Channels of Hope, Peace, Joy

Lord, our light in darkness, our hope in despair, our peace in struggle, our joy in sorrow, our way when we are lost, may your light shine in the very darkest places of our hearts and of the world, may your hope touch the hearts of those in despair. May your peace reach individuals and countries torn by war, may your joy be known to those who mourn, may those who are lost know you the Way and may we be channels of your light, your hope, your peace, your joy. And lead others in the Way of your love.

Margaret James

44. Balance

Deliver us, O God, from politics without principles, from wealth without work, from pleasure without conscience, from knowledge without character, from commerce without morality, from worship without sacrifice and from science without humanity.

M. K. Gandhi

45. Wisdom and Courage

Thank you for the wisdom you have endowed in me. Let it not drift to be craftiness that I may exploit the innocent. Thank you for the courage you have put in me but let it not be exercised to exploit the weak. Give me more and more your graciousness and gentleness, my good Lord, that those around me may understand true wisdom and courage.

Unknown

46. True Reconciliation

O Saviour Christ, Light of the world and Prince of Peace; give to those who pray a longing for your Kingdom of justice and love. Grant to those who lead the nations the true welfare of their people, and to those at war the wisdom of settlement and peace. Take from our hearts all greed, envy and pride, and equip your Church throughout the world with the gift of prophetic speech and the ministry of true reconciliation; and this we ask for your own name's sake.

Norman Wallwork

47. Justice and Compassion

O loving Lord, our country needs justice for our security and mercy for our nurture. Thank you that in yourself you link justice with mercy and combine power with love. We long for a world that is both just and compassionate. We look for a world where authority and love are inextricably joined. Challenge your Church to reach beyond the barriers that we have created. Change your Church so that we look to the interests of others rather than our own. Cleanse your Church with the Spirit of holiness and renew us with Calvary love. Focus us on Kingdom values of righteousness, peace and joy. And by the grace of Christ, in the power of the Holy Spirit, we will ever live for your glory.

Ken Todd

48. Instruments of Service

God of peace and serenity, bid the raging seas of the world's conflicts to be still. Transform all institutions of pride and domination into instruments of service for the poor and oppressed. Empower your Church to make sense of your presence as salt and light for the world, for, in the end, you are God, and in Christ you are our peace.

Akuila Yabaki

49. Open and Show

O Lord, open my eyes that I may see the need of others, open my ears that I may hear their cries, open my heart so that they need not be without succor. Let me not be afraid to defend the weak because of the anger of the strong, not afraid to defend the poor because of the anger of the rich. Show me where love and hope and faith are needed and use me to bring them to these places. Open my eyes and ears that I may, this coming day, be able to do some work of peace for you.

Alan Paton

50. Cooperative Fight

Eternal God, as the rainbow spans the heavens when the clouds are dark, so our strifes and enmities stand under the judgment of your over-arching love and righteousness. We thank you for those who in former times were our enemies and are now our friends, and for the concern for peace which grows in the hearts and minds of ordinary people the world over. Use that concern to create the structures of peace and a new atmosphere of cooperation. Help us to identify the common enemies of all the nations and to work together for the eradication of poverty, hunger and disease. Give us the will to build defences against these instead of against each other, for the sake of Jesus Christ our Saviour.

Kenneth G. Greet

51. Committing to Fullness

We commit ourselves to deepen our inner lives so that we will not fear the future. We commit ourselves to renounce private forms of faith, to live in communities of support and affirmation. We commit ourselves to the way of non-violence, cherishing forgiveness and reconciliation, being prepared to suffer for the Kingdom. We commit ourselves to develop solidarity with our sisters and brothers in every land who share with us the dream of *shalom*. We commit ourselves to light candles in the dark, to speak when all around are silent, and to live the gospel in simplicity. We commit ourselves to celebrate the promise of peace, to nurture the spirit of festivity and to grow in joy and expectation. Alleluia!

Christian Conference of Asia

52. Common Good

O God, Creator of all humankind, look with mercy upon us and, in your great goodness, give us the peace, justice and the unity for which we long. Restrain those who plan evil and encourage those who work for the common good. Protect those who live in danger, and those whose duty exposes them to harm. Uphold those who suffer and strengthen those who are afraid. Temper, O Lord, our lifestyles with simplicity, courage, humility and the love of the truth.

Lord Jesus Christ, our Brother on our way, give peace to all those who disagree with us. Take from us our fear of death and make us ready to walk beside you and to love all people. We hope for your Kingdom as we hope for peace.

Geetha de Chikera

53. Love, Truth, Life

O God of light and life and love, by your Spirit help us to live the truth; your light is stronger than darkness. Your life means more than death, your love can overcome all things. May the light of the Christ shine in us and through us, may the life of Christ free us for proper living, may the love of Christ control us; We ask this for your glory, O God of life and light and love.

Kenneth Hext

54. To Be Good

God of all goodness, make us good without our feeling of it. Help us to do good spontaneously but having no claim for us. Let our good deeds bring glory to your name. When we engage in the fight between good and evil, give us perseverance and hope that good will win in the end. Even if we are not able to see that in our lifetime, help us to be content with the realization that it will glorify you as the source of all goodness. In the good name of Jesus we pray.

Cornelius Selvamony

55. The Grace of Contentment

My Father, teach me the grace of contentment, teach me to count my blessings: I have my daily bread, while many starve; I have clothes to wear, where many have no second shirt; I have a well-built body, and enjoy good health, but there are so many who are sick, blind, dumb, or crippled or mentally challenged; I have intelligence, the opportunity and ability to learn, and to work to earn a living; I have parents and loved ones, a house to call my home, and a school to go to. There must be many who would give anything to change places with me. Holy Father, let my gratitude and contentment find expression in helping those who lack these blessings.

Vimala Arungadan

56. To Seek Equal Opportunities

Father, when we see others with possessions we do not and cannot have, let us not covet them. When others have natural gifts we lack, let us not be jealous. Instead let us cultivate and improve that which you have blessed us with, and shine in that. May all your people in this world have equal opportunities to realize their potential and improve their skills. When we are provoked to anger and lose our temper, teach us tolerance and great patience, and help us control our tongue and our actions. Teach us to spend our anger in righteous causes, in fighting for justice, and to champion the wronged. So guide, control and direct us, in your Kingdom, O Lord.

Vimala Arangadan

57. Deliver Me from Wrong Thoughts

From all my lame defeats and Oh! much more; from all the victories that I seemed to score; from cleverness shot forth on your behalf, at which, while angels weep, the audience laugh; from all my proofs of your divinity, you, who would give no sign, deliver me. Thoughts are but coins. Let me not trust instead of you, their thin-worn image of their head. From all my thoughts, even from my thoughts of you, O you fair silence, fall, and set me free. Lord of the narrow gate and needle's eye, take from me all my trumpery, lest I die.

C. S. Lewis

58. Multiply the Virtues

Lord, make my mind kindly inclined to those who are afflicted; make me melt away in tears of compassion; make my mind spotless and pure; make me crave only for the diligent performance of duties, and make me content in all circumstances of life. Let not griefs dim the brightness of the joy of the life nor cast their shadows on the lives of my fellow beings, my parents, my brothers and sisters and myself. Let not anger, envy, avarice, lust or laziness take possession of my mind. Whether I am privileged to live in a mansion, or destined to dwell in a hut, keep my mind away from the thought of unlawful gain. And fill my mind with the radiance of your presence.

With every passing moment a portion of my life ebbs away. But, I have yet to do a lot of good to lots of people in this world. So, help me discharge all my duties with diligence and discipline. Let not even an iota of error creep into the performance of my actions. Let me be a source of happiness and be an instrument of harmony in my house, in my country and in the whole world.

And let me multiply the virtues in this world several thousand-fold. Bring me in touch with the seekers after truth; and sustain me in faith in you. O Lord, Ruler of the World, and the hearts of the devotees, this is my behest; grant me this request.

S. K. Ramachandran Nair

59. Pure and Humble

Holy God, give us a pure heart that we may see you, a humble heart that we may hear you, a heart of love that we may serve you, a heart of faith that we may love you.

Dag Hammarskjöld

60. Strength to Surrender

This is my prayer to you, my Lord-strike, strike at the root of penury in my heart. Give me the strength lightly to bear my joys and sorrows. Give me the strength never to disown the poor or bend my knees before insolent might. Give me the strength to raise my mind high above daily trifles. And give me the strength to surrender my strength to thy will with love.

Rabindranath Tagore

61. Let Me Be ...

Lord, let me be true in every word, let me be earnest in every deed, let me be pure in heart, even when it is hard. Let my sincere prayers be heard, let me be led along life`s road, let me not from virtues be strayed, let me not by temptations swayed, let my life in humility at your feet be laid. Come to me Lord, as constant guide and aid.

Ramachandran Nair

62. A Vehicle of Hope and Faith

Almighty God! Give me strength to stand for the truth, to do the right according to my light, to be just and generous in all my dealings with my fellow men. Let not an angry or unkind word, or an unsympathetic look, pass from me which might hurt the feelings of others in any way. Keep me free from envy and hatred, and fill my mind and heart with love and good will. Make me, O Lord, a vehicle of hope and faith, scattering sunshine and happiness before all those with whom I come into contact in my passage through life.

K. P. Kesava Menon and S. K. Ramachandran Nair

63. The Life of Faith

(Let me affirm, O Lord that) Goodness is stronger than evil: love is stronger than hate: light is stronger than darkness; life is stronger than death; victory is ours through him who loves us.

Desmond Tutu

64. At the Beginning of a New School Week

Today is Monday, Father, and I am at the beginning of a new school week. As I set out today, I ask that your presence go with me and be with me. Let the knowledge of your presence beside me keep me pure in my thinking, speaking, and doing. Help me to have thoughts that are noble, and which will be an inspiration to good deeds. Help me to speak words that will bring comfort and joy. Help me to do things that will make life easier, and the world a better place for those around me. Let me with your help, O Father, begin a growth today that will continue through the week.

Vimala Arangadan

65. To Respect Rest

Dear Father, I am so glad today is Saturday, and my well-earned holiday. I have finished the homework for the next week. Bless these two days of the weekend for me, so they will be true relaxation for my body and mind, and an opportunity to catch up on all my other chores of home and hobby. Let me, while relaxing and enjoying my holiday, find time too to help mother with chores around the house, or father with other work or errands. If I can bring some little joy to brother, sister, neighbour or friend through some service, help me not to grudge the time or labour; for in bringing joy to others, we bring joy to ourselves. So, let my Saturday be blessed by you.

Vimala Arangaden

66. Discipline to Realize the Limit

Lord, you know better than I know myself that I am growing old and will some day be even older. Keep me from the fatal habit of thinking I must say something on every subject and on every occasion. Release me from craving to straighten out everybody's affairs. Make me thoughtful but not moody; helpful but not bossy.

With my vast store of wisdom, it seems a pity not to use it all, but you know Lord that I want a few friend at the end. Keep my mind free from the recital of endless details: give me wings to get to the point.

Seal my lips on my aches and pains. They are increasing, and love of rehearsing them is becoming sweeter as the years go by. I dare not ask for grace enough to enjoy the tales of other's pains but help me to endure them with patience.

I dare not ask for improved memory, but for a growing humility and a lessening cocksureness when my memory seems to clash with the memories of others. Teach me the glorious lesson that occasionally I may be mistaken.

Keep me reasonably sweet: I do not want to be a saint – some of them are so hard to live with – but a sour old person is one of the crowning works of the devil.

Give me ability to see good things in unexpected places, and talents in unexpected people.

And give me, O Lord, the grace to tell them so.

A Seventeenth-Century Nun

67. Self-Respect and Love

Give us, O God, at all times respect for ourselves, so that we may never do work of which we would be ashamed; So that we may never stoop to that which is mean and low; So that we may never do in the present that which in the future we would have cause to regret.

Give us, O God, at all times love for others, so that we may never refuse an appeal for help; So that we may help even before we are asked for help; So, that we may never do anything which would injure or hurt anyone else in body or in mind; So that we may find our joy in service and not in selfishness; in giving and not in getting; in sharing and not in keeping.

Give us, O God, at all times reverence for you, so that we may remember that wherever we are and whatever we do you see us; So, that we may always obey your commands; So, that we may fear nothing except to grieve you, and seek nothing except to please you.

William Barclay

68. In our Improvement

We must praise Your goodness, that You have left nothing undone to draw us to Yourself. But one thing we ask of You, our God, not to cease Your work in our improvement. Let us tend towards You, no matter by what means and be fruitful in good works, for the sake of Jesus Christ our Lord.

Ludwig van Beethoven

69. Word of God

O Lord, Heavenly Father, in whom is the fullness of light and of wisdom, enlighten our minds by the Holy Spirit, and give us grace to receive Your Word with reverence and humility, without which no one can understand Your truth. For Christ's sake.

John Calvin

70. Dedicated life

O Lord, give us more charity, more self-denial, more likeness to You. Teach us to sacrifice our comforts to others, and our likings for the sake of doing good. Make us kindly in thought, gentle in word, generous in deed. Teach us that it is better to give than to receive; better to forget ourselves than to put ourselves forward; better to minister than to be ministered unto. And unto You, the God of Love, be all the glory and praise, both now and for evermore.

Henry Alford

71. Walk of Life

O God our Father, we have come to you tonight that you may make us able to walk in your light; To act in your strength; To think in your wisdom; To speak in your truth; To live in your love; so that when all the days are done we may come to dwell in your glory: through Jesus Christ our Lord.

William Barclay

72. Not to Criticise

Help us always: To praise rather than to criticize; To sympathize rather than to condemn; To encourage rather than to discourage; To build up rather than to destroy; To think of people at their best rather than at their worst.

William Barclay

73. Choice

Grant, O God, that the ears which have heard the voice of Your songs maybe closed to the voice of clamour and dispute; that their eyes which have seen Your great love may also behold Your blessed hope; that the tongues which have sung Your praise may speak the truth; that the feet which have walked Your courts may walk in the region of light; that the bodies which have partaken of Your living Body may be restored to newness of life. Glory be to You for Your unspeakable gift.

Fifth Century Liturgy of Malabar

74. Like a Child

O God, you have said that you are specially near to those who are childlike in heart. Give us tonight, a Child's trust, that we may never doubt your love; a Child's wonder, that we may be lost in wonder at the beauty and the bounty of the universe and at the miracle of your love for us; a Child's love, that we may love you as a child ought to love a father: through Jesus Christ our Lord.

William Barclay

75. Christ's Way

Help us, O God, at all times to do the things we ought to do, to that end give us, clear sight, that we may know what to do; courage, to embark upon it; will, to find a way through all its problems; perseverance, to bring it to its appointed end; strength, to resist all the temptations which would seek to lure us aside. So, help us to begin, to continue and to end all things in you.

William Barclay

76. Bless All of Us

O God, our Father, bless our friends and our loved ones and keep them safe from harm and danger. Bless our enemies and those who dislike us and help us by caring for them to make them our friends. Bless those who are in pain of body, anxiety of mind, and sorrow of heart. Bless those who are lonely because death has taken a dear one from them. Bless those who are old and who now are left alone. Bless those who have made a mess of life and who know well that they have no one but themselves to blame. Bless those who have fallen to temptation and who are sorry now and give them grace to begin again and this time not to fall. Bless all who are in trouble and help them to win their way through it. Bless each one of us as you know we need.

William Barclay

77. Abound in Fruit

May God the Father, and the eternal High Priest, Jesus Christ, build us up in faith and truth and love, and grant to us our portion among the saints with all those who believe on our Lord Jesus Christ. We pray for all saints, for kings and rulers, for the enemies of the Cross of Christ, and for ourselves we pray that our fruit may abound and that we may be made perfect in Christ Jesus our Lord.

Polycarp

78. To Love

O Lord, grant us to love You; grant that we may love those that love You; grant that we may do the deeds that win Your love. Make the love of You to be dearer to us than ourselves, our families, than wealth, and even than cool water.

Prophet Mohammed

79. Investigation

O God, our Father, help us in our lives to have the right attitude to everyone.

Help us to have the right attitude to ourselves. Keep us from the pride which makes us conceitedly pleased with ourselves; The false modesty which is an excuse for evading responsibility; The blindness which cannot see our own faults; The selfishness which puts self in the centre of everything.

Help us to have the right attitude to others. Keep us from the critical spirit which looks for faults; The thoughtless spirit which never thinks of the feelings of others; The cowardice which is afraid of what others will say; The desire to curry favour which makes us too intent on pleasing others, even at the expense of honour, of honesty and of truth.

Help us to have the right attitude to you. Keep us from the forgetfulness which never thinks of you; The rebelliousness which takes its own way of things; The irreverence which forgets that you are here.

Help us to think of ourselves, to think of others, and to think of you as we ought.

William Barclay

80. Teach Us

O God, our Father, save us from everything which would make life useless and ugly.

Save us from: The unteachable spirit which will not learn; The ungrateful spirit which never says thanks; The unhappy spirit which is filled with complaints and discontent.

Save us from: The disobliging spirit which grudges any help it has to give; The discourteous spirit which never thinks of the feelings of anyone else; The disobedient spirit which will take nothing but its own way.

Give us: A sense of responsibility, that we may know that we can neither live nor die to ourselves; A sense of duty, that we may leave nothing that we ought to do undone; A sense of gratitude, that we may offer thanks to you by trying to live more nearly as you would have us to do.

William Barclay

81. Not to be Complacent

O God, our Father, let us not be content to wait and what will happen, but give us the determination to make the right things happen.

While time is running out, save us from the impatience which is akin to cowardice.

Give us the courage to be either hot or cold, to stand for something, lest we fall for anything. In Jesus' Name.

Peter Marshall

82. To Remember

Help us, O God, to remember that all great things have their price.

Help us to remember that, there is no achievement without work; There is no learning without study; There is no skill of body or of mind without discipline

Help us to remember that: There is no purity without vigilance; There is no friendship without loyalty; There is no love without the death of self.

Help us to remember that: There is no joy without service; There is no discipleship without devotion; There is no crown without a cross.

So, help us to be willing to pay the price that we may enter into our reward.

William Barclay

83. To be Active

O God, our Father, tonight we come to you to listen and to learn.

Take from us the laziness which will not learn, and the prejudice which cannot learn; and give us minds adventurous to think, memories strong to remember, wills resolute to do. This we ask for Jesus' sake.

William Barclay

84. Supplication

O God, Lord of all good life, give us the things which will enable us to make something worthwhile out of life.

Discipline to accept the necessity of study and of work; A sense of proportion to see the things which really matter; The ability to take the long view that we may never sell the most precious things for a moment's cheap pleasure:

Grant us these things O God.

Perseverance that we may never leave a task uncompleted; Concentration that we too may say, this one thing I do; Patience that we may never give up and never give in:

Grant us these things O God.

The teachable spirit which realizes its own ignorance; The humble spirit which will accept advice and which will not resent rebuke; The diligent spirit that whatever our hand finds to do we may do with our might:

Grant us these things, O God.

So, help us to bear the yoke in our youth that in the days to come we may serve you and serve our fellow-humans well: through Jesus Christ our Lord.

William Barclay

85. Faith, Hope, Love

O God, our Father, grant us:

The faith which is sure and certain of what it believes; The faith which unhesitatingly believes in your promises and unquestioningly accepts your commands; The faith which is loyal to you in any situation.

The hope which will never despair; The hope that no disappointment can quench; The hope which in spite of failure will never give in.

The love which is always ready to forgive; The love which is always eager to help; The love which is always happier to give than to get.

And so grant that living in faith, in hope, in love, we may live like Jesus.

William Barclay

86. Modest Life

Grant that in all things we may behave ourselves so as befits a creature to his Creator, as servant to his Lord. Make us diligent in all our duties, watchful against all temptations, pure and temperate and moderate in Your most lawful enjoyments, that they may never become a snare to us. Help us, O Lord, to act towards our neighbour that we may never transgress the royal law of Yours, of loving him as ourselves. Finally, we beseech You, O Lord, to sanctify us throughout, that our whole spirit, soul and body, may be preserved blameless unto the coming of the Lord Jesus Christ: to whom with You and the Holy Spirit be all honour and glory for ever.

Thomas à Kempis

87. Seven Virtues

Let us pray to God to give us the Seven Virtues which humans have always thought the greatest virtues of all.

O God, our Father, give us the virtues which will make life strong and lovely.

Fidelity, that we may be forever true to friendship, to love and to you;

Hope, that not all earth's setbacks and disappointments may ever drive us to despair;

Love, that we may feel towards our fellowmen as you feel to them;

Prudence, that we may be wise to choose, not that which is at the moment attractive, but that which is to our ultimate good;

Justice, that we may never be swayed by passion or by prejudice, but that in honour and in honesty we may be fair to all men;

Courage, that no cowardly and unworthy fear may ever keep us from doing the right thing and taking the right road;

Self-control, that we may be master of every impulse and of every passion, and so able to serve others because we can rule ourselves.

So let your divine grace make beautiful our human life.

William Barclay

88. To Be Good

Lord Jesus, master of all good life, help us in this fellowship always to study to make our bodies fitter; To make our minds keener and better equipped; To make our hearts purer.

Help us here to learn to be good sons and daughters in our homes; To be good citizens of the community in which we live; To be good scholars and students of our school or our college or our university; To be good workers in whatever trade or craft we are engaged; To be good members of your Church; To be good followers and disciples of Jesus.

Help us here to find week by week the joy of learning together; The joy of playing together; The joy of praying together; The joy of worshipping together.

Keep far from us anything that would hurt our fellowship or come between us. Banish from us the irritable temper; The selfish ambition; The arrogant intolerance; The false loyalty.

And help us in this place week by week to come closer to one another and closer to you.

William Barclay

89. To Make Use of Opportunities

O God, our Father, you have made life full of opportunities. Help us to miss none of these opportunities when they come to us.

Help us not to miss the opportunities of learning, and help us to work, to study, to train, and to accept discipline that we may deepen our lives; enrich our minds, to learn our trade; master our craft; be efficient at our job; be equipped on our profession.

Help us never to miss the opportunities of helping others that we may be ready to share with the poor; To sympathize with the sad; To encourage the depressed; To help those who have made mistakes back on to the rails again; To lend a hand to those who are finding things difficult.

Help us never to miss an opportunity to show where we stand that we may set a Christian example wherever we are; Always make it easier for others to do and be good, and never make it easier for them to do any wrong thing; Always be good advertisements for our faith and for our church.

So, help us to grasp every opportunity you send, and to use every gift you have given us that we may make life what you meant it to be.

William Barclay

90. Humility

O God, our Father, give to us the humility which realizes its ignorance; Admits its mistakes; Recognizes its need; Welcomes advice; Accepts rebuke.

Save us from pride in our knowledge and make us to think of the great ocean of truth all undiscovered before us. Save us from pride in our achievement and make us to remember all that we still have to do. Save us from pride in our performance and make us to remember how far short of perfection our best must still fall.

Help us in the days ahead, to study with diligence, to learn with eagerness. And give us a retentive memory to remember that which we have learned, and a resolute will to put it into action.

William Barclay

91. Friendship

Keep us, O God, from all the things which make friendship impossible.

Keep us from the sarcastic tongue; The critical eye; The ears which love malicious gossip; The mind which thinks the worst; The heart whose only love is self-love.

Give us the things which will enable friendship to flourish. Give us the ability to bear one another's burdens and to forgive one another's faults; The sympathetic, the unselfish and the understanding heart; The temper and the tongue which are always under control; The determination to treat others as we would have them treat us; The tolerance which can always see the point of view of others.

Help us to live ever remembering that in you we live and move and have our being, and that life is always in your sight.

William Barclay

92. Treating Others

Help us, O God, always to live in courtesy towards everyone whom we meet.

Help us never to speak an angry, an impatient, a boorish, an impolite or a discourteous word; Never to make people feel a nuisance; Never to do things so grudgingly and so unwillingly that it is worse than not doing them at all; Never to give anything in such a way that the gift becomes an insult; Never to treat people in such a way that it embarrasses them, or makes them feel small, or humiliates them.

Help us always to be kind; Always to make people feel that they are welcome and that we care; Always to think of the feelings of others as much as we would wish them to think of ours; Always to respect and never to laugh at the things which are important and sacred to someone else.

Help us to walk looking unto Jesus, and to make him the pattern of our lives

William Barclay

93. To Seek Truth by Serving

O God, our Father, make us so eager to seek the truth that no study may be too difficult for us and no thinking too adventurous.

Make us so willing to serve you and our fellowmen that no task may be too wearisome for us and that no one may ever appeal in vain to us for help and sympathy. Make us so to feel your love for us that our hearts may go out to you in wonder, love and praise. This we ask for your love's sake.

William Barclay

94. Handling Money

O God, you have given us all that we have. Teach us to use rightly our money and our material possessions.

Grant that we may never make money dishonestly or use it selfishly. Keep us alike from being mean and miserly, and from being spendthrift and extravagant. Help us to value independence and to have a horror of debt. Help us always to fulfil our obligations to our parents and to our home, and never to grudge what we have to contribute to the common stock. Make us always ready to give to the poor, the aged, and the needy, and to those who never have enough. Help us to be generous to our church, so that through us your kingdom may be upbuilt, and your people helped and comforted, in this place, in this land and in lands across the sea. Help us always to remember that you love a cheerful giver, and that it is always a happier thing to give than to get.

William Barclay

95. Help us to be True

O Lord Jesus, help us to be true to our faith and true to you, when things are difficult.

When we have to stand alone; When loyalty to you makes us unpopular with our fellow-humans; When doing the right thing involves us in the dislike or in the laughter of others;

Help us still to be true.

Help us to be true to our faith and true to you, when it costs us something. When our Christian duty demands more of our time than we really want to give; When our Christian duty demands more of our money than we really want to give; When our Christian duty demands more of an effort than we really want to make;

Help us still to be true.

Help us to be true to our faith and true to you, when it is all against the things we instinctively want to do. When we don't want to be unselfish; When we have no desire to think of others; When the last thing we want is to forgive someone who has injured us;

Help us still to be true.

Give us strength to do what we cannot do and to be what we cannot be; and help us to remember that by ourselves we can do nothing but that with you all things are possible.

William Barclay

96. Sense of Responsibility

O God, Lord of all good life, give us in all things a true sense of responsibility.

Help us at all times to remember our responsibility to ourselves.

Help us never to act in such a way that we shall lose our self-respect; Never to let ourselves down by doing something which is mean and low, disloyal and dishonourable; Never to do anything which we would afterwards regret, perhaps spend the rest of our life regretting.

Help us at all times to remember our responsibility to our friends, and to those whom we love, and love us.

Help us, never to disappoint those who love us; Never to fail those who trust us; Never to bring grief or heartbreak to those in whose hearts we have a special place.

Help us at all times to remember our responsibility to our fellowmen.

Help us, not to be the kind of people who are always remembering their rights and always forgetting their duties; Not to be the kind of people who want to get everything out of life and to put nothing into it; Not to be the kind of people who do not care what happens to others so long as they are all right.

Help us at all times to remember our responsibility to you.

Help us to remember that we shall answer to you for the way we have used the gifts you gave us; To remember that we shall give account for all that we have been allotted in this life; To remember at all times how you have loved us and how Jesus died for us.

William Barclay

97. Right Attitude

Give us courage and gaiety and the quiet mind. Spare us to our friends, soften us to our enemies. Bless us, if it may be, in all our innocent endeavours. If it may not, give us strength to encounter that which is to come, that we may be brave in peril, constant in tribulation, temperate in wrath, and in all changes of fortune, and, down even to the gates of death, loyal and loving to one another; through Jesus Christ our Lord.

Robert Louis Stevenson

98. To Give as We Receive

Help us, O God at all times to act towards others as we would wish them to act towards us.

Help us, to make the same allowances for others as we would wish them to make for us; To be as sympathetic and understanding to others as we would wish them to be to us; To encourage others as we would wish them to encourage us; To help others as we would wish them to help us; To be as just and fair to others as we would wish them to be to us; To forgive others as we would wish them to forgive us.

Before we criticize others, help us to remember what it feels like to be criticized. Before we find fault with others, help us to remember what it feels like to be found fault with. Before we condemn others, help us to remember what it feels like to be condemned.

Help us at all times to be like Jesus, who went about doing good; Who was among men as one who serves; Who even on the Cross prayed that his enemies should be forgiven.

William Barclay

99. Balance

O God, tonight we specially ask you to help us never to allow the great things of life to go wrong.

Help us never to allow caution to become cowardice, or courage to become recklessness. Help us never to allow carefulness to become meanness, or spending to become squandering. Help us never to allow honesty to become discourtesy, or politeness to become evasion of the truth. Help us never to allow liberty to become licence, or pleasure to become sin.

Help us never selfishly to make use of our friends, never thoughtlessly to take our loved ones for granted, never to make your love an excuse for thinking that we can do what we like. Help us always to remember how we have been loved and to try to be more worthy of it.

William Barclay

100. Taste of the Holy Spirit

Give us, O Lord, a humble, quiet, peaceable, patient, tender, and charitable mind, and in all our thoughts, words, and deeds a taste of Your Holy Spirit. Give us, O Lord, a lively faith, a firm hope, a fervent charity, a love of You. Take from us all luke-warmness in meditation, dullness in prayer. Give us fervour and delight in thinking of You and Your grace, Your tender compassion towards us. The things that we pray for, good Lord, give us grace to labour for; through Jesus Christ our Lord.

Thomas More

101. Exemplary Life

O Lord God, give us grace to set a good example to all amongst whom we live, to be just and true in all our dealings, to be strict and conscientious in the discharge of every duty, pure and temperate in all enjoyment, kind and charitable and courteous towards all; so that the mind of Jesus Christ may be formed in us, and all may take knowledge of us that we are his disciples: through Jesus Christ our Lord.

William Barclay

102. To Be Christ-like

Grant that we may walk as Christ walked; grant that what the Spirit was in him, such he may be also in us; grant that our lives may be refashioned after the pattern of his life; grant that we may do today here on earth what Christ would have done, and in the way he would have done it; grant that we may become vessels of his grace, instruments of his will, to your glory and honour: through Jesus Christ our Lord.

William Barclay

103. Save Us from Unhelpful Attitudes

O God, save us from being unwise enough to refuse the discipline which we ought to accept.

Keep us from being too proud to ask for advice. Keep us from being too self-conceited to accept guidance. Keep us from being too self-willed to endure rebuke. Keep us from foolishly disregarding the experience of those who are older and wiser than we are. Keep us from the self-confidence that cannot believe that it can be wrong, and which can see no point of view but its own.

Make us wise enough to realize our own ignorance, and to recognize our own weakness, that we may come to you who are the source of all wisdom and all strength.

William Barclay

104. Keep Us from the Valueless

O God, our Father, keep us from doing things in a way that takes all the value out of them.

Keep us from doing things unwillingly and with a grudge, in a way that makes it quite clear that the whole thing is a nuisance to us. Keep us from doing things so badly and so inattentively that they have to be done all over again. Keep us from doing things in such a hurry that they are only half done. Keep us from doing things in order to show off how good and how kind and how clever we are.

Help us to do everything in such a way that we would be happy to know that you are watching us and glad to offer what we have done to you.

William Barclay

105. Tools for Life

Give us, O Lord, a steadfast heart, which no unworthy affection may drag downwards; give an unconquered heart, which no tribulation can wear out; give us an upright heart, which no unworthy purpose may tempt aside. Bestow upon us also, O Lord, understanding to know You, diligence to seek You, wisdom to find You; and a faithfulness that may finally embrace You: through Jesus Christ our Lord.

Thomas Aquinas

106. Prolonging Patience

O God, give us the patience which we need so much.

Give us patience with people; Patience with those who need and ask our help; Patience with those who need our sympathy; Patience with those who want us to listen while they talk to us.

Give us patience with our work; Patience to work and study until we make ourselves good craftsmen; Patience to accept the discipline of learning, of training, and of practice; Patience to persevere with every task we do until we finish it.

Give us patience with life; Patience to accept things, even when we do not see either the meaning or the reason for them; Patience when hopes are very slow to come true; Patience to take the long view of things and not to be discouraged.

O God, you are the God of all eternity with all time to work in, help us to learn to wait in patience and in hope.

William Barclay

107. Selfless, Voluntary Action

O God, our Father, make us the kind of people who are really useful and really helpful.

Help us, when we are asked, to do with a good grace even that which we do not want to do, and that which no one else will do. Help us never to take offence, if someone else is asked to do what we thought we should have been asked to do. Help us never to think of praise and prestige, and credit and thanks, so long as the work is done. Help us to be equally willing to take the first place and to take the last place. Help us, when we are asked to do something, to be more ready to say yes and to say no. Help us willingly to use whatever talents you gave us in the service of others. Help us always to be volunteers and not conscripts when some job has to be done. Help us always to be willing to give up time and pleasure and leisure when someone is required to do some useful work.

Help us in all things to be like Jesus, amongst our fellowmen as they who serve.

William Barclay

108. Deliver us from Cowardice, Laziness and Arrogance

Deliver us, O Lord, from the cowardice that dares not face new truth; from laziness that is content with half-truth, and from the arrogance that thinks it knows all truth; for the sake of Christ our Lord.

Kenya

109. Righteous Life

Let me be righteous, Saviour God, without realising that I am. May the fruits of righteousness in my life be natural and spontaneous. If they bring me some recognition and appreciation, let me never delay to kneel and glorify your name.

Israel Selvanayagam

110. Equanimity of Mind

Compassionate God, console us as we mourn loss in our attempts to establish your commonwealth. Encourage us to continue the struggle and accept us again as we fall at your feet. In our success and failure, strength and weakness, life and death, let us always seek your glory.

Israel Selvanayagam

111. Bridges of Love

God of love, who enfold all the world in one embrace, help us, your people, to build bridges of love; bridges between young and old, poor and rich, black and white; bridges between those who know you and those who do not yet know you; bridges between traditionalists and modernisers, between nations and within communities. As in your self-giving, life-giving love for us, you became, in Jesus Christ, the Bridge between heaven and earth, so may we become bridges of the gospel. When we are walked over, give us courage; when we are taken for granted, give us grace; when we are despised, give us strength – so that through our lives others may catch a glimpse of Jesus the Redeemer, and entrust themselves to your saving mercy. God of love, hear our prayer, through Jesus, our Lord and Saviour.

Margaret Parker

112. Take and Make

Take our hatreds: make them into handshakes. Take our prejudices: make them into peace-offerings. Take our arguments: make them into alliances. Take our battles: make them into bonds. Take our misunderstandings: make them into music. Take our divisions: make them into dances. Take our schisms: make them into psalms.

Kate Compston

113. Accept What We Have

Lord, I may not have the great oratory of a preacher or the sensitive touches of a poet; I may not have vision of an artist or the ear of a great musician; but I will strive to be all that I ought to be in your sight, and stretch my talents and skills to the uttermost so that your world is filled with beauty, and my life becomes an offering of joy.

David Jenkins

114. To Grow to be Human

Humanizing God, you call us to go back to our position in creation which shines forth equality and integrity. Endow us with the authentic quality so that we may appreciate the dignity of every human we see. Give us a penetrating eye to see in them the divine beauty beyond their brokenness, colour, language and culture. Help us to respect their selfhood and to rejoice in their achievements and happiness. May we see the day when all communities will hoist together a multi-coloured flag and celebrate our common humanity.

Israel Selvanayagam

115. To be Civilized

Civilize me, O Divine, that I may live mindful of all things around me and sensitive to both the melodious songs and the sobbing cries. Help us to maintain civility in the path of civilization. Civilize our educational institutions that humility may regains its charm and the sore of snobbery be treated and healed. Civilize those in authority that they may adopt simplicity and servanthood. Civilize our society that even the youngest and most vulnerable may move in the thickest darkness without fear. Civilize our nation that it will outdo itself in peace making, weapons-reduction and war-avoiding. Let our satisfaction and fulfilment be secured by our conscious obedience to your holy laws of human dignity. Hear our longing, our Saviour.

Israel Selvanayagam

116. To be Free and Transparent

All knowing God, we marvel at your unrestricted glory shining even in unexpected places. Thank you for your unreserved presence surrounding us. May our lives be open letters for anyone to read, and not be covered and shelved in dark corners. Give us courage and strength to overcome the temptation to over-zealously guard our privacy, safety and security. Let us have the mindset of Christ Jesus who fully opened his person to scorching heat and jeering eyes. Reignite our mind to have a sight of the blood drops gushing from his body and words of dereliction from his mouth. Whether we are strong or weak, adequate or not, help us to walk with our heads held high but remaining humble in your sight as well as in the sight of our fellow humans.

Israel Selvanayagam

117. Enflame and Ignite

God of fire and flame, ignite in us a renewed spirit. Give us loud voices to sing your praise. Cleanse our hearts so that we may love deeply and forgive, as you have forgiven us.

Moravian

118. Compassion for the Poor and Powerless

O Lord, give us compassion for the poor and powerless. Warm our cold hearts to reflect in them your love for all people. Teach us humility and forgive our feelings of self-importance. Remind us that all we have – even our next breath – comes from you.

Moravian

119. Open our Eyes and Ears

Spirit of the living God, fall afresh on us! Open our eyes to the needs of the poor; open our ears to the cries of the suffering; open our hearts to the pain of the lonely. On this day, God, make us blessings to your people.

Moravian

120. Take the Worry and Delight

God of love, joy and peace, abide with us this day in all that we do and say. Take from us the things that worry us most and let us delight in you through all of what this day may bring. In Jesus' name we pray.

Moravian

121. Overflow with Loving Presence

God of mercy and compassion, overflow our lives with your loving presence and wash away all that would keep us from you. Our worship, love and service we gladly give in return.

Moravian

122. Make us Love and Serve the Poor

Make us worthy, Lord, to serve our fellow human beings throughout the world who live and die in poverty and hunger. Give them through our hands this day, their daily bread, and by our understanding, love. Give peace and joy.

Mother Teresa

123. Your Love Through Us

Loving Christ, you have nobody on earth but ours. Ours are the only hands with which you can do your work. Ours are the only feet with which you can go about the work. Ours are the only eyes through which your compassion can shine forth upon a troubled world. You have no body on earth but ours. Lord Jesus, make use of my body and limbs as instruments of your love, I surrender them all at your lotus-feet.

St. Teresa of Avila (adapted)

124. For Discernment

Grant me, O Lord, to know what is worth knowing, to love what is worth loving, to praise what delights you most, to value what is precious in your sight, to hate what is offensive to you. Do not let me judge by what I see, nor pass sentence according to what I hear, but to judge rightly between things that differ, and above all to search out and to do what pleases you, through Jesus Christ our Lord.

Thomas à Kempis

125. To Serve you Lord as you Deserve

Teach us, Lord, to serve you as you deserve, to give and not to count the cost, to fight and not to heed the wounds, to toil and not to seek for rest, to labour and not to ask for any reward save that of knowing that we do your will.

Ignatius Loyola

126. Surrender All

Take, Lord, all my liberty, my memory, my understanding, and my whole will. You have given me all that I have, all that I am, and I surrender all to your divine will, that you dispose of me. Give me only your love and your grace. With this I am rich enough, and I have no more to ask.

Ignatius Loyola

127. To Conform to Your Will

O Lord, let me not henceforth desire health or life except to spend them for you, with you and in you. You alone know what is good for me; do therefore what seems best to you. Give to me or take from me; conform my will to yours; and grant that with humble and perfect submission and in holy confidence I may receive the orders of your eternal providence, and may equally adore all that comes to me from you.

Blaise Pascal

128. To Breathe in Faith

Teach me, O God, not to torture myself, not to make a martyr out of myself through stifling reflection, but rather teach me to breathe deeply in faith.

Søren Kierkegaard

129. Lead to Perfection

Oh God, you put into my heart this great desire to devote myself to the sick and sorrowful; I offer it to you. Do with it what is for your service.

Oh my Creator, are you leading every man of us to perfection? Or is this only a metaphysical idea for which there is no evidence? Is man only a constant repetition of himself? You know that through all these twenty horrible years I have been supported by the belief (I think I must believe it still or I am sure I could not work) that I was working with you who were bringing every one of us, even our poor nurses, to perfection. O Lord, even now I am trying to snatch the management of your world from your hands. Too little have I looked for something higher and better than my own work – the work of supreme Wisdom, which uses us whether we know it or not.

Florence Nightingale

130. God, the Cosmic Artist

You take the pen and the lines dance. You take the flute, and the notes shimmer. You take the brush, and the colours sing. So all things have meaning and beauty in that space beyond time where you are. How, then, can I hold back anything from you?

Dag Hammarskjöld

131. Mercy and Justice

Almighty forgive my doubt, my anger, my pride. By your mercy abase me, in your strictness raise me up.

Dag Hammarskjöld

132. Simplicity and Joy

O Lord Christ, help us to maintain ourselves in simplicity and in joy, the joy of the merciful, the joy of brotherly love. Grant that, renouncing henceforth all thought of looking back, and joyful with infinite gratitude, we may never fear to precede the dawn, to praise and bless and sing to Christ our Lord.

Author Unknown

133. Freedom from all Weights

O Christ, you take upon yourself all our burdens so that, freed of all that weighs us down, we can constantly begin anew to walk, with lightened step, from worry towards trusting, from the shadows towards the clear flowing waters, from our own will towards the vision of the coming Kingdom. And then we know, though we hardly dared hope so, that you offer to make every human being a reflection of your face.

Brother Roger

134. Make Us Servants

Lord Christ, you remain, unseen, at our side, present like a poor man who washes the feet of his friends. And we, to follow in your footsteps, we are here, waiting for you to suggest signs of sharing to make us into servants of your Gospel.

Brother Roger

135. To Continue to Finish and Rejoice

O Lord God, when you give to your servants to endeavour any great matter, grant us also to know that it is not the beginning, but the continuing of the same to the end, until it be thoroughly finished, which yields the true glory; through him who for the finishing of your work laid down his life, our Redeemer, Jesus Christ.

Francis Drake

136. Give us the All-Creative Spirit

Give us the spirit of faith and devotion; to kindle a bright flame of faith in our hearts; that we may have a living knowledge of thy salvation, and that our whole life may be a thank offering for the mercies we have received.

Give us the spirit of love; that we may experience the sweetness of thy love towards us, and also love thee in return, and render our obedience not from constraint like slaves, but with the willing and glad hearts of children.

And give us the spirit of constancy and perseverance; that by the faithful practice of those things which we know to be true, our hearts may be purged of all evil thoughts and desires, and we be brought back into that pureness of spirit in which alone thou mayest be served.

Show us thy light, O thou Light of the world. Cause us to live in it; by it to pass through the shadow of death in safety, and in it to abide for evermore.

Hear us in thy mercy; through Jesus Christ our Lord.

James Ferguson

137. To Attend to your Word and Will

Grant us, O Lord, that remembering your mercy, we may never harbour hard thoughts of you, or of our fellows; and never run into the temptations which in our prayers we desire to avoid; but attending to your Word and Will, may be not foolish but understanding, and not slothful but diligent in your service, doing with all our might what you give us to do; so that, having lived lives acceptable to you, we may finish them in your fear and love; and when you call your labourers into rest, may also with them enter in.

These things we ask in the Name of our Lord and Saviour Jesus Christ.

James Ferguson

138. Fruits of the Spirit

O Lord God, whose strength is sufficient for all who lay hold on it, Grant us in thee to comfort our hearts and be strong. Humility, meekness, temperance, purity, large-heartedness, sympathy, zeal – grant us these evidences of faith, handmaids of hope, fruits of love; for the sake of Jesus Christ, our strength, our righteousness, and our hope of glory.

Christina Rossetti

139. Faith and Knowledge

Loving God, our heavenly teacher,
You are the source of our faith and of our knowledge.
Give us your wisdom to measure our faith and think accordingly.
When we see only puzzling reflections in a mirror let us long to see face to face.
When we realize that our knowledge is partial let us move on to know more.
Give us the courage to say what we know and the humility to say what we do not know.
Give us clarity of thought and charity of words to say that clearly.
Fill us with your discerning Spirit to distinguish between faith and familiarity.
Let our faith find expression in moving the mountain-like blocks and barriers.
Even if we are not able to measure our faith and enhance our knowledge,
Let it be punctuated in our heart that love is the greatest of all gifts,
Through the one who defined what is love, even Jesus Christ our Lord.

Israel Selvanayagam

140. Patience and Steadfastness

O give us patience and steadfastness in adversity, strengthen our weakness, comfort us in trouble and distress, help us to fight; grant us that in true obedience and condescension of mind we may give over our own wills unto our Father in all things, according to the example of your beloved Son; that in adversity we grudge not, but offer up ourselves unto you without contradiction. O give us a willing and cheerful mind, that we may gladly suffer and bear all things for your sake.

Miles Coverdale

141. Civilize the World

Owner of the world and its destiny, help all people everywhere to resist erroneous understanding of civilization and its propagation. When savageness continues with immeasurable magnitude along with the magical capacity to kill masses by pushing the buttons of the bombs of mass destruction in places far away, when leaders of powerful nations bargain for peace while sitting on piles of atom bombs, may we beat our chests and curse their evil intent. God of truth, let the dead words of protocol be replaced by prophetic and pastoral speeches. Civilize the world that even the least of our world sleep with adequate food in their stomach and with peace of mind, and rise in hope. Confuse the strategy of the intelligentsia so that the modest daily aspirations of the vulnerable are not shattered. Civilize us with love.

Israel Selvanayagam

142. To Seek the Worth

Grant me, O Lord, to know what is worth knowing, to love what is worth loving, to praise what delights you most, to value what is precious in your sight, to hate what is offensive to you. Do not let me judge by what I see, nor pass sentence according to what I hear, but to judge rightly between things that differ and above all to search out and to do what pleases you, through Jesus Christ our Lord.

Thomas à Kempis

143. Save Me from Snares

Save me, O Lord, from the snares of a double mind. Deliver us from all cowardly neutralities. Make us to go in the paths of your commandments, and to trust for your defense in your mighty arm alone, through Jesus Christ our Lord.

Richard Hurrell Froude

144. Treasure to be Entrusted

Kindly God, forgive our carelessness when holding the precious things entrusted to us. As we recall stories of lost things – coins, sheep, teenagers – open our eyes to the treasure to be found in people, purses and possessions. Awaken in us a longing for just giving, for tender compassion and for right relationship. When we hold holy things in tired hands, grace us with a measure of your gentleness and care.

Liz Smith

145. Help to Overcome

Help us, O Lord, to conquer anger with gentleness; to subdue greed with generosity and to overcome apathy with fervour. Help us to forget ourselves and reach out to others. Teach us to be courageous in risk-taking, patient in suffering and attentive in prayer; grant this through Christ our Lord.

Clement XI

146. Being Part of Family

O God, we thank you for the privilege of being part of a family and for all the relationships that enrich family life. Thank you for the experience of being loved and of being able to love others. Thank you for those who care for us when we're hurting. Heavenly Father, comfort and sustain the broken-hearted and give strength to the weary. May we notice when each other hurts and show we care in your name.

William Davison

147. The Greatest Goal

Lord, may our praises reach the heights, our prayers hit the targets, our giving plunge to the most needy and our love embrace the trackless, so that our hope rises on the trampoline of eternity, our patience is an endless marathon, our joy vaults over the bar and we are able to 'run the race' to the finish.

Graham Thompson

148. Eternal Source of Life

Eternal light, shine into our hearts; eternal goodness, deliver us from evil; eternal power, be our support; eternal wisdom, scatter the darkness of our ignorance; eternal pity. Have mercy upon us; that with all our heart and mind and soul and strength we may seek your face and be brought by your infinite mercy into your holy presence; through Jesus Christ our Lord,

Alcuin of York

149. God of the Dark Void

God of the dark, formless void; when we feel trapped by the bleakness of our hearts or the lack of creativity of our spirits, cross the chasm with your energy and touch us. Christ of the lonely cross; when we are unable to reach out in forgiveness to those who have wounded us, cross the chasm with your reconciling grace and empower us. Spirit who dances and yet who grieves; when we reject your strength and so fall short of our potential, cross the chasm with your life and raise us up. May we make the small steps of our journey in the name of the one who has bridged the unbridgeable out of love for us and for all.

Jill Baker

150. Patience, Humility, Constancy

Give us patience, O God, in the hour of trouble; humility in the hour of success and constancy in the hour of temptation. Grant us thankfulness for your benefits, fear of your judgement and hope in your enduring mercy; now and forever.

John Cosin

151. Teach the Basics

Lord, teach us, as your faithful followers, how to have fun without folly, to be cheerful without vanity, to have self-respect without pride, to be strict without fanaticism, to be relaxed without laziness, to be serious without gloom, to be friendly and not fickle, to be sunny but not silly, Lord teach us how.

D. M. Prescott

152. To Use Freedom Wisely

Loving God, you have generously given us all such freedom; we ask that you help us to use this freedom wisely; to love others more than we love ourselves, to care for others more than we care for ourselves, and be more selfless than selfish. And, in expressing our freedom in these ways, may we encourage others to do likewise. In the loving name of our Saviour and Lord, Jesus Christ.

Wendy Brown

153. For the Aching Vulnerable

In a world that watches as the vulnerable ache, grant us wisdom. In a world that stands by helplessly as children die, grant us a profound conscience. In a world where needs cannot be met or fed or nourished, grant us righteous anger. May we take our responsibility for the weak seriously, may we stand, attentive, by the disadvantaged and may we feel obligation, as to our own family, to those who are suffering. And in our God-expectant hope, may we act justly, love kindness and walk humbly with you, our God.

Andrea Sheppick

154. Power Towards the Highest

Give us, O God, the power to go on, to carry our share of your burden through to the end, to live all the years of our life faithful to the highest that we have seen, with no pandering to the second best, no leniency to our lower selves, no looking backward, no cowardice. Give us the power to ourselves, to break the bread of our lives for starving humanity, in humble self-subjection, as you, O God, serve your world.

J. S. Hoyland

155. Blood Relations

O God, you have made of one blood all nations to dwell upon the earth, break down we beseech you, all that divides us one from another; shame our jealousies, and lay low our pride; do away with all race-prejudice, that the bonds of fellowship and mutual service may unite the east and the west, the north and the south, that we may live in peace together, in honour preferring one another; to the glory of your Name.

G. C. Binyon

156. Empower to Be Bold

Empower me to be a bold participant, rather than a timid saint in waiting, in the difficult ordinariness of now; to exercise the authority of honesty, rather than defer to power, or deceive to get it; to influence someone for justice, rather than impress anyone for gain; and by grace, to find treasures of joy, of friendship, of peace hidden in the fields of the daily you give me to plough.

Ted Loder

157. No Other Than Your Will

Give us courage, O Lord, to stand up and be counted, to stand up for others who cannot stand up for themselves. To stand up for ourselves when it is needful to do so. Let us fear nothing more than we fear you. Let us love nothing more than we love you, for then we shall fear nothing also. Let us have no other god before you, whether nation or party or state or church. Let us seek no other peace but the peace which is yours, and make us its instruments, opening our eyes and ears and our hearts, so that we should know always what work of peace we should for you.

Alan Paton

158. Rock of Strength

Lord, our heavenly Father, who order all things for our eternal good, mercifully enlighten our minds, and give us a firm abiding trust in your love and care. Silence our murmurings, quiet our fears, and dispel our doubts, that rising above our afflictions and our anxieties, we may rest on you, the rock of everlasting strength.

New Church Book of Worship

159. Faith and Faithfulness

Help us, O Keeper of Faith, to keep the faith entrusted to us, faith in a world worth saving, faith in a dream worth sharing, faith in a heritage worth keeping even as we reinvigorate it to have meaning for us now. Help us keep faith in you, and help us not lose faith in ourselves, for faith is the substance of our hope, and hope, the assurance of love. Praise to you, O Faithful One, now and forever.

Miriam Therese Winter

160. Width of Love

O God of love, we pray you to give us love: love in our thinking, love in our speaking, love in our doing, and love in the hidden places of our souls; love of our neighbours near and far; love of our friends, old and new; love of those with whom we find it hard to bear, and love of those who find it hard to bear with us; love of those with whom we work and love of those with whom we take our ease; love in joy, love in sorrow; love in life and love in death; and that so at length we may be worthy to dwell with you who are eternal love.

William Temple

161. Simplicity

Take from me the desire to accumulate or hoard and give me in return a decluttered life and simple spirit. Help me to be content with what is and with who I am. Help me to delight in what I see, what I hear. Help me to appreciate the people I know well. Help me to see the stranger's grace.

Stephen Cherry

162. Show Another Way

Surprising God, in these times of terror, of hidden fear, of increasing uncertainty, of many betrayals, of wounding disconnections, send an email with the news that there is Another Way not of escape, but of love – where awareness, integrity of spirit, and generosity of heart, meet as companions, celebrate their connection, and transform our hesitancy of spirit for the whole earth is full of your glory and we are held in the palm of your hand.

Peter Miller

163. Seek Common Excellence

God of all excellence and integrity, we pray that your peace that transcends all understanding may guard our hearts and our minds in Christ Jesus. Help us to think always whatever is true, whatever is noble, whatever is right, whatever is pure, whatever is lovely, whatever is admirable – if anything is excellent or praiseworthy. Whatever we have learned from your servants let us put in practice. May your peace be with us.

Based on Philippians 4:7-9

XV. The Church

1. Body of Christ

Calling and covenanting God, in continuation of your people of Israel, your Son Jesus called a band of disciples who were later called Christians. You called them from a low estate with weak dispositions. You reminded them that they should form a royal, corporate priesthood; you inspired and led them by your Spirit to be light, salt, sign and foretaste, and instrument of your reign. Gracious God, because of political involvement, vile vested interests, conflicts and divisions, Christ's body is disfigured and dissected. Restore the ancient church of simplicity, passion and dedication, and infuse a new life. May the churches meaningfully celebrate your grace and salvation in worship and serve their local communities. May the presence and proclamation of the church demonstrate hope and holiness in a confused world. Even if the church is reduced to a tiny minority may we have the grace to be part of it. Reform us, sanctify the church and hallow your holy name.

Israel Selvanayagam

2. For Healthy Body

ALMIGHTY God, we pray for your Church, the Body of Christ, here in this world still broken and suffering. Confirm the faith of your Church, correct its errors, broaden its sympathies, heal its divisions; that as there is one Lord of all and one Father in heaven, so your children may be one in mind and one in Spirit.

Uphold all who teach in your Name; that rightly expounding the Wisdom of Christ, they may persuade humans to confess truth and obey him who is the Light of the world, and humans' Guide to God.

James Ferguson

3. Pilgrim People in Unity

By the grace of God we are a pilgrim people, ever moving forward and never settling down with the status quo. We bring our commitment to unity and mission, sharing with all the fullness of the blessing of the good news of Jesus Christ.

Holy God, fill us with the power of your Spirit that we may be your witnesses to the ends of the earth.

The Church of South India

4. Peace and Serenity

God of peace and serenity, bid the raging seas of the world's conflicts to be still. Transform all institutions of pride and domination into instruments of service for the poor and oppressed. Empower your Church to make sense of your presence as salt and light for the world, for, in the end, you are God, and in Christ you are our peace.

Akuila Yabaki

5. Draw Us Near

ALMIGHTY God, who has created your Church to be an abode for your Spirit, and for a tower of strength to your Church with the strength and beauty of holiness; draw the eyes of all to the Rock of their salvation; and let your House be glorious in the sight of all peoples, and its doors be open day and night on the East and the West, on the North and the South; that all nations may flow unto it; to the glory of your Son Jesus Christ.

James Ferguson

6. Pilgrim People Worldwide

Living God, thank you for the privilege of belonging to the World Church. Help us to be open to receive new insights and so experience renewal through the worship and spiritual riches that others have to share with us. Enable us to understand what it means to be a pilgrim people who travel on as part of the worldwide family of God, united in your way and time by the grace and power of Jesus.

Winston Graham

7. Integrated Church

O God our Father, Creator of the universe, whose Son, Jesus Christ, came to our world, pour your Holy Spirit upon your Church, that all the people of our world, being led through the knowledge of your truth to worship you, may offer the gold of intellect, the frankincense of devotion, and the myrrh of discipline to him who is with you and the Holy Spirit, who live and reign for ever one God, world without end.

The Church of Ceylon (Sri Lanka)

8. Unity as Sanctity

O God, the giver of life, we pray for the church throughout the world. Sanctify its life; renew its worship; empower its witness; restore its unity. Remove from your people all pride and every prejudice that dulls their will for unity. Strengthen the work of all those who strive to seek that common obedience that will bind us together. Heal the divisions which separate your children from one another, that they may keep the unity of the Spirit in the bond of peace.

Prayer used in the Ecumenical Centre, Geneva

9. Poor and Simple

Our Father, your voice has called us, you have placed your name on our lips and your work in our hands. We are your church, your pilgrim people, we ask you to open up for us a future that is new. Make us poor and make us simple, the better to know your gospel and to follow Jesus. We ask your forgiveness for our past faults, for the pride which has often driven your church to possess itself of power. Forgive your church if sometimes it has not been worthy of your trust. We are not bringing your peace to this world nor your salvation to men and women divided and distressed for we ourselves are disunited. May we who are often divided be able to be aware of so much that is madness and always to seek for unity.

Vocational Prayer Book of the seminaries of the Roman Catholic Church in Spain

10. World Church

We beseech you, O God, for your church throughout the world. May it grow in the faith of the cross and the power of the resurrection. May your spirit minister to it continually the redemption and reconciliation of all things. Keep it in your eternal unity, in great humility, in godly fear, and in your own pure and peaceable wisdom so easy to be entreated. Make it swift and mighty in the cause of the dominion of heaven. Cover, establish, and enlighten it, that it may see through all that obscures the time, and that it may move in the shadow of your wing, with faith, obedience, sacrifice, and godly power, through Jesus Christ our Sovereign.

P. T. Forsyth

11. God's *Oikoumene*

Lord, at this opportune time, we pray for the Church in the whole world, God's *oikoumene* and specially for all who are called to guide the pilgrim people.

Today we specially ask your Spirit to renew the institutional parts of the Indian Church – the congregations, dioceses, schools, colleges, hospitals, and other service organizations. We forget sometimes that we are a part of the 'movement towards the kingdom,' and that the Church is but an instrument, foretaste, sign and symbol of God's promised kingdom. As we are engaged in evangelization help us to realize that the furtherance of the kingdom is not to be measured by its numerical growth but by the impact it makes on the society towards greater justice and peace, joy and abundant life for all. Deliver us all from selfishness, self-righteousness, power mongering, corruption, litigation and lack of integrity and commitment. Open our eyes to see your presence and activity inside the Church as well as outside its borders. We praise you for adopting us as your children and for continuously renewing our minds and challenging us with your Word. In the name of Jesus Christ, Our Saviour, the Lord of the Church.

Samuel Amirtham

12. Church with Outreach

Fill the Church with the love that does not come from agreement and fellowship alone but reaches out to embrace those who are hostile and scornful. Let no task seem too heavy, no forgiving gesture too costly, because all is done in the strength of God who pardons and saves to the utmost and has made us his messengers here on earth.

Raymond Chapman

13. Revival of Brightness

God, our Shepherd, give to the Church a new vision and a new charity, new wisdom and fresh understanding, the revival of her brightness and the renewal of her unity; that the eternal message of your Son, undefiled by the traditions of humans, may be hailed as the good news of the new age; through him who makes all things new, Jesus Christ our Lord.

Percy Dearmer

14. Bond of Truth and Peace

God, the Father of our Jesus Christ, our only Saviour, the Prince of Peace, give us grace seriously to lay to heart the great dangers we are in by our unhappy divisions. Take away all hatred and prejudice and whatsoever else may hinder us from godly union and concord; that as there is but one body and one Spirit and one hope of our calling, one Lord, one faith, one baptism, one God and Father of all, so we may henceforth be all of one heart and of one soul, united in one holy bond of truth and peace, of faith and charity and may with one mind and one mouth glorify you; through Jesus Christ our Lord.

Accession Service (1715)

15. Rouse Your Church

Infinite Lord and eternal God, rouse your Church in this land, restore your people's sense of mission, and revive your work in holiness and strength. By your Spirit, teach us to give our energy, our time, our money, our service and our prayer, that your kingdom may be advanced here and in all the world; in the name of Jesus Christ our Lord.

Church in Wales

16. Signs of God's Kingdom

Guide your Church to cherish and cultivate the precious seed of the Kingdom, that all your people may be gathered into one in holiness. Teach us to recognize the old and the new treasures that have been revealed and entrusted to us, to maintain past integrity and explore new opportunities.

Raymond Chapman

17. Caring Church

Most merciful Father, you have called us to be a caring Church, reflecting in our lives your infinite care for us your children. Help us to fulfil our calling and to care for one another in an unselfish fellowship of love; and to care for the world around us in sharing with it the good news of your love and serving those who suffer from poverty, hunger and disease. We ask it in the name of Christ our Lord.

Michael Ramsey

18. Local Church

We thank you, O God, for the presence of our church in this place. We gratefully remember those who established it and all those who have maintained it thus far. May it reveal a part Christ's body, continuing the miracle of the incarnation of the divine Word. Forgive us if we have created it as a social club with a hint of piety. May the bodies and minds of the members be interlinked in their worship and service. Help us to exercise the authority in Christ's way by washing one another's feet and sharing one another's concerns. Safeguard us from the poison of corruption, competition for power and fight for position. Let our mission be intertwined with our corporate life of the congregation so that our neighbours will know what Christian love is. Give us the grace and wisdom to explore the meaning and dimensions of a living outreach.

Israel Selvanayagam

19. Community of Love

Living Christ, bring us from death to life: from being the kind of church we try to maintain to becoming a community of love, and excite us with the truth; that to die and rise again is the great mystery and challenge of the gospel for each generation. Strengthen us through prayer and give us courage to take the first step, knowing that you, whose name is Emmanuel, travel with us.

Maureen Edwards

20. Church Past and Future

Guide the Church to be faithful to the wisdom of the past and open to the revelation of the future. As we rejoice in our times of worship, keep us from lingering too long on the heights, and lead us back to do the work appointed for us.

Raymond Chapman

21. Rainbow People

Rainbow God, you have created people of many different skin colours, and given us different cultures. But in you each has its source and its fulfilment. In Jesus Christ you have made us one, breaking down the walls that we erect to protect ourselves. By your Holy Spirit you have joined us together in one body, giving to each part its special gift. We pray that in the Church we may experience, more and more, the love of your Holy Spirit, a love which honours and respects each one, which is sensitive to our hurts and hopes, which values the gifts we bring, and shares its own treasures with us.

And to you, O God, Father, Son and Holy Spirit, be all honour and glory, now and to ages of ages.

Australian Aboriginal Woman

22. Mission Partners

Loving God, we rejoice in your boundless creativity evident in every aspect of this your world; especially we thank you that, created in your image, each of us is unique. We pray for your Church throughout the world in all its diversity and thank you for the men and women whom you call to serve you across boundaries of nation and culture. We pray for our mission partners working in other countries. Through the international channels that they open for us, may your Spirit inspire us anew to work for your Kingdom to come on earth.

Gabrielle Grace

23. Fill with Truth

Gracious Father, we humbly beseech you for your universal Church. Fill it with all truth, in all truth with all peace. Where it is corrupt, purge it; where it is in error, direct it; where it is superstitious, rectify it; where anything is amiss, reform it; where it is right, strengthen and confirm it; where it is in want, furnish it; where it is divided and rent asunder, make up the breaches thereof, O you Holy One of Israel: for the sake of Jesus Christ our Lord and Saviour.

William Laud

24. Eternal Source

We praise you, O God, source of all being, eternal word and Holy Spirit: in wisdom you have brought forth the vibrancy of creation, in mercy you have called your people into the pilgrimage of faith, in weakness you have revealed the power of the gospel and in your providence you have raised up your servant Church; and so with all who long to fulfil your will, we pray that we may see your glory, hear your voice, obey your call and carry on our bodies the wounds of those faithful to your sending.

Norman Wallwork

25. Confidence to Change and Serve

Lord Jesus, where your Church is wealthy among the poor, fearful in the midst of injustice, cowardly among the oppressed, give us we pray, new confidence in your Kingdom, new hope in your purpose, new faith in your power, and new trust in your nearness. Then turn our wealth, our fear and even our cowardice into resources of strength to serve your people in your name.

Donald Hilton

26. Reconciled Community

Reconciling God, we come as old and young, male and female, black and white, employed and unemployed, and with differing degree of disability. We come with Christians far and near and discover the unity that we have in Christ. Father, Son and Spirit: Holy Trinity, you draw us into your communion of love. Make us more than a society, having things in common. Make us more than neighbours, linked by a place in common. Build us into a community; companions with you in sharing your love. Be with us as we worship, healing hurt and discord, and creating a dynamic harmony of praise.

Simon Walkling

27. Leaven of Communion

O God the Father all you ask every one of us is to spread love where the church is brought low and reconciliation where people are divided, father against son, mother against daughter husband against wife, believers against those who cannot believe, Christians against their unloved fellow Christians. You open the way for us, so that the wounded body of Jesus Christ, your church, may be leaven of communion for the poor of the earth and in the whole human family.

Author Unknown

28. Bond of Love

Bonding, loving, God, from the many peoples of the world you have made your Church a new family in Christ. It is the friendship of Jesus that binds us together, his love that gives us unity, and his care that sends us out to serve the world. We thank you that when we are strong we can give ourselves to your Church with active strength; and that in our times of weakness we can lean on the strength of others. Taught by Jesus, we have learned to rejoice with those who rejoice and weep with those who weep, so that, as friends of God, we become friends of one another.

Donald Hilton

29. Governed by the Spirit of Unity

Be gracious to all that are near and dear to me and keep us all in your fear and love. Guide us, good Lord, and govern us by the same Spirit, that we may be so united to you here as not to be divided when you are pleased to call us hence, but may together enter into your glory, through Jesus Christ, our blessed Lord and Saviour.

John Wesley

30. Church Leaders

Christ, Servant Lord, we thank you for giving to us your servants who lead the church and demonstrate the beauty of power in serving as a slave. Let them approach their positions with trembling and joy, confidence and humility, with truth and determination. Just as you called people from the margins despite rebukes from others and healed them, let our leaders not ignore the voice of even the most insignificant person. Let their diplomacy be combined with dignity and grace, and protocols with passion and prophetic outlook. As the field of administration often remains unevangelized, failing to demonstrate the kind of God we believe in, may any authority be exercised with firmness and grace. Once again anoint our church leaders with the Spirit of wisdom and of understanding, of counsel and might, and knowledge and fear of the Lord. May we all be aware that ultimately, we are accountable to your humble throne of the crucified centre.

Israel Selvanayagam

31. Words and Action

Almighty God, we are so good at talking, we excel at holding meetings and taking minutes. Forgive out tendency for endless words. By the power of your Holy Spirit, turn our words into actions, serving others as you also served. Forgive us when we sit back in the armchairs of our comfortable world, watching others in crisis and pain. Lord, help us to engage our faith to be involved, not standing at a distance, but in participation with our neighbours, that we may truly be your Church, kneeling before our communities with humility and compassion: supporting the vulnerable, seeking the lost, searching out the lonely, welcoming the stranger, with your transforming love.

Eunice Attwood

32. Together in Diversity

O God, give us grace to be communities of Christian people who travel together in all our diversity and who know how to link arms with others in solidarity; enable us all to acknowledge our wound, our hopes and our fears; give grace to the weak and the strong to help each other along the road; and may we discover and be signs of your Kingdom.

Vernon Marsh

33. Organic Unity

Triune God, Father, Son and the Holy Spirit, as you are one in a dynamic intimacy of love you have called us to be one body with one faith. Forgive the scandal and sin of our divisions which we often acknowledge but nonetheless perpetuate. Heal the wounds of many conflicts in history in the name of supposed truth and denominationalism. Defrock us and strip us bare; expose our pious gestures and rehearsed smiles. Increase our faith so that we can uproot and plant and move from our familiar ambiance and practices to new initiatives of faith. Recognizing the models of organic unity around the world, may we wake up from our slumber of complacency and at least save ourselves from wasting resources and energy. May the flame of the gospel propel us to organize, negotiate and achieve your will so that many will believe and be fascinated to your church. In the name of Christ who died, rose again and built up his body.

Israel Selvanayagam

34. Purify the Church

Gracious Father, fill your whole Church with truth and peace: where it is corrupt purge it; where it is in error, direct it; where anything is amiss, reform it; where it is right, strengthen it; and where it is divided and torn asunder, heal it and bind up its wounds; through Christ our Lord.

William Laud

35. Young's Dreams and Schemes

Ancient of days and young as each day, help us to create a world where dreams come true and the young rise up with new strength. We pray for our work with young people and for volunteers and youth workers who give time in uniformed groups, clubs and fellowships; for young people in Seed Teams, for those on Time for God Schemes. We pray for young people who long for change; for the Church that must let go of the 'manna' of yesterday to feast on the bread of today. Instil in us all a youthful longing for the Christ who 'makes all things new.'

Mark Wakelin

36. Children in Sight

Child-like God, just like the disciples of Jesus hindered the children coming to him, we also put hurdles for the children to enrich our worship and fellowship. Give us true maturity and generosity of heart to value the gifts of the children. Let us not treat them simply as objects of our teaching but symbols and primary heirs of the Kingdom of God. Loosen our tongues and lighten our hearts so that we can identify with them without inhibition and work together wherever possible. May we always be ready to learn the power of powerlessness from them and grow towards a child-like life.

Israel Selvanayagam

XVI. Christian Ministry

1. To Follow the Son of Man

Son of Man, Holy and Heavenly, you came to earth and identified with victims of oppression. Jesus, you said that you came not to be ministered to but to minister. Forgive our blunders to take the meaning and form of the church's ministry away from this core. Help us to reimagine that the beauty of authority is to serve as slaves, as you demonstrated by washing the feet of your disciples. May our structures and uniforms of ministry express this unique pattern that all around us will know that the church is there to exemplify service through ministers and members. Give us the joy of ministering to people.

Israel Selvanayagam

2. Effective Ministers

Gracious God, we thank you for the ministers by whom we have been led, guided and inspired throughout our Christian pilgrimage; for their dedication, example, preaching and leadership; for their encouragement and pastoral care, particularly in times of special need. Help us to remember that they are but human, too, and so to cherish and pray for them, support and befriend them, and be sensitive to their needs; to laugh with them and cry with them and share gladly in their ministry; that, together, we may build up the fellowship of your church and make it an effective instrument for mission and service. In Christ's name.

Derek Lyons

3. Local Preachers

Jesus the Carpenter, we pray for those you have called from different backgrounds of work and leisure to preach your Word. May their message, given by your Spirit and forged in daily experience, be relevant, vital and inspiring to all who hear, see and know them. Encouraging Lord, we pray for all who are testing their call to preach and for those with years of experience and service, that together they may find inspiration, fellowship and mutual support; and that they may grow in faith as they proclaim the good news of Jesus Christ. Risen Lord, when commitment and inspiration burn low, deepen their awareness of your living presence that brings life, newness and joy to be proclaimed in your name and through the power of the Holy Spirit.

From Kenya

4. Overseers

Loving Servant-Lord, the incense of my gratitude rises to your lotus-feet. For you have called me to an office for which I am unworthy. You have humbled me before your people but elevated me to be alongside them, particularly the poor and the needy. You have anointed me with marks of self-sacrifice and identification with the suffering. Let my girdle strengthen me to struggle for justice and fairness; my saffron hand cup and stole remind me your self-emptying incarnation; my staff to guard the true faith of your people and nourish them to grow into maturity; and my wooden cross to tell others that I represent those who labour hard, such as tree climbers, quarry workers and the fisher folk. Help me to receive reverence and honour from the people and to instantly transfer them to you. Strengthen my will and resolve not to comprise on evil and corruption. May I appear before your presence with the unspoiled robe you have wrapped around me. I pray that all my fellow bishops live up to the ideal of their calling in their working contexts. May all of us lead the pastors and people in our charge to bow down before your crucified feet, our Lord and Saviour.

Samuel Amirtham

5. Sacristy Prayers

O you who have called us to this holy ministry and set us in the blessed fellowship of all who serve you in the church of your Son, accept our thanksgiving for the high privilege which is ours. Teach us diligence, humility, and kindness in our ministry. Grant that through faithful study of your Word in the Scriptures and in the events of our time, through constant prayer, blameless living, and self-giving service we may come to understand the ways of men and of society. As we lead your people in their worship of you, and interpret to them the truth from you, may we be led to the altar of your holy love, and linger often near the cross where you make yourself known as Redeemer. As we shepherd your people, fill our hearts with love for them, and may their growth into the likeness of Christ be our chief concern.

For our brothers in the service of Christ, we ask your continuing favour. Empower them to be the prophets of your purpose and the priests of your grace. Guard and guide them and their dear ones, giving them your peace in their going out and coming in, till we all come at last to our Father's house, to go no more out for ever.

David A. MacLennan

6. Dedication to Ministry

O God, who hast kindled in me the desire to dedicate my life to your service as a minister of the gospel: grant me an abundant measure of your grace during these years of my preparation that I may use profitably the opportunities to study and walk worthy of the calling of the one to whom shall be entrusted the ministry of sacred things; through Jesus Christ my Lord.

Emil E. Fischer

7. Administration

God of grace and discipline, we thank you for the leaders of your church who have been administrators, effective, inspiring and influential, not stung by the poison of arrogance and corruption. Help us to choose our leaders with utmost sincerity, seriousness and prayer. Let our administrators always be aware that the way they administer is the best to proclaim to the world the kind of God Christians believe in. May they be prompt in correspondence, transparent in dealings and accountable for people with special concern for the poor and vulnerable.

Israel Selvanayagam

8. Meeting of Ministers

O Lord, I humbly beseech and implore you, grant me always the humble knowledge that edifies. Give unto me that gentle eloquence which is innocent of all arrogance and exaltation of one's own gifts above the brethren. Put into my mouth, I pray, the word of consolation and edification and exhortation through your Holy Spirit, that I may exhort those that are good to be better and, by word and example, recall those who are going contrary to the straight path. May the words which you shalt grant to your servant be as sharp javelins and burning arrows which will pierce the hearers and kindle them to fear and love you.

Ambrose Bishop

9. I Need You

I need you to teach me day by day, according to each day's opportunities and needs. Give me, O my Lord, that purity of conscience which alone can receive, which alone can improve your inspiration. My ears are dull, so that I cannot hear your voice. My eyes are dim, so that I cannot see your tokens. You alone can quicken my hearing, and purge my sight, and cleanse and renew my heart. Teach me to sit at your feet and to hear your Word.

John Henry Newman

10. The Busy Pastor

Teach me, good Lord:

Not to murmur at the multitude of business or shortness of time.

Not to magnify undertaken duties by seeming to suffer under them, but to treat all as liberties and gladness.

Not to call attention to crowded work, or petty fatigues.

Not to gather encouragement from appreciation by others, less this should interfere with purity of motive.

Not to seek praise, respect, gratitude, or regard from superiors or equals on account of age or past service.

Not to let myself be placed in favourable contrast with another.

Edward White Benson

11. Ongoing Preparation

Holy God, Lord of the Church and all people, thank you for your calling to be a minister in your vineyard. I gratefully remember those who shaped me and guided me for this vocation by teaching, training and counselling. I thank you for the lessons I have learned from church people whom I have served. Enable me to be open to change my approach according the context. Let me never compromise with superficial piety, conservative stubbornness and fundamentalist vigour. Give me the wisdom to prepare my order of worship relevant to the occasion, to preach your word with passion and clarity and to pray with spirit and mind. Anoint me with your Spirit that I may be able to prepare your people for their ministry and witness in their day to day life and work. In all my activities – home visits, baptisms, confirmation, Eucharist, weddings and funerals – give your counsel to share the gospel insights and values. Help me to keep my hands, mouth, and mind pure. Lead me not into the temptation of aspiring for power and position, but deliver me to do what is given to me to the best of my ability with honesty. May my dealings be transparent and accountable. Transform me into your glory again and again.

Solomon Joseph

12. Theological Educator

God of the treasures of wisdom and knowledge, thank you for teaching that fearing you is the beginning of wisdom. Throughout history you have enlightened extraordinary people to discover the hidden resources for the good of humanity. You have taught us to love you with all our heart, mind and spirit. Thank you for your Son Jesus who taught, shaped and guided his disciples for mission. Thank you for your apostles, church leaders and hosts of theologians who have warned people against false teaching, expounded your gospel for every generation and established seminaries and colleges for theological education and ministerial training. Dear Lord, it is my privilege to stand in such a long tradition to fulfil my vocation. Help me to be a creative participant in the educational ministry of my college where I currently serve. Help me to set an example in my behaviour, to be friendly with colleagues and students, and to teach with clarity and engagement. Loving God, save your church from superstition, ritual routines and misleading forces. I pray for church leaders that they might be open to welcome new ideas and encourage their ministers and congregations to experiment with alternative patterns of ministry based on the biblical paradigms. Continue to give me and my colleagues passion for truth and truthfulness, for grace and graciousness, and for the perfect combination of education and enlightenment. I pray in the name of your Spirit, the supreme teacher and guide.

Israel Selvanayagam

13. Relating to People of Other Religions

All embracing God, thank you for India being a secular country which includes people of different religions. Thank you for good people across different religious traditions, who have helped us in trouble, contributed to the common good and travelled with us in the pilgrimage of dialogue. May the church not attempt to overtly convert them, but may it be a living witness of the gospel. Keep us from bearing false witness against our neighbours of other religions; may we work together for justice, peace and integrity of creation. As your loving Son Jesus Christ appreciated the 'faith' of some extraordinary individuals from other religious traditions, help us to do the same. Give us opportunities to share one another's visions and traditions. Give us the gift of being patient to speak but eager to listen. When others ask us about reasons of our hope in Christ may we answer with gentleness and respect. Bless the ministry of interreligious dialogue all over the world. May we continue this journey with firm commitment to truth, both known and unknown, and rejoice in the hope that finally truth will win. In Christ's name we pray.

Rajamony Chellakkan

14. Love for All Humankind

Lord, we pray for people of all faiths, knowing of your love for all humankind, for the knowledge that you are present in all that is good and beautiful in the religions and cultures of the world. Give us the mind and heart to build bridges of understanding for community beyond our limited horizons. May we be open to learn truth from all sources but above all, teach us, O Lord, to share the truth of our Lord Jesus Christ, with our neighbours of whatever faith.

Herbert Jaya Singh

15. Women Leaders

Thank you, O God, for the gifts and graces the women members bring to the church. Forgive us for not recognizing them for full time ministry for so long. Raise more women leaders in the church so that the churches everywhere will grow into healing and wholeness. Where there is still prejudice, misunderstanding and confusion let the Spirit challenge and correct. By the visible presence of the women help us to share the feminine quality of the Divine and mutually enrich and grow into maturity.

Israel Selvanayagam

XVII. Christian Witness and Mission

1. Missional Church

Living God, bless your church in the world. May it stand as a sign of hope for all, and an example of love to the world. May it be faithfully Christ-like, responding to its mission, not counting the cost of commitment, but paying the praise of faith, and rejoicing in the joy of our common calling to proclaim the good news of the gospel.

Stephen Brown

2. To be Sensitive

Help us, Father God, to put the gospel into action and preach it with our lives. Help us to welcome strangers and newcomers, and make people feel wanted and cared for. Help us to listen to the ideas of other people and take their opinions seriously. Help us to notice when people are sad and be sensitive to their needs. Help us to be alert to the lonely and offer Christian friendship. Help us to hear the cry of anguish or pain and stand alongside those who need us. We dare to ask that we may grow more like Christ himself, and so help others to find his love.

Donald Hilton

3. Freed to Free

Loving God, you have set us free in Christ Jesus! As we stand in the liberty wherein you have made us free, enable your church, through prayer and action to share this freedom with all who are: oppressed by rulers, structures and systems; marginalized because of race, gender, sexuality or economic status; bound by habits which imprison and degrade; silenced because they stand by their faith and for truth; until all experience life in all its fulness and the truth which sets all people free.

Olufemi Cole-Njie

4. Freed to Free

As you free us, Lord God, from slavery to self and sin, show us how to set others free from their enslavements. May we be liberators: for the prisoners of fear, for those held fast by addictions, for those trapped in poverty and poor housing, and for all for whom disability imposes restrictions in everyday living. Help us to surrender ourselves, to be part of the answer to these prayers, giving care, compassion and time to others, as to you.

Stephen Bales

5. Enlarge My Heart

O God: Enlarge my heart that it may be big enough to receive the greatness of your love. Stretch my heart that it may take into it all those who with me around the world believe in Jesus Christ. Stretch it that it may take into it all those who do not know him, but who are my responsibility because I know him. And stretch it that it may take in all those who are not lovely in my eyes and whose hands I do not want to touch; through Jesus Christ my saviour.

An African Christian

6. Gossiping the Gospel

Lord Jesus Christ, make me today a gossip of the gospel. Help me to share good news with those who are low-spirited, to speak words of comfort to those who are broken-hearted, to give hope of freedom to those who are oppressed, and to remind those who despair of our world that you have come into it, so that through your love the world might be saved. May all my words and actions help to convince others that they are loved by you, for your sake.

Pauline Webb

7. Pierce with Truth

O God, compassionate and just, wielder of the one sword that pierces with truth and healing, penetrate the murk and fury of our hearts, that our anger may be shaped by the power of your Spirit, that we may create with you that commonwealth of justice and peace that is yours alone.

Jim Cotter

8. Building in Mission

Creator God, as new buildings and witness arise from dust and decay, help us to focus on you and your mission – not our own – for this ever-changing world. As stones and bricks are laid down, let the first one in all we do be yours, for you are the Cornerstone and the Rock upon which we must stand.

Diane Allen

9. Witness for the Saviour

Judge and Saviour, pierce the secrets of our hearts and bring to light our hidden sins. Purify and strengthen us in faith and give us courage to strive with evil and bear witness to your just and loving rule.

Jim Cotter

10. Facing Challenge

Deliver us O Lord, from the preaching that does not challenge our pleasures; from the praying that does not challenge our priorities; and from the praising that does not challenge our politics; for Jesus' sake.

Norman Wallwork

11. Responding to the Gospel

Once upon a timeless God, who imagined the unfinished story of creation, peopled it, giving it countless twists and turns, help us to discover your unfinished stories within us: stories of walking on water and through water, of red earth and dry bones spirited, of desolations becoming homecomings, and death transformed by love. Through our witness dispel wishful thinking, false promises and the desire for happy endings and replace them with generous, honest, life-giving communities of hope.

Barbara Glasson

12. Commission and Grace

Father God, show us the relationship between commission and grace. We are called to share our faith but we confess that when we hear your compelling call we are sometimes paralysed by guilt and lack of confidence. Help us, Lord, to be overwhelmed by the gospel of your love in the cross of Jesus, and to be so full of the Spirit, that the call to evangelise becomes an 'idiocy' – or like being urged to breathe. I can't stop telling what the Lord has done! It pours out through my whole life. Let it be like that, Lord. Show us Jesus' method of mission. As much about being as doing, multifaceted – meeting people on their turf, alongside the rich and the poor. Touching the untouchable, saying the unthinkable, ripping through the paraphernalia of religion with the word of truth. Instigating a way of being Church that is alive – more a movement than an institution. Travelling hopefully, living riskily 'on the edge' offering grace not condemnation, welcoming all to the Kingdom party.

Take me out of my comfort zone, Lord. Show me the doors of opportunity and give me the wit and the grace to go through them. Grant me courage to tell my story. To tell my story. To tell the story, and to trust you for harvest.

Phil Clarke

13. Life of Good News

Creating Word, bringing the world into being, for the starred sky and the songbird that tell of your being, for people diverse in colour and culture, made in your image, speaking in many tongues – we praise you.

Help us to see you at work in the world;

May our lives tell the Good News.

Living Word, seen and heard in Jesus, teacher and storyteller, speaking words of healing and forgiveness, standing silent in the face of hatred and lies, crying out on the cross – we believe in you.

Help us to hear the cries of the world today;

May our lives tell the Good News.

Breath of the Spirit, rushing wind and still small voice, challenging, changing, making connections, creating community, encouraging hope, come among us, inspire us – we need you.

Help us to communicate your love

May our lives tell the Good News.

Jan Sutch Pickard

14. To Reach Out

Lord, may your people in every country reach out to all who need the gospel of our Lord Jesus Christ, that all may hear and know Jesus as Lord and Saviour. May the wind of the Holy Spirit blow across the continents and oceans so that many may see the salvation of our Lord.

Tomasi Kanailage

15. Mission in Christ's Way

Surrendering ourselves to your love, O God, may our time be spent doing the work of Christ, all sharing and caring, teaching and learning. Witnessing and praying in the power of the Holy Spirit, so that those far and near may be loved into your family.

Methodist Church, Zimbabwe

16. With Proper Confidence

O God, grant unto us that we be not unwise, but understanding of your will: not slothful, but diligent in your work: that we run not uncertainly nor fight your battles as those that beat the air. Whatsoever our hand finds to do, may we do it with our might: that when you shall call your labourers to give them their reward, we may so have run that we may obtain; so have fought the good fight, as to receive the crown of eternal life; through Jesus Christ our Lord.

Henry Alford

17. Path of Transformation

Lord, deepen our understanding of your nature; increase in us the awareness of your ways. Draw us into those paths that lead to the transforming both of nations and of people. Strengthen us in our weakness, hold us in our trembling and form us into the servants of your mysteries, through Christ our Lord.

Donald Eadie

18. Serving as Minority

Dear Lord, help us not to lose heart when we are small minorities, and to recognise that our greatest strength lies in our weakness. Save us from preoccupation with our own safety or survival. Free us, unimpeded by power struggles, simply to obey you by witnessing and serving. Teach us how to be lowly vines, slender, struggling, yet fruitful. Show us how to be lamps, small yet shining brightly on tall lampstands; Poor ourselves, may we bring wealth to many.

Based on Genesis 49:22, Matthew 5:14-16 and 2 Corinthians 6:10
Norman Taggart

19. Fighters for Truth

Lord Jesus, make us people who fight for truth without self-righteousness who can be wrong and know ourselves forgiven, who can love and go on loving, and who can suffer if need be. May our neighbours see something of you in us and may you not be ashamed of us when you come in glory.

Christina Le Moignan

20. To be an Evangelist

Ever-sending God, thank you for the missionary heritage of extraordinary individuals and communities you have called and used. Though we are unworthy just like earthen vessels you have been so gracious to put in them your glorious gospel. Remind us of your commission that we are supposed to make disciples for Jesus, preach the gospel to the whole of creation, to be witnesses preaching repentance and forgiveness and to be as representatives of the victims of injustice, forgiving or not forgiving on their behalf. Just as the missionaries in the past have done, help us to find out the sharpened focus of the gospel in a particular context. May our churches be witnesses by the way they worship and live, particularly keeping the administration evangelical and making it witness to the meaning of authority as servanthood as our Lord Jesus demonstrated by washing the feet of his disciples. May the Christian unity help in the mission that all will believe and come forward to be transformed for a new life. Help us to deny ourselves but never deny your Son so that the message of the gospel will shine forth in splendour.

Justin Selvamony

21. Instrument of Your Peace

Lord, make me an instrument of your peace; where there is hatred let me sow love; where there is injury, pardon; where there is doubt, faith; where there is despair, hope; where there is darkness, light; and where there is sadness, joy. O, Divine Master, grant that I may never seek so much to be consoled as to console; to be understood as to understand, to be loved as to love with all my soul. For it is in giving that we receive; it is in pardoning that we are pardoned; and it is in dying that we are born into eternal life.

Francis of Assisi

22. Open Our Eyes

Open my eyes that I may see the deepest needs of my people; move my hands that they may feed the hungry; touch my heart that it may bring warmth to the despairing; teach me the generosity that welcomes strangers; let me share my possessions to clothe the naked; give me the care that strengthens the sick; make me share in the quest to set the prisoner free. In sharing our anxieties and love, our poverty and our prosperity, we partake of your Divine Presence.

Canaan Banana

23. Help Others

Lord Jesus, who came not to be served but to serve, help us to live useful lives.

Help us always to encourage, and never to discourage others; always to be readier to praise than to criticize and to sympathize rather than to condemn.

Help us always to help, and never to hinder others. Help us always to make the work of others easier and not harder. Help us not to find fault with the efforts of others, unless we are prepared to try to do the things better ourselves. Make us more ready to cooperate than to object, and more ready to say yes than to say no when anyone appeals to us for help.

Help us always to be a good example, and never bad. Help us always to make it easier for others to do the right thing, and never to make it easier for them to go wrong. Help us to remember that what is safe for us may be dangerous for others. Help us always to take our stand beside anyone who is standing for the right.

So, grant that indeed our lives may be like lights in the world.

William Barclay

24. Whole Life as Good News

Dear God, through the sensitivity of my ears, the discernment of my eyes, the clarity of my voice,

Bring joy and peace.

Through the lifting of my hands, the comfort of my arms, the journeying of my feet,

Bring joy and peace.

Through the firmness of my faith, the brightness of my hope, the genuineness of my love,

Bring joy and peace.

Through Jesus Christ, our Lord.

Ron Hoar

25. Touching Lives

Eternal God, in Christ your Son, you have touched our lives with faith and hope and love. Inspire us by your Spirit, so to touch the lives of others with gospel grace that faith may grow, hope may blossom and love abound; through Christ our Lord.

Michael Townsend

26. Joy of Serving

Eternal Father, it is your joy to call men and women to serve you across the barriers of race and language and culture: Give them strength and courage and satisfy their longing to make known the good news of Christ. Bless those who are called along the humble road, to serve and support but not to lead. When they face danger, save them from fear; when they are disheartened, be their friend; when they think they have failed, show them the cross. Give them peace in their hearts, and peace in their homes, and the joy of acceptance by whom they serve. For Jesus Christ's sake.

John Kingsnorth

27. Transforming Mission

Lord, our light in darkness, our hope in despair, our peace in struggle, our joy in sorrow, our way when we are lost; may your light shine in the very darkest places of our hearts and of the world; may your hope touch the hearts of those in despair; may your peace reach individuals and countries torn by war; may your joy be known to those who mourn; may those who are lost know you the Way and may we be channels of your light, your hope, your peace, your joy, and lead others in the Way of your love.

Margaret James

28. To Live the Truth

O God of light and life and love, by your Spirit help us to live the truth; your light is stronger than darkness. Your life means more than death, your love can overcome all things. May the light of the Christ shine in us and through us, may the life of Christ free us for proper living. May the love of Christ control us; We ask this for your glory, O God of life and light and love.

Kenneth Hext

29. Liberating Mission

Dear God, your amazing love embraces all humanity and the world you have created. We thank you for your presence, encouragement, hope and sustaining grace in the midst of human suffering. Give us renewed courage and faith to participate with you in your liberating mission. Teach us to love as Jesus did; to be in solidarity with those who are not able to develop their potential because of abuse, discrimination, injustice, or deprivation. Empower· your Church to proclaim the good news of abundant life with boldness, faith and conviction; to fulfil its prophetic role in our own time and context; in Jesus' name.

Saray Veagra

30. Witnessing Life

More than our words let our lives proclaim your gospel, O God. Just as you sent Isaiah, send us to the local area. Let our exemplary lives and honest dealings reflect aspects of the gospel. Save us from hypocrisy!

Israel Selvanayagam

31. To be Open

Lord God, you have been active in this village ever since the time of creation. Save us from the illusion that we are taking you to this area. Give us an open heart and discerning mind to identify decisive moment of your intervention in the history of these people, from generation to generation. May the Hebrew ancestors and our ancestors be together in our vision!

Israel Selvanayagam

32. Local Church Life

Gracious God, let our mission and witness start from the local church. Save us from the tendency to be enthusiastic about mission in far away places while the light of the local church is dim. Rekindle and renew us.

Justin Selvamony

33. Global Mission

Wherever we do and in whatever form, Gracious God, your mission is one. Give us a vision and solidarity of your global mission.

Based on the Methodist Church's Statement

34. Lives Tell Good News

Loving Jesus, we remember your warning to the religious teachers of the day that 'you hypocrites! You travel over land and sea to win a single convert, and when you have succeeded, you make them twice as much a child of hell as you are.' May we fear your warning and first reflect your good news in our lives.

Israel Selvanayagam

35. Living Outreach

Lord, may your people in every country reach out to all who need the gospel of our Lord Jesus Christ, that all may hear and know Jesus as Lord and Saviour. May the wind of the Holy Spirit blow across the continents and oceans so that many may see the salvation of our Lord.

Tomasi Kanailage

36. Multiple Witness

Surrendering ourselves to your love, O God, may our time be spent doing the work of Christ, all sharing and caring, teaching and learning. Witnessing and praying in the power of the Holy Spirit, so that those far and near may be loved into your family.

Methodist Church, Zimbabwe

37. Liberating Gospel

O Holy Spirit, our liberator and comforter, we are thankful that you have renewed us and given us courage and new confidence. Help us recapture our sense of mission and share in your ministry of reconciliation. Help us rediscover how to enrich the world with your justice, peace and love. Strengthen us that we may stand firm against all forms of domination, exploitation, discrimination.

Strengthen us that we may meet the challenges and opportunities of the present age to proclaim with urgency: 'Good News to the poor, liberty to the captives, recovery of sight to the blind, freedom for the oppressed and to announce the year when the Lord will save his people' (Luke 4:18,19).

Strengthen us that we may move ahead, out of the paths of divisiveness, hopelessness, powerlessness.

Strengthen us that we may go into the world with your power to fulfil our calling as servants of our Lord and Saviour Jesus Christ.

Lesley G. Anderson

38. Strength in Weakness

Dear Lord, help us not to lose heart when we are small minorities, and to recognise that our greatest strength lies in our weakness. Save us from preoccupation with our own safety or survival. Free us, unimpeded by power struggles, simply to obey you by witnessing and serving. Teach us how to be lowly vines, slender, struggling, yet fruitful. Show us how to be lamps, small yet shining brightly on tall lampstands; Poor ourselves, may we bring wealth to many.

Norman Taggart

39. Message of Love

In a world that needs your message of love so dearly, Lord, give us words to share and strength to share them. Make our lives your message to all with your words in all that we do.

Moravian

40. God's Goodness

Lord, your goodness and light fill all the world. As believers, we see that light and feel that goodness, yet many do not. Help us to open the door of faith to welcome those who desire your love. In your name we pray.

Moravian

41. Lord of Light

Lord of light, many in your world wander without direction and hope. They do not hear your word or feel your touch. Guide them, through your strength and wisdom to find the road to you. Direct them home and welcome them always.

Moravian

42. Righteous Redeemer

Righteous Redeemer, as you have blessed us with your love and power, teach us how to be blessings to those around us. Through those blessings, help us to make your world a more peaceful, grateful, loving and glorious place.

Moravian

43. Courage to be Witnesses

O God, the good news of Jesus Christ is to be neither hoarded nor withheld. Give us, we ask, the courage to be your witnesses for love, justice, and peace by our words, our actions, and our examples to others.

Moravian

44. Transformation

Wondrous Creator, we seek the transformation that takes away our resentments, prejudices, and fears, so that we may live life more fully, always seeking ways in which we can be good neighbours and advocates for the voiceless. Through Christ our Lord we pray.

Moravian

45. God's Presence

Our Lord Jesus, though we may not see you face-to-face, help us to show your presence to our neighbours, friends, family and to all whom we meet. Let us be your hands and feet in the life of someone who needs you today. In Jesus' name we pray.

Moravian

46. The Fragrance of Christ

Help me to spread your fragrance everywhere I go – let me preach you without preaching, not by words but by my example – by the catching force, the sympathetic influence of what I do, the evident fullness of the love my heart bears to you.

John Henry Newman

47. Home in God's Service

Lord, show us how we can use our homes in your service; show us a lonely person whom we can invite to a meal; show us a tired person to whom we can give a relaxing time; show us a shy person who needs mothering; show us a Christian with whom we can share fellowship that both our doors and our hearts may always be open in love.

Beryl Bye

48. Tongues in God's Service

O Lord, we confess we talk too much. We gossip about other people behind their backs. We complain about high food prices, bad weather and our own ailments. We criticize the way things are done and the people who do them. We discuss the shortcomings of our friends and neighbours, often despising them because they do not think or act in the way we think and act ourselves. We exaggerate and minimize, and repeat half-truths, seldom stopping to consider what great forests we may be setting ablaze by the small fires that we light with our tongues. Forgive us, Lord, for we need your forgiveness so much, each and every one of us.

Heavenly Father, we ask that you will take our tongues and use them in your service. Use them to speak words of comfort and encouragement. Use them to witness to your love and faithfulness. Use them for praise and thanks. Use them for laughter and merriment. Use them to soothe and to sympathize, that from our mouths may flow all that is good and pure and true, and a blessing to our fellow beings. In the name of the Lord Jesus we ask.

Beryl Bye

49. Sensitive and Tactful

Lord Jesus Christ, who commanded us to meet the needs of the hungry and thirsty, to clothe the naked and to visit the sick, the stranger and those in prison, we ask that your compassion and courage will fill our hearts, as we prepare to obey. Lead us to the lonely, the sad and the sick, and show us how we can best serve them. Prepare the way for us so that we may find them responsive. Help us to be sensitive and tactful in all we say and do. Guide us in our choice of gift and may it be given and received with graciousness. Help us to be good listeners and sparing with advice. Show us when we should speak of you and how to do it. Lord, as we go as your ambassadors, grant that we may not let you down.

Beryl Bye

50. Courage to Confess

Lord, we would be your instruments. We have nothing to offer except the desire to be workers in your harvest. But, since you have chosen the weak things of this world and the things which are not, will you not also choose us to be pour message to the world. But, we pray that you will grant us not to speak our own words but your Word, through which your people come to know and love you. Give us courage to confess the name of Jesus Christ before others. Help us to care for them, to act as neighbours unto them and to share with them what you have given to us. We do not ask to see the results of our work of salvation and that your kingdom is coming among us. Send us, Lord, as witnesses of the good news of your love made known in Jesus Christ.

Willem Visser 't Hooft

51. Interreligious Understanding

Immeasurable God, Creator and Parent of all,

we marvel at the immense variety of cultures and religious traditions in your world.

We are perplexed by conflicting truth-claims and competing interests.

We are overwhelmed by the complexity and confused by contradictions.

Help us to transcend our self-imposed limitations and be open to your future.

Motivate us to join with people of other religions in friendship and with trust,

standing together on common causes and complementary concerns.

Where our words fail, make our silence genuine and reflective.

Whatever way we turn in the journey of dialogue in Christ and with others,

let us never deviate from obeying your greatest command of

loving you with all our being and loving our neighbours as ourselves.

Help us to affirm our shared identity, concern and resources to mobilize.

Through your Son and in the fellowship of the guiding Spirit.

Israel Selvanayagam

52. Interreligious Tolerance

O God we thank you for the wholeness of the human family: for people of other faiths and none especially those who are our friends and neighbours; for the rich variety of human experience and the gifts we bring to one another when we meet in a spirit of acceptance and love; for dialogue in community, and for mutual enrichment and growing understanding; for movements to establish and sustain the legitimate rights of persons of every religious conviction. And we pray to you that people of all religions may enjoy the freedom to set forth their conviction with integrity and listen to one another in humility; that the Church may perform a reconciling ministry in a world divided by suspicion and misunderstanding, and bring healing to those places where religious intolerance fractures human community; that the Church may bear a true and loving witness to the one it calls Lord, in whose name we pray.

World Council of Churches

53. Touch Us

God of loving touch, we remember with gratitude that your holy Son Jesus touched the untouchable and transformed their lives. Touch our lips that we may be able to smile at and welcome strangers spontaneously. Touch the pulses of our nation that there will be a new impulse in those who are in decision-making positions to be straightforward and transparent. Touch the leaders of the world that they will seek the way of peace, reduce weapons and move towards civilization. Touch those who conspire in the darkness that the number of crimes and overcrowded prisons may be reduced. Touch the hearts of all Christians in our area and further afield with the flame of revival. Let the world not ignore the gospel any longer. Touch our weak frames and minds that we will be effective witnesses of your loving touch. All glory, honour and power be to you for ever and ever.

Israel Selvanayagam

54. Shine Through Us

Dear Jesus, help us to spread your fragrance everywhere we go. Flood our souls with your spirit and life. Penetrate and possess our whole being so utterly that our lives may only be a radiance of yours. Shine through us and be so in us that every soul we come in contact with may feel your presence in our soul. Let them look up and see no longer us but only Jesus! Stay with us and then we shall begin to shine as you shine; so to share as to be a light to others; the light, O Jesus, will be all from you, none of it will be ours; it will be you shining on others through us.

John Henry Newman

55. Radiant Living and Preaching

Father, we pray for all those who preach the gospel. Thank you for all who tell out your love and grace through lives of holiness and radiant living. Help those who also try to put into words the message of hope and new life to be found in Jesus Christ. Give them the help of your Holy Spirit that their words may go straight to the minds and hearts and wills of those who hear. Through Jesus Christ our Lord.

Richard Meux Benson

56. Celebrating the Messengers

Living God, we celebrate those who, stirred by your spirit, set out in boats to take the good news to faraway places. We rejoice with those who share with us now in kingdom-building work. We long for the time when your word finds a home in the hearts and minds of all.

David Coote

57. Fullness, Firmness, Fervency

Grant to us, O Lord, fullness of faith, firmness of hope, and fervency of love. For the sake of the gospel may we sit loosely to our wealth and daily embrace you in the poor of the world. As we rejoice in your generosity so may we give ourselves in the service of others; through Christ our Lord.

Thomas More

XVIII. Health and Healing

1. Tree of Life

Jesus, you are the Christ who is the Tree of Life. Your leaves are for the healing of all people. Grant us this day to shelter in your shade, that we may clearly see the things which lead to health and healing, well-being and peace. Grant us to eat of your fruit, that we may be strong to work for the health of our communities. Grant us the use of your branches, that we may shelter the homeless, defend the weak and discover creative work for unemployed hands. Grant us the sweet perfume of your flower, that in all our efforts we may never lose the wonder and delight of your presence.

David Moore

2. Healing Grace

Loving God, breathe your Spirit of healing into us, for we are like clay jars, easily broken, shattered by the fragility of life and relationships in which you place us, and may your healing grace flow through us into others. Deepen our awareness of our own need that we may recognise when others are broken and be able to share their emptiness and darkness. In the name of Christ who brings healing.

Maureen Edwards

3. Sick and Healers

As we remember the love of Jesus for all who were sick in body, mind and spirit, even when they saw only their own need – we pray for all those who care for the sick; doctors and nurses, psychiatrists and physiotherapists, receptionists and care assistants, especially those under great pressure. Renew their vision of the healing love of Jesus, and keep them as they work for health and wholeness. May the vision of your love capture anew our lives and the lives of all for whom we pray.

May the Spirit of Jesus draw us anew to trust and love you, liberating us from self-concern to love and serve others.

Peter Stephens

4. Wholistic Healing

O Lord Jesus Christ, on the cross you shed your most precious blood to bring peace with God; and by your resurrection you revitalise us with new hope that 'love is stronger than hate, good is stronger than evil and truth is stronger than falsehood.' Come to your world today by your life-giving Spirit. Come, heal the sick and restore the broken. Come, release the fearful, renew the weak with grace and save us all for your glory.

Ken Todd

5. Wholeness and Restoration

Sovereign God of compassion and care, wholeness and healing, forgiveness and love, restoration and hope, we beseech you, on behalf of a world that has been fractured, fragmented, and broken by greed, selfishness, hatred and violence, to have mercy. Grant us, we pray, a fresh intuition of your Spirit's power in order that we may be inspired to bring about transformation and reconciliation in every sector of our society. May the Spirit of love compel us to work for justice, unity, equality, inclusion, acceptance and peace for all people, from all walks of life.

Theophilus Rolle

6. Restore My Hope

Creative God, you suffered for me and suffer with me, use the energy of my anger and the depth of my despair to transform me, heal me and restore my hope.

Diane Coleman

7. Walking Along

Healer of Galilee, you come, again and again, to permeate our human condition; to take upon yourself all that harms us. And you walk with us when our bodies are racked with pain, when our minds are in confusion, when our self-esteem is lost, when our failures overwhelm, when our faith faulters, when our relationships break down, when in our sorrow even our tears dry up.

Peter Miller

8. Love Be the Deepest Truth

When the joy in my life is radiantly present, when the anguish of my life is all I can see, when the shape of my life denies the light to others; this day, every day, may your love be my deepest truth. When a long shadow falls across my life, when despair takes away hope from another's eyes, when delight lights up someone's face; this day, every day, may your love be my deepest truth. Excited or downcast, happy or sorrowful, keep us mindful of the shadows we cast upon others and turn our faces to your light in Jesus; this day, every day, may your love be my deepest truth.

David Perry

9. Depressive Illness

We pray for the mentally ill, for those whose spirits are tormented, for those lost in the inner labyrinth of the mind. May your spiritual light illuminate the valley of shadows. May your love lure them back from the far country, may your angels bring them safely home to a place of sunshine, peace and wholeness.

Tom Stuckey

10. Challenge of HIV and AIDS

Loving God, warm our hearts with the fire of your Spirit and help us to accept the challenge of HIV and AIDS. Protect the healthy, calm the frightened, give courage to those in pain, comfort the dying, and keep the departed in your unending love. May we your people, with energy and imagination, trust in your steadfast love, be united with one another to conquer all disease, fear and prejudice. We make this prayer confident in your mercy and compassion now and for ever.

Neville Smith

11. To Accept HIV/AIDS Patients

Loving God, who in Jesus willingly took on human form, come to us again in the flesh, so that in your humanity we may recognise the humanity of others. In these days, when so many feel rejected because they are HIV or have AIDS, speak to us and assure us of your presence so that we may be there for all who call on us. Lord, you dare to call us your friends, touch us with the hands of friendship so that we may reach out to those who feel untouchable. Touch us with that second touch of healing and wholeness of sight so that we may see others as you see them and offer your healing power to these your sisters and brothers. Spirit of love and life, breathe into us your compassion and care so that we may reach out in this place to touch and to share your love with all.

Daphne and Demetris Palos

12. Forgiveness and Healing

Lord God, I bring to you:

My sins for your forgiveness; my hopes, my aims, my ambitions for your blessings; my temptations for your strength; my words and duties and responsibilities for your help; my family, friends and all loved ones for your care and protection; my Sickness for your healing.

Women`s World Day of Prayer 1991 (Written by Women from Kenya)

13. Make Me Sensitive to the Pain of Others

Father, today I watched a heart operation on T.V. and I am overwhelmed by it. How you have opened the eyes of our minds, and shown us how to overcome the sickness that laid us low! Thank you, God. Thank you for this knowledge which helps doctors and nurses to heal so many people of their pains and ills or help make them less painful. Will I also some day help to ease another's pain? Father, give me that desire and concern, and a heart and mind sensitive to the pains of others.

Vimala Arangadan

14. For a Sick Friend

I am praying for my friend who is so very ill. O my Lord, you brought the touch of healing to those who crossed your path in your earthly life. You promised to respond to the prayers of your children that struggle to follow and reflect you on this earth: reach out now to this one with your healing touch. She belongs to you, O God! She yearns so deeply to serve you restore her to life and wholeness once more. And even while she suffers, may she sense your nearness and be embraced by your peace. Grant that she may have joy, even in the midst of her sufferings. And grant, blessed Lord, that she might get well again.

Leslie F. Brandt

15. Beyond Medication

Loving Lord, you have led us thus far in the rugged paths with ups and downs. You have been gracious to grant beyond the measures of our expectation. By allowing illness to capture us you have demonstrated that your children and ministers are part of the fragile common humanity. When tragedy strikes let us not confuse ourselves by asking unending questions for the reasons. Help us rather to cling to your providence and find fulfilment in your promise of Immanuel. Even now as we embark on yet a new journey towards a specialist treatment, help us to seek your grace beyond medication and medicines and to accept the outcome with humility. In the healing name of Jesus we pray.

I. R. H. Gnanadason

16. Your Healing Touch

Lord, lay your healing hand upon me, give me patience and the strength of will to swallow my bitter medicines and accept the strict diet; to bear the pains and discomfort of illness. Help me to be a good patient and not to be a nuisance to my family. Help me to get well soon. I also remember all those who are sick and in pain. May your healing touch bring relief to them. May all those who are sick with diseases that may not be cured, those wounded in accidents, so badly that they hang between life and death, and also those who watch beside them feel your unconditional acceptance of love. May strength and courage and hope be granted to them.

Samuel Amirtham

17. For Carers

Dear Lord, today I cannot forget little Siddarth whom I met in the hospital – the handsome three-year-old with those big smiling eyes. His body has grown tall and strong, but his brain has been damaged through no fault of his. And he is only one of the many like him. Open our eyes, that we may see and feel for such of your children; guide us to help them to adjust to the world around. Teach us to be kind and patient and concerned about them. Bless their parents, especially the mothers whose heart must bleed for them. Strengthen them, for they will need to be so patient, so tender, and so strong.

Lord, teach our doctors, nurses, physiotherapists, the social workers and all those who work with them, how best to help them to lead a normal and useful life, to grow up co-ordinated and disciplined like any of us. Thank you, God, for the healthy body and mind you have given me. Help me to show my appreciation by using it always to bring joy to you.

Vimala Arangadan

18. Hospital Treatment

O God, my Father, now that I know that I must go into hospital, help me not to worry. Help me to realize that worry only makes things worse, and that the more I worry the longer I will take to get better. Teach me that I am just as near you in a hospital bed as in my own home. Give me that peace of mind without which I know that I can't have health of body. Let me learn what Paul learned: I have learned, in whatever state I am, to be content.

William Barclay

19. Before the Operation

O God, help me to remember at this moment that I have a very great deal to be thankful for. I am grateful for the wisdom of the physician, and the skill of the surgeon, and the art of the anesthetist, and the kindness of the nurses. I am grateful for the merciful oblivion which anesthetics bring. Help me to be calm and relaxed, trusting the surgeon, and the skill you gave him, and trusting you. And make me quite sure that, whatever happens, nothing can separate me from your love in Christ Jesus, my Lord. Let me pray Jesus' own prayer: Father, into your hands I commit my spirit!

William Barclay

20. Depression and Hopelessness

O God, my body won't act and my mind won't think, and I feel that I can't do anything. I am too tired even to sleep. The worst of it is that I feel that I will never be able to do anything again. I get so utterly depressed. I have almost stopped hoping that I will ever be fit again; and it doesn't seem worthwhile even trying. Nothing seems to do any good, and there seems nothing left to do but to give up and give in. O God, lighten my darkness; strengthen my weakness; put hope into my hopelessness. I am beaten unless you help me. Help me to believe that you will hear this my prayer through Jesus Christ our Lord.

William Barclay

21. Old Age

Almighty and Everlasting God, we know that all who are granted a span of life one day experience the limitations of old age. If we are old, Lord, grant us a sweetness of nature that will attract others to us when we are unable to go to them. Give us patience with the human shortcomings that comes as a result of experience. Show us when to stop talking, so that we can listen instead. Help us to bear pain silently; and to share our joys and not our complaints; so that as we grow in age, we grow also in grace.

Loving God, help us to understand the problems and sorrows that old age can bring and to be ever ready to help and cheer. Help us to show interest even when we have heard the same story again and again. Reduce the speed at which we walk so that we may keep pace with slower steps. Raise our voices so that they may be more easily heard. Quicken our reactions so that we may swift to see when help is needed. Help us to be patient with ailing bodies, fussy appetites and querulous tempers, remembering that we shall one day be old and long for others to be patient with us.

Beryl Bye

22. God the Healer

We pray for all whose faith is sorely tried, whose hopes have suffered wreck, or whose love is strained to breaking; and for such as are seeking comfort because of what has been withheld or taken away. Grant them the faith that never fails; that hope which no change or loss can touch; that love which bears all things: the good portion which shall never be taken from them.

O Divine Healer of our souls and our bodies, look upon all faithful people who are sick, and who love to call upon thy Name; take their souls into your keeping, and vouchsafe to deliver them from all sickness and infirmity.

Guide all who search out the seeds and germs of disease to destroy them; and let all lay to heart the laws of good health.

James Ferguson

23. Heal the Brokenness

God our healer, in sorrow and shame, we bring you our brokenness, that you may touch, forgive and heal. We bring you the cracks and chips in our most important relationships: the misunderstandings and the hurts we engender in our families, between friends and lovers. We bring you the fissures and fractures in our worshipping communities: the petty rivalries, our avoidance of real meeting; the intolerance of difference, our wrong priorities. We bring you the shards and fragments of your wider household: nations and cultures at war – or striving for supremacy; the earth, exploited for gain, dying for want of our respect. Where there is no vision, people break loose. Give us, we pray, dreams to bind and inspire us for the future, hearts to forgive one another in the present.

Kate Compston

24. Multiple Healing

Compassionate God, you understand our true condition even beyond what the famous physicians can diagnose. When in pain we question your protection and care, reveal your presence within and around us. Cure our wounds, and challenge those who are wounding, directly and indirectly. Just as your Son Jesus did, open the eyes of the blind but expose the spiritual blindness of fanatic religious leaders and selfish economists. Help us to cooperate with you and with the physicians and carers with patience. Give us the vision of the new order of life and community you have promised where even the least will receive the dignity and respect from those who consider themselves as the greatest. May the breeze of your seas and gardens soothe us, renewing our spirit. Give us the feeling of your gentle touch and loving embrace.

Israel Selvanayagam

25. Healing of Love

When I looked at me bleeding wounds waiting for dressing. I confess, O Lord, in my moans and mourns, I suspected that either you are punishing or forsaking me. When I stopped this self-infliction of pain, I suddenly realised a flying mountain of medicinal herbs as mentioned in my religious myths. But, when I intensely realised that nothing can separate me from the love of God in Christ, there was a flash of change. Continue to heal me, my Saviour.

Israel Selvanayagam

26. Sunshine of Healing

Give me for joy, O Christ, the drying of another's tears; give me for light, the sunshine of healing their sorrows; give me for shelter, the shadow of your cross and for my heart's content, the glory of your presence.

G. A. Studdert Kennedy

27. Spirit of Multiple Healing

Grant, O Lord, to all those who are bearing pain, your spirit of healing, the spirit of life, your spirit of peace and hope, of courage and endurance. Cast out from them the spirit of anxiety and fear; grant them perfect confidence and trust in you, that in your light they may see light, through Jesus Christ our Lord.

Anon

28. Art of Patience

Lord, teach me the art of patience when I am well and give me the use of it when I am sick. In that day either lighten my burden or strengthen my back. Make me, who so often in my health have discovered my weakness presuming on my strength, to be strong in my sickness when I solely rely on your assistance.

Thomas Fuller

29. Mystery of Suffering

Lord, we pray for all who are weighed down with the mystery of suffering. Reveal yourself to them as the God of love who bears all our sufferings. Grant that they may know that suffering borne in fellowship with you is not waste or frustration but can be turned to goodness and blessing, something greater than if they had never suffered, through him who on the cross suffered rejection and hatred, loneliness and despair, agonizing pain and physical death and rose victorious from the dead, conquering and to conquer, even Jesus Christ our Lord.

George Appleton

30. Disabled Children

Dear Father God, today we are remembering in our prayers all those boys and girls who cannot run and play as freely as we can. We think about children who spend lot of time in wheelchairs and lying on bed, or perhaps sitting at a window, watching their friends at play. Help us not to be selfish; to spare time for them; to share our books, our records and our games; to tell our news and write happy letters. Help boys and girls who are shut at home, or in hospital, away from the streets and the fields, to know that we think about them and that people care for them. May they find joy in pictures and in music, in stories and in the friendship of others.

Jean Stevens

31. Change all the Unexpected into Good

I had so hoped that things would be different: that this hadn't happened, or this had, that things had not been said or that they had. How sad that today is not I had wanted. I had so hoped that things would be different. My regret is sore and painful. All my 'might have beens' haunt me. Help me, Healer of all, to give you my yesterdays for your tomorrows, to let you work together all things for good for those who love you.

Mark Wakelin

32. Fear of the Unknown

Loving Father, we acknowledge before you our fear of the unknown, our hesitancy before the oblivion of anaesthetic, our desire for life, and the recovery of health and strength. We pray for those who are to undergo surgery. Give them confidence and faith in the hands of those to whom they commit themselves, and who care for them, so that together they may work to forward the healing purpose of your love.

Neville Smith

33. Intensive Care

Father, Creator, source of all knowledge, wisdom, and skill, we rejoice in all the gifts you have bestowed upon us for the purposes of healing. We give thanks for all who work in intensive care, for their skill and expertise, and for the equipment they employ. May they use all these gifts for the benefit of those in their charge. Grant them the satisfaction of success in their endeavours. Give them serenity when their efforts are in vain. Enable them to bring courage and reassurance to all for whom they care. In the name of Jesus Christ, our Lord.

Neville Smith

34. Children in Hospital

Lord Jesus Christ, you encouraged children to approach you and be near to you, for you saw in them the signs of your kingdom. Draw near, we pray, to all children who are ill. Grant them the gifts of your kingdom: courage and cheerfulness, healing and strength. Support in your love all parents, family and staff who care for them. In your compassion look upon their stress, anxiety and fear, and grant them to know that with the children they love they are held fast in your presence, now and always.

Neville Smith

35. Those Addicted

Compassionate and merciful God, you understand that some of your children are caught up in the whirlpool of attractions and addictions. Their carelessness about thorns on the way slowly catch them up as thorny creepers. Many realise that the state they are in inflicts damage to their health and causes pain to their family. Thank you for the healing sources such as Alcoholics Anonymous and

Deaddiction centres. Help us not to distance ourselves from them but find opportunities to direct them to healing and lasting stability. In our association let them know that not only we and their dear ones but also they themselves will be able to share in the joy of heaven.

Israel Selvanayagam

36. Modern Health Care

Transforming God, thank you for modern health care, developed with your guidance and inspiration. We pray for universal access to disease prevention, diagnosis and treatment. Lay your hands on health professionals and researchers. Touch the sick and the suffering with wholeness and hope. Make us all agents of your healing love.

Ann Cooper

37. From a Hospital Bed

O God, I can't help lying here and thinking about home. I can't relax here the way I can relax at home, because everything is so strange. I keep wondering how they are getting on without me, and if they are worrying about me as much as I am worrying about them. I wouldn't be human if I didn't miss my own home and my people. But, help me to be sensible and realise that the more discontented I am, the slower will be my cure, and the longer I will be getting back to them. And help me to remember that there are other people in this ward who are home-sick too. So, help me to forget my own loneliness in doing something which will help them to forget theirs.

William Barclay

38. Mender of Minds

Jesus, healer, mender of minds, binder of bodies, saver of souls, extend your loving arm to those suffering today: those torn apart by anguish, consumed by worry, numbed by grief, trapped in prisons of loneliness, straightjackets of fear, drowning in deep pools of sadness, strangers in strange land. May we be your arms enfolding, your shoulder to lean on, your ears to listen, your voice to offer words of comfort, your heart to be wounded and to love. Grant us forbearance. And remember all carers, nurses and doctors and medical researchers, who seek to support and enable fractured lives.

Linda Hunter

XIX. Bereavement and Future Hope

1. God of Hope and Desire

God, our hope and our desire, we wait for your coming as a woman longs for the birth, the exile for her home, the lover for the touch of his beloved, and the humble poor for justice.

Janet Morley

2. Weak and Weary

May it come soon to the hungry, to the weeping, to those who thirst for your justice, to those who have waited for centuries for a truly human life. Grant us the patience to smooth the way on which your Kingdom comes to us. Grant us hope, that we may not weary in proclaiming and working for it, despite so many conflicts, threats and shortcomings. Grant us a clear vision that in this hour of our history we may see the horizon and know the way on which your Kingdom comes.

From Nicaragua

3. Surrounded by Love

We remember, Lord, the slenderness of the thread which separates life from death, and the suddenness with which it can be broken. Help us also to remember that on both sides of that division we are surrounded by your love. Persuade our hearts that when our dear ones die neither we nor they are parted from you. In you may we find peace, and in you be united with them in the body of Christ, who has burst the bonds of death and is alive for evermore, our Saviour and theirs for ever and ever.

Dick Williams

4. Spirit of Faith and Courage

Grant, O Lord, to all who are bereaved, the spirit of faith and courage, that they may have the strength to meet the days to come with steadfastness and patience; not sorrowing as those without hope, but in thankful remembrance of your great goodness in past years, and in the sure expectation of a joyful reunion in the heavenly places; and this we ask in the name of Jesus Christ our Lord.

Irish Prayer Book

5. Tragedy and Heartbreak

Lord, where tears fall through tragedy or heartbreak, enter the silence and hold me tight lest in bitterness I blame you or those close to me, when I should be trusting you with those I love and groping my way towards gratitude for the time, I have been privileged to share with them.

Further Everyday Prayers

6. Look in Pity

Lord God, you know our frame and remember that we are dust, look in pity upon those who mourn. Make your loving presence so real to them that they may feel round about them your everlasting arms, upholding and strengthening them.

Grant them such a sense of certainty that their loved one is with you, doing your high service, unhindered by pain, that they turn to life's tasks with brave hearts and steady nerves, consoled in the thought that they will meet their dear one again.

Teach us all to face death unafraid and take us at last in triumph through the shadows into your everlasting light where are reunion and never-ending joy. Through Jesus Christ our Lord.

Leslie D. Weatherhead

7. Preparing to Sleep

Compassionate God, after six days of hectic activities of creation you rested on the seventh day. When your people groaned in hard work of slavery you announced rest for them and led to celebration in the wilderness. You brought them to a land of freedom and rest. Your Son Jesus declared rest for those who laboured and were heavy laden. Your apostles considered death as sleep. Remembering all these experiences, let me properly prepare for dying. Forgive me if I have not thought of this moment every day of my life. Give me rest and keep me from disturbance. Protect me from nightmare but fill me with visions of your glory. Just as I close my eyes, gracious Father, help me glorious vision of your heavenly home.

Israel Selvanayagam

8. Giver of Comfort

Father of all mercies and giver of all comfort, deal graciously with those who mourn, that they may cast every care on you and know the consolation of your love; through Jesus Christ our Lord.

Methodist Worship Book (1999)

9. Be Near to Those Dying

Dear Lord Jesus, you have been through death yourself. Be near to those who are dying. Make yourself known to them. Give them your peace and take away their fears. Comfort the very old. May they know your company in their closing years. Be with those who minister to the dying, who seek to relieve their pain and tell them of your love.

Author Unknown

10. United in Love

O Lord our God, from whom neither life nor death can separate those who trust in your love, and whose love holds in its remembrance your children in this world and the next; so unite us to yourself that in fellowship with you we may always be united to our loved ones, whether here or there; give us courage, constancy and hope; through him who died and was buried and rose again for us, Jesus Christ our Lord.

William Temple

11. Faith and Hope

God's love fills our hearts with hope which is invincible. Lord, help us to hold fast this hope! We abide in faith's loyalty, for God's loyalty is endless. We abide in hope's certitude, for God's patience knows no bounds. We abide in love's protection, for God's goodness endures for ever. Help us to hold fast in unity. Help us to live in hope and love.

Someone Associated with Methodist Overseas Division

12. Those Cast Down

Comfort, we ask you, most gracious God, all who are cast down and faint of heart amidst the sorrows and difficulties of the world; and grant that, by the quickening power of the Holy Spirit, they may be lifted up to you with hope and courage, and enabled to go upon their way rejoicing in your love; through Jesus Christ our Lord.

Richard Meux Benson

13. Light and Hope

When dark clouds overshadow us and thick smoke obstruct our sight, God of light and hope, fill us with a vision of life beyond the grave. When the tombstones are heavy and frighten us, Lord Jesus, remind us of your raising Lazarus by ordering to take away the stone and of your own rising from the dead by the stone moving. Lift away our burdens of separation from our dear ones and lighten our heavy hearts. Just as the sunset leaves the spectacular colour combinations may rays of hope appear beyond the horizons.

Israel Selvanayagam

14. Christ the Light

O Christ the Light, illuminate and cleanse the dark corners of the world, where hang the cobwebs of apathy and the dust of neglect; shine on faces made grim by poverty and war; melt the icicles of despair, and the frozen wastes of selfishness; and let your searching rays enclose the whole in one great radiance.

Someone Associated with Methodist Overseas Division

15. New Life

Give us a vision of new life, O God of life. You bring water out of rock, plants and flowers in the wilderness and cause the sprouts of the seeds buried underneath. We marvel at the wonders of life which repeat even after long periods of remaining in darkness. When we think of oysters, we marvel at the pearls that are formed through a long period of straining and grinding. Diamonds are formed by the transformative process of pressures and temperatures caused by many successive volcanos. Our spring flowers appear to be arising from a long sleep with a promising smile. Give us the courage to have a vision of life informed by nature, now and always.

Israel Selvanayagam

16. Easter Hope

Eternal God, fount of all wisdom, the giver of life; so fill our hearts with hope that in our doubts and despair we learn to wait upon you. Sow in us the seeds of your love that we learn to die with Christ and so share the glory of his resurrection.

Let All The World ...

17. They are Yours

We give back, to you, O God, those whom you gave to us. You did not lose them when you gave them to us, and we do not lose them by their return to you. Your dear Son has taught us that life is eternal and love cannot die. So, death is only a horizon, and the horizon is only the limit of our sight. Open our eyes to see more clearly and draw us closer to you that we may know that we are nearer to our loved ones, who are with you. You have told us that you are preparing a place for us; prepare us also for that happy place, that where you are we may also be always, O dear Lord of life and death.

William Penn

18. Departed Dear Ones

Remember Lord, our fathers and mothers, our sisters and brothers who have fallen asleep in the hope of the resurrection to eternal life, and all those who have ended this life in piety and faith. Pardon their every transgression, committed voluntarily or involuntarily, in word, or deed, or thought. Bestow on them and on us your kingdom. Grant them the participation of your everlasting blessings and the enjoyment of your endless life. For you are the life, the resurrection and the peace of your departed servants, Christ our God, and to you we give glory, together with your all-holy, good, and life-giving Spirit. Now and for ever and to the ages of ages.

St. Basil the Great

19. Inspire for Hope

Eternal God, in Christ your Son, you have touched our lives with faith and hope and love. Inspire us by your Spirit, so to touch the lives of others with gospel grace that faith may grow, hope may blossom and love abound; through Christ our Lord.

Michael Townsend

20. God of Future and Hope

Living God, when we feel the shaking of the foundations and try to retreat into the security of the past,

Teach us that you are the God of the future.

Living God, when we are tempted to despair, when events move so quickly and it seems that there is no way forward,

Teach us that you are the God of hope.

Living God, when things happen beyond our understanding and we find our trust in you is threatened,

Teach us that you are the God of all faith.

Living God, in a fast-moving world, when we find our values questioned and it is not easy to perceive what is right,

Teach us that you are the God of all wisdom

So, may we learn to live each day in company with you and to follow you wherever you will lead us.

Nigel Collinson

21. A Journey of Hope

O God, only you know the truth of the burden which each of us carries. We know that some of the burdens which we wish to lay down can be picked up by the gifts and energy of others. Sometimes we can be so supported by others that the things we are carrying seem lighter. Sometimes we can change our life in ways which bring new justice and care. For other things, we have few answers, too few resources in ourselves to bring in the changes, or we simply fail in what we would hope to do or be. For this we grieve. For this we pray forgiveness. For all we pray for new ways to journey on in hope.

Dorothy McRae-McMahon

22. Our Last Awakening

Bring us, Lord our God, at our last awakening, into the house and gate of heaven, to enter into that gate, and dwell in that house, where there shall be no darkness nor dazzling, but one equal light; no noise nor silence, but one equal music; not fears nor hopes, but one equal possession; no ends nor beginnings, but one equal eternity; in the habitation of your glory and dominion, world without end.

Methodist Worship Book (1999)

23. Hope in Fear

Come to be our hope, Lord Jesus, come to set our people free; from oppression, come, release us, turn defeat to victory! Come release from every prison those who suffer in our land: in your love we find the reason still to live and understand.

Come to build your new creation through the road of servanthood; give new life to every nation, changing evil into good. Come and open our tomorrow for a kingdom now so near; take away all human sorrow – give us hope in place of fear.

Jaci Maraschin

24. Hope of Salvation

Hear us O Lord, we implore you, for who is to be our salvation if you do not take us to heart? Subdue the powers that seek our lives and give us hope for the sake of him who has conquered death – Christ, your Son, who lives with you in the fellowship of the Holy Spirit for ever and ever.

Huub Oosterhuis

XX. Special Days of the Calendar Year

1. Rhythm of the Seasons

In the rhythm of the seasons, in the turning of the days, the heartbeat of the creating God may be heard. In the soothing surge of waves, in the soft tattoo of falling rain, the heartbeat of the sustaining God may be heard. In the hungry cry of the infant, in the vacant eyes of the addict, the heartbeat of the just God may be heard. In the blush of the green against the dark earth, in the tears of peace, the heartbeat of the redeeming God may be heard. May we have the ears to hear and the ability to discern the good news of God in our midst.

Malcom Peacock

2. New Year

Lord, as we come before you today, our first meeting of a new year, we ask for your forgiveness for the past and your blessing and encouragement for the future. Forgive us for the opportunities we have not taken. Forgive us for the prayers we have not prayed. Forgive us for the people we have not visited. Forgive us for lack of faith, for lack of patience, for lack of efficiency, both in our homes and in our group. We thank you, Lord, that we can put these things behind us and reach out to new opportunities in this new year. Help us right from the beginning, Lord, and be with us to the end.

Almighty God, we approach this New Year in a spirit of adventure. We do not know what it will hold for us – but you know. We do not know how many new members will be added to us, and who they will be – but you know. We do not know which members will leave us and for what reasons – but you know. We do not know the speakers who will particularly challenge and stimulate us, and in what fields – but you know. We do not know in what ways we shall be called to work for you, and how willing and able we shall prove to be – but you know. Lord, help us to be enthusiastic and joyful in your service and at peace with you, with ourselves and with our fellow humans. We ask it in the name of the Lord Jesus.

Beryl Bye

3. The First Day Morning

Eternal and ever blessed God, you make all things new, we thank you that today you have allowed us to begin a new year.

Here in your presence we make our resolutions for the days to come.

We resolve to be faithful and true to those who love us, and loyal to those who are our friends, so that we may never bring worry to their minds or distress to their hearts. We resolve to live in forgiveness and in kindness, that, like our Master, we may go about ever doing good. We resolve to live in diligence and effort, that we may use to the full the gifts and the talents which you have given us. We resolve to live in goodness and in purity, that we ourselves may resist temptation, and that we may be a strength to others who are tempted. We resolve to live in sympathy and in gentleness, that we may bring comfort to the sorrowing and understanding to the perplexed. We resolve to live in serenity and in self-control, that no anger and no passion may disturb our own peace and the peace of others. We resolve to live in full obedience and in perfect love to you, that in doing your will we may find our peace.

O God, our Father, you have given us grace to make our resolutions, grant us also strength to keep them all this year; through Jesus Christ our Lord.

William Barclay

4. Collect for Lent

Almighty and everlasting God, you hate nothing that you have made, and forgive the sins of all those who are penitent. Create and make in us new and contrite hearts, that, lamenting our sins and acknowledging our wretchedness, we may receive from you the God of all mercy, perfect forgiveness and peace; through Jesus Christ our Lord.

Thomas Cranmer

5. Lenten Journey

Holy Father, as we begin our Lenten journey, guide us to pray as you prayed. Help us to hear your voice during this season of preparation. Despite the dark days to come, we know that light and life await us come Easter.

Moravian

6. Ash Wednesday

Almighty and Everlasting God, we come to you with penitence and confession for thinking of us more than we should think. We treat our life and enjoy to over-full as if we are going to live for centuries. Help us to count our days and consider each one as a gift from you. Let the world leaders who exploit the weak and the poor and make their citizens to be prodigal sons repent and sit in ashes. Let them renounce their demonic creed of 'we are first' and turn to serve those most deserving. May we sit in ashes publicly to represent the unrepentant. Finally, may you alone replace our ashes with your beauty and glory.

Israel Selvanayagam

7. Palm Sunday

Majestic Christ Jesus, you stunned the world by identifying yourself with the ordinary peasants and marginalized people of Galilee and being meek and simple. Help us to join the procession in spirit with hosannas on our lips. May we watch attentively the way you healed the blind and lame in the temple thus changing centuries of their alienation. You defended the shout of the masses including children against the rebuking religious leaders who latter shouted before the governor 'Crucify him!' Give us the determination and courage that we may follow you even unto the cross and witness your death. Strengthen us to proclaim the good news that you are the true royal who can make even us as the community of royal priesthood. Glorify your name!

Israel Selvanayagam

8. Maundy Thursday

We want to follow you, Jesus, at any length. Help us to watch carefully what you say and do. In a moment of temptation knowing all power and authority given to you, you overcame it by abruptly washing the feet of your disciples in the midst of your last supper. You surprised your followers and asked them to do likewise. Let us not refuse to be washed and help us to one another's feet. We want to join your song of praise even when the clouds of death overshadow us. When you anguish in prayer to seek the will of your Father, let us not sleep but give you our solidarity. May your words 'Love one another as I have loved you' never slip our memory in any circumstance.

Israel Selvanayagam

9. Good Friday Morning

O God, our Father, we thank you this day that you did so love the world that you did give your only Son for us and for all humankind. We give you thanks for Jesus Christ, our blessed Lord, and for his death upon the Cross.

That he was obedient unto death, even the death of the Cross; That he loved us and gave himself for us; That he came to seek and to save that which was lost; That he gave his life a ransom for many, a ransom for us; We give you thanks this day, O God.

Greater love has no man that this, that a man lay down his life for his friends. Help us this day to remember, and never again to forget, the love of him who laid down his life for us.

O wondrous love! To bleed and die, to bear the Cross and shame, that guilty sinners, such as I, might plead your gracious Name!

Hear this our prayer, for your love's sake.

William Barclay

10. Holy Saturday

Ever liberating Christ, your poignant words of forgiveness for your enemies on the cross continue to echo throughout the universe. Your commending of your spirit to God the source of all life continues to inspire those who care to hear. Your liberation could not be hampered by your death as you went down to the invisible world and, being alive in spirit, proclaimed liberation to the imprisoned spirits. Help us to affirm the hiddenness of life as we see nature. For some of us the Holy Saturday looks too long, and the dawn remains distant. Give us the urge to look for the morning star remembering your words about the new life.

Israel Selvanayagam

11. Watchfulness

Watching God, like your followers in times before, we sometimes cower behind closed and locked doors in fear and desperation. We long for signs, for assurance that sin and death are not the final answer. Break the grip of grief and fear with the coming announcement of the life.

Moravian

12. Spring Life

When the seeds buried and hidden sprout and manifest a spectacular and colourful life, O Creator and Saviour, you show us new life. When the renewed trees and smiling flowers meet our eyes, what else can we do but stand in awe, wonder and praise. Help us to realise that the invisible life is greater than the visible. Just as the season, expected yet unpredictable, forecasts and provides a foretaste of a greater life, we kneel before your presence with open palms waiting for the bread and wine to approach us. Make us still better.

Israel Selvanayagam

13. Easter Morning

O Lord Jesus Christ, who upon this day did conquer death and rise from the dead, and who are alive for evermore, help us never to forget your Risen Presence for ever with us.

Help us to remember, that you are with us in every time of perplexity to guide and to direct; that you are with us in every time of sorrow and comfort and to console; that you are with us in every time of temptation to strengthen and to inspire; that you are with us in every time of loneliness to cheer and to befriend; that you are with us even in death to bring us through the waters to the glory on the other side.

Make us to be certain that there is nothing in time or in eternity which can separate us from you, so that in your presence we may meet life with gallantry and death without fear.

This we ask for your love's sake.

William Barclay

14. Be Present

Be present, O risen Lord, in this your church's Easter praise; that its anthems of joy and its proclamation of your victory may worthily celebrate both the mystery of your redeeming love and the majesty of your eternal glory.

Norman Wallwork

15. Break the Bonds of Death

We give praise to you, powerful God, for breaking the bonds of death and driving away fear and hopelessness with the resurrection of your Son, Jesus. Even as he lives, so may we become alive in the Spirit and on fire with your truth and love. In Christ we pray.

Moravian

16. United to Everyone

O Christ, you are united to every human being without exception. Still more, risen from the dead, you come to heal the secret wound of our soul. And for each of us there open the gates of an infinite goodness of heart. Through such love, little by little our hearts are changed.

Brother Roger of Taizé

17. Ascension Day

Supreme God our heavenly Father, by sending your Son to the world and calling him back you have set the model of missionary movement. May we imbibe the truth of the rhythm of being near and far and rejoicing in your supremacy and intimacy. Forgive us for asking unnecessary questions about the end times of the present world and coming of your reign in full measure. Help us to ask the right questions to be authentic witnesses with the power of the Holy Spirit and the memory of Jesus and his mission in the world. May our witness ripple out from our local area to the wider regions and the whole world. Make us a living outreach with a spirit of transcendence.

Israel Selvanayagam

18. Ascending to be Universal

You are not only risen and alive, you are Lord. This is your ascension, your ascendency over the whole universe. You stand over and above all that is best in life as its source. You stand above all that is worst as ultimate victor. You stand above all powers and authorities as judge. You stand above all failure and weakness and sin as forgiveness and love. You alone are worthy of total allegiance, total commitment. You are Lord, 'my Lord and my God.'

Rex Chapman

19. Whitsun (Pentecost)

Eternal and ever blessed God, who upon this day did send your Spirit with power upon your people, let your Spirit be upon us.

Let your Spirit be in our minds, to guide our thoughts towards the truth. Let your Spirit be in our hearts, to cleanse them from every evil and unclean desire. Let your Spirit be upon our lips, to preserve us from all wrong speaking, and to help us by our words to commend you unto others. Let your Spirit be upon our eyes, that they may find no delight in looking on forbidden things, but that they may be fixed on Jesus. Let your Spirit be upon our hands that they may be faithful in work and eager in service

Let your Spirit be upon our whole lives, that they may be strong with your power, wise with your wisdom, and beautiful with your love; through Jesus Christ our Lord.

William Barclay

20 Summer Sun

Lord, we praise and thank you; giver of summer heat, wood that warms and creaks in the sun, flowers breathing scent into the still air; giver of summer rain, clear washed skies, jewelled leaves, refreshment for the land. Lord, we praise and thank you; maker of humankind and human kindness, smiles from a stranger, oneness with friends, laughing and crying, the sharing of bread and the sharing of life. Lord, we praise and thank you; far-off yet near us, God and our brother, star-clad and shining yet close as our breathing; life-giving, life-living, beginning and ending, and our life for ever.

Margaret Crofts

21. Autumn Glory

I watch the inexorable pull of the earth to leaves and pine needles. Irresistible. In succession gravity summons them. The steady flurry is obedient to the annual call, embedding into autumnal rain-sodden earth. Decomposing from recognizable identity to nurture-rich humus. No longer crisp golden scarlet and flaming russet, becoming now a friable crumble, leaf-mould black. Waiting to cradle and nurture new seeds into growth, wind-blown, rain-washed, sun-warmed. Now awaiting frost-hard stillness of winter. Then new, irresistible thrusts of spring. Atoms recycling in God's economy, infinite succession. Autumn glory on the horizon again. God open our eyes to see, wonder and worship.

Ros Murphy

22. Miracle of Life

Creator God, we thank you for your promise that while the earth endures seed-time and harvest, summer and winter, day and night, shall not fail. We thank you for the reliabilities of this good earth, for the variety of the seasons and for all the unity and contrasts of creation. We thank you for this world's agenda, for the labours of people, and permitting us to be partners to be earth's activity. We thank you that we can nourish the miracle of life upon the miracle of harvest and we praise you for the dignity of sharing in the work of your almighty hands, O God our Father, blessed for ever.

Dick Williams

23. Harvest Season

O God, you rule the times and the seasons, and in every change fulfil the unchanging purpose of your grace; who beneath all that now in winter seems dark and cold, are keeping safe germs of life, and preparing the days when the earth shall bud and blossom and bring forth again her harvest; teach us, by this your course in Nature, to trust you in your dealings with ourselves. Preserve in us the seed or that life which is life indeed: return, O Sun of Righteousness with your light and your strength: carry on the work of your grace in our hearts: and visit us with your salvation; through Jesus Christ our Lord.

Everest Tilson

24. Harvest Blessing

God, bless you yourself my reaping, each ridge, and plain, and field, each sickle curved, shapely, hard, each ear and handful in the sheaf.

Bless each maiden and youth, each woman and tender youngling, safeguard them beneath your shield of strength, and guard them in the house of the saints.

Encompass each goat, sheep and lamb, each cow and horse, and store, surround you the flocks and herds, and tend them to a kindly fold, with saints and angels.

Norman Richardson

25. Harvest of Freedom

God of love, we pray for peace that brings true freedom because weapons have been transformed into tools for agriculture; for peace where people build houses and plant gardens and live to enjoy their fruits; where food grows and people celebrate the harvest; where children play and laugh; where all live without fear and, in thanksgiving, want to share the food and good things they produce. In the name of Christ, in whom is power to heal and save.

Maureen Edwards

26. Harvest of Life

Lord, your harvest is the harvest of life; love sown in the hearts of people; love that spreads out like the branches of a great tree covering all who seek its shelter; love that inspires and recreates; love that is planted in the weak and the weary, the sick and the dying. The harvest of your love is that the life that reaches through the weeds of sin and death to the sunlight of resurrection. Lord, nurture my days with your love, water my soul with the dew of forgiveness, that the harvest of my love might be your joy.

Frank Topping

27. Power of Life

Ever living God, the Eternal I am, help us to admire the mystery of the sprout of life from buried seeds and dried tree trunks. Let us never forget the possibility of a new life out of death. In the name of the one who demonstrated that, even Jesus Christ our Lord.

Israel Selvanayagam

28. All Saints' Day

Eternal and ever blessed God, we remember this day the unseen cloud of witnesses who compass us about. We remember the blessed dead who rest from their labours, and whose works follow them. And we give you thanks for all of them.

For parents who gave us life; who tended and cared for us in years when we were helpless to help ourselves; who toiled and sacrificed to give to us our chance in life; at whose knees we learned to pray, and from whose lips we first heard the name of Jesus:

We give you thanks, O God.

For teachers who taught us; For ministers of your gospel who instructed us in your truth and in your faith; For all those who have been an example to us of what life should be; For those whose influence on us will never cease, and whose names will never depart from our memory:

We give you thanks, O God.

For the saints, the prophets and the martyrs; For those who lived and died for the faith; And, above all else, for Jesus, the captain of our salvation and the author and finisher of our faith:

We give you thanks, O God.

Grant unto us in our day and generation to walk worthily of the heritage into which we have entered; through Jesus Christ our Lord.

William Barclay

29. Communion of Saints

Gracious God, before whom the generations rise and pass away, we rejoice in the communion of saints and bless your name for all your servants who have fought the fight and kept the faith. Grant us grace to follow their good examples to continue the work which they began and enjoy with them at the last the glory of your eternal kingdom; through Christ our Lord.

John Hunter

30. Sacramental Bond

O Almighty God, you have knit together your elect in one communion and fellowship, in the mystical body of your Son Jesus Christ our Lord: grant us grace so to follow your blessed saints in all virtuous and godly living, that we may come to those unspeakable joys, which you have prepared for them that unfeignedly love you; through Jesus Christ our Lord.

Book of Common Prayer

31. Graces and Virtues of Saints

Almighty God, we offer unto you most high praise and hearty thanks for the wonderful graces and virtues which you have manifested in all your saints and in all other holy persons upon earth who by their lives and labours have shined forth as lights in the world, whom we remember with honour and commemorate with joy. For these and for all your other servants who have departed this life with the seal of faith, we praise and magnify your holy name; through Jesus Christ our Lord.

Scottish Liturgy (1560)

32. Remembrance

O God, our Father, on this Sunday of Remembrance we remember all those to whom we owe the life and the privileges we possess, and we thank you for them.

For those who lived and suffered and died to give us the freedom and good government we possess; The liberty of conscience and of speech, of thought and of worship which we enjoy;

We thank you.

For those who lived and suffered and died to find for us new continents and new lands and new countries in the distant places of the earth. New ways to heal the disease and to see the pain of the world;

We thank you.

For all who died in war, on land, at sea, and in the air; For those who were wounded in body and mind so that life could never be the same again; For those who in every age and generation have laid down their lives for their friends;

We thank you.

Above all for Jesus, the Captain of every heroic soul; That he loved us and gave himself for us; That for us he bore the cross with all its pain and shame;

We thank you.

Help us to remember this night all that this our life has cost, and help us to resolve never to waste it and never to soil it.

William Barclay

33. Remember with Gratitude

God our Father, as on this day we look back and remember with gratitude those who die in times of war, so also we look around and remember with compassion those who still suffer as the result of war: the bereaved, the lonely, the disabled, and the mentally ill. O God of love, comfort their hearts, uphold their faith, and give them peace, for Jesus Christ's sake.

Frank Colquhoun

34. Saints and Sanctification

Holy God, in Christ you have called to be saints those who are to be constantly sanctified by the Holy Spirit. Help us to emulate examples of your servants in the past and dissociate from their moments of failure and wrong views. Connect us with the communion of your blessed saints in the past and the future. May our sainthood be not distorted by self-righteousness and pride. When we scale the heights may we know how can we possibly fall to the lowest. Adorn us, O Father, with humility and resignation. Let there be no other goal of our spiritual life than reflecting your glory.

Israel Selvanayagam

35. Remember for Peace

On this Remembrance Day we come, O Lord, in gratitude for all who have died that we may live, for all who endured pain that we might know joy, for all who suffered imprisonment that we might know freedom. Turn our deep feeling now into determination, and determination into deed, that as people died for peace, so we may live for peace, for the sake of the Prince of Peace, even Jesus Christ our Lord.

Leslie D. Weatherhead

36. Collect for Advent

Almighty God, give us grace to cast away the works of darkness and put on the armour of light, now in the time of this mortal life, in which your Son Jesus Christ came to us in great humility; so that on the last day, when he shall come again in glorious majesty to judge both the living and the dead, we may rise to the life immortal, through him who is alive and reigns with you and the Holy Spirit, now and ever.

Thomas Cranmer

37. Humbling God

Almighty and everlasting God, you have stooped to raise fallen humanity by the child-bearing of blessed Mary; grant that we who have seen your glory revealed in our human nature, and your love made perfect in our weakness, may daily be renewed in your image, and conformed to the pattern of your Son, Jesus Christ our Lord.

David Silk

38. Winter Glory

God of winter glory, of pale sunlight cut to ribbons by bare black branches, of cut-glass ice intricately etched with your imagination, what desperate love drove you to the Mary-stable-shepherd idea? Help us to see in this story of poverty, struggle, hope and fear, your most beautiful creation.

Penny Worth

39. Make Us Humble

O Lord our God, as we celebrate again the festival of Christmas, we ask you to make us humble and loving like Jesus, who did not come to be served but to serve, and who said that it is better to give than to receive; so that, in his name, we may devote ourselves to the care and service of all those who are in need. We ask this through the same Jesus Christ, our Lord.

Stephen S. Smalley

40. Prepare Us

Loving Father, help us remember the birth of Jesus, that we may share in the song of angels, the gladness of the shepherds and the wisdom of the wise men. Close the door of hate and open the door of love all over the world. Let kindness come with every gift and good desires with every greeting. Deliver us from evil by the blessing which Christ brings, and teach us to be merry with clean hearts. May the Christmas morning make us happy to be your children and the Christmas evening bring us to our beds with grateful thoughts, forgiving and forgiven, for Jesus' sake.

Robert Louis Stevenson

41. Christmas Eve

Let us remember before God all those who rejoice with us but upon another shore and in a greater light – that multitude which no one can count or number, whose hope was in the word made flesh and with whom in the Lord Jesus we for evermore are one.

David Waterman

42. Christmas Morning

O God, our Father, we thank you for Christmas time, and for all that it means to us.

We thank you that, when Jesus, your Son, came into this world, he came into a humble home. We thank you that, he had to grow up and to learn like any other boy. We thank you that, he did a good day's work, when he grew to manhood, as the carpenter in the village shop in Nazareth. We thank you that, he was tempted and tired, hungry and sad, just as we are. We thank you that, he was one with his brethren in all things, that he truly shared this life with its struggles and its toils, its sorrows and its joys, in trials and its temptations. We thank you that, he knew what it is to live in a home circle, just as we do; to earn his living, just as we do; to know friendship and to know the failure of friends, just as we know it. We thank you for the service of his life; the love of his death; and the power of his Resurrection.

Grant O God, that, when he comes to us, he may not find that there is no room in our hearts for Him; but grant that this Christmas day he may enter into our hearts and abide there for evermore.

hear this our prayer, for your love's sake.

William Barclay

43. Guiding Light

O God our Father, who by the bright shining of a star led the wise men to the city of David: guide us by the light of your Spirit, that we too may come to the presence of Jesus and offer our gifts and our worship to him, our Saviour and our Lord.

Alan Warren

44. Christmas Acclamation

Child of Bethlehem, Light of our world, whose parents found no room in the inn and became refugees in Egypt, we pray for all those forced to flee their homes, all who, like you, our Son of Man, have nowhere to lay their head.

Hope of our world: ***Hear our prayer.***

Child of Bethlehem, Light of our world, born in a stable, your bed a cattle manger, we pray for all who, for whatever reason, live in poverty in our own country, that the greed which impoverishes others may yet give way to generosity and compassion.

Hope of our world: ***Hear our prayer.***

Child of Bethlehem, Light of our world, born through the painful labour of your beloved Mother, even in birth shadowed by death, we pray for all (especially those known to us), who suffer in body or mind and are fearful for their future.

Hope of our world: ***Hear our prayer.***

Child of Bethlehem, Light of our world, whom Herod sought to kill, we pray for all oppressed by rulers arrogant with despotic power, for all who face persecution because of race or belief, remembering especially at this time Christians in the Middle East and Pakistan, and Muslims in Burma; that Mary's song of a new and just world may be fulfilled.

Hope of our world: ***Hear our prayer.***

Child of Bethlehem, Light of our world, we pray for all children everywhere, but especially for those abused inhumanly by others.

Hope of our world: ***Hear our prayer.***

Child of Bethlehem, Light of our world, radiating the love and glory of God, help us to see your divine image in people everywhere, for your name's sake.

Eric Lott

45. A Humble Prayer

God, our Creator, we offer this humble prayer on Christmas Day. We come to worship with a song of thanks in our hearts—a song of redemption, a song of hope and renewal. We pray for joy in our hearts, hope in our God, love to forgive, and peace upon the earth. We ask for the salvation of all our family members and friends, and we pray your blessings on all people. May there be bread for the hungry, love for the unlovable, healing for the sick, protection for our children, and wisdom for our youth. We pray for the forgiveness of sinners and abundant life in Christ. Holy Spirit, fill our hearts with your love and power. In the name of Jesus Christ we pray.

Lia Icaza Willetts

46. True Gift

The gifts I'd leave beneath your tree, aren't those that you can touch or see, No toys meant just for pointless play, but gifts to bless you every day. The gift of friendship warm and true, is one that I would leave for you. Good health and happiness and cheer to keep you smiling through the year. The gift of peace that comes from God, with prayer to guide each path you trod. And when your heart has lost its song, the gift of hope to cheer you on. These are the gifts I'd leave for you.

Kay Hoffman

47. Peace to Prevail

In a world where worry, not peace, prevails, stir up that good news again. This Christmas, make it real in our hearts. Never have we needed your joy and peace more than now. Thank you for the gift of Jesus, our Immanuel, the Word made flesh. Forgive us for forgetting – that your love never changes, never fades, and that you never abandon the purpose for which you came: to save us from our sinful condition, and to give us life eternal, the joy of relationship with a holy God. Your birth—and your death—sealed your promise to us for ever.

Rebecca Barlow Jordan

48. Work Begins

When the song of the angels is stilled, when the star in the sky is gone, when the kings and princes are home, when the shepherds are back with the flocks, then the work of Christmas begins: To find the lost, to heal those broken in spirit, to feed the hungry, to release the oppressed, to rebuild the nations, to bring peace among all peoples, to make a little music with the heart. And to radiate the Light of Christ, every day, in every way, in all that we do and in all that we say. Then the work of Christmas begins.

Howard Thurman

49. Comfort the People

Heavenly Father, please comfort the people who won't be happy this Christmas: those who won't get any Christmas presents, or even any Christmas cards: those who won't have the money to buy the presents they would love to give their friends; those who won't have a Christmas dinner, or won't get the things they are longing for; and those who will be sad because someone they love will not be with them.

Zinnia Bryan

50. Thanksgiving of New Year Eve

O God, our Father, today we are remembering all the way by which You have brought us to this present hour, and we thank you for every step of it.

We thank you for every experience which has come to us, because we know that in it and through it all you have been loving us with an everlasting love.

For gladness and for grief; for sorrow and for joy; for laughter and for tears; for silence and for song;

We give you thanks, O God.

That you have kept us in our going out and our coming in; that you have enabled us to do our work, and to earn our living; that you have brought us in safety to this present hour:

We give you thanks, O God.

For any new things that we have learned, and for any new experiences through which we have passed; if we can do our work a little better, and if we know life a little better; for friends who are still closer to us, and for loved ones who are still more dear;

We give Thee thanks, O God.

And today, as we remember the passing years, we thank you most of all for Jesus Christ, the same yesterday, today and for ever. Help us to go on, certain that, as You has blessed the past, so the future is also forever in your hands; through Jesus Christ our Lord.

William Barclay

51. Preparing for Entering into a New Year

Almighty God, as we prepare to go forward into a new year, give us your wisdom and your strength. Open our minds to new ideas and modern methods. Help us to keep the things that are good and useful, and discard what is dated and useless. Give those who have something to offer confidence and courage to serve on our committee. Save us from getting into a rut and wanting to stay there. Guard us from the danger of allowing social projects to take precedence over spiritual ones. Show us how can we attract outsiders and retain their interest. And, most of all, grant that each one of us may live a life worthy of you and the high calling to which you have called us.

Beryl Bye

XXI. In Solidarity

1. Encouraging Presence

Dear God, your amazing love embraces all humanity and the world you have created. We thank you for your presence, encouragement, hope and sustaining grace in the midst of human suffering. Give us renewed courage and faith to participate with you in your liberating mission. Teach us to love as Jesus did; to be in solidarity with those who are not able to develop their potential because of abuse, discrimination, injustice, or deprivation. Empower your Church to proclaim the good news of abundant life with boldness, faith and conviction; to fulfil its prophetic role in our own time and context; in Jesus' name.

Saray Veagra

2. Voice for the Voiceless

God of us all, we thank you that you place us in community, to enable and encourage each other, to share and grow together. Help those of us who are usually silent or silenced, to speak and be heard. Help those of us who are always heard, to learn to make space for others to have voice. Help us all to be people who listen with our hearts, value each other's differences, and work together as we listen to your word and your wisdom. Please broaden our minds and hearts to be in tune with yours, that we may see as you see, and love as you love. Help us to recognize that, in enabling and encouraging each other with your kindness, our communities, and each of us in them, may grow and flourish.

Ruth Yorke

3. Those Struggling

We bring before you, O God, the troubles and perils of people and nations, the sighing of prisoners and captives, the sorrows of the bereaved, the necessities of strangers, the helplessness of the weak, the despondency of the weary, the failing powers of the aged. O God, draw near to each, for the sake of Jesus Christ our Strength.

Saint Anselm

4. Liberation and Full Life

God, heart-illumining Light of the World, we pray for a new vision within our souls, that our blindness and arrogance may be removed, that we may yet learn to walk your way of unselfish service to others.

Lord, in your mercy; ***Hear our prayer.***

God of our one world, our broken world; we pray for people in places where there is violence, that people living in uncertainty and fear, may yet live in hope and peace with each other.

Lord, in your mercy; ***Hear our prayer.***

God of our one earth, source of all life, we pray for more wise and unselfish sharing in earth's resources, remembering local tribal peoples who are disregarded and whose lands are exploited ruthlessly for selfish gain.

Lord, in your mercy; ***Hear our prayer.***

God of great compassion, we pray for those in our one world oppressed by the unjust, uncaring ways of the strong, that justice for the poor and powerless may yet be found.

Lord, in your mercy; ***Hear our prayer.***

God of healing, whose purpose is wholeness of life for all, we pray for the sick, those who suffer in body, mind, or spirit, remembering too those distressed by loneliness, and grieving the loss of loved ones; especially for those known to us (*we name them silently*).

Lord, in your mercy; ***Hear our prayer.***

In the Name of Jesus, the Pain-bearer, and Light-bringer.

Eric Lott

5. Migrants

Migrant God, free from borders, your presence spans the universe. In all our journeys we find you with us and within us. In Jesus you reveal yourself taking sanctuary on earth, in flesh and blood, choosing to pitch a tent among mortals, with nowhere to lay your head. We behold you still in the face of those who are uprooted from their homes by war, poverty and persecution. We bless you for their courage and resilience in seeking freedom and sanctuary. Grant to them safety in all their trail and travels. Give to all who receive them the capacity to listen as they share their stories of a search for justice, freedom and peace.

Inderjit Bhogal

6. Sorrowful and Suffering

Have mercy, O God, on all who are sorrowful, those who weep and those in exile. Have pity on the persecuted and the homeless who are without hope; those who are scattered in remote corners of this world; those who are in prison and ruled by tyrants. Have mercy on them as is written in your holy law, where your compassion is exalted.

Jewish

7. Perseverance, Faith, Zeal

Lord Jesus, you understand the sufferings of the weak and the oppressed. Although you are strong, you allowed yourself to be taken prisoner. You were the victim of bullying and ill-treatment, punishing blows and insulting words. You suffered an agonizing death for us and for our sins. Be near to those who suffer innocently as political prisoners and give peace and comfort to them by your presence. O God, the father of the forsaken, the help of the weak, the supplier of the needy; you teach us that love towards the human race is the bond of perfectness and the imitation of your blessed self. Open and touch our hearts that we may see and do, both for this world and that which is to come, the things that belong to our peace. Strengthen us in the work which we have undertaken; give us wisdom, perseverance, faith and zeal, and in your own time and according to your pleasure prosper the issue; for the love of your Son, Christ Jesus.

Lord Shaftesbury

8. Struggling for Justice

Show me the suffering of the most miserable so I will know my people's plight.

Free me to pray for others for you are present in every person.

Help me to take responsibility for my own life so that I can be free at last.

Grant me courage to serve others, for in service there is true life.

Give me honesty and patience so that I can work with other workers.

Bring forth song and celebration so that the spirit will be alive among us.

Let the spirit flourish and grow so that we will never tire of the struggle.

Let us remember those who have died for justice for they have given us life.

Help us love even those who hate us, so that we can change the world.

United Farm Workers (United Church of Christ)

9. Victims of Wealth and Weapons

Lord God, in Jesus your body was broken by the cowardly and the powerful. The judgement hall of Pilate knew your silence as surely as your critics knew your voice. In word and silence, take on the powerful of the world today: those whose word sentences some to cruelty or unmerited redundancy; those whose word transfers wealth or weapons for the sake of profit or prejudice; those whose silence condones the injustice they have the power to change. O Saviour of the Poor, liberate your people.

Iona Community

10. Young People

Lord, we pray for young people taking on new responsibilities – in school, work, church, sport teams, young groups or at home; for those who are fallen under bad influences – members of destruction gangs, those who abuse drugs, young girls who are pregnant, inmates of brothels and prisons; for young people needing school places or employment with very poor prospects of finding them, and for those who find freedom beyond their grasp because of personal or national circumstances; for young people for a thirst for justice, yearning for brotherhood and a need for love. May our church and society not ignore, scorn and exploit the young.

Someone associated with Methodist Overseas Division

11. Those Unfortunate

God of bounty, beauty and variety, we celebrate your creation, love and faithfulness. You know that we are grieved by those unfortunate ones living amongst us - land labourers without land of their own, house builders who do not have their own houses, climbers of trees who do not own any tree, and quarry workers whose rest is often robbed. May your children and the churches awake to see this contradiction. Help us to identify authentic mission fields where people struggle for their survival and are exploited. Enlighten us and our political leaders that we are saved from the sin of confusing contradictions with diversity. Through Christ our Lord, the friend of labourers and the marginalized.

Israel Selvanayagam

12. Foes and Friends

Each thing we have received, from you it came, O God. Each thing for which we hope, from your love it will be given. Kindle in our hearts within a flame of love to our neighbours, to our foes, to our friends, to our loved ones all, from the lowliest thing that lives, to the name that is highest of all.

Iona Community

13. Refugees

O Brother Jesus, who as a child was carried into exile, remember all those who are deprived of their home or country, who groan under the burden of anguish and sorrow, enduring the burning heat of the sun, the freezing cold of the sea, or the humid heat of the forest, searching for a place of refuge. Cause these storms to cease, O Christ. Move the hearts of those in power that they may respect the men and women whom you have created in your own image; that the grief of refugees may be turned into joy, as when you led Moses and your people out of captivity.

African Prayer

14 Victims of Injustice

God of history, you share our joys and crushing sorrows, you hear the cries of the afflicted, you fill the hungry, and you set free the oppressed. We pray for the end to all injustice. Inspire us with the all-embracing love of God, challenge us with the sacrificial love of Jesus, empower us with the transforming love of the Spirit, that we and all God's people may live and be free!

Iona Community

15. Those in Darkness

We pray for light where the dark is doubly dark; where wrong dresses up as right and saints are unsure what to believe; where life has gone into a tunnel and all that is known are confusing noises and stumbling blocks in the blackness; where faith, hope and love are in ashes, needing an angel to blow on them.

Iona Community

16. Palmyra Climbers

God of hard work, thank you for the awesome Palmyra with a canopy of green leaves, juice-containing flowers and long trunk. Thank you for my strength to hop up, hugging the tree with my tools bag. When parts of my body become rough and disfigured causing people to despise me, let me think of the nail marks of Jesus your Son and my friend. When I squeeze the flowers and cut the nibbles I feel how wonderful that I am an instrument to sweeten the life of many! In the late night after the last tree when I enjoy a half pot of fermented juice you will kindly understand. If I fail to understand your protection and slip out for a fatal fall, please take care of my wife and children. Let them always remember that I started with the first tree and finished with the last with an acted prayer involving some of my tools. Just as the tender leaves face up to heaven for new life, let me always look above. In your sweet name I delight.

Israel Selvanayagam

17. Meanest Cities

Living God, as we see your glory in the grandeur of the mountains and in the beauty of the lochs, help us to seek that same glory in the meanest streets of our cities. Enable us to walk there with you that we may find the breadth, height and depth of your love for all in Jesus Christ our Lord.

Alan Anderson

18. Bricklayers

The bricklayer laid a brick on the bed of cement. Then, with a precise stroke of his trowel spread another layer and without a by-your-leave, laid on another brick. The foundations grew visibly, the building rose, tall and strong, to shelter humans. I thought, Lord, of that brick buried in the darkness at the base of the big building. No one sees it, but it accomplishes its task, and the other bricks need it. Lord, what difference whether I am on the roof-top or in the foundations of your building, as long as I stand faithfully at the right place?

Michel Quoist

19. Other Patients

O God, keep me from praying to you, as if there was no one in this ward except me. Help me to remember that I am only one person and one voice in this ward and in this hospital, and in a world in which there are so many people in trouble. Bless everyone in this ward, anyone who is lonely or frightened, anyone who is shy and nervous; anyone who is suffering a lot of pain; anyone who is making slow progress and who is discouraged; anyone who has had a setback today and who is disappointed; anyone who is worried and anxious; anyone for whom there is no recovery. And help me to help others, and so to forget my own troubles by sharing the troubles of others.

William Barclay

20. Widows and Orphans

We, your servants, offer you, O God, prayers and intercessions on behalf of the peace of the churches and the tranquillity of the monasteries; keep your ministers in righteousness, forgive sinners who turn to you, make the rich in almsgiving, provide for the poor, support the widows, educate the orphans, sustain the aged, guard the youth by your cross, gather the dispersed, convert those in error; and let our prayers and intercessions prevail with you, and we will offer praise and honour to your high trinity, now and always and for ever.

Syrian liturgy

21. Subjects of Local Government

We pray for those who serve as councillors; may they be thoughtful and wise in their decisions and open in their approach to changing conditions. We pray for council employees; may their skills and experience be respected by elected councillors and their dealings with the public be marked by helpfulness, courtesy and tact. We remember the services to people for which local government is responsible; may the most vulnerable members of the community be supported and encouraged in their quest for a full and useful life. May our area be one in which people are happy to live.

Further Everyday Prayers

22. Distressed and Afflicted

O Lord, the nurse of all, let us not die of starvation because of our greediness and contempt

for our needy brothers and sisters. Therefore, fountain of goodness, send upon the earth peaceful and seasonable rains to bring forth fruit for our nourishment. Ocean of compassion, cease the drought and the barrenness which distress and afflict us. Mingle together with the warmth of the sun the dew of your kindness for us and your beasts. Do not neglect us because we neglect your commandments, nor turn your face away from us and shut your ears against us because we disobey your ordinances. For you are a God of mercy, compassion and love to humankind, and to you, the Father who is without beginning, we send glory, together with your only-begotten Son and your all-holy, good and life-creating Spirit, now and ever and unto ages of ages.

St. Symeon of Thessaloniki

23. Miners, Traders, Trappers

O God, help me to walk in the boots of the miner, the shoes of the trader, the moccasins of the trapper, and in the sandals of Jesus Christ the Master, and to see others as he would see them.

A Canadian Indian

24. Those Deprived

As we remember the love of Jesus for the outcast in society; the beggar and the criminal, the swindler and the prostitute – we pray for all your people, especially those who work in deprived areas. Renew their vision of the universal love of Jesus and strengthen them in seeking to serve the most needy and neglected. May the vision of your love capture anew our lives *and the lives of all for whom we pray.*

May the Spirit of Jesus draw us anew to trust and love you, liberating us from self-concern to love and serve others.

Peter Stephens

25. The Family

Loving, creating God, we thank you that you did not create us to be alone but set us to live in relationship with other people and with you. Thank you for the people who are important in our lives; those who have made us what we are and those whose lives have enriched ours; for friends and family, and those who bring us joy; for those for whom we care and those who care for us.

We pray for all who are finding life difficult today; those who are separated from friends and family; those whose relationships are oppressive or violent, or broken beyond repair; those whose daily life is a struggle against poverty or discrimination. We pray for all in the world who will die this day and for those who will be born; for those who grieve for loved ones they have lot and those who will celebrate new life.

David Gamble

26. Prisoners and Their Families

Lord, you offer freedom to all people, we pray for all who are in prison and for those who are affected by, or involved in their imprisonment. Break the bonds of fear and isolation and support with your love; prisoners and their families and friends, prison chaplains, prison staff and all who care. Heal those who have been wounded by the acts of others, especially victims of crime. Help us to forgive one another, to act justly, love mercy and walk humbly together with Christ.

William Davis

27. Those Broken and Rejected

Creator God, you made us in your image, to love and to be loved. You gave us *eyes* to see those whom we can love. You gave us *ears* to hear those who cry for lack of love. You gave us *voice* and *speech* to console those broken by rejection. You gave us *touch* to bring without word the warmth of recognition and understanding to those who dwell alone in fear and sorrow. Creator God, teach us the skills of *seeing* and *listening,* of *speaking* and *touching*, for with these tools you gave us the power to mirror your Love.

Peter Fox

28. Vulnerable Child

Light of my life, little child, God be thanked, God be praised; for the laughter and love; for the shouting of glee; for the soft baby sleep; for the radiant beauty that shines from each movement. God keep you, God guide you, God build up your life in fullness, God fill you with her pure grace, so that day by day, through this quiet and simple home life, all perfections grow in you and a life that shall ever glow.

Lily Amirtham

29. Street Children

Father, today I remember the hundreds of children living on the streets, orphans, and many who run away from drunken and abusive parents. They live on the streets, sleep inside drain pipes, in the drains, on the pavements; in the open, braving the cold and the rain. Older men and rowdies bully them, make them pay protection money, or make them steal for them; they harass them, beat them up and maim them. Bless those who run homes for these unfortunate children; who try to teach them and to be honest; and help to bring some security and peace and joy into their lives. We pray to you to raise more people like them, who will open their hearts to them. Give me courage to join this salient work in solidarity and guide me to do so at the right time.

Vimala Arangadan

30. Those Aspiring to Improve

I am only a spark, make me a fire. I am only a string; make me a lyre. I am only a drop; make me a fountain. I am only a hill; make me a mountain. I am only a feather; make me a wing. I am only a rag; make me a king.

Author Unknown (Mexico)

31. A Mother with a Mentally Challenged Child

All mighty Father and Gracious Mother, we praise you for giving Sujatha who is retarded in her mental growth. We believe she is, first of all, your special child and that is why you gave her to us, our child. Our dear God, by her birth you have tested us in many ways and changed our lives through unknown challenging and life-changing events.

By giving her to us you have showered on us love and joy beyond all understanding. Every day you have renewed our youthfulness by her companionship. Sujatha, the eternal child, connects us to more and more people every day, widening our horizon of friendship. Her love knows no bounds, her love is unconditional, she challenges me to slow down my pace of life, and to be more and more patient with people.

She also challenges me in her difficult movements, when the fits overpower her, when she gets into bouts of depression, is unable to relate herself to anyone around her, and all that she can do is cry bitterly and helplessly, while I know I am not responsible for all her states of mind.

In such moments I remember the mothers and parents of mentally challenged persons, their anguish and tears, their worries and anxieties for their children. I pray that their sorrows have an end. And to this purpose, a place may be created where they can come together to share their pain, receive comfort and strengthen and thus create a space for solace and peace.

Ritamma David

32. Friends

Help me, O God, to be a good and true friend, to be always loyal and never to let my friends down, never to talk about them behind their back; my word be honest before their faces, never to betray a confidence or talk about things about which I might be silent; always to be ready to share everything I have, to be as true to my friends as I would want them to be to me. This I ask for the sake of him who is the greatest and truest of all friends, Jesus' sake.

Vimala Arumgadan

33. Those who Value Sports and Games

Thank you, O Lord, for your word through your servant that says physical training is of some value, but godliness has value for all things (I Tim 4:8). Help me to grow up physically and spiritually fit. Thank you, Lord, that we can run and jump, swim and dance, feeling refreshed and well. Thank you for all the intelligence we need in playing games like chess, badminton, football, cricket, *kabadi* and *onam* ball. Help all of us to have an attitude of good sports-personship so that we always play fair and win or lose graciously; and bless all those who arrange national, continental, international and Olympic games that they be diligent and honest. Through Jesus Christ.

Lily Amirtham

34. Grandparents

Dear God our Father, we thank you for the joy of being grandparents. We are grateful for our children and their children. It is a special joy for us to see our grandchildren play with us and allow us to play with them. We pray for your blessing upon them, so that they may grow with healthy bodies, with wisdom and knowledge, that they may love God, that they may take good care of God's creation and fulfil your purpose for which you have sent them into this world. Father, enable their parents to provide them proper nourishment and encouragement. May they be models whom the children to look up to. We know that they are not ours but yours, and indeed, they belong to the world. Use them as instruments for the new heaven and new earth of which we the parents have been dreaming about and praying for. May we be found not binding them to our traditions and ideas but liberate them to have their own dreams and visions and commit themselves to realise them. May they all be truly world citizens, thinking globally and acting locally for your kingdom. Let our grandchildren grow up like Jesus, the boy who grew up in Nazareth, and in whose name we offer this prayer.

Gnana Robinson

35. Those Anxious to Grow in Love

O God, our Heavenly Father, you have commanded us to love one another as your children, and have inculcated the highest friendship in the bond of your spirit, we beseech to maintain and preserve us always in the same bond, to glory, our mutual comfort, with all those to whom we are bound by any special tie, either of nature or of choice; that we may be perfected together in that love which is from above, and which never fails when all other things shall fail. Send down the dew of your heavenly grace upon us, that we may have joy in each other that pass not away, and having lived together in love here, according to your commandment, may live for ever together with you, being made one in you, in your glorious Kingdom hereafter, through Jesus Christ, our Lord.

George Hickes

36. Disabled

Heavenly, Compassionate Father, we pray for all who are handicapped in mind or body. May their bravery, endurance and cheerfulness inspire us. Give us imagination and sympathy to see how best we can help them, and how they can have opportunity to help us.

Sid G. Hedges

37. Seeking Your Blessings

O God our Father, bless those for whom life is very difficult; those who have difficult decisions to make, and who honestly do not know what is the right thing to do; those who have difficult tasks to do and to face, and who fear they may fail in them; those who have difficult temptations to face, and who know only too well that they may fall to them, if they try to meet them alone; those who have a difficult temperament and nature to master, and who know that they can be their own worst enemies; those who have difficult people to work with; those who have to suffer unjust treatment, unfair criticism, unappreciated work; those who are sad because someone they loved has died; those who are disappointed in something for which they hoped very much; those who have been hurt by their enemies, or, what is far more bitter, by the faithlessness and the disloyalty of their friends. Bless us, O God, with whatever we need and we are bringing to you now.

William Barclay

38. For All Humankind

Holy God, we pray for all human beings, though divided into nations and races. Yet are all humans, your children, drawing from you their life and being, commanded by you to obey your laws, each in accordance with the power to know and understand them. Cause hatred and strife to vanish, that abiding peace may fill the earth, and humanity may everywhere be blessed with the fruit of peace. So, shall the spirit of brotherhood and sisterhood prevail among humans, showing forth their faith that you are the Father of all.

Jewish Prayer from the Liberal Jewish Prayer Book

39. God of Love, God of Justice

God of Love, God of Justice, wonder of wonders, we adore you! Your love fuels justice, your foolishness makes for wisdom. Bearing their burden and showing your wounds you bring freedom to the oppressed; sharing their pain, you bring healing to the afflicted. You turn wolves into lambs!

Your love wins, inspires and empowers; your justice stands for ever and ever; your peace comes over all everywhere.

Dhyanchand Carr

40. For Ourselves

Loving Holy Spirit of God, we pray that we and all people may increasingly work together to establish the Kingdom of God on earth; that the resources of the world may be gathered, distributed and used with unselfish motives and scientific skills for the greatest benefit for all; that beauty may be given to our towns, and left to our countryside; that children may be finely bred and finely trained; that there may be open ways, and peace, and freedom from end to end of the earth; and that all people may learn to be lovers through keeping your company. In the name of Jesus.

G. C. Binyon

41. Life-Sustainers

Compassionate God, today we pray for those who in different ways sustain our lives: vegetable vendors, hawkers, suppliers of milk and distributers of newspapers; shoppers and pullers of heavy loads; drivers on roads and railways, captains on waterways and pilots in the air; cleaners on grounds as well in sewage tunnels. May the educated ones working in offices and institutions be kind, courteous and corrupt free. Let those who sustain our lives by their service have a sense of satisfaction and joy and help us to make them feel we are grateful to them. Beautify your world, O Lord.

Israel Selvanayagam

42. Resourceful Trees

O God, you dwell above the tallest Palmyra trees, may your presence be praised. Let the Palmyra groves flourish; and their products be used to nourish all those in need. You give us our daily *neera* (palm juice), roots, and fruits. O Lord, we are not the sinners but rather the sinned-against in society. Forgive us for not caring for the trees and for felling them at our pleasure. Lead us not into perils but save us from slipping down the trees and falling into death. May our labour be saved from the exploitation of the traders and protect us from the sugar lobby that our jaggery brings fair price to us. All power, glory, and Kingdom are yours.

Godson Samuel

43. Justice for Women

Dear Lord, you know about the lives of women – all those ordinary handmaidens whose lowliness you have regarded throughout all generations. You will call them blessed, because they work without resting, feeding their families, maintaining their households, helping each other, raising chickens and crops and children to your glory. You will not send them empty away.

Dear Life

44. My Sisters

Gentle, compassionate God, I weep for my sisters – women in joy, women in pain, unsure of who they are as humans, unsure who they are as women ... Unsure! They work so hard, too hard, trying to hold it all together. They long for the sweet gentleness of love; tender, loving, caring gentleness; and receive a different kind of love off-handed, well meaning, rough yet genuine; this love is rarely expressed in a way that really touches their inner needs, their inner longing. They struggle to come to terms with unfulfilled relationships; with being the main child carer, child raiser; being locked into the smallness of a country community; being wife, mother, housewife, farm worker, economic expert. God, they are beautiful women, hurting women, longing, aching, needing women. They have such courage, so many inner resources and strengths; I am in awe of them. I rejoice in my sisters in the country; I weep for my sisters. I weep for my sisters.

Noel Nicholls

45. A Dalit

O God, as a Dalit, I get exceedingly tired and so filled up with confronting and fighting caste, that formidable foe. It passes its poison from one generation to another. Untouchability has polluted all of the wellsprings of the nation's institutional life. More widespread than the drug scourge; more explosive than nuclear weapons; more crippling than germ warfare; casteism has washed upon the shores of our nation, since ancient times. Yet as I bow before you, O God, I pledge to you, to my ancestors sacrificed greatly, so that I might enjoy whatever rights and privileges are mine to experience and to my children and to their children, that I will keep the noble fight of faith and perseverance. I will not accept the invincibility of caste and the inviolability of its mythical, sacred precepts. I know that greater is the One that is in me than the one that is in the world. May that Spirit`s presence and power direct and inspire me now and evermore until victory is won for my people, and all people, and until the kingdoms of this world become the Kingdom of our Lord and of his Christ. I thank you for choosing me to be an instrument for this purpose.

Y. Jesudasan (adapted)

46. Physician

Dear Lord, You Great Physician, I kneel before you. Since every good and perfect gift must come from you, I pray. Give skill to my hands, clear vision to my mind, kindness and sympathy to my heart. Give singleness of purpose, strength to lift at least a part of the burden of my suffering people and a true realization of the privilege that is mine. Take from my heart all guile and worldliness, that with the simple faith of a child, I may rely on You.

Anonymous

47. Pharmacist

Dear God, Giver of life and health, make me an instrument of your healing grace. All through this working day, help me find the right medicine to restore health and the adequate words to comfort the ailing. As many prescriptions flow through my hands, give me a watchful eye to check the correct dosages and to discern any dangerous drug interactions. Fill me with the sensitivity to hear the unspoken cry for healing as Our Lord Jesus did when the bleeding woman touched his garment. And when the suffering gets beyond the human medical science of healing, when anger or frustration and despair set in, give us all, patients, their families, doctors, nurses and pharmacists, the patience and understanding to trust in your grace.

Asha Anne Simpson - Amirtham

48. Ordinary People

Give us wisdom, give us patience, and above all, give us the power to discern and to cherish those people who we may consider ordinary workers and disposable cog wheels in the immense machination of our enterprise: our customers who generously contribute to our revenues, and all others who we think constitute but the tools and means in the realisation of our corporate objectives, are indeed, the very precious objects of your creation. Help us to be considerate of the ordinary people.

Arun Amirtham

49. Industry

We are asked to watch out for our completion and the way they might twist trends in the industry. We are asked to have a keen eye on our customers and create the right product road maps for them. We cannot forget the supplier base nor ignore the imperative that we need them to supply us with the technologies that our best-in-class. We are taught to manage the right portfolio mixes to sustain our growth patterns, watch out for substitute products that might wipe our competitive advantages and build entry and exit barriers to safeguard our market territory. Lord, in all this, give us humility and instil in us the understanding that all our plans and programmes, roadmap and target settings are subordinate to your grand master plan for humankind as it continually and joyfully unfurls through the evolutionary process.

Arun Amirtham

50. Flow for Writing

Great Creator and Supreme Artist, thank you for the panorama of your creation-scudding clouds, scalloped beaches, and the roar of waves. I realise the creative force that permeates all your creations. God of Creativity, make me a channel of your creative energy. Help me to align with the energy pulsating in the universe and connect with the source of GOD – Good Orderly Direction. For the nearer I come to GOD-head, the more I 'write with the flow'. help me overcome my artistic blocks; quell my inner censor when I work on my initial drafts; and eschew perfectionism in my writing. From one creator to another, it seems natural to seek your help in this creative alliance. Grant me humility and wisdom to accept and acknowledge that we are instruments and not the authors of our creative work. Augment my inner creative voice with your own that I may resonate in harmony with the divine.

Thank you, Divine Alchemist, for the alchemy of life experiences and wisdom. May I through my writing metabolise experiences. In doing so may I move towards the source of all divinity. The Writer's Way is a spiritual pilgrimage. Help me to realise my dreams and my writer`s vision with clarity and singleness of purpose. I have faith that you will.

Nandini Murali

51. Technocrat

Dear Lord and CEO of the universe, we thank you for the wonder, beauty, and attention-to-detail in your creation. For all that is seen and unseen; for that we comprehend; and for all that we fail to comprehend and merely seek to model. We thank you for the physical forces, the natural laws and the abundant matter that bestow upon us the technological marvels of our achievements, govern the creativity of our grand innovations and ensure the perpetuity of optimisation and productivity increase in our global industrial process which, of course thanks to our management expertise, work with clock-work precision to the delight of our stake-holders.

Arun Amirtham

52. Those Sick

Lord, we want to pray today for those people who we know are sick at home or in hospital. We ask that today each of them would realise your presence and love of them; we pray that they would turn to you for strength to face their pain. Help them to learn something special about you and those who care for them, during this time of healing, help them to get well and go home as early as possible.

Lily Amirtham

53. Nursing the Sick

Dearest Lord, may I see you today and every day in the person of your sick, and whilst nursing them minister unto you. Though you hide yourself behind the unattractive disguise of the irritable, the exacting, the unreasonable, may I still recognise you and say, 'Jesus, my patient, how sweet it is to serve you.' Lord, give me this seeing faith, then my work will never be monotonous. I will ever find joy in humouring the fancies and gratifying the wishes of all poor sufferers. And, O God, while you are Jesus, my patient, design also to be to me a patient Jesus, bearing with my faults, looking only to my intention, which is to love and serve you in the person of each of your sick. Lord, increase my faith, bless my efforts and work, now and for evermore.

Daily Prayer of Mother Teresa of Calcutta

54. Those in Pain

Lord Jesus Christ, befriend your pain, says the book; bear it bravely, says my friend; see the goodness in it, says the pastor; forget it and do it boldly, tells the counsellor; understand its ABC, says the physician. It is part of life, no one is spared I know. But Lord, is there any way of handling it without agony? You should know, for you bore it on the cross.

Sam and Lily Amirtham

55. An Eternal Bond

O Lord, our God, from whom neither life nor death can separate those who trust in Thy love, and whose love holds in its embrace your children in this world and the next; so unite us to yourself that in fellowship with you we may always be united to our loved ones whether here or there. Give us courage, constancy and hope. Through him who died and was buried and rose again for us, Jesus Christ our Lord.

William Temple

56. Ageing Gracefully

Dear God, we pray for the elderly and the old that they will remain young in spirit. Keep them from being unthinkingly critical of young people whose ways are not their ways. Give them understanding of the present world, of the ideas and ideals of teenagers, many of whom hate war and fear and despise the establishment. Help the old not to fear the change nor to cling to institutions which have ceased to have meaning for other generations. Let us pray that the old may be able, out of their experience, to help the young people in an understanding and uncondescending way. And teach us all, O Lord, how to learn from each other and to find you in everyone we encounter.

Etta Gullick

57. Heal our Sorrows

Loving Lord, the long days of our sorrow still endure. Father, grant to the soul you have been chastening what you have promised, the healing and the cure. Should it be ours to drain the cup of grieving even to the drugs of pain at your command we will not falter, thankfully receiving all that is given by your loving hand.

Dietrich Bonhoeffer (before being executed)

58. Grace Under Pressure!

Lord, let me not pray to be sheltered from dangers: but to be fearless in facing them. Let me not beg for the stilling of my pain: but for the heart to conquer it. Let me not look for allies in life's battlefield: but to my own strength. Let me not crave in anxious fear to be saved: but hope for the patience to win my freedom.

Anon

59. Graceful Acceptance

If through the stony paths of pain my way should lie, save from the vain unfaith of asking 'Why?' Help me to grasp in patient faith the mystery that you are Sovereign Lord, yet this infirmity is not from you, but not without your knowledge to pray in earnest faith, assured that you can heal and eagerly embrace the means you use – Doctors, nurses, radiotherapists and healing hands, and oil and prayer on prayer. Yet all the time to know your love is free to heal or else to use all gifts of offered pain to do the Suffering Servant's ministry. So, give me strength that, in your armour clad, I may meet pain, wrestle, grasp and bear and soak it in the cross's glow and offer it to you. And so, O Lord, accept in grace immense my gifts of gold and myrrh and frankincense.

Bill Harris

60. Preparation for Death

Dear God, I pray that when my time comes, I may not grumble that my body has worn out too soon, but hold on to gratitude that I have been so long at the helm of the most wonderful creation the world has ever known and look forward to meeting the Great Designer face to face.

Paul Brand

61. In Anticipation

Lord of compassion, it is so hard to feel useless, to be unable to escape from difficulties, to be dependent on the will of others, to have no control. When there is nothing I can do to decide the future, give me the power to wait; to wait without anger, to wait without tiring of my life.

L. Samuel

62. Rulers

Almighty and Eternal God, the Disposer of all the affairs in the world, there is not one circumstance so great as not to be subject to Your power, nor so small but it comes within Your care; Your goodness and wisdom show themselves through all Your works, and Your loving kindness and mercy appear in the several dispensations of Your Providence. May we readily submit ourselves to Your pleasure and sincerely resign our wills to You, with all patience, meekness and humility; through Jesus Christ our Lord.

Queen Anne

63. God of Justice and Mercy

God of Justice and Mercy, we affirm with your devout ones of old that your judgments are true, just and holy. We in global solidarity confess that we may deserve moments of crisis such as natural calamities and pandemics. Yet we also repeat that your mercy is boundless, and it is our only hope. Equip us with analytical tools to investigate where we have gone wrong. When we are in your intensive care, sharpen our vision of joy in the future that may overcome the pain of the present. Keep us from swerving from our covenanted bond that we belong to you.

Israel Selvanayagam

64. Those Inspiration and Example

Tonight, O God, we bring our thanks to You, and specially our thanks for people.

For those who are an example to us, and those who in their lives show us what life ought to be; For those who are an inspiration to us, and who fill us with the desire to make of life a noble thing; For those who are a comfort to us when life has hurt us; For those who are a strength to us, and in whose company we feel fit to tackle any task; For those who, although we do not know them personally, have by their words or by their wirings influenced us for good; For those whose love and care and service and understanding we so often take for granted; For those who give us loyal friendship and for those who give us true love: We this night thank you, O God.

And most of all we thank you for Jesus to be the Pattern of our lives, the Companion of our way, and the Saviour of our souls.

William Barclay

65. Those in Need

Tonight, O God, we want to forget ourselves and to remember others.

Those who are ill and in pain; Those who are waiting for an operation; Those who are waiting for a doctor's diagnosis and verdict, and who fear the worst:

Bless all such.

Those who are nervous, worried, anxious, afraid of life; Those who are on the verge of a nervous breakdown; Those who feel that they cannot cope with life:

Bless all such.

Those who are hungry and cold; Those who are refugees with no home; Those who are unemployed with no work; Those who are persecuted and those who have lost their freedom:

Bless all such.

Out of your great riches supply the need of those distressed in body, mind or heart.

William Barclay

66. Relief and Comfort

Relieve and comfort, O Lord, all the persecuted and afflicted; speak peace to troubled consciences; strengthen the weak; confirm the strong; instruct the ignorant; deliver the oppressed from them that spoil him; and relieve the needy that has no helper; and bring us all, by the waters of comfort and in ways of righteousness, to the kingdom of rest and glory: through Jesus Christ our Lord.

Jeremy Taylor

67. Sewage Workers

Holy God, forgive our madness of treating the sewage workers as untouchable around the world. Just as you clean and sanctify us, they clean our sewages, often without protective covers. By treating them untouchable we deny your sanctifying grace. Give us a sense to respect all those who do cleaning jobs and create a healthy condition for our living. May we express our sincere gratitude for them!

Israel Selvanayagam

68. Prisoners

Lord, you offer freedom to all people; we pray for all who are in prison and for those who are affected by or involved in their imprisonment. Break the bonds of fear and isolation and support with your love; prisoners and their families and friends, prison chaplains, prison staff and all who care. Heal those who have been wounded by the acts of others, especially victims of crime. Help us to forgive one another, to act justly, love mercy and walk humbly together with Christ.

William Davis

69. Refugees and Victims of Oppressions

Compassionate God, whose Son Jesus as a child was carried into exile, remember all those who are deprived of their home or country, who groan under the burden of anguish and sorrow, enduring the burning heat of the sun, the freezing cold of the sea, or the humid heat of the forest, searching for a place of refuge. Cause these storms to cease, O Christ. We also pray for the victims of oppressions including domestic violence and of war and conflicts. Move the hearts of those in power that they may respect the men and women whom you have created in your own image; that the grief of refugees and other victims of injustice may be turned into joy, and hope of your kingdom.

Author Unknown

70. You are Everything

Sustaining Creator, in our weakness you give us strength; in hardship, an oasis; in persecution or calamities, protection. You are everything to us, dear Lord. Beyond our temporal concerns you bring love and hope. May we be such beacons in the lives of others.

Moravian

71. Happiness

Lord of love and kindness, help us to show your true power. May we seek not our own joy but to bring happiness to others; not our own security but to help others find hope; not our own peace but a harmony that brings others together. Grant us your love.

Moravian

72. Kindness

Generous Lord, infuse our spirits with your love and compassion that we might see the broken spirits of others and respond as you have shown us. Where there is need, help us to meet it with your kindness. May all that is good be seen in us, your children.

Moravian

73. Submission

We command our beings to submit to your authority, Lord Jesus. Where there is evil, blot it out and fill those spaces with your Holy Spirit. Fill us to be fruitful members of your body, and thereby equip others to be likewise.

Moravian

74. Conform My Will

O Lord, let me not henceforth desire health or life except to spend them for you, with you and in you. You alone know what is good for me; do therefore what seems best to you. Give to me or take from me; conform my will to yours; and grant that with humble and perfect submission and in holy confidence I may receive the orders of your eternal providence, and may equally adore all that comes to me from you.

Blaise Pascal

75. Animals

Hear our humble prayer, O God, for our friends the animals. We entreat for them all your mercy and pity, and for those who deal with them we ask a heart of compassion, gentle hands and kindly words. Make us ourselves to be true friends to animals and so to share the blessings of the merciful. For the sake of your Son, the tender-hearted Jesus Christ our Lord.

Author Unknown

76. Father of the Forsaken

O God, the father of the forsaken, the help of the weak, the supplier of the needy; you teach us that love towards the race of man is the bond of perfectness, and the imitation of your blessed self. Open and touch our hearts that we may see and do, both for this world and that which is to come, the things that belong to our peace. Strengthen us in the work which we have undertaken; give us wisdom, perseverance, faith, and zeal, and in your own time and according to your pleasure prosper the issue; for the love of your Son Jesus Christ.

Lord Shaftesbury

77. Love of Life

Lord, may we love all your creation, all the earth and every grain of sand in it. May we love every leaf, every ray of your light.

May we love the animals: you have given them the rudiments of thought and joy untroubled. Let us not trouble it; let us not harass them, let us not deprive them of their happiness, let us not work against your intent.

For we acknowledge unto you that all is like an ocean, all is flowing and blending, and that to withhold any measure of love from anything in your universe is to withhold that same measure from you.

Fyodor Dostoevsky

78. Sufferers

You are love, and you see all the suffering, injustice, and misery, which reign in this world. Have pity, we implore you, on the work of your hands. Look mercifully on the poor, the oppressed, and all who are heavy laden with error, labour and sorrow. Fill our hearts with deep compassion for those who suffer, and hasten the coming of your kingdom of justice and truth.

Eugène Bersier

79. Interdependence

O God, you have bound us together in this bundle of life; give us grace to understand how our lives depend on the courage, the industry, the honesty and integrity of our fellow men; that we may be mindful of their needs, grateful for their faithfulness, and faithful in our responsibilities to them, through Jesus Christ our Lord.

Reinhold Niebuhr

80. The Work of Peace

Give us courage, O Lord, to stand up and be counted, to stand up for those who cannot stand up for themselves, stand up for ourselves when it is needful for us to do so. Let us fear nothing more than we fear you. Let us love nothing more than we love you, for thus we shall fear nothing also. Let us have no other God before you, whether nation or party or state of church. Let us seek no other peace but the peace which is yours, and make us its instruments, opening our eyes and our ears and our hearts, so that we should know always what work of peace we may do for you.

Alan Paton

81. Daily in Solidarity

Gracious God, today we pray for those who long for love and acceptance while living in strange lands, protection from the safeguarding authorities and care from agencies of health. Touch the pulse and heartbeats of those who lack the capacity of loving the strangers in whatever form they may appear. When we see authorities for whom the lives of vulnerable minorities do not matter, may the love of Christ compel us to march on and kneel in solidarity with them.

Israel Selvanayagam

82. Prayer of the Ox

Dear God, give me time. Men are always so driven! Make them understand that I can never hurry. Give me time to eat. Give me time to plod. Give me time to sleep. Give me time to think

Carmen Bernos de Gasztold

83. Prayer of the Butterfly

Lord! Where was I? Oh yes! This flower, this sun, thank you! Your world is beautiful! This scent of roses ... Where was I? A drop of dew rolls to sparkle in a lily's heart. I have to go ... Where? I do not know! The wind has painted fancies on my wings. Fancies ... where was I? Oh yes! Lord, I had something to tell you.

Carmen Bernos de Gasztold

84. Go Between Friends

I shook hands with my friend, Lord. And suddenly when I saw his sad and anxious face, I feared that you were not in his heart. I am troubled as I am before a closed tabernacle when there is no light to show that you are there. If you were not there, Lord, my friend and I would be separated.

For his hand in mine would be only flesh in flesh and his love for me that of man for man. I want your life for him as well as for me. For it is only in you that he can be my brother.

Michel Quoist

85. The Wire Fence

The wires are holding hands around the holes: To avoid breaking the ring, they hold tight the neighbouring wrist, and it's thus that with holes they make a fence.

Lord, there are lots of holes in my life. There are some in the lives of my neighbours. But if you wish we shall hold hands. We shall hold very tight and together we shall make a fine roll offence to adorn Paradise.

Michel Quoist

86 The Lord's Thirst

Lord, you did not thirst on the cross, only for the drinking water. You thirst after the salvation of the body, mind and soul of the humans. Lord, let us also thirst not for money and fame, but for justice and grace. Lord, let us also thirst not for comfort and pleasure, but for equality and welfare of the world. Living Lord, we thirst after you as the deer thirsts for streams of water.

Johnson Gnanabaranam

87. Voice of the Voiceless

Lord, give us a deaf ear in this world of noise. Give us a sensitive heart to turn to the cries of those who have no voice, no eyes and no ears.

Assembly of the Presbyterian Church in North East India

88. Cries of Labourers

Lord, we hear the cries of people who are being oppressed and who are under fetters in this country. The exploited labourers who receive unjust wages, the bonded labourers who don't have freedom to live as they wish. Give us courage to speak against injustice, corruption and violence aimed against these labourers and to transform their lives of misery into lives of happiness. We pray also for the oppressors and request you to transform them as life-giving agents.

Madhya Pradesh Christian Council

89. Open the Prison Doors

O God, the Father and Mother of all, we bring to you the varied people of the earth. We pray in solidarity with all who suffer unjustly. Remove from our own hearts our lingering prejudices. Open the prison doors for all who are in bondage to unjust social habits and laws and are oppressed unjustly. Bind us all together in love as brothers and sisters in one family of God.

North West India Christian Council

90. Church, Town, Nation

Loving Lord Jesus, take our group and transform it by the power of your Holy Spirit so that all our members may work together for the cause of love. Take our church and revive it with our Holy Spirit, so that all who worship there may become vitally concerned for the spiritual health of their neighbours, their families and their friends. Take our town and grant that its affairs may be ordered by those who are your servants, directed by your Spirit's power. Take our nation and forgive us where we need forgiveness and give us a longing to live under your laws and subject to your Spirit's will. In your name we ask it.

Beryl Bye

91. With Women

Almighty God, we unite today with women everywhere to pray for the whole world. We know that the sin and suffering that abound have been brought upon ourselves through our own wilfulness and disobedience.

Lord, forgive us.

We confess that we have valued wealth and possessions above spiritual gifts, and we have failed to love other people as ourselves.

Lord, forgive us.

The unrest and greed of our nations reflect the same in our individual hearts.

Lord, forgive us.

We pray for a renewed sense of responsibility in us and in all humankind.

Grant this, O Lord.

We pray for a transforming love, in humans for humans.

Grant this, O Lord.

We pray for a fresh determination to obey your commandments.

Grant this, O Lord.

We pray for new values, new outlooks and new priorities.

Grant this, O Lord.

And in the coming days fill our hearts and homes with your Holy Spirit and give us your peace.

Beryl Bye

92. People in Crises

Almighty God, we pray for all those who have found the burdens and difficulties of this life too much for them. We think of those who contemplate suicide – reach out to them, Lord. We think of those who are unmarried and are to bear a child and are frightened of the consequences of their guilt – comfort them, Lord. We think of those in financial difficulties and who cannot see a way out – help them to get things in proportion. Lord, we think of the old and the lonely and the unwanted – show them how they can contribute to life. Lord, all these are your children – touch them and make them whole.

Beryl Bye

93. Women in Public Office

Gracious God, guide and direct those women who have been called to public office: our women members of Parliament and Assemblies, council members, magistrates, police, revenue officers, and school governors. Grant them wisdom to discern between right and wrong, justice and injustice, progress and retreat. Grant them courage to stand alone when necessary. May they never become so involved in service to the community that they have no time to consider their own problems and concerns. Help them to listen patiently as well as to speak forcefully, and keep them fit and sound in body, mind and spirit. We ask this in your name.

Beryl Bye

94. Use of Media

Lord of wisdom, while we thank you for the reason, discovery and the role of many who produce programmes, teach us discernment as we listen to our radio and watch our television sets. Save us from becoming hardened to violence and brutality. Grant that we may not find cause for laughter in things that are cruel or obscene. Give us increased appreciation of refreshing sceneries, fine music, good plays and informative documentaries, and a healthy and untainted sense of humour so that we may enjoy what is good and switch off what is unprofitable for our mental and spiritual development.

Beryl Bye

95. Victims of Accidents

Lord, today our thoughts are with those who have suffered as a result of road, train, air accidents. We pray for the mothers and wives and sisters of those who have died, asking that your comfort and love will surround them. We pray for the children left fatherless or motherless or orphaned, and for those who will care for them. We pray for those who feel responsible for the accident, that you will sustain them. We pray for the doctors and nurses who are caring for the injured, that their work may be inspired by your divine compassion. You suffered, O Lord, so we know you understand their suffering.

Beryl Bye

96. Pray in His Name

O Lord our God, Father of the Crucified, the comfort of the sorrowful and the strength of sufferers, we give you thanks for him who came forth from you, a light unto our darkness, who in divine love carried upon his own soul our sins and woes through the thick shadows, and went down the ways of death, so that no soul of all your children should cry in vain for the light of your face.

In his name, therefore, we pray:

For all who are tyrannized, illtreated, and slain for Christ's sake; let no trial shake their or embitter their hearts but keep them faithful and true.

For all who wronged, oppressed, defrauded, or betrayed; defend them from despair and anger.

For all who are downcast by fruitless toils or shattered hopes, who, hurt and bruised in spirit, serve without thanks and toils without recompense; preserve them by your good Spirit from utter grief of heart.

For all who are friendless and homeless, the refugees, the wanderers, and the prisoners; succour them O Lord and have pity on every waif and child of misery.

For all who are left behind and forgotten, all who are alone and afraid, the defeated, the timid, the broken hearted; befriend, comfort, and abide with them.

For all who are tempted to destroy themselves, the enslaved, the despairing, the victims of strong drink whose feet are caught in the net, and all who are reaping the evil they have sown; let the power of Christ break of their fetters and set them free.

For all penitents who despaired to do your will, yet falter continually; all who with doubtful feet stumble on in search of love, those who, struggling after purity, are vexed with evil imagination, all who would fain follow you, but fear your cross; give strength to them that have no might and grant them victory.

For all who are disquieted and troubled in spirit, all who are in soul straits and bound in miseries, the deranged and mentally ill; loose their burden and break the yolk of evil that they may know your peace.

For all who are sick, feverish, and worn by disease or stricken by accident, all who are deprived of sight, speech or hearing, and all the helpless; relieve their suffering, expel their maladies, revive their spirits, heal their wounds, and make them whole.

For all old frail folk and those to whom drawing nigh; sustain them in unclouded faith and perfect peace.

For all the dying; let light perpetual shine upon them, that they may fall asleep in peace and awake in the light of your face.

For all who mourn, for those bereft of those in whom their souls delighted, saddened with memories of vanished faces and loved voices stilled; give them comfort in hope of that day when heart shall find heart and those sundered on earth shall foregather in heaven.

Relieve and comfort them all, O God, and make us, too, to rejoice in every experience, however hard, bitter, or costly, by which we are schooled in humble faith and in charity with our fellows; through the power and mercy of Jesus Christ, our Saviour and Good Physician..

Church and Leadership, London, 1945.

97. Divine Presence in Creation

The tree, dependent on the soil in which it grows, a home for animals, birds and insects, fungi and other parasites, the beautiful orchid ... absorbing the impurities of the air we breathe and giving out oxygen, it heals and gives life to the world. Fragile, it can be broken and smashed by wind and hurricane, but in the process of falling to the ground and dying, it gives life again to the soil that nourished it. Trees hold the land together and save it from becoming a desert, shedding leaves to be broken down by the forces of nature to renew the earth.

Creating God, trees speak to us of the mystery of your presence, and your words to us; 'I created you. I love you and care for you. You belong to me like branches of the tree. My name is Emmanuel. I will be with you until the end of time and beyond with all the energy and love that are needed to heal and nourish the nations and their peoples; and to bring all things into a unity in Christ.'

Creator God, help us to care for the trees which you planted that we may have abundant life.

Maureen Edwards

98. Resources of the Earth

Creator God, you made the wells of this earth and continue to replenish them. You send rain on the righteous and on the unrighteous and invite us to drink the water of life. We pray for all lands which cry out for rain, that they may be blessed. We pray also for those places where floods destroy. May we thirst until we find a vital harmony with the earth, replenished and whole. To you we turn.

World Council of Churches

99. A Better World

O God, whose nature it is to be generous; we confess to you our share of the guilt for a world of hungry families and homeless peoples; forgive us for our self-centred living and spending; forgive those who blame you for their failures. Grant that this week some who have given nothing may start to give; those who have given something may give more; that both our church and our nation may give due place to the cries of those who have nothing to eat and nowhere to live; for the sake of Jesus Christ.

Christopher Idle

100. With All Creation

Have mercy on us, God. All creation is subjected to futility – our futility, our folly which spoils, pollutes and poisons. As your children, grant us that glorious liberty which can set all creation free. Let clean water come forth from the desert and fresh streams in the wastelands until the trees of the field clap their hands and the floods lift up their voice in praise of your name.

Worshipping Ecumenically, WCC

101. Close Family

Lord Jesus Christ, I praise and thank you for my parents and my brothers and sisters, whom you have given me to cherish. Surround them with your tender loving care, teach them to love and serve one another in true affection and to look to you in all their needs. I place them all in your care, knowing that your love for them is greater than my own. Keep us close to one another in this life and conduct us at last to our true heavenly home. Blessed be God for ever.

Michael Buckley

102. Neighbours

Lord, you taught us that all who come our way are our neighbours. But hear our prayer for those with whom we come in daily contact because they live close to us. Help us to be good neighbours to them. Give us the grace to overlook petty annoyances and to build on all that is positive in our relationship, that we may love them as we love ourselves, with genuine forbearance and kindness. For Jesus' sake.

Brooke Foss Westcott

103. To be a True Friend

Lord, when I have failed friends, I have failed you. Give me the courage to be a true friend. In those times when friends are needed, let me not be afraid of opinion, nor of failure. Let me not run from sorrow or grief, but let me stand, with you, beside my friends in their hour of need. Let my friendship be a pledge of my faith in you.

Frank Topping

104. Different Kinds of Workers

Lord, we pray for all manner of men and women, boys and girls, in their working lives: Give courage and cheerfulness to those who work on assembly lines, in supermarkets, and in routine jobs. Give patience and wisdom to those who deal with people: to social workers, teachers, police, nurses and ambulance drivers. Give skill to doctors and surgeons, scientists and researchers. Give integrity and inspiration to skilled workers and creative artists. Give wisdom to all leaders and judges, magistrates and those who make laws. Give patience and love to those who work in the home. Give motive and inclination to learn to those who study at school, college or university. Let us never despise or envy the work of others but help us to recognize that we are all needed in order to supply the needs of all.

Marjorie Holmes

105. Those in Sports

I pray, Lord, for all engaged in sports activity: in the big events that catch headlines, and in the numerous matches and contests in my own area, in schools and clubs, and among families and friends. Let pleasure and healthy exercise be the motive, and let the enjoyment and friendly rivalry contribute to the building up of community life.

More Everyday Prayers

106. God of All Games

Creator God, thank you for all the opportunities to be creative and thus participate in your continued creation. Thank you for the relaxation, refreshment, friendship and bondedness which we experience in games. Forgive us if we are obsessed with professional games with the support of wealthy and mighty. Give us confidence to identify numerous local and village games which do not get publicity and media coverage. When we applaud and sing congratulatory songs in huge stadiums, let us remember millions of children and young people around the world who do not have the opportunities to realise their potential through encouragement and skill training. In our plays may we renounce the instinct of aggressiveness and cherish friendly laughter. Above all, let all our activities of sports glorify your name.

Israel Selvanayagam

107. Creative Talents

Father, we give you thanks for all who enrich our lives with their talents. We thank you for story-tellers, playwrights and poets. We thank you for music-makers, those who compose and those who play. We thank you for writers and journalists, programme makers and cameramen who enlarge our understanding and give us new knowledge. We thank you for those who make us laugh. Use their gifts in your service; through Jesus Christ our Lord.

More Everyday Prayers

108. Exemplary Prisoner

O Lord, please give me the strength to carry me through my imprisonment. Let me concentrate, not on feeling sorry for myself, but on what I am doing while I am here. Let me comfort those left behind, for they are suffering more than I. Let me not be lonely, for there are many more lonely than I. I can have friends here' Let me not feel anger or bitterness, for they are negative; instead let me have the strength not to give in to temptation and make use of my talents. Above all, Lord help me to see what I can do best and give me strength to do these things.

Author Unknown

109. Prisoners in Christ

Almighty God, we thank you for the men and women in prison who have become children though faith in Jesus Christ. We pray that when they are released they may find love, acceptance and security within the church and grow to maturity in Christ. We ask this for your greater glory.

Author Unknown

110. Prisoners of Conscience

Lord Jesus, you experienced in person torture and death as a prisoner of conscience. You were beaten and flogged and sentenced to an agonizing death though you had done no wrong. Be now with prisoners of conscience throughout the world. Be with them in their fear and loneliness, in the agony of physical and mental torture, and in the face of execution and death. Stretch out your hands in power to beak their chains. Be merciful to the oppressor and the torturer and place a new heart within them. Forgive all injustice in our lives and transform us to be instruments of your peace, for by your wounds we are healed.

Amnesty International

111. Liberating Joy

For so long, dear God, I stared with dreadful fascination at the thick heavy chains binding my burdened life. When all the while you were waiting for my personal consent to break the chains and set me free. Oh, what liberating joy when I finally said Yes!

Ruth Harms Calkin

112. With Great Anxiety

Lord, there is nothing I can do to alter the situation, and there is nothing that you do not know – even the hairs on our head are numbered by you. My anxiety is great, and I cannot face thinking about my problems. But you have promised to help. Please give me the necessary faith to unburden my worries on you knowing that you care.

Prisoner's Lantern

113. Do Help Me

Lord Jesus Christ, you were poor and in misery, a captive and forsaken as I am. You know all man's distress; you abide with me when all others have deserted me; you do not forget but seek me. You will that I should know you and turn to you. Lord, I hear your call and follow you; do help me.

Dietrich Bonhoeffer

114. Fellow Prisoners

Chiefly do I remember all my loved ones, my fellow prisoners and all who in this house perform their hard service. Lord have mercy, restore me to liberty, and enable me so to live now, that I may answer before the world. Lord, whatever this day may bring, your name be praised.

Dietrich Bonhoeffer

115. Judges and Magistrates

Heavenly Father, at whose hand the weak shall suffer no wrong nor the mighty escape just judgement: pour your grace upon your servants our judges and magistrates, that by their true, faithful and diligent execution of justice and equity to all people equally, you may be glorified, the commonwealth daily promoted and increased and we all live in peace and quietness, godliness and virtue; through Jesus Christ our Lord.

Thomas Cranmer

116. Those Hungry

O God our Father, in the name of him who gave bread to the hungry we remember all who through our human ignorance, selfishness and sin are condemned to live in want; and we pray that all endeavours for the overcoming of world poverty and hunger may be so prospered that there may be found food sufficient for all; through Jesus Christ our Lord.

Christian Aid

117. Those Redundant and Unemployed

Almighty God, we pray for those who have been made redundant or who cannot find employment. Help them to discover renewed self-esteem and feel valued and needed. Give them a sense of calling within the work of your kingdom, here on earth. In Jesus' name.

Prayers for Times and Seasons (WYS Book No. 15)

118. Drivers

God of life and liveliness, thank you for the facility to travel fast by this vehicle and the skill to drive. Thank you for those who have worked to create and maintain this vehicle. Let me drive carefully and confidently and keep me from the temptation to overspeed. Help me awake while driving and fill me with mindfulness and loving kindness about myself and those fellow drivers. May my eyes be fixed on my way and look to the destination of journey. Whoever accompanies me in my vehicle may they have a pleasant experience and peaceful mind. Surround us with your presence and kindle our imagination so that we will reflect on the ongoing journey and ultimate goal of our life. Bless my again, me Saviour.

Israel Selvanayagam

119. Corporate Commissioning

Into your hands, O God, we commend our souls and our bodies, our families and our friends, all our neighbours and all who have blessed us with their goodness, those who have confessed their faith in Christ and those who stand in need of your protection. Enfold us in your love and grant us never to be parted from you in time or in eternity; for your own mercies' sake.

Edmund of Abingdon

120. Those in Pain

For the joys of embodiment, for the exhilaration of exercise, for touch, sight, hearing, smell and taste, we give you thanks, incarnate Christ. May the aching muscles that scream out to us after unaccustomed exercise, remind us of the pain of those often-forgotten parts of his body: those who endure physical pain, those who are prevented from reaching their full potential, those who are hungry, those who live in fear, those who are forgotten or ignored. Challenging Christ, may we stand with you among the forgotten and the marginalized. Crucified Christ, may we the hope and joy of your risen life.

Ruth Gee

121. To See the Crown of Thorns

O most loving Christ, let us see your crown of thorns in every tear-filled eye; your bleeding and naked body in every suffering soul; your nail-pierced hands in every forgotten prisoner and your wounded feet in every broken traveller; and take us to the place of healing, both ours and theirs; for your own name's sake.

Thomas Traherne

122. Chaplains for Armed Forces

Compassionate God, as we grieve for the horrors of war and commit ourselves to be peace-makers, we pray with gratitude for all the chaplains serving with the armed forces. Knowing your presence, may they be wholly attentive; knowing your forgiveness, may they offer your mercy; knowing your truth, may they offer your freedom; and may your love strengthen them in every trouble and sorrow and danger. In the name of the Prince of Peace.

Alison Tomlin

123. Those Lost in Course

Lord Jesus, we pray for those we know in loveless relationships, separated by a chasm of betrayal: those who dreams have been shattered, and who feel ignored and worthless. We pray that you will break into their lives with power, and give us power to proclaim that our God knows each one of them by name and that each one is special, loved and honoured by God.

Susan Sutton

124. The Homeless

Lord, we ask you to help families who are homeless and helpless. We pray that your will be done in their lives, that they would find food and shelter and that they would not die or suffer because of other people. Lord, we pray that you will lift them up from where they are now and keep your guard of angels surrounding them, keeping them safe.

Ashish Jaffey

125. The Abandoned

Loving God, we pray for those who feel themselves to be abandoned and forgotten, cut off without hope or help. We pray for those who have lost their security and a sense of purpose in life or who lack a sense of their own worth. We pray for those who feel separated from you by guilt, failure, past mistakes or a lack of trust. We pray for those whose dreams have been shattered, their trust abused and their love betrayed. Bridge the gap of hopelessness and isolation with the outstretched arms of your compassion and forgiveness. May all who seek your presence find you; may all who long for your acceptance know your peace; may all who ask for forgiveness and healing be blessed. In the name of our Christ our Saviour and bridge-builder.

Keith Davies

126. Rainbow People

Holy God, in the sign of the rainbow you promised life to all people, each one wonderfully made in your image: lesbian, gay, bisexual, transgender, intersex, queer and straight. Lead us all to the fullness of life which is your will and your gift, through Jesus Christ our Lord.

Mark Rowland

127. Law and Judiciary

For judges, defendants, and plaintiffs and particularly for barristers, we pray to you. How much 'palavering' there often about trifles! How often formalities rule and not true law. Often they have not people in mind but legal paragraphs;

and none of us can cope with the cunning of lawyers. We are grateful that your judgement is entirely different. Perhaps it is more severe, but your grace is there as well. For that we praise and thank you. Let the courts of justice here on earth reflect your justice and grace.

Ghana's Young Christians

128. Strength in Struggle

Lord, strengthen those who are trying to help the apathetic and who are struggling for the underprivileged and discriminated against. When they seem to fail, save them from the bitterness of spirit, from cynicism, from loss of faith and hope, and when they have success give them humility. Encourage them always to be bold and patient and fill them with the joy and love which the gift of your Spirit brings; make them realise how much they may learn from those they try to help.

Michael Hollings and Etta Gullick

129. Victims of the Covid-19

Loving God, we are in shock while the virus is spreading here and everywhere and taking an alarming number of lives. Once again, we realise that our lives are so vulnerable. If we have lost, please return to us a vision, purpose and meaning of life. Comfort the mourning and strengthen the anxious. Give us a new life of reverence and join us with the faithful affirming that, live or die, we are for the Lord.

Israel Selvanayagam

XXII. Physical and Material Needs

1. Basics

Two things I ask of you; do not deny them to me before I die:
Remove far from me falsehood and lying; give me neither poverty nor riches; feed me with the food that I need, or I shall be full, and deny you, and say, 'Who is the LORD?' or I shall be poor, and steal, and profane the name of my God.

Agur (Proverbs 30:7-9)

2. Moon of Joy

May you be for us a moon of joy and happiness. Let the young become strong and the grown man maintain his strength, the pregnant woman be delivered and the woman who has given birth suckle her child. Let the stranger come to the end of his journey and those who remain at home dwell safely in their houses. Let the flocks that go to feed in the pastures return happily. May you be a moon of harvest and of calves. May you be a moon of restoration and of good health.

Masai, Tanzania

3. Joy and Peace

Dear God, through the sensitivity of my ears, the discernment of my eyes, the clarity of my voice,

Bring joy and peace.

Through the lifting of my hands, the comfort of my arms, the journeying of my feet,

Bring joy and peace.

Through the firmness of my faith, the brightness of my hope, the genuineness of my love,

Bring joy and peace.

Through Jesus Christ, our Lord.

Ron Hoar

4. Awareness of a Child's Experience

As infants, so recently from the womb, we cry and with our mother's touch are calmed and made secure,

In our isolation, Lord we cry to you!

As children, shaken by the pain of a fall, seeking solace in a parent's arms,

In our isolation, Lord we cry to you!

As confused adolescents, enduring the pain of transition from child to adult,

In our isolation, Lord we cry to you!

As adults in a hostile world seeking others to share our personal island,

In our isolation, Lord we cry to you!

As age leads to loss of those whose touch we have valued,

In our isolation, Lord we cry to you!

(Pause)

Your healing touch we recognise in the touch of others, but in our lonely times, when no human touch is near and the fears of life beset us, hold us in your love as

In our isolation, Lord we cry to you!

Peter Fox

5. The Daylight of Dialogue and Hope

Lead us, O lord, from the night of doubt and despair into the daylight of dialogue and hope. Lead us out of the tomb of suspicion and fear, into the life of faith and trust. Lead us out of the darkness of terror and hate into the sunlight of security and love; and lead us out of the gloom of isolation and hurt into the healing presence of your glory; through Jesus Christ our Lord.

Norman Wallwork

6. Free from Cowardice, Laziness, Arrogance

Deliver us, O Lord, from the cowardice that dares not face new truth; from laziness that is content with half-truth, and from the arrogance that thinks it knows all truth; for the sake of Christ our Lord.

Edward Pender

7. Timely Blessing

Dear Father, give us our daily bread, good seasons and health. Protect us from war, disease and drought. If you would tempt me a bit by withholding your blessings for a while, then your will be done. If my time is up and my hour has come, deliver me from all evil. If not, give me strength and patience.

Martin Luther

8. Disturbing God

God of the poor, we long to meet you yet almost miss you; we strive to help you yet only discover our need. Interrupt our comfort with your nakedness, touch our possessiveness with your poverty, and surprise our guilt with the grace of your welcome in Jesus Christ.

Janet Morley

9. Best Companion

Lord, when I walk in the darkness be my light; when I am lonely be my companion; when I am weak come to my help; when I am restless grant me your peace and when I am bitter fill me with your patience and love; for Jesus' sake.

Dietrich Bonhoeffer

10. Quicken our Consciences

God our Father, in this house of prayer you bless your family on its earthly pilgrimage; so quicken our consciences by your holiness, nourish our minds by your truth, purify our imaginations by your beauty, and open our hearts to your love, that, in the surrender of our wills to your purpose, the world may be renewed in Jesus Christ our Lord.

William Temple

11. Sustain and Fill

Behold, Lord, an empty vessel that needs to be filled. My Lord, fill it. I am weak in the faith; strengthen me. I am cold in love; warm me and make me fervent, that my love may go out to my neighbour. I do not have a strong and firm faith; at time I doubt and am unable to trust you altogether. O Lord, help me. Strengthen my faith and trust in you.

Martin Luther

12. Safety and Quietness

Lord may nothing perturb us and nothing make us frightened; for all things are passing and you alone are changeless. Those who possess you lack nothing and you alone meet all our needs.

St. Teresa of Avila

13. Celebration of Diversity

O God, the Lord of the Universe, we thank you for the beauty of the hundreds of languages in our country and in the whole world. Help us with the right aptitude to appreciate the languages other than our own. Help us to accept 'unity in diversity' as your precious gift to humanity, a treasure to be guarded for generations to come. Help us to respect cultures that differ from us and to believe that this adds to the wealth of our country and richness of your world. Above all teach us the right word for love and justice and the right method to establish them.

Samuel Amirtham

14. Gifts of Life

O God, give us the gifts which we need most of all.

Wisdom always to choose the right, and courage always to do it; Strength to overcome temptation, and produce ever to stay in the straightway; Clear sight to see what to do, and perseverance never to give up trying to do it:

Grant us these things, O God.

Diligence in study, and fidelity in work; Purity in pleasure, and delight in simple things; Honour in every action, and truth in every work:

Grant us these things, O God.

Loyalty to our friends, and forgiveness to our enemies; Sympathy for all in sorrow, help for all in need, understanding for those who have made mistakes; Love for our fellows, and love for you:

Grant us these things, O God.

William Barclay

15. Relaxing Home

May our homes be a refuge from the stress and injustice in the world around us where we are safe, rejuvenated, and loved. May our schools inspire a love of learning where students and teachers feel safe, loved and happy. Bless our homes and schools, that they may be places where we grow closer to you.

Like the woman at the well, we seldom realize that our souls are utterly dry, deprived of your living water, so wallowed in the sins that squeeze your breath from our mortal beings, cisterns become normal. Purge us, Lord, and fill us with your living water!

Moravian

16. A Child

Lord we need your help.
We need a calm mind ; grant us your peace.
We need a clear head; grant us your wisdom.
We need to be very careful; grant us your patience.
We need to be inspired; grant us your enthusiasm.
Keep us from all panic as put our trust in your power
to keep us this day.

Name unknown

17. A Child's Prayer

Make me, dear Lord, polite and kind to everyone, I pray: And may I ask you how you find Yourself, dear Lord, today?

Author Unknown

18. To be Used

Use me then, my Saviour, for whatever purpose, and in whatever way, you may require. Here is my poor heart, an empty vessel; fill it with your grace. Here is my sinful and troubled soul; quicken it and refresh it with your love. Take my heart for your abode; my mouth to spread abroad the glory of your name; my love and all my powers, for the advancement of your believing people; and never suffer the steadfastness and confidence of my faith to abate; so that at all times I may be enabled from the heart to say, 'Jesus needs me, and I am his.'

Dwight L. Moody

19. Stop Land Burning (*Nikosi Sikilel i Africa*)

Have compassion, Lord, upon this land. Let your mercy come upon it, Lord. Hold your hands out, Lord, and bless this land, land that burns, Lord, land that burns. Let our people stand before you all. Judge them with your judgement hard, O Lord. Let justice triumph in this land that burns, Lord, land that burns.

Author Unknown

20. Balancing

Lord, if we are bitter, sweeten us; if we are rebellious, reason with us; if we are resentful, be understanding with us; if we are sad, comfort us; if we are downcast, lift us up; if we are doubtful, reassure us. Lord, we need you. Meet our need, we pray you.

Beryl Bye

21. Holy Spirit, the Highest Gift

O Eternal God, have mercy upon us. Through your Holy Spirit unite us with yourself and kindle us with true light and righteousness. Your Son's words tell us of your loving-kindness, the gift of your Holy Spirit and your earnest desire to help us: 'How much more shall your heavenly Father give you his Holy Spirit, when you ask it of him.' From this we know that when we ask you will willingly give us this good gift. We are confident, therefore, that you will hear our prayers and petitions. To you with your son and the Holy Spirit be all honour and glory, for ever and ever.

Philip Melanchthon

22. Freedom from Noise

We live in a restless noisy world. The crash of waves on a small boat. The noise of gunfire and the explosion of bombs. The shouts of the market-place and the wail of hungry child. The dumb pleading of the addict's needle and the protests of the oppressed. The frustrated anger of the unemployed and the scream of the tortured. The restless noise of machines. The clamant knocking of the prisoner and the noisy silence of unforgiveness. Out of the depths of our noise we cry to you, O Lord, the never ceasing prayer of your people, with your people, for your people, that the discordant clamour of your world maybe turned into symphonies of peace, love and joy. May the voice of prayer be never silent. God is not deafened by our noise, he opens his ears wider when we cry.

Author Unknown

23. Future Security

Faithful God, you have promised to supply all your children's needs out of your riches in glory by Jesus Christ. In these days of political uncertainty, economic depression, social unrest, fear on our streets and across our world, we thank you that you are totally dependable, and the source of all true and lasting happiness. Help us to recognize you as the 'pearl of great price' with which our future security is guaranteed, but without which we will continue to struggle alone. May we invest our lives wisely in pursuit of this treasure which will never lose its value.

Noel Fallows

24. Light in Complexity

You are the God of dark matter and dazzling galaxies; war-torn countries and growing economies; broken communities and thriving neighbourhoods; hidden thoughts and healthy conversations. Pierce the shadows that surround and threaten to overwhelm us with your light. Bring the hope and joy of your Son which can never be overcome.

John Hellyer

25. Sustaining Hope

Great God of love, fill our lives with your hope; hope that gives birth to justice; hope that builds well-being in community; hope that reaches out hands to make peace; hope that finds expression in daily acts of love, and so your kingdom comes.

Bill Anderson

26. Needs of Others

O Lord God, since you have called us to devote ourselves to the needs of others, grant us the strength of your grace. In the midst of our work let us not lose sight of your great purposes. Let us not snatch the management of your world from your hands, lest we faint and fall in the presence of your wisdom; this we beg for Jesus' sake.

Florence Nightingale

XXIII. Meetings in Local Congregation

1. Today is Sunday

Father, Today is Sunday-your day of rest. I thank you for this day. Let me take this opportunity to spend time meditating on your Word, in prayer, in praise, in intercession. On this day, I join your children everywhere praising your name. I remember once more with joy that you are my Father and my Mother and you chose to love me as your child. Once more I ask you for your forgiveness for the many times I have failed you. Give me a truly repentant heart, and strengthen me to keep from doing that which hurts you or other people. Teach me to wait on you and try to listen to you, so that I will learn what is your will for me and do it. May the time I spend in your presence this day, my Creator, help to bring me closer to you, and make me a more obedient child of yours; and if it be your will, use me for the good of your children everywhere.

Vimala Arangadan

2. The Lord's Day

O Lord, God of our life, who has given us the rest of this sacred day; grant that the benediction of its restfulness may abide upon us throughout the week. Enable us to carry the influence of its consecration into all we do; let the praises of our lips rendered to you this day become praise in our lives. May the power of your love be with us in every duty, that by pureness, by knowledge, and by tenderness we may glorify you; through Jesus Christ our Lord.

William Barclay

3. The Day of Rejoicing

Father, we rejoice that you have given us Sunday: the day when we remember that you created the word and all that is within it, the day when Jesus was raised from the dead and death and hell laid waste, the day in which all things were made and re-made. Father, we may approach Sunday with longing and expectation; as the hungry seek for bread, so may we yearn for word and sacrament; save our worship from all that is trivial; rooted in the reality of the world in which we live, may it yet glimpse the glory of your presence, and stand in awe at the light of your holiness; may we sense the presence of all who have gone before us, hearing in your own songs the echo of unseen heaven's praise.

More Everyday Prayers

4 At the Start of Worship

O Lord our God! You know who we are; some with good consciences and some with bad, persons who are content and those who are discontent, the certain and the uncertain, Christians by conviction and Christians by convention, those who believe, those who half-believe, those who disbelieve.

And you know where we have come from: from the circle of relatives, acquaintances and friends or from the greatest loneliness, from a life of quiet prosperity or from manifold confusion and distress, from family relationships that are well ordered or from those disordered or under stress, from the inner circle of the Christian Community or from its outer edge.

But, now we all stand before you, in all our differences, yet alike in that we are all in the wrong with you and with one another, that we must all one day die, that we would all be lost without your grace, but also in that your grace is promised and made available to us all in your dear Son Jesus Christ. We are here together in order to praise you through letting you speak to us. We beseech you to grant that this may take place in this hour, in the name of your Son our Lord.

Karl Barth

5. Join the Praise of the Church

O most great and mighty God, whose glory is above all our thoughts whose mercy is over all your works: Let the inspiration of the Holy Spirit assist us in all the duties of this sacred day; let us join in the praise of your church with ardent affection; let us hear your Word with earnest attention and let the prayers and sacrifices of your holy church, offered unto you this day, be graciously accepted. Being created by you, let us even act for your glory and being redeemed by you, let us render unto you what is yours; through Jesus Christ our Lord.

John Wesley

6. Worship at All Times

This day, as are all days, loving God, is the day to worship you. This time, as are all times, loving God, is the time to give you praise. This moment, as are all moments, loving God, is the moment to turn to you in faith. And so, this day, at this time, from this moment onwards, we worship you, we praise you, we turn again in faith. Fill our hearts with joy and gladness, we pray, and take away strain and stress, that we may feel free to worship you with our whole beings. In Christ's name.

Stephen Brown

7. Worship/Prayer Fellowship

Gracious God, give us the ears to hear voice, the eyes to see your glory, the hearts to know your love, and then the will to worship – for you are God, we are your people, and it is right that we offer you praise. Bless our time together, and bless us as we go, that here and at home we may know your ceaseless presence in the power of your Spirit. In the name of our living Lord Jesus Christ.

Stephen Brown

8. Bread and Wine

Lord Jesus Christ, you are for us our bread of life, as vulnerable as bread placed in the hand, to be accepted with joy or cast aside; as satisfying as bread to the hungry, and giving life for the future; broken like bread before all can share, and as necessary as bread to sustain our living.

Lord Jesus Christ, you are for us our spiritual drink; rich as the blood-red, sun-filled grape, taken, pressed and destroyed to new-create; welcome as the clean, fresh draught to the weary traveler, drawn from the deep, clear well that never fails; gift to our thirst to meet our need, poured in love that all might share. Bread and wine you are; food and drink – to our eternal satisfaction.

Donald Hilton

9. Worship with Many Gifts

Loving God, we come to worship you. We bring our gifts and bring ourselves; we bring our hopes and we bring our fears; we bring our experience of this last week, its hurt and its delight; we bring our thoughts of those for whom we want to pray. We bring our families and friends, those close to us and those far away; we bring the work we have done this week, and the work we have failed to do; we bring our relationships within this church, and all our contacts in the wider community of town and nation. These all, Lord, we lay before you. If anything we bring is good in your sight – affirm and bless us. If anything we bring is lacking in purpose and truth – enlighten and guide us. If anything we bring is fragmented and broken – heal and mend us. If anything we bring is twisted and tawdry – forgive and renew us. But, Lord, whatever we bring, do not reject us; welcome us in your Son's name.

Donald Hilton

10. Committee to Choose

Lord, we need your guidance especially today as we meet to appoint our committee and officers for the coming year. Help us to choose the right people for the right jobs. Restrain us from choosing people just because they are our friends without considering their capabilities. Show us clearly those who will be of greatest spiritual strength to our group. Indicate new people who may have a great deal to offer but are shy about putting themselves forward. Give those of our members who may have served for many years the courage to step back if they feel it is right to do so. Lord, we long for this group to be greatly used in your service. Take it now and mould it as you will.

Beryl Bye

11. Meeting for Common Purpose

Gracious and compassionate God, thank you for this meeting and all opportunities it brings to us to enjoy fellowship and to work together for a common purpose. Give us at this time clarity of thought, and selflessness in intent. When we share ideas and plan together let nothing else be our guiding principle than your love, justice and fairness. We pray for all those who are affected by the decisions we make. Give them your grace to know the truth and gain understanding. Whether delight or disappointment, let our decision arise from our deep convictions and equanimity of mind. In Christ's name we pray.

Israel Selvanayagam

12. At the Start of a Meeting

In our thoughts and speaking, may the Lord be with us. In our argument and agreement, may the Lord be with us. In our concerns and anxieties, may the Lord be with us. In our exploration and deciding may the Lord be with us. May we discern God's will, through the power of the Holy Spirit and in the name of Jesus Christ.

Annette Sampson

13. Opening a Meeting

Thank you, O Lord, for the privilege of working in your vineyard. Help us to be faithful in our dealings, truthful in our speaking and deep in our commitment. Guide our meeting with the wisdom and integrity of your Holy Spirit. Bless us with a purity of heart and clarity of mind. May we be quick to listen, slow to speak and give space for silence. In all we decide and do let your holy name be glorified. In the name of our servant Lord.

Israel Selvanayagam

14. In the Vestry

A. God of community and congregation, as your Son Jesus has taught us, where two or three are gathered, you are in our midst. Prepare the servant who is going to lead the service and preach the word with the gift of confidence, humility and holy imagination. May s/he be endowed with wisdom to speak the right word in the right tone. Let all who worship rejoice in the presence of God and renew their commitment. In Christ's name, we pray.

B. Holy, holy, holy, Lord God Almighty, help us to worship in the beauty of holiness with an imagination of the heavenly church joining us. Let us never seek success of our standard but faithfulness to your revelation.

C. Be present O God in our midst of your people's gathering. May we realise that the sanctity of the church lies in the unity of the people. Prompt people to go and be reconciled with those with whom they need to be reconciled. (In the Eucharist may we once again experience the sacramental blood relation of all God's people).

D. Gracious God, thank you for the privilege of worshiping in this place with your other children. As your Son Jesus said to a Samaritan woman, neither on this mount nor in Jerusalem, but in every place the true worshippers of the Father will worship in Spirit and in truth. Help us to follow this guideline.

E. Prepare us O God to worship you with undivided minds and unfaltered movements. Let our songs, adoration, confession, petitions and your words give us a wholesome experience. Help us to feel renewed in our spirit at the end and clarity of our faith and life.

Israel Selvanayagam

15. With the Choir

A. May we sing with our spirit and our understanding that the listeners may know your message clearly. May the words of our mouths and music of our hearts harmonise the voice of our congregation.

B. Just as the words and music join together to give a new experience, O God, let our singing join the congregation together for a new life. All glory and joy be to you our creator and redeemer.

C. Just our breath turns to be the music, joyful God, let our hearts join your mysterious presence. Let our whole being have a share in your joy which may melt and transform us.

D. May our creator rejoice and delight us in his holy presence. In the name of the one on whose lips the words of the psalms were hummed, even Jesus Christ our Lord.

E. Accept our fruits of the sacrifices from our mouth, O gracious God. May we step into your presence with trembling and proclaim your words rejoicing. Forgive our weakness.

Israel Selvanayagam

16. Before the Sermon

A. May I speak the truth in love overcoming the temptation to twist in order to create a certain impression. May we all hear your truth even irrespective of the quality of my voice and purity of all our thought.
B. May the words of my mouth and meditation of all our hearts be acceptable in your sight, O Strength and Saviour.
C. God of all truth, let me speak what I hold as truth. Let the truth lead us from all sorts of untruth and falsehood. Whatever may the consequence, let us stand firm in truth.
D. God the source of all wisdom, we acknowledge that your word is a lamp for my feet and a light on my path. Help us to focus your light to our path we walk every day.
E. God of all grace, thank you for the privilege of preaching and hearing your words. Our preparation is inadequate and our completeness rests in your grace and guidance.

Israel Selvanayagam

17. Offertory Prayer

A. Thank you, O God, for the gift of life and gifts of abundance we enjoy. Our gifts cannot match your generosity. We offer these gifts as a token of our gratitude and love. Accept us and ours.
B. Merciful God, we come to your presence with tiny gifts but with our eyebrows raised, incense burning in our inner sanctuary, along with flowers of smile and tears of joy.
C. From the air we breathe, the food we eat, the clothes we wear to the friendship and fellowship we enjoy:

All gifts come from you, our bounteous God. All power and glory are yours.

D. Ours are your gifts, graces and guidance, O God of all blessings:

Yours is kingdom, power and glory for ever and ever.

Israel Selvanayagam

E. God, Your Spirit breathes through all creation, you have made our bodies your dwelling place and home. You offer yourself through everything:

Transform our lives through grace and love.

F. We bring to you bread and wine for our communion; lives and gifts for your kingdom. You offer yourself through everything:

Transform our lives through grace and love.

G. We bring to you the miracle that is our human body, our joy, our pain. You offer yourself through everything:

Transform our lives through grace and love.

H. We bring to you our vulnerability, doubts and questions. You offer yourself through everything:

Transform our lives through grace and love.

Donald Eadie 'An offertory prayer' (in a Service for Healing and Wholeness)

I. You know us, God. You know all about us. We tell you what we want, not to inform you but to be honest with ourselves in your light.

What we want now is to make our offerings to you. Help us to know what to do with those things we want that are not worthy of you or us.

Accept our lives, our loves, our integrity. What we offer to you make whole, so that we may go on from strength to strength and continue to find your meaning in our lives, now and always.

John B. Coburn

XXIV. Nations, Countries and the World

1. Nations

O God, send peace upon earth, that the nations no longer may prepare for war, and that they may try, not to destroy, but to understand each other.

O God, bless those parts of the world where they are learning the meaning of freedom and of liberty, and where new nations are being born. Take away all bitterness and hatred, and grant that people of all colours and races may learn to live in fellowship together.

O God, bless those places in the world where the name of Jesus is not known, or where it is rejected. Strengthen and uphold all missionaries in the peril and the loneliness of their task; and bring quickly the day when all people everywhere will confess that Jesus Christ is Lord.

O God, bless those parts of the world where people are homeless and hungry, and grant that those of us who have may ever be ready to share their plenty with those who have too little.

O God, bless those nations who have a different political creed and a different way of life from ours; and save us from being too quick to condemn that which we do not understand just because it is different, and help all people everywhere to find a fellowship in Jesus Christ which will cross all creeds and frontiers and weld them into one.

And help us to work, and to pray, and to give, and to sacrifice to bring the day when the kingdoms of the world will be the Kingdom of the Lord: through Jesus Christ our Lord.

William Barclay

2. Whole World

O God, who made of one blood all nations who dwell in the world, bless this world. Bring quickly the day when colour and race shall no longer divide us. Give your help in those places where new nations are being born, and grant that bitterness and hatred may not destroy brotherhood and peace. And hasten the time when the knowledge of yourself will cover the earth as the waters cover the sea and when none shall any longer even speak of war.

William Barclay

3. A Leader

Create in me, O Lord, a new heart, and so renew my Spirit that your law may be my study, your truth my delight, your Church my care, your people my crown, your righteousness my pleasure, your service my government; so shall this kingdom through you be established with peace.

Queen Elizabeth II

4. Common Good

Almighty God, who has ordained that humans should serve you in serving one another by their labours: have regard, we pray you, to this nation, oppressed at this time by many burdens. Grant to its citizens grace to work together with honest and faithful hearts, each caring for the good of all; that seeking first your kingdom and its righteousness, they may have added to them all things needful for their daily sustenance and the common good; through Jesus Christ our Lord.

Geoffrey F. Fisher

5. Politicians and Authorities

Lord God, in our prayers for our country we remember especially the men and women who powerfully influence the life of society: those who fashion our politics, those who frame and administer our laws, those who mould public opinion through the press, radio and television, those who write what many read. May all such recognise their responsibility to you and to the nation, that people may be influenced for what is good, not evil; for what is true, not false; for the glory of your name.

Frank Colquhoun

6. Response to Challenges

Your people tremble, wonder and are perplexed as they see their nation grappling with creeping materialism, atheism and gnawing corruption in high and low places. Grant your Church strength, wisdom and courage to confront the people of this nation and announce the Good News of eternal life through Jesus Christ.

John Banda

7. For Our Country

Lord, save our country, from the social sins of wealth without work, education without character, commerce without morals, pleasure without conscience, science without human values, politics without principles, religion without sacrifice. Make us a nation that re-catches the vision of *dharma* (just order).

M. K. Gandhiji (adapted by Samuel Amirtham)

8. Towards a True World

Where there is passion to know the truth and abide by it;

Where positions are not considered to be beyond being responsive and accountable;

Where people live with dignity and self-reliance without depending on trickling charity;

Where human dignity is discerned and respected beyond statures, fancies and fashions;

Where there are equal opportunities for all people to realise their full potential;

Where there is commitment to persevere on peace before rushing to war;

Where production of food is given more importance than production of weapons of war;

Where every person feels at home with genuine friends and loving neighbours;

Where even a little girl will travel in the night without fear but humming in joy;

Where there is a constant search for true civilization and development with civility;

Into that true world let our people and leaders awake.

Israel Selvanayagam

9. Justice and Peace

O loving Lord, our country needs justice for our security and mercy for our nurture. Thank you that in yourself you link justice with mercy and combine power with love. We long for a world that is both just and compassionate. We look for a world where authority and love are inextricably joined. Challenge your Church to reach beyond the barriers that we have created. Change your Church so that we look to the interests of others rather than our own. Cleanse your Church with the Spirit of holiness and renew us with Calvary love. Focus us on Kingdom values of righteousness, peace and joy. And by the grace of Christ, in the power of the Holy Spirit, we will ever live for your glory.

Kenneth Todd

10. For Nation at War

Grant, O merciful God, that with malice toward none, with charity to all, with firmness in the right as you give us to see the right, we may strive to finish the work we are in; to bind up the nation's wounds; to care for him who shall have borne the battle and for his widow and his orphan; to do all which may achieve and cherish a just and lasting peace among ourselves and with all nations.

Abraham Lincoln

11. Our Beautiful Land

Bless our beautiful land, O Lord, with its wonderful variety of people, of races, cultures and languages. May we be a nation of laughter and joy, of justice and reconciliation, of peace and unity, of compassion, caring and sharing. We pray this prayer true patriotism, in the powerful name of Jesus our Lord.

Desmond Tutu

12. A Vision of our Land

Grant us, O God, a vision of our land, fair as she might be; a land of justice, where none shall prey on others; a land of plenty, where poverty shall cease to fester; a land of brotherhood, where success shall be founded on service and honour be given to worth alone; a land of peace, where order shall not rest on force, but on the love of all for their land, the great mother of the common life and welfare.

George Appleton

13. Our Country

Lord, bless our country, may we take pride not in the might of our people, not in the mere length of years, not in things achieved or gained for ourselves, but in the unselfishness we have displayed, the times when we have turned the other cheek, the willingness we have shown to serve without reward, and above all the efforts we have made to unite all humans as equal members of your world family.

Did G. Hedges

14. Justice of Sharing

Heavenly Father, may your Holy Spirit lead the rich nations to support the poor, and the strong nations to support the weak; so that every nation may develop in its own way, and work together with other nations in true partnership for the promotion of peace and the good of all humankind; through Jesus Christ our Lord.

Source Unknown

15. A Heaven of Freedom

Where the mind is without fear and the head is held high; where knowledge is free; where the world has not been broken up into fragments by narrow domestic walls; where words come out from the depth of truth; where tireless striving stretches its arms towards perfection; where the clear stream of reason has not lost its way into the dreary sand of dead habit; where the mind is led forward by you into ever-widening thought and action; into that heaven of freedom, my Father, let my country awake.

Rabindranath Tagore

16. Our Country India

We praise you for our country, its beauty, the riches it has for us and gifts it showers on us. We thank you for your people, the gift of languages we speak, the variety of races we have, the cultural heritage we cherish and the latent possibilities there are for our country to be great. Grant that we accept these gifts with thankfulness and use them for the good of the human race and to bring glory to you. Through Jesus Christ our Lord.

From India

17. Republic Day (India)

Our Heavenly Father, the sounds of music from all around awaken me this morning. It is Republic Day. Thank you, O Father, for this our land with its high mountains, its many rivers, its fertile plains, its wealth of forests and minerals, the seas around abounding in marine life.

O what a rich land is ours! We remember before you, the many communities and multi-cultures that make up our nation. Teach and help us, Father, each one to be proud of this our land, and so to be united as one people; forgetting our differences, working only for the good of each other as one whole.

Show us that we are many colours making one pretty rainbow; different silks weaving one rich and beautiful tapestry. Put in our hearts a great love for this land, love for every Indian. whatever the language or religion; help us to spend our lives working for the good of all people in this country, and never knowingly serve the cause of disunity.

So guide and help us, O Father, to be one.

Vimala Arangadan

18. For India

O Almighty, Create thoughts and actions in the minds of the people of my nation so that they live united. Help all religious leaders of my country to give strength to the people to combat the forces of division. Embed the thought 'The nation is bigger than the individual' in the minds of the leaders and people. O God, bless my people to work and transform the country into a prosperous nation soon.

A. P. J. Abdul Kalam

19. Clean India

Lord of all nations, we pray particularly for India and her millions. Lord, grant us a deep sense of responsibility that everyone may do his/her duty and strive for the good of the nation. We beseech you to aid us to fearlessly love truth and boldly stand up against injustice. Assist us to vigilantly watch any erosion of democratic way of life. Grant us a structure in which the lowly and the lost too will participate in the decision-making process.

Holy Lord, eradicate corruption from our public and private life. Forgive our foolishness in accepting corruption as a way of life. Protect the integrity and independence of our judiciary that justice may flow with ease. Strengthen law and order that people may not despair. Preserve the freedom of the press and uphold everyone's right to worship and propagate their faith, without hatred or hindrance.

Good Lord, help our people, the government, the political parties and voluntary agencies to assiduously endeavour for the establishment of a truly secular, egalitarian, democratic and just society. Save the nation from black laws and fissiparous tendencies of disintegration. Make India strong that she may shed pride and live in lasting peace with her neighbours.

Bless our country and all her inhabitants to live in dignity and charity to all. Grant your grace that we may all live in humility as members of one world human family.

M. A. Thomas.

20. Peace in India

O God, our heavenly Father and Mother! You are the 'Prince of Peace' and you have left your peace with us, your children, men and women of different races, colours, regions, languages and creeds, living in India. Grant us your grace to make this your heavenly gift our eternal heritage, and to learn to live with one another and with our neighbouring nations in peace and harmony. Teach us to see in our diversities the beauty of your creation and to accept one another as brothers and sisters in love and trust. Help us to realise that you have spoken to our fathers and mothers '*in many and various ways*' that we may use our religion not as an instrument to divide us, but as a means to unite us. We acknowledge that you are '*God and not man*' and that you never come down to destroy. Restrain us, therefore, gracious Lord, from indulging ourselves in any unjust activity that may hurt and destroy our neighbours. Help us to see in our life that '*justice and peace kiss each other*' and bind us together in equity. In the name of our Lord, Jesus Christ, we pray.

Gnana Robinson

XXV. Universe and Environment

1. Earth and Environment

Lord, thank you for letting me find my friend who was lost: my friend, the earth.
The earth, after all, is made up of the same stuff as I, and it needs the light and warmth of the same sun.
We had lost touch with each other for a time. I no longer saw, or visited, or even spoke to my friend. I thought, or rather we thought, my brother and I, that we no longer had need of the earth.
Lord, we have found our friend again, but it is sick, wounded, and exhausted.
You gave it to us once, and we took it into our hands when it was unspoiled, savage,
but able to be tamed.
Some of us betrayed it to the 'developers' who forced it to prostitute itself, so that they may take their unbridled pleasure from it. And now, disfigured and contaminated, the earth sickens us when we draw near. Lord, the earth has no arms, it has no voice, let me be its defender, let me fight on its behalf.
For it was you who gave me the earth, Lord; you gave it to me and to all people.
In protecting it and developing it as you wish, once more I will save it, and, in saving it, save all my brothers.

Michel Quoist

2. Sustaining Presence

You nourish and sustain the world from day to day, and wherever we go you are present more fully than we dare presume. We thank you for this presence, this hidden, vulnerable, yet faithful presence here and now. We believe in it and live from you as we live from bread as we hunger and thirst for peace.

Huub Oosterhuis

3. Confession and Restoration about Nature

Eternal God, maker of the skies above, lowly Christ, born amidst the growing earth, Spirit of life, wind over the flowing waters, in earth, sea and sky, you are there. O hidden mystery, sun behind all suns, soul behind all souls, in everything we touch, in everything we meet, your presence is around us, and we give you thanks. But when we have not touched but trampled you in creation, when we have not met but missed you in one another, when we have not received but rejected you in the poor, forgive us, and hear now our plea for mercy.

Iona Community

4. Teach by Nature

Lord, isn't your creation wasteful? Fruits never equal the seedlings' abundance. Springs scatter water. The sun gives out enormous light. May your bounty teach me greatness of heart. May your magnificence stop me being mean. Seeing you a prodigal and open-handed giver, let me give unstintingly … like God's own.

Helder Camara

5. Celtic Prayer of Creation

O Christ, there is no plant in the ground but it is full of your virtue.
There is no form in the strand but it is full of your blessing.
There is no life in the sea, there is no creature in the ocean,
There is nothing in the heavens but proclaims your goodness.
There is no bird on the wing, there is no star in the sky,
There is nothing beneath the sun but proclaims your goodness.

Iona Community

6. Wonderful Earth

Creator God, yearning and striving to bring harmony out of chaos, so fill with your wisdom the inscape of our being, and so move with the wind of your presence among the landscapes of our world, that the earth may reflect the wonder of the universe, in the glory of the transfigured, at one with you in the cost of creating.

Jim Cotter

7. Birth Pangs

Lord: help us to see in the groaning of creation, not death throes but birth pangs; help us to see in suffering a promise for the future, because it is cry against the inhumanity of the present. Help us to glimpse in protest the dawn of justice, in the Cross the pathway to resurrection, and in suffering the seeds of joy.

Rubem Alves

8. Surprise with Nature

God of ancient calm, let your peace still us. God of fearful storm, fill us with awe. God of mountains, widen our vision. God of shining stars, illumine our journey. God of lonely plains, touch these empty spaces within us where we are vulnerable enough to meet you.

Peter Miller

9. Agents of Change

Gracious God, grant to us a vision of a world transformed by your love; a world where resources are shared and clean water is available to all; a world where the hungry are fed and the naked clothed; a world where the diversity of nature flourishes, and pollution and destruction has ceased; a world where love is shared and differences are peacefully resolved. Gracious God, grant to us we pray: courage to speak out, that the voiceless may be heard; willingness of heart and mind to be agents of change in this world; strength to be channels through which your transforming love will flow.

Sandra Goodwin

10. All in Peace

'O You King of kings and Lord of lords, who desire that all people should dwell together in unity; let your will be known and done among the nations; guide their feet into the way of peace. Remember us and all humanity in your mercy. Deliver us from the sins which give rise to war and conflict, and strengthen within our hearts the will to establish righteousness and justice in the earth. Give unto us and to all who worship you the sincere desire to live in peaceful and loving fellowship with all people. Fix our minds and hearts upon your eternal purposes for your children on earth.'

Moravian

11. Justice Triumphant

We pray, O Father, for justice on the earth. When no justice can be found, help us to know that justice will ultimately triumph because you are a God who will judge with complete fairness. Thank you, God.

Moravian

12. Justice and Truth

God of justice and mercy, guide the nations of the world into the way of justice and truth. Establish among them that peace which is the fruit of righteousness that they may become the kingdom of our Lord and Saviour Jesus Christ.

Moravian

13. Sights and Smells

Creator of life and light, we bless you this day for the beauty of your world, for the sunshine and flowers, storm-cloud and starry night, for the first radiance of dawn and the last smouldering glow of the sunset. We thank you for physical joy, for the ecstasy of swift motion, for deep water to swim in, for goodly smell of rain on dry ground, for hills to climb, and hard work to do, for all skill of hand and eye, for music that lifts our hearts in one breath to heaven, for the hand-grasp of a friend, for the gracious loveliness of children … for all these your sacraments of beauty and joy, we thank you, our Lord and our God.

Godfrey Pain

14. Father's Eyes to See the Universe

I would like to rise very high, Lord, above my city, above the world, above time. I would like to purify my glance and borrow your eyes. I would then see the universe, humanity, history, as the Father sees them. I would see in the prodigious transformation of matter, in the perpetual seething of life, your great body that is born of the breath of the Spirit. I would see the beautiful, the eternal thought of your Father's love taking for step by step, everything summed up in you, things on earth and things in heaven. And I would see that today, like yesterday, the most minute details are part of it.

Michel Quoist

15. World United in Love

Guide our nation and world leaders, grant them wisdom, conviction, courage, and compassion. We pray for an end to hatred and war, for a world united in love and peace. We pray for the ecological healing of our world, that we may be conscious of our impact on your creation. Help us to be better stewards of the world we live in and all those who inhabit it.

Moravian

16. Real Peace

We pray for peace, but not the easy peace built on complacency and not the truth of God; we pray for real peace, the peace God's love alone can seal.

We pray for peace, but not the cruel peace leaving God's poor bereft and dying in distress; we pray for real peace, enriching all humanity.

We pray for peace, and not the evil peace defending unjust laws and nursing prejudice, but for the real peace of justice, truth and brotherhood.

We pray for peace: Holy Communion with Christ our risen Lord and all humanity; God's will fulfilled on earth, and all his creatures reconciled.

We pray for peace, and, for the sake of peace, look to the risen Christ, who gives the grace we need to serve the cause of peace and make our own self-sacrifice.

God, give us peace; if you withdraw your love there is no peace for us, nor any hope of it. With you to lead us on, through death or tumult, peace will come.

Alan Gaunt

17. Power to be Gentle

Lord, we pray for the power to be gentle; the strength to be forgiving; the patience to be understanding; and the endurance to accept the consequences of holding to what we believe to be right.

May we put our trust in the power of good to overcome evil and the power of love to overcome hatred. We pray for the vision to see and the faith to believe in a world emancipated from violence, a new world where fear shall no longer lead men to commit injustice, nor selfishness make them bring suffering to others.

Help us to devote our whole life and thought and energy to the task of making peace, praying always for the inspiration and the power to fulfil the destiny for which we and all people were created.

Prayer for World Peace (1978)

18. Environmental Responsibility

Lord God, we praise you for the brotherhood and sisterhood that we share across the world as followers of the way shown to us by Jesus. As our need of each other's care and love becomes ever more obvious in matters of environmental responsibility and sustainable pattern of life, encourage and enable us, as people of faith, to understand the responsibility with which you have entrusted us, both for stewarding the earth's resources and for respecting and cherishing each other's integrity and welfare. We give particular thanks for friendship of the people. We thank you for all particular links between churches in different parts of the world, and we ask that these contacts may become vehicles of greater understanding and unity.

Martin Dodds

19. Climate Change

We give thanks for the commitment of climate change advocates who boldly challenge the status quo, and give a voice to the voiceless all around the world who are actually suffering the effects of climate change right now. We pray for politicians and negotiators, that they will make ethical and just decisions, based on science, and not political interests; for the voiceless and the people who suffer most and contribute least to climate change; for climate justice and fairness, that everyone may be able to have a dignified existence; that we will open our ears to hear the cries of the suffering and acknowledge that climate change is a problem for everyone.

Julia Edwards

20. Sacred Earth

God of bush bog-myrtle, of old man banksia and dancing birch, of sheltering banyan and red rowan, of whispering aspen and Huon pine, of heather and of eucalyptus, illumine our minds that we may embrace your sacred earth with a renewed tenderness imbued with wisdom and rooted in wonder.

Peter Miller

21. The Sanctity of Earth

Creator of earth and of earth's children, creator of soil and sea and sky and the tapestries of stars, we turn to you for guidance as we look on our mutilated planet, and pray it is not too late for us to rescue our wounded world. We have been so careless. We have failed to nurture the fragile life you entrusted to our keeping. We beg you for forgiveness and we ask you to begin again. Be with us in our commitment to earth. Let all the earth say:

Miriam Therese Winter

22. Temple of the Universe

In the temple of my inner being, in the temple of my body, in the temple of earth, sea and sky, in the great temple of the universe I look for the light that was in the beginning, the mighty fire that blazes still from the heart of life, glowing in the whiteness of moon, glistening in night stars, hidden in the black earth, concealed in the unseen depths of my soul. In the darkness of the night, in the shadows of my being, O God, let me glimpse the eternal. In both the light and the shadows of my being let me glimpse the glow of the eternal.

J. Philip Newell

XXVI. The Lord's Prayer - Different Versions

1. Traditional

Our Father, who art in heaven,
hallowed be thy Name;
thy kingdom come;
thy will be done;
on earth as it is in heaven.
Give us this day our daily bread.
And forgive us our trespasses,
as we forgive those who trespass against us.
And lead us not into temptation;
but deliver us from evil.
For thine is the kingdom,
the power, and the glory,
for ever and ever. Amen.

2. Modern

Our Father in heaven
hallowed be your Name,
your kingdom come,
your will be done,
on earth as in heaven.
Give us today our daily bread.
Forgive us our sins
as we forgive those who sin against us.
Do not bring us to the time of trial
but deliver us from evil.
For the kingdom, the power,
and the glory are yours
now and for ever. Amen.

3. Sung Version

Our Father, who art in heaven,
hallowed be thy name.
Thy kingdom come, thy will be done,
hallowed be thy name.

On this earth as it is in heaven.
Hallowed be thy name.
Give us this day our daily bread,
hallowed be thy name.

Forgive us all our trespasses,
hallowed be thy name.
as we forgive those who trespass against us.
Hallowed be thy name.

Lead us not into temptation,
hallowed be thy name.
but deliver us from all that is evil.
Hallowed be thy name.

For thine is the kingdom, the power, and the glory,
Hallowed be thy name.
for ever and for ever and ever.
Hallowed be thy name.

Amen, amen, it shall be so.
Hallowed be thy name.
Amen, amen, it shall be so.
Hallowed be thy name.

Caribbean

4. Millennium Scottish (Sung) Version

Our Father, who art in heaven,
hallowed be thy Name;
thy kingdom come;
thy will be done;
on earth as in heaven.
Give us today our daily bread.
And forgive our sins,
as we forgive each one of those who sins against us.
And lead us not to time of trial;
but deliver us from evil.
For thine is the kingdom, the power and the glory,
Amen.

5. In Expansion

Our Father in heaven, Mother, Friend and Companion, living in the highest of all heights,
Hallowed be your name which has been profaned by bloodshed and wrongdoing and selfish use.
Your kingdom come, the kingdom of justice, peace and love, and the kingdom of the poor.
Your will be done, the holy will, connecting heaven and earth, fascinating yet not forcing.
Give us today our daily bread, strength to earn and grace to share, without anxiety and greed.
Forgive us our sins, as you always do because of your infinite compassion and mercy;
as we forgive those who sin against us, without reserve, count and limit, though we shudder to say.
Do not bring us to the time of trial, to fall in the traps of making our name and fame great,
but deliver us from evil, the evil of oppression, corruption, manipulation and deception.
For the kingdom, the power, and the glory are yours, for you alone give them back to us with joy now and for ever, without any gaps in time, space and restrictions to follow your ways.

Israel Selvanayagam

6. An Interpreted Version

Our Father, you are in this our land, may your name blessed in our incessant search for Justice and peace. May your Kingdom come for those who have for centuries awaited a life with dignity. May your will be done on earth as in heaven and in the Church of the whole world, a Church on the side of the poor. Give us today our daily bread to build a new society. Forgive us our trespasses; do not let us fall into temptation of believing ourselves already new men and women. And deliver us from the evil of war and from the evil of forgetting that our lives and the life of this country are in your hands.

Christian Communities in Nicaragua

XXVII. Benedictions and Blessings

1. Triune

May the grace of the Lord Jesus Christ, and the love of God, and the fellowship of the Holy Spirit be with you all.

St. Paul (2 Cor. 13:14)

2. Whatever is Good

Finally, brothers and sisters, whatever is true, whatever is noble, whatever is right, whatever is pure, whatever is lovely, whatever is admirable – if anything is excellent or praiseworthy – think about such things. Whatever you have learned or received or heard from me, or seen in me – put it into practice. And the God of peace will be with you.

St. Paul (Phil. 4:8-9).

3. Whole Person

May God himself, the God of peace, sanctify you through and through. May your whole spirit, soul and body be kept blameless at the coming of our Lord Jesus Christ. The one who calls you is faithful, and he will do it.

St. Paul (1 Thess. 5:23-24)

4. Glory to God

To our God and Father of Lord Jesus Christ who is the blessed and only sovereign, the King of kings and Lord of lords. It is He alone who has immortality and dwells in unapproachable light whom no one has ever seen or can see, to Him be honour and eternal dominion.

(I Timothy 6:15-16)

5. God of Peace

Now may the God of peace, who through the blood of the eternal covenant brought back from the dead our Lord Jesus, that great Shepherd of the sheep, equip you with everything good for doing his will, and may he work in us what is pleasing to him, through Jesus Christ, to who be glory for ever and ever.

An apostle (Heb. 13:20-210)

6. Stand without Blemish

Now to him who is able to keep you from falling, and to make you stand without blemish in the presence of his glory with rejoicing, to the only God our Saviour, through Jesus Christ our Lord, be glory, majesty, power, and authority, before all time and now and for ever.

Jude 24

7. Ancient Benediction

The Lord Jesus Christ be near to defend you, within you to refresh you, around you to preserve you, before you to guide you, behind you to justify you, above you to bless you, who lives and reigns with the Father and the Holy Spirit, God for evermore.

Anon

8. Comprehensive Wishes

May the road rise up to meet you; may the rains fall gently on your fields.

May the wind be always at your back; may the sun shine warm upon your face;

And until we meet again; may God hold you in the palm of his hand.

Gaelic

9. Through Nature

May God, who is present in sunrise and nightfall, and in the crossing of the sea, guide your feet as you go. May God who is with you when you sit and when you stand, encompass you with love and lead you by the hand. May God, who knows your path and the places where you rest, be with you in your waiting, be your good news for sharing, and lead you in the way that is everlasting.

Gaelic

10. Peace of the Shining Stars

Deep peace of the running wave to you.
Deep peace of the flowing air to you.

Deep peace of the quiet earth to you.
Deep peace of the shining stars to you.
Deep peace of the Son of Peace to you.

Celtic

11. Abundant Life

May the power of God this day enable me; the charm of God disarm me; the beauty of God silence me; the justice of God give me voice; the integrity of God hold me; the desire of God move me; the fear of God expose me to the truth; the breath of God give me abundant life.

Author Unknown

12. God Ahead

May God stride out before you on your journey through life and through prayer.

May Jesus, your playful brother, pace you in his holy way to the end.

May the Holy Spirit greet you at each corner and cuddle you to her breast.

Sian Swain Taylor

13. From Despair to Hope

And now to him who is able to keep us from falling, and lift us from the dark valley of despair to the bright mountain of hope, from the midnight of desperation to the daybreak of joy, to him be power and authority, for ever and ever.

Martin Luther King Jr.

14. From You to Us

The peace of God which passes all understanding, keep our hearts and minds in the knowledge and love of God and of his Son Jesus Christ our Lord; and the blessing of God Almighty, the Father, the Son and the Holy Ghost, be amongst you and remain with you always.

Book of Common Prayer

15. The Aaronic Blessing (with response)

The Lord Bless you and keep you;
We will be a blessing for others.
The Lord make his face shine upon you;
We will shine in darkness.
The Lord turn his face toward you and give you peace;
We will live as channels of peace.
Numbers 6:24-26; extension by Israel Selvanayagam

16. After Communion

As you have been fed at this table go to feed the hungry. As you have been set free go to set free the imprisoned. As you have received – give. As you have heard – proclaim. And the blessing which you have received from Creator, Son and Spirit go with you.

Worshipping Ecumenically, WCC

17. Prosperity and Hope

May God Almighty bless you, blessings of heaven above, blessings of the deep lying below, blessings of the breasts and womb, blessings of the grain and flowers, blessings of the eternal mountains, bounty of the everlasting hills (Gen. 49:25-26) be with you and go with you until we meet again. In the name of the Father, Son and Holy Spirit.

Worshipping Ecumenically, WCC

18. Promise and Commission

Go out into the world in peace; have courage; hold on what is good; return to no one evil for evil; strengthen the faint-hearted; support the weak, and help the suffering; honour all people; love and serve the Lord, rejoicing in the power of the Holy Spirit and may the blessing of God almighty, the Father, the Son, and the Holy Spirit, be amongst you and remain with you always.

CSI Book of Common Worship

19. Motherly Blessing

May the blessing of the God of Abraham and Sarah, and of Jesus Christ born of our sister Mary, and of the Holy Spirit, who broods over the world as a mother over her children, be upon you and remain with you always.

The New Century Hymnal, 873

20. For the Departed and the Living

May the God of the departed and the living, continue to be your companion, counsellor, comforter and guide. When you walk through deep waters and coals of fire, when you experience cold and heat, may God be your protecting shield and encouraging presence. When you have to step in slippery paths, on new thresholds and confusing crossroads, may the Emmanuel hold your hands tightly with tender care. May your fear of the unknown be removed by the promise of a joyful future. May the God of unfailing love be your eternal home, precious prize and ultimate goal. Peace be upon you, now and always.

Israel Selvanayagam

21. Spirit's Blessing

Sense the warm passion of the Spirit's flame. Speak with the fervour of the Spirit's voice. Move with the music of the Spirit's dance. May God's Spirit bless you and confirm you in your calling as a disciple of Christ.

Michael Youngson

22. Blessing for Limbs

God bless our eyes, so that we may recognize injustice. God bless our ears, so that we may hear the cry of the stranger. God bless our mouths, so that we may speak words of welcome to newcomers. God bless our shoulders, so that we may be able to bear the weight of those struggling for justice. God bless our hands, so that we will be able to work together to establish peace.

Olwyn Holden

23. Christmas Blessing

May the joy of the angels, the eagerness of the shepherds, the perseverance of the wise men, the obedience of Joseph and Mary, and the peace of the Christ child be yours this Christmas. And the blessing of God almighty, the Father, the Son and the Holy Spirit, be upon you and remain with you always.

The Promise of His Glory

24. God Bless in all Moments

God bless you when you run; for God himself runs with you. God bless when you walk; Christ's Spirit is beside you. God bless you when your feet are sore; Christ Jesus washes them. Go out and live and hope and love, for our God leads on, the flame held high. God's blessing now, and all the way, on you and those whom you love.

Margaret Woodcock

25. Bless the Fundamentals

Bless, O God, the thing on which rests my eye;
Bless, O God, the thing on which rests my hope;
Bless, O God, my reason and my purpose;
Bless, Oh bless them, you God of life.

Alexander Carmichael

Authors and Printed Materials

(*with minimal details if available. Wikipedia is consulted where necessary*)

Abbreviations

MMCB – Minister of the Methodist Church in Britain (*without stating the special positions/periods*)

MC – Methodist Church

LPMCB – Local Preacher in Methodist Church in Britain

CSI – The Church of South India

URC – United Reformed Church

USPG – United Society for the Propagation of The Gospel (London-based)

WCC – World Council of Churches

Adam, David, (b. 1936) is an Anglican priest who worked in North Yorkshire for over twenty years, where he began writing prayers in the Celtic pattern, and he later became Rector of Holy Island, Lindisfarne, where he lives retired. (97)

African Prayer (303)

Alcott, Louisa May (1832-1888) was an American novelist, short story writer and poet. (83)

Alcuin of York (735-804) was an English scholar, clergyman, poet, and teacher from York, Northumbria. (232)

Alford, Henry (1810-71) was a Dean of Canterbury, one of the most variously-accomplished churchmen of his day – poet, preacher, painter, musician, biblical scholar, critic, and philologist. (211, 257)

Allen, Diane, USA, is an author; her books include *Daughter of the Dales* and she has written devotions as well. (254)

Alves, Rubem (1933-2014) was a Brazilian theologian, philosopher, educator, writer and psychoanalyst. Alves was one of the founders of liberation theology. (360)

Ambrose, Archbishop of Milan who became one of the most influential ecclesiastical figures of the 4th century. (50, 249)

Amirtham, Arun, A Solar Energy Engineer, Zurich. (313-314)

Amirtham, Lily, member of the CSI, former lecturer in Lady Doak College, Madurai and painter of water colours. (155, 307-308, 314)

Amirtham, Samuel (1932-2017), ecumenical theological educator and bishop in the CSI. (xxviii, 16, 145, 240, 248, 271, 314, 338, 353)

Amnesty International is a non-governmental organization founded in 1961 based in London focused on human rights. (91, 329)

Anderson, Alan, a former member of the Central House of the Selly Oak Colleges, Birmingham. (192, 204, 304)

Anderson, Bill, MMCB. (341)

Anderson, Lesley G., (Panama). (20, 40, 105, 262)

Anglican Church of Canada (134)

Anglican Church of New Zealand. (134)

Anon, Aotearoa (New Zealand). (48, 274, 315, 370)

Anselm (1033-1109), an Italian Benedictine monk, abbot, philosopher and theologian, who held the office of Archbishop of Canterbury from 1093 to 1109. (47, 180, 300)

Appleton, George (1902-1993), an Anglican bishop, writer, composer of prayers. (17, 106, 186, 196, 274, 354)

Aquinas, Thomas, St. (1225-1274) was an Italian Dominican friar, philosopher, Catholic priest, and Doctor of the Church. An immensely influential philosopher, theologian, and jurist in the tradition of scholasticism. (78-79, 163, 181, 199, 222)

Arangadan, Vimala (1915-2016), writer of stories and editor of magazines for Children, Bangalore. (207, 209-210, 270-271, 307-308, 343, 345)

Archbishop of Canterbury. (331)

Arndt, Johann (1555-1621) was a German Lutheran theologian who wrote several influential books of devotional Christianity. He was a forerunner of pietism, a movement within Lutheranism that gained strength in the late 17th century. (83)

Arnold, Thomas (1795-1842) was an English educator and historian, an early supporter of the Broad Church Anglican movement and reformer of schools education. (146, 156)

Ascension Rite, The Worship Book of the United College of the Ascension, Selly Oak, Birmingham (1996-2006). (4-5, 37)

Attwood, Eunice, Vice President of the Methodist Conference, 2010/2011. (245)

Augustine, St. of Hippo (354-430), a Roman African, early Christian theologian and influential writer. (6, 39, 57-58, 73, 77, 119, 153, 168, 180)

Austin, John (1939-2007) was the Bishop of Aston (Midlands) from 1992 to 2005, filling a post which had been long vacant. (63)

Australian Aboriginal woman. (242)

Baillie, John (1886-1960) was a Scottish theologian, a Church of Scotland minister. His books include *A Diary of Private Prayer.* (37, 159)

Baker, Jill, Lay leader, MCB. (232)

Bales, Stephen, MMCB. (254)

Banana, Canaan, Former President of the Methodist Church in Zimbabwe. (258)

Banda, John. (352)

Banyard, Edmund, a minister and former Moderator of the General Assembly of the URC. (196)

Barclay, William (1907-1978), minister of the Church of Scotland, Biblical Scholar and theologian. (18, 24-26, 34-36, 145-149, 151-153, 157-158, 167, 169-170, 202-203, 211-223, 258, 271-272, 276, 284, 286-288, 291-292, 295, 297, 304, 309, 317, 338, 343, 351-352)

Barry, Rosy Morgan, LPMC, SE Berkshire Circuit. (14)

Barth, Karl (1868-1986), a great Swiss Theologian and Pastor, associated with the anti-Nazi Confessing Church. (9, 344)

Basil the Great (330-379) was the Bishop of Caesarea Mazaca in Cappadocia, Asia Minor. He was an influential theologian who supported the Nicene Creed and opposed the heresies of the early Christian church. (55, 167, 281)

Beckingham, Keith, MMCB. (189)

Beethoven, Ludwig van (1770-1827) was a German composer and pianist. A crucial figure in the transition between the classical and romantic eras in classical music, he remains one of the most recognized and influential musicians of this period and is considered to be one of the greatest composers of all time. (211)

Benedict (born in Nursia and died in 547 AD in Monte Cassino, Italy, is a Christian saint venerated in the Catholic, Orthodox and Anglican Churches. He is a patron saint of Europe. (68, 79)

Benson, Richard Meux (1824-1915) was a priest in the Church of England and founder of the Society of St. John the Evangelist, the first religious order of monks in the Anglican Communion since the Reformation. (250, 266, 279)

Benson, White Edward (1829-1896) was Archbishop of Canterbury from 1883 until his death. Prior to this, he was the first Bishop of Truro, serving from 1877 to 1883. (250)

Bernos, de Garztold Carmen (1919-1995) was a French poet. After World War II she went to live at the Benedictine Abbaye Saint Louis du Temple at Limon-par-Igny. (321)

Bersier, Eugene (1831-1889) was a pastor of the Swiss Reformed Church. He founded the Evangelical Church l'Etoile. (320)

Betham-Edwards, Matilda (1836-1919) was an English novelist, travel writer and Francophile, and a prolific poet, who corresponded with several well-known English male poets of the day. (65)

Bhogal, Inderjit, MMCB. (123, 300)

Bidaux, Josianne Bhutan. (60, 172)

Bingham, Jane, Learning and Development Coordinator, East Central Region (2016/17). (70)

Binyon, ***G.C.*** is a writer on and promoter of Christian social thought in Britain. (234, 310)

Birch, John, LPMC. (165)

Blakey, Wesley, MMCB. (108, 127)

Bonar, Horatius (1808-89) was a minister of the Free Church of Scotland. He was reputed as a religious writer and authored the influential 'Kelso Tracts,' and also, he was a hymn-writer. (161)

Bonaventure of Bagnoregio (1221-1274) was a Franciscan friar, Master of Theology at the University of Paris, Minister General of the Franciscan Order, and Cardinal of the Catholic Church. (109)

Bonhoeffer, Dietrich (1906-1945) was a German Protestant theologian, martyred for opposition to the Nazi genocide in the WW2, important for his support of ecumenism and his view of Christianity's role in a secular world. (74, 154, 172, 186, 315, 329-330, 337)

Book of Christian Prayer (1974). (162)

Book of Common Prayer of the Church of England (52, 291, 371)

Booth, Howard, Senior Lecturer in the University of Manchester, author of books on health care and healing. (8)

Booth, Jim, MMCB. (190)

Bouillon, Dorothée, United Protestant Church of Belgium. (115)

Bouverie Pusey, Edward (1800-82) was an English clergyman and scholar, and one of the major figures of the Oxford Movement. (144)

Boyd, Malcom (1923-2015), an American Episcopal priest and author, was active in the Civil Rights Movement as one of the Freedom Riders in 1961. (37)

Brand, Paul (1914-2003), pioneering physician/surgeon in the field of leprosy. Born in Tamil Nadu of missionary parents and worked there. (316)

Brandt, Leslie F., author, Christian Prayer and Meditations including *Book of Christian Prayer* (1974). (270)

Bridget of Sweden (1303-73) was a mystic and saint, and founder of the Bridgettines nuns and monks after the death of her husband of twenty years. (91, 193)

Bright, William (1824-1901) was a famous church historian and Regius Professor of Ecclesiastical History in Oxford. (82, 124, 168, 197)

Brown, Anne, MMCB. (189)

Brown, Stephen, Minister, URC, UK. (42, 253, 345)

Brown, Wendy, West Hertfordshire and Borders Circuit. (233)

Bryan, Zinnia is an author of prayers; her books include *Prayers for Every Day.* (297)

Buckley, Michael. (136, 327)

Burdon, Adrian, MMCB. (109)

Burgess, Stuart, MMCB. (60, 171)

Bye, Beryl (1973), Writer of Prayers, Cheltenham, England. (24, 263-264, 272, 283, 298, 322-324, 340, 346)

Calkin, Ruth Harms is a popular English author of devotional books. (130, 329)

Calvin, John (1509-1564) was a French theologian, pastor and reformer in Geneva during the Protestant Reformation. (154, 211)

Camara, Dom Helder (1909-1999), a Roman Catholic pro-poor and anti-rich priest in Brazil, who became the Archbishop. (50, 184, 360)

Canadian Indian (105, 175, 305)

Carmichael, Alexander was born in Scotland in 1832. Though a civil servant, his life-long vocation was the recording and translating of Gaelic prayers and stories, for which he is revered now. (373)

Carmichael, Amy (1867-1951) was a Christian missionary in India, who opened an orphanage and founded a mission in Dohnavur in Thirunelveli Dt., Tamil Nadu. She served in India for 55 years and wrote extensively about the missionary work there. (67)

Carr, Dhyanchand, presbyter of the CSI, New Testament scholar and activist, former Mission & Theology Secretary of the Christian Conference of Asia and Principal of the Tamil Nadu Theological Seminary, Madurai. (310)

Carter, Graham, MMCB. (204)

Catherine of Genoa (1447-1510) was an Italian Roman Catholic saint and mystic, admired for her work among the sick and the poor and remembered because of various writings describing both these actions and her mystical experiences. (119)

Catherine of Siena (1347–1380), a laywoman associated with the Dominican Order, was a mystic, activist, and influential author. (84, 114)

'Celtic' indicates a tribe, language and ancient civilization that flourished over a thousand years BCE in the British Isles. The Celtic church was founded in the early centuries of the CE until it got assimilated with the Roman Church and was driven out of England by the Saxons in the 5th century. A number of Celtic abbeys and pilgrim centres such as Iona have survived. St. Patrick, a Briton, worked as a bishop in Ireland in 5th cent. In the next cent Columba, a Celtic missionary, found several monasteries in Ireland. Celtic spirituality is said to be wholistic combining nature, human depth and justice. (39, 166, 371)

Ceril (125)

Challoner, Richard (1691-1781) was an English Roman Catholic bishop, a leading figure of English Catholicism during the greater part of the 18th century. (108)

Chapman, Raymond, Emeritus Professor of English in the University of London and a non- stipendiary priest in the Diocese of Southwark. (240-242)

Chapman, Rex. (288)

Charlton, Gwen. (61, 174)

Chellakkan, Rajamony (b. 1942) is a presbyter of the CSI, Kanyakumari Diocese. (251)

Cherry, Stephen, is the Dean of King's College, Cambridge, and was formerly a residentiary canon of Durham Cathedral. (128, 235)

Chikera, Geetha de, Sri Lanka.(206)

Chinnakone, Jackie, Burgess Hill Methodist Church. (142)

Christian Aid, a large charity based in London. (330)

Church Army, is an evangelistic organisation founded in 1882 in the Church of England and now operating in many parts of the Anglican Communion. (42)

Church in Wales (241)

Church of Bangladesh (199)

Church of South India (238, 372)

Clark, Geoffrey. (168)

Clarke, Phil, MMCB. (255)

Clement of Rome (Saint, Pope) is listed by Irenaeus and Tertullian as Bishop of Rome, holding office from 88 to his death in 99. He is considered to be the first Apostolic Father of the Church, one of the three chief ones together with Polycarp and Ignatius of Antioch. (126)

Clement XI, (1649-1721) was head of the Catholic Church and ruler of the Papal States from 1700 to his death. He was a patron of the arts and of science. (231)

Clowes, David, MMCB. (45)

Clutterbuck, Diane, MMCB. (xxvii, 20, 107)

Coburn, John B. (1914-2009) was bishop of the Episcopal Diocese of Massachusetts, USA, from 1976 to 1986. His best known book is *Prayer and Personal Religion.* (62, 90, 349)

Coggan, Donald (1909-2000), Baron Coggan, PC was the 101st Archbishop of Canterbury from 1974 to 1980, supporter of women's ordination and revived dialogue with Rome. (120)

Coleman, Diane, LPMCB. (268)

Cole-Njie, Olufemi, MMCB. (253)

Collinson, Nigel, MMCB. (105, 173, 175, 282)

Colquhoun, Frank (1909-1997) was a Canon Residentiary and Vice-Dean of Norwich Cathedral. Previous to that he was Chancellor of Southwark Cathedral.

Ordained for over sixty years, he exercised a varied ministry, half of which was spent in parish life. (292, 352)

Compston, Kate, a modern English poet and writer. (224, 273)

Cooper, Ann, LPMCB, Newcastle West Circuit. (276)

Coote, David, MMCB. (166, 266)

Cornick, Ray, LPMCB, Poole and Swanage. (116)

Cosin, John (1594-1672), English bishop and theologian. (65, 130, 232)

Cotter, Jim (b. 1942), an Anglican priest, retreat leader, creative liturgist of our day, a lecturer at Lincoln Theological College and Chaplain of Gonville and Caius College, Cambridge. (28, 36, 47-48, 50, 162, 164-165, 197-198, 254-255, 360)

Coverdale, Miles (1488-1569) was an English ecclesiastical reformer, puritan preacher and a Bible translator. (82, 97, 183, 230)

Crane, Josette, MMCB. (35, 128, 190)

Cranmer, Thomas (1489-1556) was a leader of the English Reformation and Archbishop of Canterbury during the reigns of Henry VIII, Edward VI and, for a short time, Mary I. (284, 293, 330)

Crofts, Margaret, LPMCB, Sherburn circuit. (288)

Cumings, Llewellyn is an English author and composer of prayers including *Prayers from Cradle to Grave*. (135)

Cyril (378-444) was the Patriarch of Alexandria from 412 to 444. He was enthroned when the city was at the height of its influence and power within the Roman Empire. (125)

Daily Prayer (5, 112)

Daniel, Gill, MMCB. (94)

David, Ritamma, Lecturer, Social Activist, Madurai, Tamil Nadu, India. (308)

Davies, Andrea, LPMCB. (95)

Davies, Keith, MMCB (332)

Davies, Paul, MMCB. (49)

Davis, William, MMCB, (306, 318)

Davison, William, MMCB. (232)

Dearmer, Percy (1867-1936) was an English priest (socialist) and liturgist best known as the author of *The Parson's Handbook*, a liturgical manual for Anglican clergy. (109, 240)

Denning, Bill, late MMCB (artist and poet, and a part time pastoral tutor, Wesley College, Bristol in 1990s). (63)

Devanesan, Chandran (b.1943) was the first Indian Principal of the Madras Christian College. (64-65, 183)

Dewey, Margaret (USPG). (172)

Didache, The, also known as 'The Lord's Teaching Through the Twelve Apostles to the Nations', is a brief anonymous early Christian treatise written in Koine Greek, dated by most modern scholars to the first century. (190)

Dionysius of Alexandria (c.200-265), the Great, was the 14th Pope and Patriarch of Alexandria from 248 until his death in 264. (195)

Divine Liturgy of St. Mark was at one time the primary worship service of the Orthodox Church of Alexandria. The oldest extant copy of this liturgy dates from the fourth century (*Daily Prayer* 84). (51)

Dodds, Martin, Cumbria/Argentina Contact Group, 2010/2011. (363)

Donne, John (1572-1631) was a prominent English metaphysical poet and cleric in the Church of England. (80)

Dostoevsky, Fyodor was a Russian novelist, philosopher, short story writer, essayist, and journalist. (320)

Drake, Francis (1540-1596) was an English sea captain, privateer, slave trader, pirate, naval officer and explorer of the Elizabethan era. (229)

Dunkerley, Roderic (1884-1966) was a Congregational minister and Christian writer, of prayers for school children, with Gregor. (35)

Dunstan, Paul, Cumbria District Evangelism Enabler. (117)

Dutton, Susan, Social Care Facilitator at Methodist Home for the Aged, Claybourne, 2010-2011. (27)

Eadie, Donald, MMCB, spiritual director, writer of prayers and meditations. (15-16, 19, 60, 62-63, 90, 97, 99, 106, 149, 175, 185, 201, 257, 349)

Ebert, Mary Ann, an American author. (86, 171)

Ecumenical Centre, Geneva (239)

Edmund of Abingdon, St. (1175-1240), a former Archbishop of Canterbury (331)

Edwards, Julia, Mission Partner Fiji. (364)

Edwards, Maureen (d. 2018), LPMCB, prayer writer and editor. (19, 21, 104, 175, 242, 267, 290, 326)

Elizabeth II, Queen of England. (352)

***Ellis,* Jenny**, Connectional Spirituality and Discipleship Officer, 2009-2010. (140, 149)

Emerson, Ralph Waldo (1803-1882), American essayist, poet, philosopher and transcendentalist. (13)

Ephrem the Syrian (306-363) was a Syriac Christian deacon and a prolific Syriaclanguage hymnographer and theologian. (39)

Erasmus, Desiderius (1466-1536) known as Erasmus of Rotterdam, was a Dutch philosopher and Christian humanist, and the greatest scholar of the northern Renaissance. (7, 73, 182)

Esquivel, Julia (1930-2019) was a Guatemalan poet, theologian and peace activist. (55)

Falla, Terry C., Professor at New Zealand Baptist Theological College, University of Auckland. (78)

Fallows, Noel, Lay leader MC Ireland. (340)

Farrer, Austin (1904-1968), an English Anglican philosopher, theologian, and biblical scholar. (38)

Fénelon, François (1651-1715) was a French Roman Catholic archbishop, theologian, poet and writer. (86, 163)

Ferguson, J. M. Macdougall, a 20th century English writer of books including *A Prayer Project for Juniors and Young Seniors* (1946) and *The School Assembly: Services Of Worship For Schools* (1957). (27-28)

Ferguson, James (20th century), Crieff, Scotland; Minister of Kensington Chapel, London. (17, 26, 76, 184, 229, 237-238, 272)

Fischer, Emil E. (1852-1919) was a German chemist and 1902 recipient of the Nobel Prize in Chemistry. (249)

Fooler, Michael. (110)

Forsyth, P. T. (1845-1921) was a Scottish theologian and minister of the Congregational tradition. (239)

Foucauld, Charles de (1858-1916) was a cavalry officer in the French Army, then an explorer and geographer, and finally a Catholic priest, a hermit who lived among the Tuareg in the Sahara in Algeria. (80)

Fox, George (1624-1691) was an English Dissenter, who was a founder of the Religious Society of Friends, commonly known as the Quakers or Friends. (84)

Fox, Peter, Methodist medical mission partner, *LPMCB,* Tavistock Circuit. (123, 144, 170, 306, 336)

Francis of Assisi (1182-1226), born and died in Assisi, Italy, he came to be an Italian Catholic Friar, and regarded as saint. (23, 70, 258)

Froude, Richard Hurell (1803-36) was an Anglo-Catholic thinker who joined the Oxford Movement, which he drove more and more towards the Catholic tradition of the Mediaeval period. (163, 231)

Fuller, Thomas (1608-1661) was an English churchman and historian. He is now remembered for his writings, particularly his *Worthies of England*, published in 1662 after his death. (274)

Gaelic (Scottish-Irish language). (370)

Galloway, Kathy is an ordained Church of Scotland minister and was, in 2002 the first woman to be elected leader of the Iona Community. She has held the position of Head of Christian Aid Scotland and has been a patron of the Student Christian Movement. (165)

Gamble, David. (306)

Gandhi, M. K. (1869-1948), Father of the Independent India. (204, 353)

Gaunt, Alan (b. 1935), a Congregationalist hymn writer who has served in Congregational and URC churches in the north of England. (363)

Gee, Ruth, MMCB. (81, 94, 144, 331)

Gelasian Sacramentary is a book of Christian liturgy, containing the priest's part in celebrating the Eucharist. It is the second oldest western liturgical book that has survived. It dates from the late 7th century. (180, 384)

Gelasius I (born in Tunisia and died in Rome, 496) was the Supreme Pontiff of the Catholic Church from 492 to his death in 496; a prolific author. (77)

George, Rosa. (136)

Ghana's Young Christians. (7, 333)

Gnanabaranam, Johnson (1933 – 2008), former Bishop, Tamil Evangelical Lutheran Church, southern India. (322, 384)

Gnanadason, I. R. H. (1915-1973), a bishop in the CSI, Kanyakumri Diocese. (270)

Good, Peter (Ireland) MMCB, was killed just before retirement in Omagh at the time of the bombing in 1998. Two of his church members died in the explosion. (91)

Goodwin, Sandra, MC women leader, UK. (361)

Grace, Gabrielle was the Secretary of the Overseas Relations of the Methodist Church Office in the 2000s. (242)

Graham, Winston, MMCB, Ireland. (238)

Green, Fiona, LPMCB, Ashbourne Circuit. (8, 27, 37)

Greenwell, Dora (1821-1882) was an English poet whose name came to be the pseudonym of a writer of rare spiritual insight and fine poetic genius. (95)

Greet, Kenneth (1918-2014), was a prominent Methodist minister in Britain. (206)

Gregory of Nazianzus (c.329-389), was a 4th-century Archbishop of Constantinople, and Theologian. (7)

Guigo the Carthusian (1174-1193), sometimes referred to as Guy, was a Carthusian monk and the 9th prior of Grande Chartreuse monastery, from 117480, in France. (11)

Gullick, Etta, Catholic prayer composer, often jointly with Michael Hollings (see below) (110, 120, 315, 333)

Habermann, Johann (1516-90) was a German Lutheran theologian. (121)

Hammarskjöld, Dag (Hjalmar Agne Carl) (1905-1961) was a Swedish economist and diplomat who served as the second Secretary-General of the United Nations. (208, 228)

Hancock, Peter MMCB. (188)

Hardwicke, Clare. (59, 171)

Hare, Maria (1798-1870) was an Irish mystic and writer. (39)

Hedges, Sid G., English writer of prayers for schools. (28, 309)

Hellyer, John, MMCB. (45, 189, 341)

Henderson, Ian, Ireland. (92, 126)

Henry, Matthew (1662-1714) was a nonconformist minister and author, born in Wales but spending much of his life in England. (140)

Hext, Kenneth, MMCB. (58, 207, 260)

Hickes, George (1642-1715) was an English divine and scholar. (124, 309)
Hildegard of Bingen (1098-1179) was a German Benedictine abbess, writer, composer, philosopher, Christian mystic, visionary, and polymath. (110, 385)

Hilton, Donald (1932-2012), Minister of URC, Moderator of Synods and of the General Assembly. (6-7, 25, 71, 87, 93, 127, 243-244, 253, 345)

Hoar, Ron (1929-2005) was an American academic who served as the Director of the Pasadena City College and later its Director. (259, 336)

Hoffman, Kay. (296)

Holden, Olwyn, worship leader, Haxby and Wigginton MC. (373)

Holland, Sheila, mission partner in UK from Togo (2010-11). (120)

Hollings, Michael (1921-1997) was a famous Roman Catholic priest, Chaplain of the Westminster, London and a prolific writer. His books include *The Living Priesthood* (1977). (110, 120, 333)

Holmes, Marjorie (1910-2002) was an American columnist and prolific Christian author of 134 books, 32 of which were best sellers. (131, 136, 327)

Holy Qur'an (124)

Howarth, Ian, MMCB. (191)

Hoyland, J. S. (1750–1831) was an English Quaker author. Known as a writer on the Romani people, he also published a religious work. (167, 192, 233)

Hunter, John (1849-1917) was a famous Scottish hymn writer. (197, 291)

Hunter, Linda, writer, Darlington. (276)

Hutt, Robin, MMCB. (104, 172)

Ibiam, Akanu (1906-1995), a distinguished medical missionary who was appointed governor of the Eastern Region of Nigeria. (186)

Idle, Christopher (b. 1938), British Hymnodist, (326)

Ignatius of Antioch, 5th century. (203)

Iona Community was founded in 1938 in the Iona Island of Scotland as an ecumenical Christian Community centred around an abbey working for peace and social justice, rebuilding of community and the renewal of worship. It attracts pilgrims. (11, 16, 38, 41, 49, 53-54, 85, 90, 142, 163, 165, 200, 302-303, 360)

Irish Prayer Book (278)

Jacobs, Jo, MMCB. (137)

James, Margaret (1920-2009), a Methodist mission partner to southern India, Local Preacher, Wareham. (149, 204, 260)

James, Walter (1879-1908). (81)

Jasper, Tony, an English author. (20)

Jeffery, Connie, LPMCB, Thames Valley Circuit. (195)

Jaffey, Ashish, priest of the St Mar Thoma Church, Bristol (332)

Jenkins, David, URC Minister from 1967, was Moderator of Northern Synod 1987-1997 and Moderator, General Assembly 1997-1998. (34, 224)

Jenks, Benjamin (1646-1724) divine, eldest son of John Jenks, vicar of Eaton-under-Haywood, Shropshire. He became an Anglican priest. His book of *Prayers* became popular. (68, 199)

Jesudasan, Y. (312)

Jewish. (1-3, 185, 301, 310)

Johansen-Berg, John, author of many books on spirituality including *Prayers of the Way* (Paperback), 1992. (200)

Johnson, Samuel (1709-1784), was an English writer who made lasting contributions to English literature as a poet, playwright, essayist, moralist, literary critic, biographer, editor, and lexicographer. He was a devout Anglican. (44, 145)

Jones, Crompton, An English author and prolific writer. His books include *A Book of Prayer in Thirty Orders of Public Worship*, 2015. (157, 184)

Jones, David, MMCB. (118)

Jones, Ward, MMCB. (83, 188)

Jordan, Rebecca Barlow is an inspirational author of spiritual books. (296)
Jordan, Stuart, MMCB. (190)

Joseph, Solomon (b. 1947) is a presbyter from the CSI and has served the MCB as Recognised and Regarded (1998-2020). (250)

Julian of Norwich, St. (73)

Kaan, Fred (1929-2009), was a clergyman of Dutch origin who served in the Congregational Church in Britain and a prodigious hymnwriter. (166)

Kalam, A. P. J. Abdul (1931-2015) was an aerospace scientist who served as the 11th President of India from 2002 to 2007. (356)

Kanailage, Tomasi, Fiji. (256, 261)

Kelly, Liam (aged 13), Ealing Trinity Circuit. (166)

Kempe, Margery (1373-1438) was an English Christian mystic, known for writing through dictation *The Book of Margery Kempe*, a work considered by some to be the first autobiography in the English language. (82)

Kempis, Thomas à (1380-1471) was a German-Dutch canon regular of the late medieval period and the author of *The Imitation of Christ*, one of the most popular and best known Christian devotional books. (83, 86, 97, 110, 143, 171, 179, 181, 215, 227, 231)

Ken, Thomas bishop (1637-1711), an Anglican cleric but anti-establishment, who was considered the most eminent of the English non-jurying bishops, hymn writer. (128, 200)

Kendall, Joan is an American author of Christian themes. (130)

Kennedy, Studdert, G. A. (1883-1929) was an English Anglican priest and poet. (273)

Kenseth, Arnold (1915-2003), Harvard scholar, pastor of the southern Congregational Church and a New England poet of the sacred. (56)

Kerry, Jonathan. (94)

Kierkegaard, Søren (1813-1855) was a Danish (first) existentialist philosopher, theologian, poet, social critic and religious author. (74, 79, 91, 187, 227)

Kingsnorth, John (USPG). (259)

Kingston, Ken, LPMCB, High Wycombe. (45)

Kingston, Thomas, Ireland (b. 1967). (27, 104)

Kirby, ***Ermal,*** MMCB. (110, 114)

Kozak, Pat. (121)

Kupke, ***Annette,*** LPMCB, Sterling. (6)

Lakota Prayer, a Native American prayer to awaken one's spirit. (56, 387)

Lancelot Andrewes, Bishop (1555-1626), was an English bishop and scholar, who held high positions in the Church of England during the reigns of Elizabeth I and James I. (51)

Langton, Stephen (1150-1228) was an English Cardinal of the Roman Catholic Church and an Archbishop of Canterbury. The dispute between King John of England and Pope Innocent III over his election was a major factor in the crisis which produced Magna Carta in 1215. (106)

Latin American Council of Churches. (164)

Laud, William (1573-1645) was an English churchman, appointed Archbishop of Canterbury from 1633 during the personal rule of Charles I. (243, 245)

Lawley, John, LPMCB, Telford Circuit. (161)

Lawton, David, LPMCB, South East Berkshire. (116)

Le Moignan, Christina (d. 2020) MMCB. (175, 257)

Let All The World … Ecumenical and International Worship Resource by USPG et al. (16, 18, 33, 51, 280)

Lewis, C. S. (1898-1963) was a British writer and lay theologian. He held academic positions in English literature at both Oxford University and Cambridge University. (208)

Lincoln, Abraham. (354)

Liturgy of Malabar, of the Syro-Malabar Catholic Church based in Kerala, India, founded in 1923 (*Daily Prayer*, 113). (52, 198, 212)

Loder, Ted, a retired minister of the United Methodist Church of America, an activist and creative preacher. (56, 234)***Lott, Eric***, MMCB, mission partner in southern India for about 30 years. (51, 98-99, 111, 295, 300)

Lord Shaftesbury (1801-1885) - Anthony Ashley Cooper, 7th Earl of Shaftesbury KG, styled Lord Ashley from 1811 to 1851 and then Lord Shaftesbury following the death of his father, was a British politician, philanthropist and social reformer. (301, 320)

Loyola, Ignatius (1491-1556) was a Spanish Basque Catholic priest and theologian, who co-founded the religious order called the Society of Jesus and became its first Superior General at Paris in 1541. (78, 80, 198, 227)

Lunn, Andrew, MMCB. (120)

Luther King Jr., Martin (1929-1968), a black American Baptist minister, champion of human rights and race justice, martyr and popular for his speech 'I have a dream.' (27, 65, 371)

Luther, Martin (1483-1546) was a German professor of theology, composer, priest, monk, and a seminal figure in the Protestant Reformation. (165, 183, 198, 337)

Lyons, Derek is associated with the Redhill Methodist Church. (247)

MacLennan, David A. (1948-2014) was a Scottish actor, director, writer and producer. (249)

Malik, Sarah, a former youth President of the MCB. (133)

Maraschin, Jaci (1929-2009), at the end of his career Maraschin was Emeritus Professor at the São Paulo Methodist University and an ordained priest of the São Paulo Anglican Diocese of the Brazilian Episcopal Anglican Church, part of the Anglican Communion. (282)

Marsh, Clive, Methodist Theologian, Principal, Queen's Foundation for Ecumenical Theological Education, Birmingham. (123)

Marsh, Vernon, MMCB. (245)

Marshall, Peter (b. 1926) is an American author, television and radio personality, singer, and actor. (214)

Martin, Nancy (b.1953) is an American writer, known mainly for the *Blackbird Sisters Mystery Series.* (187)

Martin, Paul, MMCB. (164, 189, 197)

Massai (a tribe) -Tanzania. (335)

Mathesan, George (1842-1906) was a Scottish minister and hymn writer. (68)

Matta, Margaret, Deaconess, MCB. (58)

McIlhagga, Kate, Minister, United Reformed Church, UK. (71, 107)

McKnight, Thomas (b. 1941) in Lawrence, Kansas, American artist. (61, 193)

McRae-McMahon, Dorothy (b. 1934) is a retired Australian Uniting Church minister and activist, renowned for human rights work and local 'street level' activism. (282)

Mechthild of Magdeburg (1207-1282), German mystic and medievalphilosopher. (21, 50, 181)

Melanchthon, Philip (1497-1560) was a German Lutheran reformer, collaborator with Martin Luther, the first systematic theologian of the Protestant Reformation, intellectual leader of the Lutheran Reformation, and an influential designer of educational systems. (340)

Menon, Kesava K. P., a Hindu thinker, Kerala. (209)

Methodist Church of Zimbabwe. (256, 261)

Methodist Worship Book (MWB), 1999. (133, 279, 282)

Millar, Peter, an Anglican priest, a former warden of the Iona Community. (54, 63, 235, 268, 361, 364)

Milner-White, Eric (1884-1963) was Dean of York from 1941 until 1963 and a leading figure in the religious, educational and cultural life of the city. (38, 197)

Mirabai (1498-1546) was a poet saint in Maharashtra, was intensely devoted to Lord Krishna. (64, 389)

Moody, D. L. (1837-1899) was an American evangelist and publisher connected with the Holiness Movement, who founded the Moody Church. (125, 339)

Moore, David, MMCB. (92, 267)

Moravian Church is one of the oldest Protestant denominations in the world, with its heritage dating back to the Bohemian Reformation in the 15-16th century and the Unity of the Brethren established in the Kingdom of Bohemia, in Germany. They publish prayers for every year, and most of the prayers in this collection with their name come from the 2015 yearbook. (24, 40, 43-44, 68-69, 71-73, 87, 93, 176-180, 225-226, 262-263, 284, 286-287, 318-319, 339, 361-362)

More, Thomas (1478-1535) is venerated in the Catholic Church as Saint. He was an English lawyer, social philosopher, author, statesman, and noted Renaissance humanist. (182, 221, 266)

Morley, Janet, a Methodist lay theologian, author and prayer writer. (200, 277, 337)

Murali, Nandini, Madurai, a writer. (313)

Murphy, Ros, MMCB. (289)

Nair, Ramachandran, S. K., Hindu thinker, Kerala. (6, 208-209)

National Council of Churches in Korea. (193)

Nestorian Liturgy, East Syriac, 5th century. (60, 173)

New Church Book of Worship, Presbyterian Church, USA,1876. (234)

Newell, Philip J. (b. 1953) is a poet, peacemaker, minister and scholar, internationally acclaimed for his work in the field of Celtic spirituality. (28-29, 141, 159, 364)

Newman, John Henry (1801-90) was an English theologian and poet, first an Anglican priest and later a Roman Catholic priest and cardinal, who was an important and controversial figure in the religious history of England in the 19th century. (145, 249, 263, 266)

Newton, ***Gill,*** MMCB. (96)

Ngurliana, MC of Upper Myanmar. (108)

Nicaragua (367)

Nicholls, Noel, member of Kepa The Advisers Institute. (311)

Niebuhr, Reinhold (1892-1971) was an American Reformed theologian, ethicist, commentator on politics and public affairs, and professor at Union Theological Seminary for more than 30 years. (162-163, 320)

Nightingale, Florence (1820-1910) was an English social reformer and statistician, and the founder of modern nursing. (228, 341)

Nouwen, Henri (1932–1996) was a Dutch Catholic priest, professor, writer and theologian with special interest in psychology and spirituality. (75)

Nuchopa, Naboth from Zimbabwe, former Secretary for Racial Justice in the Methodist Church. (40)

Odell, Christine, Methodist author of prayers (43)

Oosterhuis, Hubb (Gerardus Josephus Henricus (b. 1933) is a Dutch theologian and poet, mainly known for his contribution to Christian music and liturgy in the Dutch language, used in both Protestant and Roman Catholic churches. (88, 116, 196, 282, 359)

Osborn, Leo, Jewish writer. (118)

Oxenham, John (1852-1941), English journalist, novelist and poet. (12)

Oxley, Simon, Baptist minister, UK, former Executive Secretary of the WCC. (70)

Pain, Godfrey, writer of prayers '*For Senior Schools' Youth.*' (362)

Palos, Daphne and Demetris, from South Africa, Mission Partners in MCB, 1990s. (269)

Parker, Margaret. (224)

Parkinson, Rachel, MMCB. (96)

Pascal, Blaise (1623-1662) was a French mathematician, physicist, inventor, writer and Catholic theologian. (227, 319)

Paton Alan (1903-1988), a South African author and anti-apartheid activist. (187, 205, 234, 320)

Patrick (c. 389-461), was born in Britain, captured by Irish pirates, rescued and became an Irish bishop. (67, 86, 141, 171)

Peacock, Malcom, MMCB. (283)***Pearce, Steve***, Children Ministry and South Asia Secretary, the Methodist Church in Britain. (20)

Peck, Scott (1936-2005) was an American psychiatrist and best-selling author who wrote the book *The Road Less Travelled*, published in 1978. (41)

Pender, Edward. (336)

Penn, William (1644-1718) was the son of the admiral and politician Sir William Penn. Penn was a writer, early member of the Religious Society of Friends, and founder of the English North American colony, the Province of Pennsylvania. (281)

Perry, David, MMCB. (82, 269)

Philaret, Metropolitan of Moscow, one of Rowan William's favourites, written in his own hand in the opening page of Rupert Shortt's *Rowan's Rule: The Biography of the Archbishop* (2008). (139)

Pickard, Jan-Sutch is a writer and storyteller living on the Isle of Mull, and a former warden of the Abbey on Iona. (69, 119 122, 256)

Pillai, Krishna (Henri Alfred, 1827-1900), Tamil poet and convert from the Vaishnava Hinduism. (127)

Pillinger, Peter, MMCB. (7)

Plant, Stephen, Faculty of Divinity, University of Cambridge, Dean of Trinity Hall. (143)

Polycarp (69-155) was a Christian bishop of Smyrna. According to the *Martyrdom* of Polycarp, he died a martyr, was bound and burned at the stake, then stabbed when the fire failed to consume his body. (213)

Prescott, D.M. (233)

Procter, M.E., British writer. (168)

Prophet, Mohammed (571-632) was an Arab religious, social and political leader and the founder of Islam. He is regarded by Muslims as the final messenger from God. (213, 391)

Pusey, Edward Bouverie (1800-1882) was an English churchman, Regius Professor of Hebrew at the University of Oxford; one of the leading figures in the Oxford Movement. (144)

Queen Anne (1665-1714), Queen (1702-1707) of England, Scotland and Ireland (316)

Quintelier, André. (66)

Quoist, Michel (1918-1997), a French Catholic priest, theologian and writer, most known for his bestselling book, *Prayers of Life.* (32, 136, 158, 202, 304, 321, 359, 362)

Rabia of Basra (Rabi`a al-Adawiyya al-Qaysiyya, 713-801) was a Muslim saint and Sufi mystic. (66)

Ramsey, Michael (1904-1988) was bishop of Durham, Archbishop of York, 100th Archbishop of Canterbury. (241)

Rauschenbusch, Walter (1861-1918), an American Baptist minister, key figure in promoting social gospel including tax justice. (12-13, 154)

Ren, British Christian Poet. (96)

Richard of Chichester (1197-1253) is a saint who was Bishop of Chichester. In Chichester Cathedral a shrine dedicated to Richard became a richly decorated centre of pilgrimage. (65, 181)

Richard, Ex-offender, Lincoln. (46)

Richardson, Kathleen, MMCB. (61, 174)

Richardson, Norman Honorary Fellow; Lecturer (retired/part-time) in Education for Religious & Cultural Diversity, Belfast. (289)

Robinson, Susan, Organist, St. Andrews MC, Pudsey. (47)

Robinson,Gnana (1935-2019) was a presbyter of the CSI, Kanyakumari Diocese, theological educator and activist. (309, 357)

Roger of Taizé (Roger Schütz, popularly known as Brother Roger), was a Swiss Christian leader and monastic brother. In 1940 he founded the Taizé Community, an ecumenical monastic community in Burgundy, France, serving as its first prior until his murder in 2005. (106, 227-228, 287)

Rolle, Richard (c. 1290-1349) was an English hermit, mystic, and religious writer who at the end of his life lived near a Cistercian nunnery in Hampole, Yorkshire. (95)

Rolle, Theophilus, bishop, Bahamas/Turks and Caicos Islands District Chair of the MC. (268)

Roman Catholic Church in Spain. (239)

Rossetti, Christina (1830-1894) was an English poet who wrote a variety of romantic, devotional, and children's poems. (77, 107, 183, 187, 230)

Rowland, Mark, MMCB. (332)

Runcie, Robert (1921-2000) was a British Anglican bishop. He was the Archbishop of Canterbury from 1980 to 1991, having previously been Bishop of St. Albans. (121)

Rupp, Joyce (b. 1943) is an American award-winning author, a retreat and conference speaker. the co-director of The Institute of Compassionate Presence, a member of the Servite Order, and a volunteer for Hospice. (164)

Ruskin, John (1819-1900) was a writer, artist, art critic and polymath who was precocious at all stages of his life. He was the first Professor of Fine Art appointed at Oxford. (201)

Salmon, Virginia. (13)

Sampson, Annette, LPMCB, Birmingham. (346)

Samuel, Godson, Methodist minister, Mumbai. (311)

Samuel, Lilly. Rtd Teacher, Madurai. (216)

Sargent, Barbara. (56)

Saward, Michael (1932-2015) was a British Anglican priest, author and hymnodist. (135)

Schaffran, Janet, formerly Sister Helen Anthony, entered religious life from St. Theresa's parish in Parma, Ohio. She was a campus minister at Walsh University in Canton, OH (1980-89), and since 1992, she has been a hospice chaplain with Forbes Hospice/West Penn Allegheny Health System in Pittsburgh. (121)

Scottish Liturgy (291)

Scotus Erigena, John (815-877) was an Irish theologian, Neoplatonist philosopher, and poet. (48)

Sellick, David. (201)

Selvamony, Cornelius (1915-2010), theological educator, bishop in the CSI, Kanyakumari Diocese. (207)

Selvamony, Justin (b. 1950) is a presbyter of the CSI, Kanyakumari Diocese, Missioner. (258, 261)

Selvanayagam, Gnana Leelal (b. 1950), a member of the CSI. (xxv, 49, 135, 155)

Selvanayagam, ***Israel,*** (originally Presbyter, CSI), theological educator and writer, MMCB. (xxvii, 4-5, 9, 12, 29, 32, 42-43, 49, 61, 70, 74-75, 81-82, 89, 92, 95, 98, 101-104, 109, 112-113, 115, 117-118, 129, 131-132, 135, 138, 140, 142, 150, 155, 168, 173, 188, 201, 224-225, 230-231, 237, 241, 244-247, 249, 251-252, 260-261, 265-266, 273, 276, 278, 280, 285-286, 288, 290, 293, 302-303, 310, 316, 318, 321, 328, 331, 333, 346-348, 353, 367, 372)

Shaw, Gilbert (1886-1967), an Anglo-Irish Church of England priest, from 1940 vicar of St. Anne's Soho. (33)

Sheasby, Peter, MMCB. (126)

Sheppick, ***Andrea,*** LPMCB, Shropshire and Maches Circuit. (233)

Silk, David (b. 1936) is an English priest of the Roman Catholic Church. He was formerly an Anglican bishop and was the Bishop of Ballarat in the Anglican Church of Australia. (293)

Simpson, Asha Anne, Pharmacist and Teacher, Geneva. (312)

Singh, Herbert Jaya, Researcher in Christian Institute for the Study of Religion and Society and Lecturer in Religions and Interreligious Dialogue at UTC (1980s), Bangalore. (251)

Singh, Jogendra (1877-1946) was a member of the Viceroy's Executive Council in India. He served as Chairman of the Department of Health, Education and Lands. (200)

Singh, Sadhu Sundar (1889-1929), convert, mystic, preacher and Indian Christian theologian. (59, 66, 156)

Smalley, Stephen S. (b. 1931) was Dean of Chester in the last part of the 20th century and the first year of the 21st: he is also an eminent Anglican scholar. (294)

Smith, Anne, MMCB. (107)

Smith, Liz, MMCB. (108, 120, 139, 192, 231)

Smith, Neville, a former Training Officer for the Hospital Chaplaincies Council, London. (269, 275)

Snowden, Rita (1907-1999) was born at Brightwater and grew up in Hope, in the south of the Nelson province, New Zealand. While still a young girl she felt a call to be an overseas missionary. (143)

Soubirous, Mary Bernarde (1844-1879), also known as Saint Bernadette of Lourdes, was the firstborn daughter of a miller from Lourdes, France. (96)

Sowden, Sue, MMCB. (149)

Srisand, Koson, Thailand. (188)

Starck, Johann (1741-1816) of Königsberg (historic Prussian city that is now Kaliningrad, Russia) was a prolific author and controversial theologian, as well as a widely read political writer. (122)

Stephens, Peter, MMCB. (267, 306)

Stevens, Jean A. (b. 1951) was a member of the Primary General Presidency of The Church of Jesus Christ of Latter-day Saints (LDS Church) from 2010 to 2015. USA. (274)

Stevenson, Robert Louis (1850-1894) was a Scottish novelist and travel writer, most noted for the *Treasure Island.* (70, 79, 150, 157, 220, 294)

Stuart, Janet (1857-1914) was a Roman Catholic nun- 'mother' (convert from Anglicanism) and educator. She founded a number of schools. (87, 174)

Stuckey, Tom, MMCB. (269)

Sulston, Peter, MMCB. (190)

Sundaram, V.P.K. (1915-2003) was a genius in Tamil language, music and hand-drumming. He was on the faculty of the Tamil Nadu Theological Seminary, Madurai. (42)

Sutton, Susan (332)

Swami, Ramalinga (1823-1874), of Chidambaram, Tamil Nadu, India, was a sage who claimed to transcend particular form of religion and have the supreme power of light. (67)

Symeon, St. of Thessaloniki (c. 1381-1429) was a monk, bishop and theologian in Greece. (305)

Syrian Liturgy. (304).

Syrian Orthodox Church. (143)

Taggart, Norman (b. 1935), is a Methodist minister of Ireland and was installed the President of the Methodist Church in Ireland in 1997. (257, 262)

Tagore, Rabindranath (1861-1941) was a Bengali poet, playwright and artist who was awarded the Nobel prize in literature. (65, 169, 208, 355)

Takenaka, Masao (1925-2006) was a Japanese theologian who taught for over 40 years at Doshisha University in Kyoto, Japan, where he was a Professor of Christian Ethics and Sociology of Religion. (142)

Taylor, Jeremy (1613-67), was a cleric in the Church of England who achieved fame as an author during the Protectorate of Oliver Cromwell. (52, 86-87, 185, 317)

Taylor, John, MMCB. (57, 93)

Teal, Richard, MMCB. (83, 192)

Teilhard De Chardin, Pierre (1881-1955) was a French idealist philosopher and Jesuit priest who trained as a palaeontologist and geologist and took part in the discovery of the Peking Man. (78, 137)

Temple, Sophie, a pupil, Shebbear College, Devon, at the age of 17/18. (95)

Temple, William (1881-1944) was an English Anglican priest and social thinker, who served as Bishop of Manchester, Archbishop of York and Archbishop of Canterbury. (xxviii, 81, 172, 235, 279, 315, 337)

Teresa of Avila, St. (1515-1582), probably a female saint, Carmelite and mystic with the great influence in the religious world. (226, 338)

Teresa, Mother (Mary Teresa Bojaxhiu, 1910-1997), honoured in the Catholic Church as Saint Teresa of Calcutta, was an Albanian-Indian Roman Catholic nun and missionary who founded the 'Missionaries of Charity.' (226, 314)

Thayumanavar (1705-1744) was a Tamil Saiva spiritual philosopher from Tamil Nadu, India. (150, 395)

The Church of Ceylon. (239)

The Whole Duty of Man is an English high church 'Protestant' devotional work, first published anonymously, with an introduction by Henry Hammond, in 1658. (196)

Thomas, M. A., a Mar Thoma priest from Kerala who founded in 1963 the Ecumenical Christian Centre, Bangalore. (356)

Thomas, Megan, Methodist Youth President, 2014-15. (46)

Thomas, R. S. (1913-2000) was a Welsh poet and Anglican priest who was noted for his nationalism, spirituality and dislike of the anglicisation of Wales. (62)

Thompson, Graham, MMCB. (127, 144, 199, 232)

Thorogood, Bernard. (67, 130)

Thurman, Howard (1899-1981) was an African-American author, philosopher, theologian, educator, and civil rights leader. (296)

Tillotson, John (1630-1694) was the Anglican Archbishop of Canterbury from 1691 to 1694. (167)

Tilson, Everest, Methodist Professor, Ohio. (289)

Toc H. is an international Christian movement. The name is an abbreviation for Talbot House, a resting place for soldiers in the WWI founded in 1915 at Poperinghe, Belgium. (143)

Todd, Ken, MMCB, Ireland. (92, 205, 268, 353)

Tomlin, Alison MMCB (331)

Topping, Frank (b. 1937) is an English actor and writer enjoying an active retirement, preaching and performing. He lives in the Forest of Dean, UK. (79, 137, 159, 290, 327)

Townsend, Michael. (259, 281)

Traherne, Thomas (1636-1674) was an English poet, clergyman, theologian, and religious writer. (331)

Train, Daphne. (87, 174)

Tukaram (Sant) was a 17th century Hindu poet who belonged to the Varkari Bhakti movement in Maharashtra, India. (41, 64, 66)

Tullett, Maureen, Burgess Hill MC. (189)

Turner, Philip (1925-2006) was an English writer best known for his children's books. (40)

Tutu, Desmond (b. 1931) is a South African Anglican cleric, Archbishop and theologian known for his work as an anti-apartheid and human rights activist. (209, 354)

Tyrwhitt, Elizabethe Oxenbridge (c. 1519-1578) was an English gentlewoman, courtier, and writer. She was also a lady of the privy chamber to Kathryn Parr and shared the Queen's views on religion. It is probably at this time that her book of prayers was written. (85, 156)

Underhill, Evelyn (1875-1941) was an English Anglo-Catholic writer and pacifist known for her numerous works on religion and spiritual practice, in particular Christian mysticism.(86, 173)

United Church of Christ (USA). (301)

Uniting Church of Australia. (105, 106)

Vaughan, Charles (1816-1897) was an Anglican churchman, effective preacher and prolific author. (81)

Vautrey, Richard, Vice President, British Methodist Conference, 2009-2010. (137)

Veagra, Saray was a Methodist Mission Partner in Britain (1990s) from Panama. (260, 299)

Veater, Selwyn. (93)

Visser't Hooft, Willem, W. A. (1900-1985) was a Dutch theologian who became the first Secretary General of the World Council of Churches in 1948 and held this position until his retirement in 1966. (264)

Wade, Alan is an American singer-songwriter from Chattanooga, Tennessee, USA. (78)

Wakelin, Mark, MMCB. (246, 275)

Walkling, Simon, Minister, URC, UK. (243)

Wallwork, Norman, MMCB. (39, 42, 118, 170, 193, 205, 243, 255, 287, 336)

Walton, Roger, MMCB. (46, 191)

Warren, Alan. (295)

Waterman, David (1936-2006), MMCB. (294)

Watters, Rosemary. (61, 174)

WCC (World Council of Churches) is a Fellowship of about 350 Churches from around the world. It was formed in 1948 and is based in Geneva. (20, 44, 54, 55, 113, 122, 265, 326, 32)

Wearing, Michael (1939-2017) was a British Television producer. (41)

Weatherhead, Leslie D. (1883-1975) was an English Christian, Non-conformist. (8, 278, 293) ***Webb, Pauline*** (1927-2017), a much-loved broadcaster and writer, a prominent Methodist woman leader both at home, overseas and in the ecumenical movement. (149, 254)

Wells, Herbert George (1866-1946) was an English writer. He was prolific in many genres, from novels and short stories to war games. (185)

Wesley, John (1703-1791), an Anglican clergyman, founder of the Methodist movement (Church). (33, 53, 58, 78, 94, 145, 192, 244, 344)

Wesley, Susanna (1669-1742), the mother of the Wesley Brothers (John and Charles), known for dedication and disciplining. (8, 57, 191)

Westcott, Brooke Foss (1825-1901), a New Testament scholar, former professor of divinity in Cambridge, and bishop. (48, 116, 196)

Wigley, Stephen, MMCB. (191)

Wilding, Pamela, an Anglican priest from Kenya. (22, 102)

Willetts, Lia Icaza, ordained minister, United Methodist Church, USA. (296)

Williams, Dick (SPCK). (277, 289)

Williams, Yvonne, LPMCB. (139)

Wilson, Thelma. (94)

Winter, Miriam Therese (b. 1938) is a Roman Catholic Medical Mission Sister, theologian, writer and songwriter. (128, 234, 364)

Women's World Day of Prayer. (xxviii, 269)

Woodcock, Margaret, LPMCB, Wimborne. (373)

Worth, Penny, MMBI. (293)

Wren, Brian A. (b. 1936) is a United Methodist pastor of America, hymn-poet and writer with profound theology. (57)

Yabaki, Akuila, Methodist minister and leader, Fiji. (205, 238)

York, Alcuin of (c. 735-804), an English scholar, clergyman, poet and teacher from York. (232)

Yorke, Ruth, Deacon, MCB. (299)

Youngson, Michael. (373)

Youngson, Michaela, MMCB. (191)

The Sources Consulted and Used

Amirtham, Samuel and Lily (ed.), *Prarthananjali*, Madurai: Leo Prints, 2004.

Appleton, George, *Acts of Devotion*, London: SPCK, 1963.

Backhouse, Robert (initial draft), *The SPCK Book of Christian Prayer*, London: SPCK, 1995.

Banyard, Edmund, *Reaching for the Infinite*, Birmingham: National Christian Education Council, 2000.

Barclay, William, *Everyday Prayers* (originally published as *The Plain Man's Book of Prayers,* 1959), San Francisco: Harper and Row, 1959.

Barclay, William, *Epilogues and Prayers*, London: SCM, 1963.

Barclay, William, *Prayers for Health and Healing*, London: Hodder and Stoughton, 1968.

Barclay, William, *Prayers for Help and Healing*, London: Collins, Fontana Books, 1976.

Batchelor, Mary, (selected and arranged), *The Lion Prayer Collection,* Oxford: Lion Publishing plc, 1994.

Bell, John L. and Graham A. Maule (ed.), *Iona Community: A WEE Worship Book,* Govan, Glasgow: The Wild Goose Worship Group, The Iona Community, 1989.

Brokering, Herbert F., *Luther's Prayers,* Minneapolis: Augsburg Publishing House, 1967.

Brook, Avery (from the collection of Alexander Carmichael), *Celtic Prayers*, New York: The Seabury Press, 1981.

Bye, Beryl, *Prayers for All Seasons,* Guilford: Lutterworth Press, 1973. (24, 263-264, 272, 283, 298, 322-324, 340, 346)

Chapman, Raymond, *Hear Our Prayer,* Norwich; The Canterbury Press, 2003.

Cherry, Stephen, *Barefoot Prayers – A Meditation a Day for Lent and Easter*, London: SPCK, 2013.

Cotter, Jim (with music composed by Paul Payton), *Out of the Silence ... Into the Silence: Prayer's Daily Round*, Harlech: Cairns Publications, 2006.

Daily Prayer, London: Oxford University Press, 1941.

Daily Watchwords Year Book (2015 edition) of the Moravian Church, Germany.

Dunkerley, Roderic and Gregor H., *Prayer-Time in the Junior School,* London: University of London Press, 1958.

Eadie, Donald, *Grain in the Winter*, Peterborough: Epworth, 1999.

Eadie, Donald, *Into the Foothills of Transformation*, Glasgow: Wild Goose Publications, 2019.

Everyday Prayers, Further Everyday Prayers (1987), More Everyday Prayers: Church of England (www.churchofengland.org).

Doberstein, John W. (ed.), *Minister's Prayer Book,* Philadelphia: Muhlenberg Press, undated.

Edwards, Maureen (comp.), *Called to Prayer: An Anthology of Prayers for Public Worship and for Personal Use*, Peterborough: Methodist Publishing House, 2001.

Falla, Terry C. (ed.), *Responsive Prayers and Readings for Contemporary Worship*, Adelaide: Lutheran Publishing House, 1981.

Ferguson, James, *Prayers for Common Worship*, London: Allenson and Co., 1956.

Ferguson, J. M. Macdougall, *Sing Praises! 100 Services for the Infants Assembly*, Surrey: The Religious Education Press, Ltd., 1958.

Felch, Susan M. (ed.), *Elizabeth Tyrwhitt's Morning and Evening Prayers*, Hampshire: Ashgate Publishing Limited, 2008. (useful reference: 'A Brief History of English Private Prayer Books' (pp. 19-32).

Francis, Dayanandan (ed.), *The Christian Witness of Sadhu Sundar Singh: A Collection of his Writings,* Madras: The Christian Literature Society, 1989.

Hamman, A (ed.) and Walter Mitchell (tr.), *Early Christian Prayers*, London: Longmans, Green, 1962.

Harling, Per (ed.), *Worshipping Ecumenically,* Geneva: WCC Publications, 1995.

Hedges, Sid G. (Comp.), *Down to Earth and Up to Heaven ... Prayers for the Youthful*, Surrey: The Pilgrim Press and National Sunday School Union, 1964.

Hilton, Donald (Comp.), *The Word in the World – Prayers for Christian Worship Book 2*, Birmingham: Christian Education Publications, 2001.

Iona Abbey Worship Book, Glasgow: Wild Goose Publications, 2001.

Iona Community Worship Book, Iona: The Abbey, 1994.

Iona Community: *A Wee Worship Book: Fourth Incarnation*, 2009.

Johnson, Gnanabaranam, *The Passion of Christ*, Chennai (E. M. S. Johnson), 2016.

Lemopoulos, Georges (ed.), *Let us Pray to the Lord – A Collection of Prayers from the Eastern and Oriental Orthodox Traditions*, Geneva: WCC Publications, 1996.

Mabey, Juliet (compiled), *One World Book of Prayer*, Oxford: One World Publications,1999.

Manschreck, Clyde (comp.), *Prayers of the Reformers*, Philadelphia: Muhlenberg Press, 1958.

Micklem, Caryl (ed. + other authors: Anthony Coates, John Gregory, David Stapleton and Roger Tomes), London: SCM Press, 1970.

Miller, Peter, *Remembering Dorothy – A Few Prayers for Life, Healing, Hope and Laughter*, Newtonmore (Scotland): Groverprint and Design, 2011.

Morley, Janet (ed.), *Bread of Tomorrow*, London: SPCK and Christian Aid, 1992.

Newell, J. Philip, *Sounds of the Eternal: A Celtic Psalter*, Norwich: The Canterbury Press, 2002.

Oosterhuis, Huub, *Your Word is Near, Contemporary Christian Prayers,* tr. by N. D. Smith, London: Newman Press, 1968.

Pain, Godfrey S. (comp.), *Prayers for Senior Worship*, London: Methodist Youth Department, 1947.

Pawelzik, Fritz (ed.) and Robbins Strong (tr.) *I Lie on My Mat and Pray*, New York: Friendship Press, 1964.

Paynter, Neil (selected), *50 Great Prayers from the Iona Community*, Glasgow: Wild Goose Publications, 2009.

Pawelzik, Fritz (ed.), *I Sing your Praise – Young Africans at Prayer*, New York: Friendship Press, 1967.

Prayers Encircling the World – An Anthology, Louisville: Westminster John Knox Press, 1999.

Prescott, D. M. (Ed.), *The Senior Teacher's Prayer Book*, London: Blandford Press, 1962.

Quoist, Michel, *Prayers of Life*, London: Gill and Macmillan, 1963.

Quoist, Michel, *Meet Christmas And Live!* Dublin: Gill and Macmillan Ltd., 1973.

Robins, Wendy S. (comp. and ed.), *Let All the World: Liturgies, Litanies and Prayers from Around the World*, London: USPG, 1990.

Sellick, David, *Christianity and Teenage Thinker: A Book of Prayer for Schools Morning Assemblies*, Oxford: A.R. Mowbray, Co. Ltd., 1969.

Selvanayagam, Israel, *In Spirit and Mind – 100 Prayers* (in Tamil), Nagercoil: Kanyakumari Diocese Communication Dept, 2007.

Singh, Godwin R. (comp. and ed.), *Ecumenical Prayer Calendar*, Delhi: ISPCK (for NCCI), 1983.

Singing the Faith, London: Hymns Ancient and Modern Ltd., London: Methodist Publishing, 2011.

Smith, Neville, *Prayers for People in Hospital*, Oxford: Oxford University Press, 1994.

Suter, John Wallace (comp. and ed.), *Prayers for New World*, New York: Charles Scribner's Sons, 1964.

Tagore, Rabindranath, *Gitanjali: Songs Offerings*, Calcutta: Rabindra-Bhavana; Santiniketan,1999.

The Church of South India Book of Common Worship, Chennai: CSI Centre, 2004.

The Methodist Worship Book, Peterborough: Methodist Publishing House, 1999.

The Methodist Prayer Handbook, 2009-2020, London: Methodist Publishing, 2009-2020.

The New Century Hymnal, Cleveland (Ohio): The Pilgrim Press, 1995.

The World Calls Christians to Prayer, London: Cargate Press (for Methodist Overseas Division) – year not mentioned.

Thomson, Ian, *Two Hundred School Assemblies*, London: A. R. Mowbray and Co Ltd, 1966.

Tilson, Everett and Phyllis Cole, *Litanies and Other Prayers for the Common Lectionary (Year B)*, Nashville: Abingdon Press, 1990.

Tutu, Desmond, *An African Prayer Book*, London: Hodder and Stoughton, 1996.

Zundel, Veronica, *The Lion Book of Prayers: A Treasury of Christian Prayers Through the Centuries*, Tring (Herts, England): Lion Publishing, 1987.